POWER / KNOWLEDGE / LAND

AFRICAN PERSPECTIVES

Kelly Askew and Anne Pitcher
Series Editors

Power / Knowledge / Land: Contested Ontologies of Land and Its Governance in Africa
Laura A. German

In Search of Tunga*: Prosperity, Almighty God, and Lives in Motion in a Malian Provincial Town*
André Chappatte

The Infrastructures of Security: Technologies of Risk Management in Johannesburg
Martin J. Murray

There Used to Be Order: Life on the Copperbelt after the Privatisation of the Zambia Consolidated Copper Mines
Patience Mususa

Animated by Uncertainty: Rugby and the Performance of History in South Africa
Joshua D. Rubin

African Performance Arts and Political Acts
Naomi André, Yolanda Covington-Ward, and Jendele Hungbo, Editors

Filtering Histories: The Photographic Bureaucracy in Mozambique, 1960 to Recent Times
Drew A. Thompson

Aso Ebi*: Dress, Fashion, Visual Culture, and Urban Cosmopolitanism in West Africa*
Okechukwu Nwafor

Unsettled History: Making South African Public Pasts
Leslie Witz, Gary Minkley, and Ciraj Rassool

A complete list of titles in the series can be found at www.press.umich.edu

Power / Knowledge / Land

Contested Ontologies of Land and Its Governance in Africa

Laura A. German

University of Michigan Press
Ann Arbor

Published in the United States of America by the University of Michigan Press
Manufactured in the United States of America
Printed on acid-free paper
First published October 2022

A CIP catalog record for this book is available from the British Library.

Library of Congress Cataloging-in-Publication data has been applied for.

ISBN 978-0-472-07533-1 (hardcover : alk. paper)
ISBN 978-0-472-05533-3 (paper : alk. paper)
ISBN 978-0-472-22011-3 (e-book)

Publication of this volume has been partially funded by the African Studies Center, University of Michigan

For Eli and Ella, may you continue to find wonder in other life forms, joy in one another, and meaning in belonging—to both community and place.

and

For Esther Mwangi, may you live on through all of those who gained knowledge, courage and inspiration from you.

Universalist discourses and globalist projects are grounded in a unitary ontology and imperialist epistemologies which assume that the world is one, that it is knowable on a global scale within single modes of thought, and is thus manageable and governable in those terms.

—Conway and Singh (2011: 701)

CONTENTS

Digital materials related to this title can be found on the Fulcrum platform via the following citable URL: https://doi.org/10.3998/mpub.12071412

ACKNOWLEDGMENTS

I am a mother and wife, and a professor of anthropology. If I had always remembered my priorities as enumerated, there would have been fewer sacrifices in the 2.5 years it took me to write this book (but I would still be writing!). So let me start in the proper order, and give my deepest thanks to my husband Jeff—for all the early morning drop-offs, weekend and afternoon parenting, copyediting, and moral support that provided the opportunities to write in the context of a heavy teaching and mentoring load, and for always being there on so many levels. I could not have hoped for a more committed and loving life partner. And to Eli and Ella, for your patience and empathy on the days when I gave too much at work to give my all at home, and for your love and sense of humor—which continue to fill and inspire, and keep the fire burning bright. My biggest motivation for finalizing this book is to be able to turn to you, unconditionally.

For a book that took this long not just to write, but to gather the necessary insight, the credits undoubtedly spread far beyond those named here. Let me start with Penney Stringer, medical doctor, visionary, and soul sister extraordinaire. Those who have ever lost sight of it will know that health is the foundation of everything. Thank you again and again for the distance you travelled and generosity you showed to restore me to health so I could write this manuscript. And to our pandemic pod, who made living and working during a pandemic possible by bringing not just sanity to our Covid-19 lockdown, but also times of great joy and connection.

Broadening the circle further are all of those I have collaborated with most closely in recent years—starting with the incredibly talented graduate students with whom I journeyed into the realms of critical agrarian and legal studies, ontological anthropology, and settler colonialism, and whose own processes of intellectual discovery enrich the intellectual lives of faculty every day. Suneel Kumar, Anya Bonanno, Katie Foster, Walker DePuy, Jacob Weger, Rachel Arney, Maya Henderson, and Lowery Parker deserve special mention. Acknowledgement is also due to those I collaborated with closely in the context of various research projects—from the review of discourse and evidence on inclusive business (Lorenzo Cotula, Katie Foster, and Anya Bonanno), to land titling and community-investor partnerships in Mozambique (Eunice Cavane, Almeida Sitoe, and Carla Braga), large-scale agricultural/biofuel investments and their implications for customary tenures and local livelihoods (George Schoneveld, Lowery Parker, Davison Gumbo, Esther Mwangi, and Pablo Pacheco), and shifting contours of property and authority in the context of conservation and enclosures in Kenyan rangelands (Paul Wachira Naiputari, Ryan Unks, and Lizzie King). I owe a particular debt of gratitude to Carla Braga for the intellectual exchange and motivation that enabled some of these ideas to first be committed to paper (German and Braga 2021), and for some of the literature and ideas this exposed me to—from Mignolo and Yngstrom, to "mobilizing metaphors." For your critical eye and sharp intellect, and for the sustained collaboration and friendship over the years, *obrigada, irmã.*

The next layer of gratitude goes to Daniel Bromley—who inspired in me a sizeable dose of courage to start this project, whether through seeing a renowned economist critique establishment views of land governance (was it not economists themselves, albeit of the neoclassical persuasion, who wrote that book?), or accompanying the project during its early stages and shaming me by example to get these chapters written. While a coproduced manuscript would have had broader appeal, I have no regrets for the path taken. The phrase "prospering in place" is all yours.

To Ellen Bauerle, Flannery Wise, Kelly Askew, Mary Hashman, and the editorial, production, and marketing teams at the University of Michigan Press, thank you for the time and energy invested in this project. You are a small team, but your expertise—and your patience, support and guidance at every step—have made all the difference.

I would also like to extend my gratitude for the thoughtful feedback provided by the anonymous and not-so-anonymous reviewers. My deepest debt of gratitude goes to Pauline Peters, for the care taken to review each and every sentence and footnote of this volume, and to reach into your intellectual archive to suggest new literature to deepen the evidence and perfect the arguments. I am particularly indebted to you for repeated reminders of the centrality of descent-based landholdings, for the insight that connections to land in Africa are often best understood through the lens of belonging, and for pointers in navigating the francophone scholarship (for which Google Translate does a remarkable job, after you know what to look for).

Last but most definitely not least, I owe my deepest gratitude to the countless individuals who took their time from their busy and overburdened lives to sit with me and share their experiences with land governance and land loss—from those whose livelihoods were displaced by jatropha plantations in the Brong Ahafo region of Ghana, to those affected by tourism, mining, forestry, and agricultural investments in the Manica and Nampula Provinces of Mozambique and the Copperbelt, Northern and Southern Provinces of Zambia, and those living under the growing territorial control of conservation NGOs in Laikipia, Kenya. While the research taking place with your gracious support had many of the hallmarks of an extractive enterprise, it was carried out with your concerns at the forefront. I can only hope that the insights gathered herein, inspired by the stories you shared, will help in some small way to alleviate the discursive and material aggressions that continue to be leveraged on your ways of life.

Introduction

Every year from 1999 until the onset of the Covid-19 pandemic,[1] the World Bank has held an international Land and Poverty Conference, bringing together representatives of government, academia, civil society, and the private sector to deliberate on land governance. In 2015, I attended a session in which a representative of an eastern Africa farmers' association was a speaker alongside representatives of multinational corporations, in a session chaired by a staff member of the International Finance Corporation. This was a rare chance to hear the voice of an actual farmer at an event purportedly focused on addressing their needs. The farmer's voice on the matter of land was both emphatic and clear: "We do not need people to invest in our land, we need them to invest in *us*." Yet the session chair thanked him and moved on to the other speakers, never returning to the vision for land and investment that he had so clearly articulated. I was struck by the magnitude of this erasure in a space of (evidently performative) inclusive dialogue, but in looking around the room saw no indication that anyone had even noticed. The agenda moved on, with apparently little concern for truly hearing what he and those he was there to represent had to say. This was not the first time such a vision had been articulated. It had been advanced by the Eastern Africa Farmers' Federation (EAFF) at least five years earlier, for example, in "The Entebbe Declaration on Large Foreign Land Acquisitions," which states,

> EAFF firmly believes that small-holder farmers, producers, fisher-folk and pastoralists should be recognized as *the key investors on land and in agriculture* in Africa . . . EAFF strongly believes that the win-win model is *sound investments in African farmers* that increase their productivity on the land. (EAFF 2010: 3, 5, emphasis added)

I start with this vignette because that room was a microcosm, if you will, of a global land governance regime purporting to serve the interests of poor rural communities in the global South, but often running roughshod over their needs, interests, and visions for their own future.

The vision articulated by the EAFF and other organizations working to elevate the voice of small-scale farmers, pastoralists, and fisherfolk within national and international land governance fora includes food that is produced by smallholders rather than by agribusiness firms; recognition of smallholder farmers, pastoralists, and fisherfolk as Africa's most important investors and producers; and public and private investment in these producers rather than in land and natural resources and their expropriation (EAFF 2010; La Via Campesina 2017, 2018).[2] It also includes a vision of farmers retaining their land and freedom of choice, rather than being made laborers in someone else's business or bound by long-term contractual agreements. And for some, it centers on food grown to meet the needs of local households through flexible consumption and sale rather than exclusively for export; an agri-food system built around the principle of food sovereignty, in which individuals have direct, democratic control over how they feed and nourish themselves and the lands, water, forests, fishing areas, seed, and other resources they depend on; and a land governance and political system that favors the common good, guarantees personal security, and ensures social, economic, political, and environmental justice (La Via Campesina 2017, 2018; Rosset 2013).

As this book will show, this vision is hardly visible within the discourses and practices surrounding land and its governance that have consolidated within international development circles over the past decade. Instead, many of the organizations whose very raison d'être is to advance the interests of the rural poor—multilateral development banks, bilateral development agencies, and socially conscious non-governmental organizations (NGOs)—have helped to advance a global land governance system that is compatible with, and in many ways serves to legitimate, a neoliberal order in which land and water are increasingly commodified, concentrated, and made available to those deemed most "efficient," without regard for whether they are struggling local households or highly capitalized foreign firms. They have helped to legitimate a system in which takings of the land[3] on which rural households sustain themselves are legitimated, provided they can be defended on procedural grounds. And they have helped to bring into being a system in which the rights to and products from land move freely across national borders toward those most able to pay rather than most in need and in which yields take precedence over diverse values of land in the name of an elusive "food security" at a global scale. Finally, we have inherited a world order in which those who dare to stand up and defend their own and others' means to a livelihood are met by growing levels of violence and personal insecurity.[4] *How did we get here?*

This book profiles the consolidation of a relatively coherent, although not uncontested, land governance orthodoxy in which the seemingly progressive language of rights, tenure security, and women's empowerment have been deployed to redirect the 2007 outcry over "global land grabs" to garner support for land titling and procedural forms of rights recognition, while obscuring the relationship between these instruments, the commodification of land, and growing transnational interests in Africa's farmland. In stark contrast to Western notions of land as (individualized and alienable) property, alternative ontologies of land from across the African continent center place-based social identities and embed land in webs of (more-than-human) relationality and reciprocity in which people may not own land, but belong to it. This contrast exposes the coloniality of the project of "improving" Africa's land governance by projecting onto the continent conceptions of land as a thing that must be extracted from these webs of relationality in order to "secure" it. Far from safeguarding the interests of the rural poor, these dominant conceptions play a crucial part in efforts to grease the wheels of the commodification of land and the appropriation of land and its productive and financial value by powerful commercial interests—both domestic and foreign.

By nature of the book's subject matter, its ethnographic content, and its politics, it dovetails with Nancy Postero and Eli Elinoff's (2019) call for a new anthropology for this "post-political" era of neoliberal governance (Swyngedouw 2009), which has ushered in "a transformation in modes of governing, living, and relating defined entirely by economic logics" while "substituting political struggle with market-based social reconciliation" (Postero and Elinoff 2019: 4; see also Brown 2015; Swyngedouw 2009). This "anthropology of politics" calls for placing our (and others') ethnographic material at the service of world-making, in which scholarship may serve as "both a site of politics and a resource for future transformation" (Postero and Elinoff 2019: 7).[5]

THE ARGUMENT

This book's journey begins in recent history, toward the end of the 2000s when the global financial crisis dovetailed with other mounting "crises"—food, energy, environmental—to spur a renewed interest in land in the global South (Anseeuw et al. 2012; Borras et al. 2011). While a host of studies profiled continuities with the past (Byerlee 2012; Edelman and León 2013), rising energy and food prices, EU policy commitments to renewable energy and the investments in biofuel feedstock it generated, and the financial crisis dovetailed to stimulate renewed commercial interest in Africa's farmland (Cotula, Dyer, and Vermeulen 2008; Fairbairn 2014; German, Schoneveld, and Pacheco 2011). The growing financialization of land enabling the conversion of global farmland real estate into an asset class in global financial markets, the salience of green credentials to justify land and resource expropriation, and a strong foundation of land and investment policy reforms carefully laid through the lending and technical assistance (and aid conditionalities) of the World Bank and IMF helped grease the wheels for a massive transfer of land out of the "customary" domain (Daniel and Mittal 2010; Fairbairn 2014; Fairhead, Leach, and Scoones 2012), while poking "massive structural holes in the tissue of national sovereign territory" (Sassen 2013: 26).

This trend was welcomed by many in the international development establishment. According to a 2008 article in the *Wall Street Journal*,[6] the director-general of the Food and Agriculture Organization of the United Nations (FAO), Jacques Diouf, had campaigned for years for more foreign investment in the global agriculture sector, declaring that, "Foreign direct investment in agriculture is the only way we are going to eradicate global poverty." And in 2009, the World Bank published a report entitled "Awakening Africa's Sleeping Giant: Prospects for Commercial Agriculture in the Guinea Savannah Zone and Beyond" that decries the sorry state of African agriculture—from the limited competitiveness of export crops, to the high dependence on imported food crops and low yields—and calls the African Guinea Savanna "one of the largest underused agricultural land reserves in the world" (World Bank 2009: 2). The successful agricultural commercialization observed in the Brazilian Cerrado and northeastern Thailand—regions formerly seen as "relatively backward"—could also be achieved in Africa, it argues, if only policies and institutions could be strengthened and public and private investments in agriculture scaled up. While the report states that large-scale farming is unlikely to be the most appropriate pathway for achieving this vision in most cases, land policy reforms involving "secure transferable land rights" were needed to enable land to move "to those who can use it most productively" (World Bank 2009: 3).

Socially conscious NGOs, on the other hand, responded with an outcry against what they saw as a "global land grab." In a 2008 report entitled "SEIZED! The 2008 Land Grab for Food and Financial Security," GRAIN[7] declared,

> Today's food and financial crises have, in tandem, triggered a new global land grab. On the one hand, "food insecure" governments that rely on imports to feed their people are snatching up vast areas of farmland abroad for their own offshore food production. On the other hand, food corporations and private investors, hungry for profits in the midst of the deepening financial crisis, see investment in foreign farmland as an important new source of revenue. As a result, fertile agricultural land is becoming increasingly privatised and concentrated. If left unchecked, this global land grab could spell the end of small-scale farming, and rural livelihoods, in numerous places around the world. (GRAIN 2008: 1)

The debate thus became rapidly polarized, with proponents speaking in terms of "investment" and "commercial agriculture" and critics advancing a series of reports profiling the scale and impact of "land grabbing" through a look at both global trends (Anseeuw et al. 2012; Schoneveld 2011) and localized experiences with dispossession (e.g., FoEE 2010; JA and UNAC 2011; Oxfam 2011). A host of country studies soon followed under the auspices of the Land Deal Politics Initiative (LDPI), the International Land Coalition (ILC), the International Institute for Environment and Development (IIED), and national and international NGOs,[8] with the agrarian studies community soon engaged in academic critiques.[9] By 2011, the global assembly of the International Land Coalition had advanced the Tirana Declaration—denouncing land grabbing and calling for "pro-poor, people-centred and environmentally sustainable" governance of land and natural resources (ILC 2011).

The global development community was thus at a crossroads. The vision of the World Bank and FAO of a more globally competitive agricultural sector in which foreign firms would supply the capital and know-how to revitalize African agriculture was closer than ever to being realized with this new wave of investment, and yet also at the greatest risk of being fully discredited. However, within a few years, the global hype around land grabbing had died down in international development circles and "land governance" emerged as a prominent object of development discourse, funding, multi-stakeholder collaboration, knowledge production, and donor programming—with significant buy-in from many previously antagonistic actors. A 2011 World Bank report, *Rising Global Interest in Farmland: Can it Yield Sustainable and Equitable Benefits?*, was a centerpiece to this transition, acknowledging the polarization, highlighting opportunities presented by the new wave of investment, and centering tenure security and land governance as the crucial elements on which these opportunities rested:

> When done right, larger-scale farming can provide opportunities for poor countries with large agricultural sectors and ample endowments of land. To make the most of these opportunities, however, countries will need to better *secure local land rights* and *improve land governance*. (Deininger et al. 2011: xv, emphasis added)

These concepts had broad appeal, and by 2012 the new consensus had been codified in the form of the "Voluntary Guidelines on the Responsible Governance of Tenure of Land, Fisheries and Forests in the Context of National Food Security" (CFS and FAO 2012) and endorsed at a special session of the Committee on World Food Security (CFS 2012). This shared commitment, commonly referred to as "the VGGTs", has since been further codified in the African Union's "Guiding Principles on Large Scale Land Based Investments in Africa" (AU, AfDB, and UNECA 2014) and the land governance targets and indicators within the Sustainable Development Goals, the set of global commitments enshrined in the United Nations' 2030 Agenda for Sustainable Development.[10] The broad buy-in to the VGGTs rested in part on the wide aspirational net that was cast—from legal recognition of informal and customary tenures to land markets, investments, and changes to tenure rights and duties. Yet, crucially, it served to legitimate the expropriation of land through the language of "mutually beneficial transfers" (CFS and FAO 2012: 19), "responsible" and "smallholder-sensitive" investments (20, 21), and relevant safeguards.

A second idea central to efforts to reconcile the growing interest in farmland with the needs and aspirations of rural communities that has also gained traction in the international development community is "inclusive business"—the notion that it is possible to generate a profit while addressing poverty through community-investor partnerships or efforts to more

equitably share value with low-income groups (SNV and WBCSD 2008; Woodhill 2016). While there is no globally codified set of standards for what this means and how to achieve it as exists for land governance, an exercise at mapping the state of play suggests that the alignment of multilateral agency initiatives, donor programs, business platforms, NGOs, practitioner networks, and financing around this idea is no less impressive (Woodhill 2016: 45). Efforts are also underway to codify this idea for the international community (Kelly, Vergara, and Bammann 2015; German et al. 2018;[11] Chamberlain and Anseeuw 2019).

Does this alignment of previously antagonistic actors around a set of common ambitions—and codified norms and instruments to operationalize them—represent a major achievement in the recognition of customary land relations? Or a massively successful effort to normalize and de-politicize land transactions and the wider political economic order in which they are embedded? This book explores the role of a global knowledge regime in which mobilizing metaphors of "rights," "security," and "empowerment" (and crisis narratives of tenure insecurity and poor governance), and the particular ways these concepts are defined and codified, have helped to frame and justify interventions that advance the commodification of land and its alienation from customary rights holders, while forestalling critiques that threaten this project. The unqualified and persuasive endorsement of a few key instruments in the global arsenal of land rights protections—the formalization of alienable rights and voluntary codes of conduct enshrining procedural interpretations of collective rights—stands in stark contrast with mounting evidence, both historical and contemporary, of their ambiguous and often harmful effects. And the taming of critique in international development circles over the past decade stands in stark contrast to the ongoing and in some cases increasing tenure, livelihood, and physical *in*security. While the pace of agricultural land deals has slowed (Lay et al. 2021; Nolte, Chamberlain, and Giger 2016; Cotula and Berger 2017), pressure on land and resources is being felt more acutely in many places; land access and livelihoods continue to be threatened; land-related conflict is on the rise; and there is growing inequality in land relations "based on gender, age, wealth, socio-economic status and ethnicity" (Cotula, Anseeuw, and Baldinelli 2018: 10; see also Cotula and Berger 2017; Lay et al. 2021; Nolte, Chamberlain, and Giger 2016). In 2020, eight years after the codification of a major global agreement on land governance, the murder of land and environmental defenders was at an all-time high—with the mining and agribusiness sectors the primary culprits (Global Witness 2020). With the hype having shifted from "land grabs" to "land governance" and "inclusive business" (a transition that is explored in Part I of this book), attention to the underlying drivers of land loss and growing land and livelihood insecurity—namely, the neoliberal push for transnational investment and secure land access *for investors* has been muted.

Here, it is worth reflecting on the term "customary," which comes with a fair share of conceptual baggage. While once taken to apply to unchanging tradition, what passes today as "custom" has been shown to be profoundly shaped—some would say fully constituted—by colonial rule (Chancock 1991; Colson 1971; Schimdt 1990), as well as by interactions with the post-colonial state, adaptation and reinterpretation of customs in light of changing socio-economic conditions, and ongoing social struggles within rural and urban societies (Diala 2017; Ewelukwa 2002; Okech 2019; Schmid 2001; Ubink and Amanor 2015). Just as the colonial interests of consolidating indirect rule or more contemporary interests in advancing market-based property arrangements have shaped customary legal orders (Alden Wily 2000; Schmid 2001; Schmidt 1990), values emanating from within African societies are also found in the official legal systems of African countries (Frémont 2009). The very boundaries between customary and state legal orders are thus often difficult to pin down. Yet legal anthropologists and institutional theorists have demonstrated time and again the crucial importance of recognizing the existence of legal orders outside of the (admittedly porous) boundaries of the nation state—whether customary, religious, or other (Bromley 1991; Ostrom 1990; F. and K. von Benda Beckmann 2006). While neither static nor uncontested, they matter because of their salience and traction in the everyday governance of rural affairs across Africa and beyond (Alden Wily 2011). They are also crucial to understandings and the governance of land and property.

This book draws on a diverse suite of evidence to make its arguments, from texts and websites of international development organizations, to published reviews and ethnographies, to primary data and personal observations from fieldwork and participation in global knowledge fora. While the discursive and political economic trends discussed in this volume are global in reach, the book's geographical focus is Africa. This is justified by the region's prominence within both discourses of improvement surrounding land governance and transnational land deals over the past 15 years. It has also been the terrain of various professional engagements that serve as inspiration for the volume and dovetail with the book's themes.

My interest in the growing commercial interest in Africa's farmland began with ethnographic fieldwork to document the dynamics and outcomes of large-scale land acquisitions and private investments across sub-Saharan Africa. From 2008 to 2011, I managed a European Commission grant to the Center for International Forestry Research to analyze the social and biophysical impacts of biofuels. This work put me on the ground in 2009, studying the impact of large-scale land acquisitions as the topic was just gaining recognition in international circles. I worked with colleagues to carry out case studies in Ghana and Zambia, while collaborating with colleagues working in Asia and Latin America to carry out global comparative work (German, Schoneveld, and Pacheco 2011).[12] I gained additional insights from case studies on agriculture, forestry, and mining investments across southern and central Africa (Cerutti et al. 2011; Mandondo et al. 2014; Mwitwa et al. 2012). Upon returning to academia in 2012, I poured my energy into fieldwork in Mozambique, in a bid to learn from the country's "successes" based on what was then considered one of the most progressive land laws on the continent (Alden Wily 2011) and what I understood at the time to be an ambitious effort to level the playing field for local communities vis-à-vis the influx of private investment in rural areas under the aegis of the *Iniciativa de Terras Comunitarias* (iTC), or Community Lands Initiative. Working in partnership with Drs. Eunice Cavane, Carla Braga, and Almeida Sitoe of Eduardo Mondlane University, we found that in most respects, land dynamics in Mozambique were no better than those observed elsewhere—with legal recognition and growing formalization of customary land rights doing little to safeguard customary land relations, secure their land access and control, or support local livelihoods. These studies highlighted all that goes wrong for rural communities in land-based investment and large-scale land acquisitions. With iTC playing a decidedly ambiguous role with respect to local interests in land, this work also sparked an interest in the role played by the state, NGOs, and so-called "community participation" in these processes. Systematic qualitative reviews on biofuel sustainability (Hunsberger, German, and Goetz 2017),[13] the implications of "the global land rush" for agricultural communities (German 2016), and the inclusiveness of agricultural value chains (German et al. 2020) have since complemented observations from these isolated cases, allowing first-hand observations to be contextualized within wider trends.

A second source of inspiration comes from my somewhat regular attendance, since 2011, of the annual World Bank Conference on Land and Poverty, where I have witnessed first-hand the shift from antagonistic engagements surrounding "land grabs" to the growing discursive alignment and collaboration of the donor community, private sector, and civil society on the land question. While this transition has been interpreted by some as a strategic move by NGOs to influence the land agenda in favor of customary land users (see, for example, Kapstein 2018), the so-called "business turn" (Hall, Scoones, and Henley 2016) in which NGOs seek to make common cause with multinational corporations, international financial organizations, and bilateral agencies on a growing number of issues has rightfully begun to receive closer scrutiny (Baur and Schmitz 2012; Chapin 2004; Sachedina, Igoe, and Brockington 2009).

Finally, recent scholarship and consulting work on core themes of this volume, from inclusive business to the formalization of customary land rights and women's tenure security, have given me the opportunity to systematically contrast the discourse from major players in the international development community with evidence from the published literature. This work has helped to crystalize the vast disconnect between the theories of change populating international development circles and the actual relationships between investment, land dynamics (titling, consultations, acquisitions), and rural livelihoods. It has also shown how a surface level of consensus on spheres of common interest (e.g., "respect for land rights") may mask vastly different visions of rural futures, and the negative reactions invoked by those with positions of influence in the land governance arena when bringing these differences to the surface. These ideas were first committed to paper through a scholarly critique of the emergent land governance regime published with Dr. Carla Braga in *The Journal of Peasant Studies* (German and Braga 2019). I have since gained additional empirical and theoretical insights from a foray into dominant and marginalized ontologies of land, water, and biodiversity governance (DePuy et al. 2021), and coloniality (Arney et al. 2022).

THEORETICAL UNDERPINNINGS

This volume draws its primary insights from scholarship on the knowledge-power nexus, or the "politics of knowledge," and its recent turn to ontological questions in a bid to make sense of the global knowledge regime surrounding land and its governance. Yet to stop there would leave the crucial question of the work being done by these discursive-ontological formations unaddressed. For this, I draw on (agrarian) political economy to connect these discursive formations to wider economic and political ideologies and the material conditions produced by them—and to critical theories of law and property for insights into the institutional mechanisms through which the two connect.

The Politics of Knowledge

> Western civilization's ability to manage knowledge explains its success in expanding itself politically and economically.
> —Mignolo (2012: xiii)

POWER/KNOWLEDGE

Social scientists have long argued for the inseparability of power and knowledge and the intimate association between regimes of truth and regimes of rule. Michel Foucault, in particular, is widely credited with observations related to *productive* forms of power—namely, how power operates not just through overt repression, but by shaping the concepts that are thinkable and the practices and ways of being that become normalized (Bazzul 2016). In his own words, "We are subjected to the production of truth through power and we cannot exercise power except through the production of truth" (Foucault 1980: 93). Along these lines, power is not considered as something located in a particular place or held by particular actors and absent elsewhere, but rather something that circulates among and is exercised by individuals who are simultaneously the targets of and the "vehicles of power or elements of its articulation" (Foucault 1980: 98).

Foucault and those inspired by his work trace the relationship between the political rationalities and techniques involved in efforts by powerful actors to "govern others" on the one hand, and processes of subject formation through which actors "govern themselves" on the other (Foucault 1979, 1990; see also Agrawal 2005; Dean 2010; Lemke 2002). What makes this form of power accepted is the fact that it "does not weigh on us as a force that says no, but that it traverses and produces things, it induces pleasure, forms knowledge, produces discourse" (Foucault 1980: 119). Truth—including that held by marginalized groups, or those working to defend their interests—is thus not something that lies outside of power or is devoid of power, but a manifestation of it.

Cris Shore and Susan Wright (1997) highlight the role often played by "mobilizing metaphors"—keywords that succeed in attracting mass popular support—in this process. These metaphors, "become the centre of a cluster of keywords whose meaning extend and shift while previous associations with other words are dropped. Their mobilizing effect lies in their capacity to connect with, and appropriate, the positive meanings and legitimacy derived from other key symbols" (Shore and Wright 1997: 20). In the land sector, metaphors of "rights," "security," and "empowerment" serve as powerful metaphors that resonate with deeply held values; it is inconceivable that one would disagree with them. Together with "crisis narratives" that construct one particular story (while excluding others) about problems demanding urgent attention (Rocheleau, Steinberg, and Benjamin 1995)—such as "tenure insecurity" and "poor land governance," or any number of sub-crises invoked in tandem (e.g., climate change, food security, domestic abuse, or Covid-19[14]) —these metaphors form powerful mechanisms of actor enrollment while part and parcel of the making of self-evident truths about the world.

The operation of certain "apparatuses of knowledge" ("methods of observation, techniques of registration, procedures for investigation and research, apparatuses of control") is said to produce and contribute to the construction of shared and largely unconscious *"regimes" of thought, knowledge and discourse* (Foucault 1980: 93, 81, 102, 112, 113). In a 1970s interview entitled "Truth and Power," Foucault explored how these new knowledge and discursive regimes often emerge over the course of only a few years (Foucault 1980: 112), constituting self-evident "truths" that are difficult to see or diagnose as they permeate our very modes of thought and understanding of reality:

> Each society has its regime of truth, its general politics of truth: that is, the types of discourse which it accepts and makes function as true . . . the techniques and procedures accorded value in the acquisition of truth; the status of those who are charged with saying what counts as true . . . "Truth" is the object of immense diffusion and consumption . . . ; is produced and transmitted under the control, dominant if not exclusive, of a few great political and economic apparatuses . . . and linked in a circular relation with systems of power which produce and sustain it, and to effects of power which it induces and which extend it. (Foucault 1980: 131–32)

Such discourses do not just make the world in a flat way, in which all voices have equal weight. Rather, certain voices and versions of truth are privileged over others, and those that are elevated tend to align with powerful actors and interests in society. Writings in political ecology, for example, have shown that environmental knowledge can be as much a manifestation of power and ideology as a reflection of actual material conditions, and may demonize disenfranchised land users while advancing the interests or legitimacy of the powerful (Fairhead and Leach 1996; Peet and Watts 2004). Knowledge practices categorizing the "other" have also been shown to justify and thus advance colonialism and imperialism (Abu Lughod 2013; Said 1978; Spivak 1993). This points to the need to "provincialize" dominant modes of thought, exposing them not as universal, objective truths but as the products of particular times, places, interests, and power relations (Chakrabarty 2000; see also Maldonado-Torres 2017; Mignolo and Walsh 2018). This has long been the project of political ecologists, Black feminist and critical race theorists, and Indigenous, postcolonial, and decolonial scholars, among others, who have struggled to de-center and deconstruct received wisdoms about environmental conditions and their causes (Fairhead and Leach 1995, 1996; Sivaramakrishnan 1999), gender (Amos and Parmar 2005; Abu-Lughod 2013; Haraway 1988; Oyewumi 1997), race (Baker 1998; Buck 2012; Gould 1981; Mbembe 2017) and European superiority (Cohn 1996; Coulthard 2010; Escobar 1995; Gruffydd Jones 2013; Mignolo 2012; Ndlovu-Gatsheni 2018; Sousa Santos 2014; Spivak 1993).

For a volume such as this, however, to treat scholarship on coloniality as but one of many equally relevant strands of thinking within the politics of knowledge would obscure some of the fundamental dynamics that have enabled singular land governance logics to gain purchase across such far-flung locales as the Peruvian Amazon, the Great Rift Valley, the Guinea Savanna zone, and the humid tropical forests of Southeast Asia. Engaging with coloniality is one of the most powerful ways to move the power/knowledge framing outside the inner workings of the West and onto the global stage in which European knowledge, ontology, and history have been positioned as universal (Quijano 2007; Chakrabarty 2000).

Differentiated from colonialism as a formal system of political domination over others,[15] coloniality is framed by Aníbal Quijano (2007) as an ongoing system of intersubjective constructions posing as objective truths that perpetuate relationships of domination between European culture and its others. In other words, coloniality is "a pattern of power that operates through the naturalization of racial and social hierarchies that make possible the reproduction of relationships of territorial and epistemic domination" (Gomez-Quintero 2010: 89, in reference to Quijano 2000). It is rooted in the cultural complex of European-Western modernity/rationality that was constituted alongside colonialism, which framed history as an,

> evolutionary continuum from the primitive to the civilized; from the traditional to the modern; from the savage to the rational; from pro[to]-capitalism to capitalism, etc. And Europe thought of itself as the mirror of the future of all the other societies and cultures; as the advanced form of the history of the entire species. (Quijano 2007: 176)

Coloniality, then, is rooted in epistemology—constituted as forms of absolute knowledge in which discourses of the rationality and modernity of the West invoke the inferiority of other peoples, places, nations, and cultural orientations. Coloniality is not just far-reaching, but ongoing—connecting colonial experience to the present and making it hard to differentiate the postcolonial from the neocolonial "as mutually exclusive states of being" (Ndlovu-Gatsheni 2013: xi). The reasons for this continuity lie, in large part, in the ongoing reproduction of the narratives of modernity and hierarchy within the ontologies and institutions in the West and, through this, in "the imagination of the dominated" (Quijano 2007: 169; see also Merino Acuña 2014). Yet, crucially, these epistemological continuities are not divorced from material realities or geopolitical concerns, but constitute those very conditions, while "hiding their own geopolitical grounding" (Mignolo 2012: xiii). By invoking the inferiority of other peoples and places, discourses of the rationality and modernity of the West help to justify outside interventions in the name of progress—from "the Christian mission of the early modern (Renaissance) colonialism [to] the civilizing mission of the secularized modernity, and the development and modernization projects after World War II" (Mignolo 2012: 22). And the knowledges so carefully cultivated and curated in the centers of economic and political power in the West are thus a crucial and central part of the ability of Western civilization to expand itself politically and economically both in the past and present. Coloniality thus undergirds a broader world order involving not just hierarchies of race and nationality, but forms of economic and political domination. For these scholars, "development," "modernization," and "good governance" are but the latest permutations of this process (Escobar 1995; Gruffydd Jones 2013; Mignolo 2012). "As a concept, process, discourse and practice, [development] remains caught up in coloniality of power, which hampers the formulation of possibilities for decolonized, democratic and inclusive development" (Ndlovu-Gatsheni 2012: 48).

Coloniality and modernity are thus two faces of the same coin, in which problems in the contemporary world order are rooted in the tendency for coloniality to be constantly masked by the rhetoric of modernity:

> It is the very logic of coloniality, that moves the world, but it has to be disguised with the rhetoric of modernity, of salvation and progress. (Mignolo 2012: xvi)

ONTOLOGICAL ANTHROPOLOGY: [DE]CENTERING THE CONCEPTS WE THINK WITH

As discussed above, postmodern scholars have long argued for how concepts make the world by shaping the thoughts which are thinkable and normalizing certain practices and conceptions of self. In the interplay of *logos* and the constitution of things, Foucault grants historical-analytical primacy to the former (Pellizzoni 2015: 49)—demonstrating the conditions that are sustained by the concepts through which the world is thought at different historical moments. Naming, as with the formulation of categories marking socially deviant acts from "normal" behavior, the designation of "culture" as something separate from "nature," and the delineation of boundaries between the "developed" and the "undeveloped" world, is part and parcel of the constitution of those same subjects (Escobar 1995; Foucault 1980; Hacking 1986). "Once the distinctions were made, new realities effectively came into being" (Hacking 1986: 164). Put differently, "the ways in which we know and represent the world are inseparable from the ways we choose to live in it" (Jasanoff 2004: 2)—with realities enacted in our everyday practices.

Yet many of the questions addressed by these social theorists represent epistemological questions—the study of "how people create knowledge and what is possible to know" (Moon and Blackman 2014: 1169), "how one sees things" (Holbraad and Pedersen 2017: 4), or how the world can be known. More recently, anthropologists have turned to ontological questions—questions about reality itself, the study of what *is* and of "what exists for people to know about" (Moon and Blackman 2014: 1169). While many scholars emphasize the inseparability of epistemology and ontology (e.g., Crotty 1998), a shift to ontological questions enables far greater insights into other worlds than is possible if assumptions about "*what is*" and "*what is X*" (the concepts we think with) go unquestioned. By forcing us to question our assumptions about reality and the concepts through which we think the world (or filter and interpret the worlds of others), the situatedness and provinciality of our own world-making come to light. Interrogating the concepts used to think and write with is key, as they embody "basic commitments and assumptions about *what things are, and what they could be*" (Holbraad and Pederson 2017: 5) and enable these assumptions to be called into question.

A commitment to provincialize our assumptions about the world and the concepts through which we think it requires that we move beyond conceiving of ontologies different from our own as simply questions of belief, or stories that have no bearing on the world—in which our own ways of knowing the world are synonymous with some singular, objective, and all-encompassing reality (a "one-world world," to quote Law 2011). What ontological questions ask is that we see these differences instead as "different realities being done in different practices" (Law 2011: 2). And that requires not just taking other worlds seriously, but de-centering the ontological underpinnings of the modern/Western world—such as the nature/culture divide and the humanism it gives rise to (Latour 1993).

Those working in the ontological vein of contemporary scholarship vary in the degree of emphasis on metaphysical and ontological questions, and the degree to which they explore reality beyond human representations of it (or commit to multiple realities). The broader turn to human language and social construction that the power/knowledge framing is heir to, and the embeddedness of the anthropologist in their own cultural-historical-semiotic contexts, make it hard to "conceptualize that which is outside of language or culture" and thus to explore reality beyond human representations of it (Kohn 2015: 314). One of the most ambitious efforts to do so is Eduardo Kohn's own pioneering study of human relationships to rainforest beings in the Ecuadorian Amazon (Kohn 2013), in which he explores how humans communicate with a host of nonhuman beings beyond the constraining forces of human language and symbolism. This volume makes no such effort to move outside of language, but rather uses a combination of a Foucauldian-style archaeology of language and cross-cultural inquiry to explore how worlds are made through both the constructive force of language and the "ontological assumptions drawn from it," and the legitimation these constructs provide for a set of political economic relations that further entrench hierarchies of knowledge, being, and material entitlement.

Such a project calls on us not to assume the words "land," "property," "rights," or "security" exist in other languages or in the ways in which other societies conceptualize the world and their place within it. Where similar concepts do exist, it demands that we not assume these entities designate the same semantic field, or relate to one another in the same ways. Better yet, it asks us to approach the land question in its entirety as an open-ended question, asking what "land" *is*—both for those advancing interventionist logics on the world stage, and for the people and places deemed deficient and in need of (land programming) intervention.

A number of scholars have begun to explore ontologies of land in the context of contemporary debates surrounding land and environmental governance. In Tania Li's 2014 article "What is land?," she explores the "materialities, relations, technologies and discourses" through which land has been assembled as a resource for global investment (Li 2014: 589)—yet does so through a distinctly ontological lens. In a bid to provincialize dominant constructs, Li highlights how what land *is* for the farmer is not the same as what it is for the tax collector; while its materiality matters, its uses and meanings are not stable and are often contested. She highlights a host of legitimation tactics and "inscription devices" through which land's contemporary singularity has been constructed—highlighting the "great deal of complex cultural work" required to assemble land as a resource available for some purposes (global investment) to the exclusion of others (customary uses) (Li 2014: 592). She poses a set of questions that are central to both locating and contesting dominant land governance constructs. By asking, "what land is (its ontology), what it can do (its affordances) and how humans should interact with it" (Li 2014: 590) across differently situated social formations, it is possible to provincialize constructs increasingly advanced as universal. Further, in an article entitled "Rethinking land grab ontology," Philip McMichael (2014) seeks to expand this ontological analysis of the current land governance moment. He highlights two contested ontologies of land—the "neoproductivist," in which land is conceived of as an economic resource available for agribusiness-driven expansion in the name of sustainable intensification, and "land sovereignty," in which land is understood as essential to smallholder livelihoods and environmental stewardship and resilience.

These debates should be contextualized within wider fields of scholarship juxtaposing settler colonial with Indigenous ontologies of land and being, and their instrumental roles in advancing Indigenous dispossession and settler futurities on the one hand, and motivating Indigenous resistance on the other. According to Glen Coulthard (Yellowknives Dene and associate professor at the University of British Columbia), while most Western societies tend to derive meaning from the world in historical/developmental terms and thus place time as the "narrative of central importance," Indigenous metaphysics tend to revolve around *place* and "the central importance of land to Indigenous modes of being, thought, and ethics" (Coulthard 2010: 79). Coulthard cites the late Lakota philosopher Vine Deloria in saying, "it is a profound misunderstanding to think of land or place as simply some material object of profound importance to Indigenous cultures (although it is this too); instead, it ought to be understood as a field of 'relationships of things to each other' (Deloria 2001)" (Coulthard 2010: 79). This profound relationality—with living humans and ancestors, and with other-than-human beings (animals, plants, spirits)—is a defining feature of Indigenous ontologies of land and environment across world regions (Burow, Brock, and Dove 2018; DePuy et al. 2021). Place and the animate beings that inhabit it are not passive objects, but are regularly called upon to anchor Indigenous systems of morality (Basso 1996) and are often capable of intervening in human affairs, typically to encourage people to live right (Di Giminiani 2015; Lentz 2006). The nature of these relationships to land is rarely one of ownership, and more often one of respect, reciprocity, care, kinship and belonging (Benöhr and Lynch 2018; Kohn 2013; Shipton 2009; Tsing 2003). Place is also wrapped up in social identities—a repository of social norms and shared history; a means for connecting with ancestors; a teacher and a source of strength (Basso 1996; Coggeshall 2018; Coulthard 2010; Simpson 2014). And, increasingly, place and the politics of belonging are being leveraged within struggles over resources and power in the context of migration and globalization, reaffirming the relationship between rights to land and membership in particular communities and often hardening boundaries between autochthons and strangers (Geschiere and Gugler 1998; Lentz 2007; Mujere 2010; Shipton 2009).

Settler colonial ontologies of land, on the other hand, are said to operate through a logic of elimination (Tuck and Yang 2012; Wolfe 2006); ontological foreclosures whereby "other modes of perceiving, representing, and experiencing land" are occluded (or belittled and weaponized) (Burow, Brock, and Dove 2018: 57); and settler moves to innocence[16] that serve to rescue settler futures (Tuck and Yang 2012). With territoriality argued to be settler colonialism's "specific, irreducible element," settler colonialism must "destroy to replace" (Wolfe 2006: 388)—a logic that is apparent in these ontological forms. "Negatively, it strives for the dissolution of native societies. Positively, it erects a new colonial society on the expropriated land base" (Wolfe 2006: 388). These seemingly benign mechanisms of discursive and ontological erasure and replacement are argued by Coulthard (2014) to be the contemporary version of the overtly violent means once used under colonialism to eliminate native societies and erase and re-make landscapes to their own liking. The onset of more "polite" times (German and Braga 2019) means that legitimation tactics are instrumental to new regimes of exclusion and dispossession. Scholars of settler colonialism and neocolonialism push back at efforts to situate these processes in the past, emphasizing instead the ongoing need to justify the settler (and, I would argue, imperial) present (Wolfe 2006). "Negative" discourses of *terra nulius* (Kosek 2006; Voyles 2015), underutilization and inefficiency (Li 2014), and "abstract, empty and exchangeable space" (Moore 2005: 20), as well as "positive" efforts to narrow relationships to land to only that between owner and property (Moreton-Robinson 2015), resonate deeply with the ontological reimaginings of land in the contemporary moment. Without the force of such erasure and reconstitution of land and property relations, "land could not be wrested from those who belong to it and to whom it rightfully belongs" (Simpson 2014: 100).

Yet settler colonial and neocolonial ontologies of land do not take hold uniformly. As argued by Mario Blaser, conflict and contestation with contemporary projects of dispossession—whether extractivist or conservationist—are often motivated by ontological ruptures surrounding "the very definition of the 'things' that are at stake" (Blaser 2013: 14). In profiling environmental conflicts between Indigenous peoples and the state in the Peruvian Amazon and Paraguay, he found indignation surrounding,

> the values and assumptions with which others approach their territories, without care and without a personal relationship with the nonhuman inhabitants of these territories. One is warranted in saying that in these cases the indigenous peoples are defending not simply access to and control over resources; they are defending complex webs of relations between humans and nonhumans, relations that, for them, are better expressed in the language of kinship than in the language of property. (Blaser 2013: 14)

These "place-based imaginaries" often ground relational ethics (Basso 1996; Blaser 2013)—a foundation from which many Indigenous people and communities resist both state sovereignty and capitalist accumulation (Blaser 2013; Coulthard 2010).

Efforts to center place-based ontologies of land in wider debates over property tend to receive knee-jerk reactions from mainstream property theorists. "You don't mean to tell us that you are proposing we look to *premodern* forms of thought for insight?!," retorted one attendee to such ideas at the 2019 Workshop on the Ostrom Workshop at Indiana University. Such disbelief can only emanate from a place of ontological arrogance—the idea that Western and modernist conceptions of nature/culture and property are not situated (culturally, historically, politically), but universal. Only the non-Western Other has culture; what we have here in the West is knowledge. One does not have to glance far afield—whether to the havoc wreaked by the institutionalization of fire and flood suppression as "good environmental management" (Delcourt and Delcourt 1998; Long and Lake 2018; Morita and Jensen 2017) or the politics of the post-truth era—to understand the shaky ground on which this assumption rests.

Theoretical work on power/knowledge and ontology is not just an academic exercise of exposing knowledges that stand above and apart from material and social reality, but an exercise in understanding how the very world is made—from "rights" to regimes of rule and material reality itself. Foucault and other contemporary scholars working in this power/knowledge tradition make exposing the conditions that give rise to certain concepts, and the (social, ecological, material) conditions that these concepts in turn sustain, a core analytical project. Here, it is important to draw on other areas of scholarship to situate these discursive and ontological dynamics within the wider landscape of changing economic, political, and material configurations on the world stage.

Political Economy of the "Global Land Grab"

> It is impossible to separate the ideas and symbolism of subordination from a process of material exploitation.
>
> —Scott (1990: 188)

Knowledge and ontology do not exist as mere thoughts disconnected from material relations and place, but are inextricably linked to them. A parallel focus on political economy highlights the material interests behind—and material relations produced and legitimated by—the emergent knowledge regime. This section situates the politics of knowledge surrounding land and its governance within the underlying shifts in political economic conditions shaping the evolving role of land in Africa and beyond.

While there are undoubtedly historical continuities in both domestic and transnational land relations, scholars highlight the shifting role of land in lower-income countries over the past 15 years and the wider political economic trends in which these shifts have taken place. Following the post-independence period in Asia and Africa in which states enlisted agriculture in support of import substitution policies to achieve rapid industrialization, agriculture was largely neglected. Under structural adjustment, the state institutions directing agricultural development were dismantled and the support formerly provided to farmers removed (De Schutter 2011). During this time, agricultural value chains tended to concentrate returns in processing and distribution, with the risks falling on primary producers (Selby 2009)—creating incentives for agribusiness companies to invest in upstream and downstream activities while sourcing agricultural produce from local suppliers (Cotula 2012). Yet in the mid- to late-2000s, a shift occurred in which agribusiness began to take a greater interest in agricultural production, and together with investment funds and government agencies, began to acquire long-term rights over large tracts of farmland in the global South.

Studies of the scale, geography, and character of these land acquisitions corroborate the existence of a "worldwide rush for land" in line with the outcry from civil society (Anseeuw et al. 2012). A global report of the phenomenon by the Land Matrix published in 2011 suggested that between 43.7 and 83.2 million hectares[17] of land (in deals involving areas in excess of 200 ha) had changed hands between 2000 and 2011. Out of these global totals, Africa was found to be the most targeted region, with 754 land deals covering an estimated 56.2 million ha of transactions being reported. Of these, legally formalized transfers were estimated to cover 26.2 million ha, and deals where project implementation had commenced, 21 million ha. While these numbers are notoriously slippery (Scoones et al. 2013), two separate analyses highlight the high concentration of these deals in a handful of African countries, including Sudan, Ethiopia, Mozambique, Tanzania, Madagascar, Zambia, DR Congo, Ghana, South Sudan, and Liberia (Anseeuw et al. 2012; Schoneveld 2011). While discursive maneuvers sought to frame African land as idle and available, in practice land acquisitions have often been sited in prime cropland near roads and railways and displaced local land uses. An estimated 45% of deals were found in the first Land Matrix report to be targeting cropland or crop-vegetation mosaics (Anseeuw et al. 2012), and a separate study found deals larger than 2000 ha in a sample of 32 African countries to account for an area equivalent to 8.3% of the annual area harvested across all of sub-Saharan Africa (Schoneveld 2011; see also Cotula et al. 2009). These investments were clearly not targeting unutilized land. While the pace of land deals declined after 2013 (Lay et al. 2021), land acquisitions continue and their local impacts have increased as deals formerly existing only on paper materialize as operational investments (Nolte, Chamberlain, and Giger 2016).

With agriculture characterized by high levels of uncertainty and risk (Woodhill 2016) and Africa's rural areas once considered an investment backwater, what accounts for this seismic shift in global interest in Africa's farmland? An early review of the international political economy of the "global land rush" by Lorenzo Cotula of the International Institute for Environment and Development (IIED) pointed to both market and policy forces (Cotula 2012). One key market force has been the changing supply and demand of agricultural commodities, and the fear induced by the 2008 spike in food prices over future supply and its implications for national food security (Figure 1). This spike followed a long period of food price decline accompanying the expansion of agricultural frontiers and trade (Cotula 2012). The spike is thought to have been induced by rising energy costs, the diversion of food crops to biofuels and the devaluation of the dollar, and exacerbated once prices started to rise by export restrictions on staples, agribusiness monopoly pricing and the increased role of financial speculators in markets for agricultural commodity derivatives (Cotula 2012; De Schutter 2010; Headey and Fan 2008; McMichael 2009).

Yet this is not a simple story of supply and demand of agricultural commodities. As investors sought more dependable investments in the wake of the 2008 financial crisis, farmland was seen as an increasingly attractive investment. A deepening trend toward the financialization of agriculture enabled this shift, with a host of new farmland funds emerging to lure investors in search of alternatives (Fairbairn et al. 2014). To understand the parameters of this shift, it is important to distinguish between profit-making through productive activities such as commodity production and trade, and profit-making through financial channels (Arrighi 1994; Krippner 2011). Financialization is a historically recurrent phenomenon in which, midway through a "cycle of accumulation," capitalist accumulation shifts its emphasis from commodity production and trade to finance (Arrighi 1994; Fairbairn 2014). The unique features of farmland as an investment class dovetailed with the food price spike and the growing disillusionment with the latest financial era[18] to generate renewed excitement in farmland among investors. As geographers have pointed out, "capitalism cannot survive without being geographically expansionary and perpetually seeking out spatial fixes for its problems" (Harvey 2001: 25) or without new commodity frontiers (Moore 2011). Africa's farmland had become the spatial fix to the financial crisis and the erosion of faith in purely financial assets.

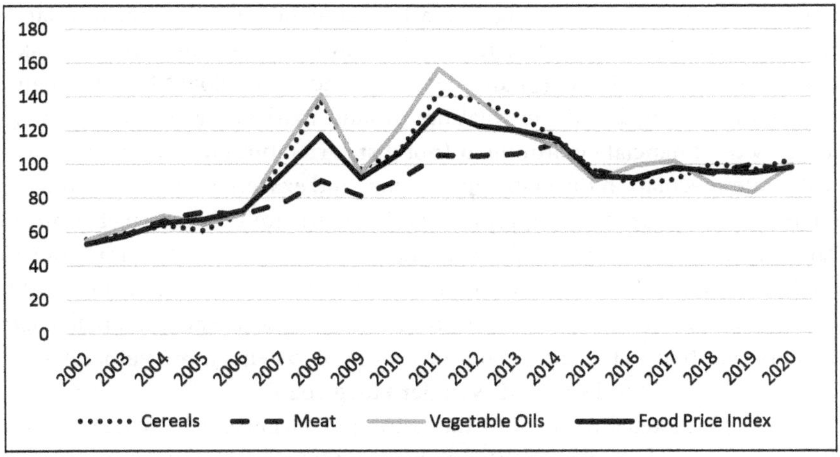

Figure 1. Price indices for food and key food commodities. (Source: FAO; Available at: http://www.fao.org/worldfoodsituation/FoodPricesIndex/en.)

According to Madeleine Fairbairn, "the new farmland investments are premised on the land's profitability as both a productive and a financial asset" (Fairbairn 2014: 785). Fairbairn identified two farmland investment strategies: "own-lease out," in which land is purely a financial asset (with returns from rental income and capital gains on appreciation), and "own-operate," in which land's function is both productive and financial (capital gains). Among these sources of value, farmland investors were found to place a heavy emphasis on capital gains from land appreciation and on land as an inflation hedge (with land expected to retain its value more than most financial assets).

> Investors who are drawn to farmland are often motivated by a desire to get the right kind of exposure to long-term trends or extreme events that would alter the political economy of global agriculture . . . such as global population growth and increasing resource scarcity; or "value investing" aiming at capturing long-term intrinsic value of an asset (and where farmland's productive capacity is key to its value as an investment—whether that investment is in production or just the land itself). (Fairbairn 2014: 783–784)

The "realness" of farmland as a source of profit has become second to its financial value, with financialization enabling farmland to become "a store of value first and foremost and a means of production only as an afterthought"

(Fairbairn 2014: 786). This suggests a fundamental shift in what farmland "is"—both symbolically and materially. In addition to its central role in making customary land in Africa and beyond attractive to global capital, financialization has enhanced the volatility of land markets by subjecting them to the wider financial environment (not just agricultural use value); fostered real estate speculation through appreciation; and exacerbated unequal power relations within agri-food supply chains (Fairbairn 2014; Fairbairn et al. 2014; van der Ploeg 2020). These shifts are deeply consequential to rural households, and not only in the ways represented in the discourses of the World Bank, with the drive for financial profits harming workers and small-scale farmers (Fairbairn et al. 2014) and making food systems more vulnerable to shocks (Clapp and Isakson 2018; van der Ploeg 2020).

A third market force behind the rising global interest in Africa's farmland, and closely related to the aforementioned trends in supply-demand and financialization, has been the restructuring of the global food regime. Some scholars have argued that we are in the process of transitioning into a new global food regime, although "the form and content of that putative regime" is debated (Burch and Lawrence 2009: 267). A food regime may be defined as "stable periodic arrangements in the production and circulation of food on a world scale, associated with various forms of hegemony in the world economy: British, American, and corporate/neoliberal" (McMichael 2009: 281). The emergent food regime, led by global corporations profiting from the reorganization of and control over agri-food chains (van der Ploeg 2020), is said to have followed two earlier regimes: the first based upon colonial trade in bulk commodities like wheat and sugar, and the second typified by industrial agriculture and manufactured foods (Burch and Lawrence 2009). Attempts to explain and characterize the transition to the third food regime have emphasized the "clean and green" aspects of food (Le Heron and Roche 1995); the international flows of commodities and finance capital (Pritchard 1998); the increasing power of supermarkets and the food retail sector's ability to restructure agri-food supply chains (Friedmann 2005); the reconstruction of the agricultural sector as an extractive economy (Ye et al. 2020); and the tension between the corporate imperative for global agri-food expansion and the desire of marginalized peoples for food sovereignty (McMichael 2005). The land grab may be seen as one expression of this restructuring in which growing food prices, declining Northern productivity and widening land costs between North and South find expression in the acquisition of cheap land, water, and labor in the global South (McMichael 2012).

These more theoretical treatments find support in the value chain literature, which highlights two interrelated trends in global agribusiness value chains that were already reshaping production and processing in the global South by the onset of the financial crisis. The first is the growing importance of product and process standards driven by the increasingly stringent food safety requirements of importing countries; a shift from product standards enforced at borders to controls over production and processing; and the growth of private standards to complement mandatory public standards (Humphrey and Memedovic 2006). The second trend consists of increasing concentration along value chains, driven in part by the need to satisfy the requirements of demanding global buyers—whether product safety and sustainability or customization and specifications related to the volume, speed, and reliability of supply (Humphrey and Memedovic 2006). Value chains are increasingly characterized by greater vertical integration, either through explicit inter-firm coordination replacing tacit coordination through markets or through consolidation of ownership, and by the growing influence of lead firms in constructing value chains to "deliver what is required by global buyers and food safety regimes" (Humphrey and Memedovic 2006: 5; see also Gereffi et al. 2001; Mausch et al. 2009). For example, consumer demand for high-quality fresh produce year-round has led to the restructuring of horticultural value chains from a mostly wholesale-based produce market involving middlemen buying produce from farmers and selling it to grocers, to tightly integrated supply chains in which supermarkets maintain their own regulatory standards over each point in the chain (Barrett et al. 1999; Dolan and Humphrey 2004). Tightening standards and growing vertical integration across a host of value chains, alongside the search for ever greater production and processing efficiencies, is squeezing out smallholders and farm workers alike (German et al. 2018).

Policy forces have also been instrumental to these dynamics, from the policies directly surrounding the late-2000s spikes in food prices and land transactions, to the longer arc of neoliberal policy reforms in which the very boundaries of state and market are no longer easy to discern. The rapid growth in biofuels in the 2000s is widely understood to be driven by government policies (mandates, targets and subsidies) enacted for a mix of energy independence, environmental/climate, and rural development motives (Duffield, Xiarchos, and Halbrook 2008; European Commission 2009; Hochman and Zilberman 2016; Kristoufek, Janda, and Zilberman 2012). They were also shown to have had a significant impact on both food prices and the increased pace of transnational land deals in the late 2000s

(Anseeuw et al. 2012; Cotula 2012; Kristoufek, Janda, and Zilberman 2012). Government support to land acquisition overseas has also played a role, given widespread expectations of rising food and agricultural commodity prices linked to fundamentals of global supply and demand (Anseeuw et al. 2012; Cotula 2012). Early analyses often pointed to China and the Gulf States as drivers of farmland acquisitions (Anseeuw et al. 2012; Edelman, Oya, and Borras 2013), yet recent evidence points to Europe and the US in terms of both investor origin and efforts to liberalize Africa's economic policy and land markets (Daniel and Mittal 2010; Maganga et al. 2016; Nolte, Chamberlain, and Giger 2016). The latest Land Matrix report, for example, identifies Malaysia and the United States as the top investor countries in terms of the area of land in concluded land deals between 2000 and 2020 (Lay et al. 2021). Thus, while private companies rather than government entities account for most land transactions,[19] government policies have played a crucial role in supporting agribusiness-led acquisitions (Cotula 2012; Nolte, Chamberlain, and Giger 2016).

The agency of host country economic and political elites should not be underestimated. Driven not just by "benevolent strategic choices to promote economic development" but also by opportunities to attract international capital to provide "national elites with opportunities for business activities, political patronage and personal gain" (Cotula 2012: 671), host countries have embraced reforms opening up their markets and land to foreign entities. This alignment in the interests of foreign capital and domestic elites is one of the crowning achievements of the political economic regime that is reconfiguring land and livelihoods in the global South, and a hallmark of Western imperialism (Quijano 2007). While the G8 and Africa's leading "land donors" continue to rely on aid conditionalities to encourage neoliberal reforms (Maganga et al. 2016)—what James Ferguson calls "a crude battering open of Third World markets" (Ferguson 2009: 173), there are now opportunities for elites of all stripes to profit from the entrenchment of capitalism's reach into rural areas.

Many have drawn connections between these shifts and the deepening of neoliberalism, what David Harvey defines as "a theory of political economic practices that proposes that human well-being can best be advanced by liberating individual entrepreneurial freedoms and skills within an institutional framework characterized by strong private property rights, free markets, and free trade" (Harvey 2005: 2). With *neo*liberalism once thought to be distinguished from classical liberalism by the retrenchment of the state, recent scholarship points instead to the changing nature of the state and "the active role it imagines for government in creating the conditions for diffusion of markets and market-like mechanisms" (Collier 2012; see also Hilgers 2012). While one may need to do some digging to identify the neoliberal ideals within state-centered efforts to shift to biofuels,[20] policy shifts within host countries to attract foreign investors, streamline business transactions, liberalize land markets, and open borders to trade in agricultural commodities are clearly an entrenchment of the neoliberal ideals espoused by the West (Brown 2005; Daniel and Mittal 2010; Maganga et al. 2016). And they have been part and parcel of the capitalist drive to transform the role and function of African farmland in the process of establishing new frontiers for capitalist expansion (Edelman and Wolford 2017; Moore 2011; Peluso and Lund 2011). Unsurprisingly, neo-liberal policies restructuring agriculture and international commerce have also been deeply consequential for rural households, exposing them "to a variety of interrelated threats, including: competition from subsidized industrial agricultural products from the North, streamlined supply chains that reduce the market power of small producers, rising input costs and reduced access to formal credit, and increased competition for farmland" (Fairbairn et al. 2014: 658).

The parallels between the political economic shifts traced herein and the politics of knowledge and ontology profiled in the previous section echo Alexander Dunlap and Sian Sullivan's call to explore "the iterative and consequential connections between objective/material and subjective/psychological dimensions" of alienation (Dunlap and Sullivan 2019) or the relationship between "symbolic humiliation" and material domination and its role in facilitating appropriation (Besteman 2014: 181). Marxist scholars arguing for a twin analysis of these two domains tend to assume that the subjective consequences of alienation emanate from its material dimensions, in which "objective conditions have subjective consequences" (Zhang 2011) or whereby "changing objective conditions produce shifts in political subjectivities" (Harvey 2018: 142). In line with ontological scholarship, this book flips this causality on its head, arguing instead for the generative role of the subjective-ontological in enabling and legitimating the shifting material conditions profiled above.

Without losing track of this coupling of the ideological-ontological and material in land governance, I turn now to a third set of ideas surrounding the crucial role of the law as a central terrain through which abstract notions of "what land *is* or *could be*" become codified and instrumentalized—a crucial mediator, so to speak, between cognitive-discursive and material realms.

Critical Theories of Rights, Law and Property

> If possession of land was (and remains) the ultimate objective of colonial power, then property law is the primary means of realizing this desire . . . Laws of property also reflect and consolidate language, ways of seeing, and modes of subjectivity that render indigenous and colonized populations as outside history lacking the requisite cultural practices, habits of thought, and economic organization to be considered as sovereign, rational economic subjects.
>
> —Bhandar (2018: 3)

> The law itself now becomes the instrument by which people's land is stolen.
>
> —Marx (1990: 885)

In establishing the rules of the game that are to be recognized by the state, law is a crucial mediating device between persons, between persons and things, and between motivation and behavior. It sanctions rightness and wrongness by establishing the rules governing economic and political activity; identifying the boundaries between legality and illegality; identifying the spaces and persons to be governed; and distinguishing those with rights from those without. As a constitutive force in society, it has long been recognized as a site of struggle (Terdiman 1987). Yet the law is constitutive not just of norms of behavior, but of thought. In codifying concepts, drawing boundaries, inscribing aspirations, and legitimating and thereby helping to normalize social behavior, the law is a vehicle for the "emergence of beings, things, power, institutions, offices, and jurisdiction" (Motha 2015: 328). Pierre Bourdieu, in particular,

> devotes particular attention to this special linguistic and social power of the law "to do things with words." Essential to that capacity—to the law's reproduction and continuation, to its legitimation in the eyes of those under its jurisdiction—is what Bourdieu terms the law's "power of form." This power inheres in the law's constitutive tendency *to formalize* and to *codify* everything which enters its field of vision. Bourdieu connects this tendency with Max Weber's speculations about "formal rationality." He argues that this formalization is a crucial element in the ability of the law to obtain and sustain general social consent, for it is taken (however illogically) as a sign of the law's

impartiality and neutrality, hence of the intrinsic correctness of its determinations. (Terdiman 1987: 809–810, emphasis in original)

This productive or constitutive dimension of law has also been recognized for its role in helping to inscribe the conditions of possibility—enabling certain presents and futures while foreclosing others (Burow, Brock, and Dove 2018; Moreton-Robinson 2015). The functions of the law in both inscribing the boundaries of socially sanctioned behavior and doing things with words, while obscuring its political dimensions, underlie the call to connect analyses of contemporary land grabbing to its legal contexts (Edelman, Oya, and Borras 2013).

The law has been a crucial mediating device between foreign capital and local landscapes, reconfiguring international trade and investment, finance and property. WTO rules, for example, have "required states in the global South to open their economies to the Northern-dominated international food trade, dismantle farm sector protections and adopt intellectual property protections" while encouraging export-oriented agriculture (McMichael 2012: 682). Similarly, with the world of finance: in addition to the "material infrastructures required to establish the connections sustaining the workings of finance capital, there is a need for rules, instructions and standards that guide and frame the operative principles at stake in these dynamics" (Mezzadra and Neilson 2013: 15). And while the current era of titling has been legitimated again and again as an instrument for enhancing tenure security and customary rights recognition, turning land to so-called productive use requires "regimes of exclusion that distinguish legitimate from illegitimate uses and users, and the inscribing of boundaries through devices such as fences, title deeds, laws, zones, regulations, landmarks and story-lines" (Li 2014: 589). Property also plays a central role in financialization, lying at the core of the value creation process, with its future value deriving from both the generation of constant income streams and its value appreciation over time (Ouma 2016). "To fully realize this value, one needs to be able to sell the asset with the underlying ownership rights" (Ouma 2016: 90). The interests surrounding these more recent trends toward financialization of farmland rest conveniently on more longstanding theories and practices of property emphasizing alienability. "Property is usually defined as equivalent to alienation. Property rights systems that do not have the right to alienate are considered defective" (Merino Acuña 2014: 948). Investors and land speculators have thus invested in titling (and land consolidation) as a means to "cultivate" appreciation in land value (Fairbairn 2014) and enable its alienation and circulation. "All of these rules have institutionalized market and property relations privileging agribusiness in the name of production 'efficiencies,' 'free trade' and global 'food security'" (McMichael 2012: 682). The law has thereby enabled the political economic trends profiled above by remaking the rules, entitlements, and conditions of possibility.

A few key ideas from critical theories of rights, law, and property resonate with these observations. The first is that law and institutions are not neutral arbiters of social interests, but a manifestation of power relations in society—reflecting and perpetuating the interests of the powerful. In Ulrike Schmid's words, "law is never apolitical" (Schmid 2001: 42). A key source of inspiration for this view is found in Critical Legal Studies (CLS) and its various offshoots—Critical Race Theory (CRT), Latinx Critical Legal Theory (LatCrit), Feminist Legal Criticism (FemCrit), and others—which advanced the idea that "law is politics" (Tushnet 1991) and challenged a number of key components of modern legal thought. These include its assumed formalism (that legal reasoning is impersonal, restrained, and apolitical), objectivism (that the law may be deciphered through its underlying moral order, rather than contingent power struggles), and neutrality/equality (Frug 1992; Unger 1983). Those working in the CLS/CRT tradition have shown that the law is instead biased along the lines of race and ethnicity (Delgado and Stefancic 2017; Moran 1997; Valdes 1997); gender (Frug 1992; MacKinnon 1982); and political economy (Horowitz 1977; Stone 1981). CRT and its sister disciplines call on us to question "the very foundations of the liberal order, including equality theory, legal reasoning, Enlightenment rationalism, and neutral principles of constitutional law" (Delgado and Stefancic 2017: 3).

Another key idea lies in the need to critically interrogate the discourse and practice of "rights." These critiques lie in multiple academic fields. From CLS and CRT, critiques include the tendency for rights to be framed in procedural rather than substantive terms; to be rolled back when conflicting with the interests of the powerful; to be alienating, separating people from one another and from collective life; and to be gradually "cut back by narrow interpretation, administrative obstruction or delay" (Delgado and Stefancic 2017: 29). Other critiques emanate from decolonial theory, in which the emancipatory potential and universality of human rights is shown as conceptually and historically delimited by what constitutes the state of being human (Maldonado-Torres 2017), and land rights are shown to be circumscribed by settler colonial logics aiming to reinscribe colonial power relations on the ground through "a finite set of legal forms and practices" (Blomley 2014: 1292). Historian Samuel Moyn traces how the rise of human rights on the global stage was accompanied by the erosion of international commitment to material equality in the context of market fundamentalism (Moyn 2010). Rights discourses, Moyn argues, are part of a defensible political program, but only a very minor part—helping to defend a few principles but failing to engage wider political struggles, including those surrounding liberalism itself. Moyn suggests that the rise of human rights is therefore complicit within the global rise in inequality, enabling questions of social and economic justice, distributional ethics, and political economy to retreat into the background. In reference to the work of Gayatri Spivak and Walter Mignolo, Maldonado-Torres (2017) draws attention to how the definition of human rights (and, I would argue, land rights) "leads to the creation of experts who are designated to speak to the colonized and other marginalized peoples about the rights that they possess" (Maldonado-Torres 2017: 130). Having conceptions of property codified and popularized by nations whose own legal systems are shaped by histories of settler colonialism and neoliberal political philosophy, and by "development experts" trained in these schools of thought, has been instrumental to rendering alternative legalities invisible (Merino Acuña 2014).

Insights also come from front-line struggles to defend Indigenous land claims. Mark Stevenson, Metis lawyer and founding member of the Indigenous Bar Association of Canada, levels a fundamental criticism of the exercise of rights—namely, its demand for the clear identification of the substantive rights and correlated duties of all parties. The law thus demands certainty, a

> legal technique that is intended to define with a high degree of specificity all of the rights and obligations that flow from a treaty and ensure there remain no undefined rights outside the treaty. The certainty jargon has now replaced the less fashionable term "extinguishment" which had been used to describe the certainty provisions in earlier treaties and land claim agreements. Fundamental to the concept of certainty is the notion of a land surrender or an exchange of very specific treaty rights for *the complete and absolute cession of all undefined rights to the land and the territory.* (Stevenson 2000: 114)

Property law, in particular, is "heavily invested in drawing sharp lines around our entitlements, so that we can identify the relevant property subjects, objects, and relations at play in any given context" (Blomley 2014: 1296). And yet such certainty has been observed to be a double-edged sword—

desirable for defending one's claims or entitlements in the face of growing interest in land, yet all too often deployed as a means of extinguishing other claims, enhancing security for those wishing to appropriate customary land, or rationalizing that appropriation through the lines drawn around legitimate property holders. Mapping customary rights onto the formal legal system in Canada, for example, entailed not a simple process of formal state recognition of an existing normative order, as argued by Hernando de Soto (2000), but "an attempt to stabilize or remake their very reality" (Blomley 2014: 1295). Formalizing rights through treaties or property law is also said to require a break from Indigenous history and culture by conforming to the authority system of the majority (the state or Crown), and/or by giving up other constitutionally protected[21] or customary rights (Stevenson 2000). Stated somewhat differently, it involves inserting Indigenous "identity, law and title into the conceptual space of a settler legal system"—pointing to the ambiguous promise of using settler law, an "instrument of dispossession," to sustain Indigenous territorial sovereignty (Blomley 2014: 1292, 1293). Similar arguments have been made with respect to the postcolonial neoliberal state (Merino Acuña 2014). Fee simple, for example, while recognized to be the most complete form of ownership, nevertheless denotes a feudal relationship in which the Crown holds the allodial title (Blomley 2014).

Several recent volumes have also begun to connect the development of property law with processes of racialized state formation, in which "racial regimes of ownership" (Bhandar 2018) or the "possessive logics of patriarchal white sovereignty" (Moreton-Robinson 2015) operate to legitimize settler colonial practices and affirm the sovereignty of the (white, patriarchal) nation-state. This is shown to work through processes of racialization through which some people are deemed unfit to own property or viewed as "a deficit model of humanity" (Moreton-Robinson 2015: xiii), while white settlers are recognized in the law as property-owning subjects or as embodying property forms equated with civilized life. While the political logics of "postcolonial" states and the legal regimes underlying them cannot be assumed to embody the same logics as settler colonialism, legal reforms carried out under neoliberalism share many of the same features—from discursive regimes invoking global hierarchies of persons, practices, and legalities, to reliance on the very post-colonial states working to transform Africa's farmland for capitalist expansion for the protection of the customary rights affected by this expansion.

A final set of theoretical insights is drawn from what might be called processual interpretations of land and property. These perspectives contest notions of land and property as a singular or stable essence, highlighting instead their relational, contingent, and performative character—land and property as process or assemblage, rather than a thing (Blomley 2013, 2014; Li 2014). Land and the essences it is imbued with (e.g. resource, commodity) are therefore not intrinsic, but rather "made up" (Hacking 1986), an "assemblage of materialities, relations, technologies and discourses that have to be pulled together and made to align" (Li 2014: 589). "What land *is*" varies from place to place, and deep cultural work is required to imbue it with a singular or stable essence to the exclusion of others (Li 2014: 590). Property too, in this conception, may be thought of as "a relational effect, performed into being through the alignment of human and nonhuman resources . . . [and] stabilized . . . through complex assemblages of land titling, jurisprudence, belief, everyday practice, maps, hedges, fences, and so on" (Blomley 2014: 1296). Our property representations do not simply describe, but also enact worlds into being, and the making of certain stabilized notions of property involves boundary-work in which certain notions are normalized and others are obscured from view. The production of liberal conceptions of property, in particular, is said to involve two conceptual cuts: the conversion of a network of social relationships into a set of discrete, bounded parcels of land from which others are to be excluded; and the spatial circumscription of the subject-owner as "a presocial, autonomous and distinctive subject, protected from others by the shield of rights" (Blomley 2010: 206). The work of E.P. Thompson (1963) on the parliamentary enclosure of the English commons, and the work of African legal scholars on the role of law reform in fostering the privatization of customary tenures in Africa (Boone 2007; Manji 2006), provide crucial insights into the struggles involved in these stabilizations. When we deploy property in this way, relationships are severed "to the collective, to individuals, to things, to ancestors, to the divine, to the past, and to the future" (Blomley 2014: 1292). At stake are the visibility and legitimacy of contextual, contingent, and relational conceptions of property (Blomley 2007; DePuy et al. 2021).

ORGANIZATION OF THE VOLUME

To place dominant land rights discourses and practices within this power/knowledge framing, it is important to both crystallize key facets of the knowledge-truth regime and the techniques through which they are operationalized, and to "provincialize" them by exposing their "situatedness" in particular times, places, actor constellations, and interests. Where the evidence fails to neatly stack up in support of the truth claims therein, it will be possible to expose the emergent land governance regime as a historically and politically situated project, and to begin to highlight all that is obscured from view—from other ways of conceiving of land relations, to the conditions that these dominant framings sustain.

Part I, *Emergence of a Global Knowledge Regime*, profiles the emergence of a shared set of constructs surrounding (a particular form of) "land governance" through a look at key milestones in the reframing effort, and by tracing its contours—from key concepts, to the instruments through which those concepts are enacted in land and development programming. Chapter 1, Discursive Transformation, profiles how the problem space and terms of debate have shifted over time, from "land grabs" to "land governance" and "inclusive business," and seeks to unpack the discursive and programmatic elements of an emergent land governance orthodoxy. Chapter 2, Enrollment, explores the growing conceptual and programmatic alignment among actors in the land governance arena, with a focus on multilateral financial institutions, bilateral donors, and socially progressive NGOs, to demonstrate how diverse actors have enrolled in the emergent knowledge regime.

Part II, *Decentering Emergent Truths*, draws on published and primary evidence to hold this global knowledge regime up to scrutiny, profiling why the emergent truths—self-evident as they appear—need to be decentered, denaturalized, and provincialized. It is divided into four chapters, each of which explores an element of the knowledge regime. Chapter 3, Women's Tenure Security and the False Promise of Titling, draws on published evidence to scrutinize the self-evident truth that women's tenure security is at risk, and titling is the best means to enhance that security. It points to both the shaky evidence on which this project stands, and the other ways in which tenure security has been conceptualized and practiced, with a focus on sub-Saharan Africa. Chapter 4, Collective Titling and Community Consultation, asks whether formalizing collective tenures and community consultation represent a shift away from the dominant 20th-century strategy of extinguishing community-based and customary tenure in the name of progress, as Alden Wily (2018) suggests, or part of that very same process. This chapter uses a comparative analysis of experiences in Mozambique and Peru, countries identified by Wily to be among those in which collective land rights are strongest, yet with contrasting dynamics concerning the recognition of Indigeneity—a key parameter in international legal protections of both territory and the rights to consultation and consent. Drawing on evidence from fieldwork and peer reviewed literature suggests that formal state recognition of collective rights and consultations do as much to erode as to safeguard collective tenures.

Chapters 5 and 6 explore alternative ontologies of land and the role played by the "inclusive business" concept in the land governance arena, respectively. Chapter 5, Contested Ontologies of Security, uses a qualitative review of discourses and the ethnographic record to dig into the concepts of "land" and "security" from two lenses: the emergent land governance orthodoxy, and situated ontologies of land from across the continent. It exposes dominant conceptions of security as strongly aligned with the commodification of land, and highlights how place-based conceptions of security stand in sharp contrast to these dominant constructs in their multifaceted relationality. Chapter 6, The Strategic Importance of "Inclusive Business" to Land Governance, contrasts prominent framings of "inclusive business" within international development with evidence on inclusiveness from review papers published by myself and others to interrogate the concept. This analysis exposes how what is centered in the public imagination, such as big business being an opportunity rather than a threat to the interests of rural land users, silences other realities—from farmers' visions for rural futures, to how the structuring of global value chains is working at cross-purposes with truly inclusive forms of territorial ordering and economic relations.

Part III, *Prospering in Place*, draws out the main conclusions of the manuscript and moves beyond critique to explore how land and its governance might be conceived "otherwise." Chapter 7, Rethinking Land and Rural Futures, examines all that the emergent knowledge regime obscures to trace elements of alternative possibilities for land, investment, and development. The chapter draws on the place-based and relational ontologies of land profiled in Part II and contemporary political visions of rural people (to unambiguously center the conversation in the present) to ask, "If we de-center 'land governance' and 'inclusive business' and think beyond the corresponding commodification of customary land, what alternatives might be embraced as visions for rural futures?"

REFERENCES

Abu-Lughod, L. 2013. *Do Muslim Women Need Saving?* Boston: Harvard University Press.

Agrawal, A. 2005. Environmentality: Community, intimate government, and the making of environmental subjects in Kumaon, India. *Current Anthropology* 46(2): 161–190.

Alden Wily, L. 2000. Reconstructing the African commons. Paper presented at the 'Eighth Biennial Conference of the International Association for the Study of Common Property,' Bloomington, IN, May 31–June 4, 2000.

Alden Wily, L. 2011. The law is to blame: The vulnerable status of common property rights in Sub-Saharan Africa. *Development and Change* 42(3): 733–757.

Amos, V. and P. Parmar. 2005. Challenging imperial feminism. *Feminist Review* (80): 44–63.

Anseeuw, W., M. Boche, T. Breu, M. Giger, J. Lay, P. Messerli, and K. Nolte. 2012. *Transnational Land Deals for Agriculture in the Global South: Analytical Report based on the Land Matrix Database*. Bern, Montpellier and Hamburg: Centre for Development and Environment, Agricultural Research Centre for International Development and German Institute of Global and Area Studies.

Arney, R., M. Henderson, H. Deloach, G. Lichtenstein, and L. German. 2022. Connecting across difference in environmental governance: Beyond rights, recognition and participation. *Environment and Planning E: Nature and Space* 1–27. https://www.doi.org/10.1177/2514848622108892.

Arrighi, G. 1994 *The Long Twentieth Century: Money, Power, and The Origins of Our Times*. New York: Verso.

AU, AfDB, and UNECA. 2014. *Guiding Principles on Large-Scale Land Based Investments in Africa*. Addis Ababa: African Union, African Development Bank and United Nations Economic Commission for Africa.

Baker, L.D. 1998. *From Savage to Negro: Anthropology and the Construction of Race, 1896–1954*. Berkeley, CA: University of California Press.

Barrett, H., B. Ilbery, A. Browne, and T. Binns. 1999. Globalization and the changing networks of food supply: The importation of fresh horticultural produce from Kenya into the UK. *Transactions of the Institute of British Geographers* 24(2): 159–174.

Basso, K. 1996. *Wisdom Sits in Places: Landscape and Language among the Western Apache*. Albuquerque: University of New Mexico Press.

Baur, D. and H.P. Schmitz. 2012. Corporations and NGOs: When accountability leads to co-optation. *Journal of Business Ethics* 106(2012): 9–21.

Bazzul, J. 2016. *Ethics and Science Education: How Subjectivity Matters*. Basel, Switzerland: Springer.

Benöhr, J. and P.J. Lynch. 2018. Should rivers have rights? A growing movement says it's about time. *Yale Environment* 360. Available at: https://e360.yale.edu/features/should-rivers-have-rights-a-growing-movement-says-its-about-time (accessed Apr 5, 2022).

Bhandar, B. 2018. *Colonial Lives of Property: Law, Land and Racial Regimes of Ownership*. Durham, NC: Duke University Press.

Blaser, M. 2013. Notes towards a political ontology of "environmental" conflicts. In: L. Green (Ed.), *Contested Ecologies: Dialogues in the South on Nature and Knowledge*, 13–27. Cape Town, South Africa: HSRC Press.

Blomley, N. 2007. Making private property: Enclosure, common right and the work of hedges. *Rural History* 1(1): 1–21.

Blomley, N. 2010. Cuts, flows, and the geographies of property. *Law, Culture and the Humanities* 7 (2): 203–216.

Blomley, N. 2013. Performing property, making the world. *Canadian Journal of Law and Jurisprudence* 27(1): 23–48.

Blomley, N. 2014. Making space for property. *Annals of the Association of American Geographers* 2014(6): 1291–1306.

Boone, C. 2007. Property and constitutional order: Land tenure reform and the future of the African state. *African Affairs* 106 (425): 557–586.

Borras, S.M. Jr., R. Hall, I. Scoones, B. White, and W. Wolford. 2011. Towards a better understanding of global land grabbing: an editorial introduction. *The Journal of Peasant Studies* 38(2): 209–216, https://www.doi.org/10.1080/03066150.2011.559005.

Bromley, D. 1991. *Environment and Economy: Property Rights and Public Policy*. Cambridge, MA: Basil Blackwell.

Brown, T. 2005. Contestation, confusion and corruption: Market-based land reform in Zambia. In: S. Evers, M. Spierenburg, and H. Wels (Eds.), *Competing Jurisdictions: Settling Land Claims in Africa*, 79–102. Leiden, Netherlands: Brill Academic Publishers.

Brown, W. 2015. *Undoing the Demos: Neoliberalism's Stealth Revolution*. Brooklyn: Zone Books.

Buck, P.D. 2012. Wither Whiteness? Empire, state, and the re-ordering of Whiteness. *Transforming Anthropology* 20(2): 105–117.

Burch, D. and G. Lawrence. .2009. Towards a third food regime: Behind the transformation. *Agriculture and Human Values* 26(4): 267–279.

Burow, P.B., S. Brock, and M.R. Dove. 2018. Unsettling the land: Indigeneity, ontology, and hybridity in settler colonialism. *Environment and Society: Advances in Research* 9 (2018): 57–74.

Byerlee, D. 2012. Are we learning from history? In: M. Kugelman and S.L. Levenstein (Eds.), *The Global Farms Race: Land Grabs, Agricultural Investment, and the Scramble for Food Security*, 21–34. Washington, DC: Island Press.

Cerutti, P., S. Assembe, L. German, and L. Putzel. 2011. Is China unique? Exploring the behavior of Chinese and European firms in the Cameroonian logging sector. *International Forestry Review* 13(1): 23–34.

CFS. (2012). *Report of the 38th (Special) Session of the Committee on World Food Security (11 May 2012)*. Rome: Committee on World Food Security. Available at: http://www.fao.org/3/md958e/md958e.pdf (accessed Nov 8, 2020).

Chamberlain, W. and W. Anseeuw. 2019. Inclusive businesses in agriculture: Defining the concept and its complex and evolving partnership structures in the field. *Land Use Policy* 83(2019): 308–322.

CFS and FAO. 2012. *Voluntary Guidelines for the Responsible Governance of Tenure of Land, Fisheries and Forests in the Context of National Food Security*. Rome: Committee on World Food Security and Food and Agriculture Organization of the United Nations.

Chakrabarty, D. 2000. *Provincializing Europe: Postcolonial Thought and Historical Difference*. Princeton, NJ: Princeton University Press.

Chancock, M. 1991. Paradigms, policies, and property: A review of the customary law of land tenure. In: K. Mann and R. Roberts (Eds.), *Law in Colonial Africa*, 61–84. Portsmouth, NH: Heinema.

Chapin, M. 2004. A challenge to conservationists. *World Watch Magazine* November/December 2004: 17–31.

Clapp, J. and S.R. Isakson. 2018. Risky returns: The implications of financialization in the food system. *Development and Change* 49(2): 437–460.

Coggeshall, J.M. 2018. *Liberia, South Carolina: An African American Appalachian Community*. Chapel Hill, NC: The University of North Carolina Press.

Cohn, B.S. 1996. *Colonialism and its Forms of Knowledge: The British in India*. Princeton, NJ: Princeton University Press.

Collier, S.J. 2012. Neoliberalism as big Leviathan, or . . . ? A response to Wacquant and Hilgers. *Social Anthropology/Anthropologie Sociale* 20(2): 186–195.

Colson, E. 1971. The impact of the colonial period on the definition of land rights. In: V. Turner (Ed.), *Profiles of Change: African Society and Colonial Rule*, 193–215. Cambridge: Cambridge University Press.

Conway, J. and J. Singh. 2011. Radical democracy in global perspective: Notes from the pluriverse. *Third World Quarterly* 32(4): 689–706.

Cotula, L. 2012 The international political economy of the global land rush: A critical appraisal of trends, scale, geography and drivers. *Journal of Peasant Studies* 39(3–4): 649–680.

Cotula, L. and T. Berger (2017) *Trends in Global Land Use Investment: Implications for Legal Empowerment*. London: International Institute for Environment and Development.

Cotula, L., N. Dyer, and S. Vermeulen. 2008. *Fuelling Exclusion? The Biofuels Boom and Poor People's Access to Land*. London: IIED.

Cotula, L., W. Anseeuw, and G.M. Baldinelli (2018) Between promising advances and deepening concerns: A bottom-up review of trends in land governance 2015–2018. *Land* 8(7): 106.

Cotula, L., S. Vermeulen, R. Leonard, and J. Keeley. 2009 *Land Grab or Development Opportunity? Agricultural Investment and International Land Deals in Africa*. London and Rome: International Institute for Environment and Development, Food and Agricultural Organization of the United Nations, and International Fund for Agricultural Development.

Coulthard, G. 2010. Place against empire: Understanding Indigenous anti-colonialism. *Affinities: A Journal of Radical Theory, Culture, and Action* 4(2): 79–83.

Coulthard, G. 2014. *Red Skin, White Masks: Rejecting the Colonial Politics of Recognition*. Minneapolis: University of Minnesota Press.

Crotty, M. 1998 *The Foundations of Social Research: Meaning and Perspectives in the Research Process*. London: Sage.

Daniel, S. with A. Mittal. 2010. *(Mis)investment in Agriculture: The Role of the International Finance Corporation in Global Land Grabs*. Oakland, CA: The Oakland Institute.

Dean, M. 2010. *Governmentality: Power and Rule in Modern Society*, 2nd Edition. London: Sage.

Deininger, K., D. Byerlee, J. Lindsay, A. Norton, H. Selod, and M. Stickler. 2011. *Rising Global Interest in Farmland: Can it Yield Sustainable and Equitable Benefits?* Washington, DC: World Bank.

Delcourt, P.A. and H.R. Delcourt. 1998. The influence of prehistoric human-set fires on Oak-Chestnut forests in the southern Appalachians. *Castanea* 63(3): 337–345.

Delgado, R. and J. Stefancic. 2017. *Critical Race Theory: An Introduction*. New York: New York University Press.

Deloria, V. Jr. 2001. Power and place equal personality. In: V. Deloria Jr. and D. Wildcat (Eds.), *Power and Place: Indian Education in America*, 21–28. Golden, CO: Fulcrum Publishing.

DePuy, W., J. Weger, K. Foster, A.M. Bonanno, S. Kumar, K. Lear, R. Basilio, and L. German. 2021 Environmental governance: Broadening ontological spaces for a more livable world. *Environment and Planning E: Nature and Space*, https://www.doi.org/10.1177/25148486211018565.

De Schutter, O. 2010. *Food Commodities Speculation and Food Price Crises*. Geneva: United Nations Special Rapporteur on the Right to Food.

De Schutter, O. 2011. How not to think of land-grabbing: Three critiques of large-scale investments in farmland. *The Journal of Peasant Studies* 38(2): 249–279.

de Soto, H. 2000 *The Mystery of Capital: Why Capitalism Triumphs in the West and Fails Everywhere Else*. London: Basic Books.

Diala, A.C. 2017. The concept of living customary law: A critique. *The Journal of Legal Pluralism and Unofficial Law* 49(2): 143–165.

Di Giminiani, P. 2015. The becoming of ancestral land: Place and property in Mapuche land claims. *American Ethnologist* 42(3): 490–503.

Dolan, C. and J. Humphrey. 2004. Changing governance patterns in the trade in fresh vegetables between Africa and the United Kingdom. *Environment and Planning* 36(3): 491–509.

Duffield, J., I.M. Xiarchos, and S.A. Halbrook. 2008. Ethanol policy: Past, present, and future. *South Dakota Law Review* 53(3): 425–453.

Dunlap, A. and S. Sullivan. 2019 A faultline in neoliberal environmental governance scholarship? Or, why accumulation-by-alienation matters. *EPE: Nature and Space* 3(2): 552–579.

EAFF. 2010. *The Entebbe Declaration on Large Foreign Land Acquisitions*. Nairobi, Kenya: East African Farmers' Federation. Available at: https://www.landcoalition.org/sites/default/files/documents/resources/EAFFPositionLargeLandAcquisitions_3.pdf (Oct 18, 2019).

Edelman, M. and A. León. 2013. Cycles of land grabbing in Central America: An argument for history and a case study in the Bajo Aguán, Honduras. *Third World Quarterly* 34(9): 1697–1722.

Edelman, M. and W. Wolford. 2017. Introduction: Critical Agrarian Studies in theory and practice. *Antipode* 49(4): 959–976.

Edelman, M., C. Oya, and S.M. Borras Jr. 2013. Global land grabs: Historical processes, theoretical and methodological implications and current trajectories. *Third World Quarterly* 34(9): 1517–1531.

Escobar, A. 1995. *Encountering Development: The Making and the Unmaking of the Third World*. Princeton, NJ: Princeton University Press.

European Commission. 2009. *Directive 2009/28/EC of the European Parliament and of the Council of 23 April 2009 on the Promotion of the Use of Energy from Renewable Sources and Amending and Subsequently Repealing Directives 2001/77/EC and 2003/30/EC.* Available at: https://eur-lex.europa.eu/legal-content/EN/ALL/?uri=CELEX%3A32009L0028 (accessed Dec. 14, 2020).

Ewelukwa, U.U. 2002. Post-colonialism, gender, customary injustice: Widows in African societies. *Human Rights Quarterly* 24(2): 424–486.

Fairbairn, M. 2014. "Like gold with yield": Evolving intersections between farmland and finance. *The Journal of Peasant Studies* 41(5): 777–795.

Fairbairn, M., J. Fox, S.R. Isakson, M. Levien, N. Peluso, S. Razavi, I. Scoones, and K. Sivaramakrishnan. 2014. Introduction: New directions in agrarian political economy. *The Journal of Peasant Studies* 41(5): 653–666.

Fairhead, J. and M. Leach. 1995. False Forest History, Complicit Social Analysis: Rethinking Some West African Environmental Narratives. *World Development* 23(6): 1023–1035.

Fairhead, J. and M. Leach. 1996. *Misreading the African Landscape: Society and Ecology in a Forest-Savanna Mosaic*. Cambridge, UK: Cambridge University Press.

Fairhead, J., M. Leach, and I. Scoones. 2012. Green grabbing: A new appropriation of nature? *The Journal of Peasant Studies* 39(2): 237–261.

Ferguson, J. 2009. The uses of neoliberalism. *Antipode* 41(S1): 166–184.

Foucault, M. 1979. *Discipline and Punish: The Birth of the Prison*. New York: Vintage.

Foucault, M. 1980. *Power/Knowledge: Selected Interviews and Other Writings 1972–1977*. Edited by C. Gordon. New York: Pantheon Books.

Foucault, M. 1990. *The History of Sexuality: An Introduction*. New York: Vintage Books.

Frémont, J. 2009. Legal pluralism, customary law and human rights in Francophone African countries. *Victoria University Wellington Law Review* 40(1): 149–165.

Friedmann, H. 2005. From colonialism to green capitalism: Social movements and emergence of food regimes. In: F. Buttel, and P. McMichael (Eds.), *New Directions in the Sociology of Global Development*, 227–264. Amsterdam: Elsevier.

FOEE. 2010. *Africa: Up for Grabs, The Scale and Impact of Land Grabbing for Agrofuels*. Brussels: Friends of the Earth Europe.

Front Line Defenders. 2020. *Front Line Defenders Global Analysis 2020*. Dublin, Ireland: Front Line Defenders.

Frug, M.J. 1992. A postmodern feminist legal manifesto. *Harvard Law Review* 105: 1045–1075.

Gereffi, G., J. Humphrey, T. Kaplinsky, and T.J. Sturgeon. 2001 Introduction: Globalisation, value chains and development. *IDS Bulletin* 32(3): 1–8.

German, L.A. 2016. The global land rush: Implications for agricultural communities. *CAB Reviews* 10(33): 1–19.

German, L. and C.M.T. Braga. 2019. Decentering emergent truths on tenure security: Archaeology of a global knowledge regime. *Journal of Peasant Studies*, https://www.doi.org/10.1080/03066150.2019.1682555.

German, L., G. Schoneveld, and P. Pacheco. 2011. The local social and environmental impacts of biofuels: A global comparative assessment and implications for governance. *Ecology & Society* 16(4): 29.

German, L.A., A.M. Bonanno, L.C. Foster, and L. Cotula. 2020. "Inclusive business" in agriculture: Evidence from the evolution of agricultural value chains. *World Development* 134(2020): 105018.

German, L., L. Cotula, K. Gibson, A. Locke, A. Bonanno, and J. Quan. 2018. *Land Governance and Inclusive Business in Agriculture: Advancing the Debate.* State of the Debate Report 2018, Land: Enhancing Governance for Economic Development (LEGEND). London: Overseas Development Institute.

German, L. and G. Schoneveld. 2012. A review of social sustainability considerations among EU-approved voluntary schemes for biofuels, with implications for rural livelihoods. *Energy Policy* 51(2012): 765–778.

Geschiere, P. and J. Gugler. 1998. The urban-rural connection: Changing issues of belonging and identification. *Africa* 68(3): 309–319.

Global Witness. 2020. *Defending Tomorrow: The Climate Crisis and Threats Against Land and Environmental Defenders*. London: Global Witness.

Gomez-Quintero, J.D. 2010. La colonialidad del ser y del saber: La mitologización del desarrollo en América Latina. *AGO.USB Medellin-Colombia* 10(1): 87–105.

Gould, S. J. 1981. *The Mismeasure of Man*. New York: W.W. Norton & Company.

GRAIN. 2008. SEIZED! The 2008 Land Grab for Food and Financial Security. *GRAIN Briefing*, October 2008.

Gruffyd Jones, B. 2013. "Good Governance" and "State Failure": Genealogies of Imperial Discourse. *Cambridge Review of International Affairs* 26(1): 49–70.

Hacking, I. 1986. Making up people. In: M. Baigioli (Ed.), *The Science Studies Reader*, 161–171. London and New York: Routledge.

Hall, R., I. Scoones, and G. Henley. 2016. *Strengthening Land Governance: Lessons from Implementing the Voluntary Guidelines*. London: Department of International Development.

Haraway, D. 1988. Situated Knowledges: The Science Question in Feminism and the Privilege of Partial Perspective. *Feminist Studies* 14(3): 575–599.

Harvey, D. 2001. Globalization and the "spatial fix." *Geographische Revue* 2: 23–30.

Harvey, D. 2005. *A Brief History of Neoliberalism*. Oxford, UK: Oxford University Press.

Harvey, D. 2010. *The Enigma of Capital and the Crises of Capitalism*. Oxford, UK: Oxford University Press.

Harvey, D. 2018. Universal alienation. *Journal for Cultural Research* 22(2): 137–150.

Hilgers, M. 2012. The historicity of the neoliberal state. *Social Anthropology / Anthropologie Sociale* 20(2012): 180–194.

Headey, D. and S. Fan. 2008. Anatomy of a crisis: The causes and consequences of surging food prices. *Agricultural Economics* 39: 375–391.

Hochman, G. and D. Zilberman. 2016. Corn ethanol and us biofuel policy ten years later: A systematic review and meta-analysis. Paper presented at the Agricultural and Applied Economics Association Annual Meeting, Boston, July 31–August 2, 2016.

Holbraad, M. and M.A. Pederson. 2017. *The Ontological Turn: An Anthropological Exposition*. Cambridge, UK: Cambridge University Press.

Horowitz, M.J. 1977. *The Transformation of American Law 1780–1860*. Cambridge, MA: Harvard University Press.

Humphrey, J. and O. Memedovic. 2006. Global Value Chains in the Agrifood Sector. United Nations Industrial Development Organization. Available at: https://www.unido.org/sites/default/files/2009-05/Global_value_chains_in_the_agrifood_sector_0.pdf (accessed Dec. 14, 2020).

Hunsberger, C., L. German, and A. Goetz. 2017. "Unbundling" the biofuel promise: Querying the ability of liquid biofuels to deliver on socio-economic policy expectations. *Energy Policy* 108: 791–805.

International Land Coalition. 2011. *Tirana Declaration: Securing Land Access for the Poor in Times of Intensified Natural Resources Competition*. Rome: International Land Coalition.

Jasanoff, S. 2004. The idiom of co-production. In: S. Jasanoff (Ed.), *States of Knowledge: The Co-production of Science and Social Order*, 1–12. London and New York: Routledge.

JA and UNAC. 2011. *Lords of the Land: Preliminary Analysis of the Phenomenon of Land Grabbing in Mozambique*. Maputo, Mozambique: Justiça Ambiental and União Nacional de Camponesas.

Kapstein, E.B. 2018. Governing the global land grab. *Global Policy* 9(2): 173–183.

Kelly, S., N. Vergara, and H. Bammann. 2015. *Inclusive Business Models: Guidelines for Improving Linkages between Producer Groups and Buyers of Agricultural Produce*. Rome: Food and Agriculture Organization of the United Nations.

Kohn, E. 2013. *How Forests Think: Towards an Anthropology beyond the Human*. Oakland, CA: University of California Press.

Kohn, E. 2015. Anthropology of ontologies. *Annual Review of Anthropology* 44: 311–327.

Kosek, J. 2006. *Understories: The Political Life of Forests in Northern New Mexico*. Durham, NC: Duke University Press.

Krippner, G. 2011. *Capitalizing on Crisis: The Political Origins of the Rise of Finance*. Cambridge, MA: Harvard University Press.

Kristoufek, L., K. Janda, and D. Zilberman. 2012. Correlations between biofuels and related commodities before and during the food crisis: A taxonomy perspective. *Energy Economics* 34 (2012): 1380–1391.

Landesa. 2012. Land rights and food security. *Issue Brief.* Seattle, WA: Landesa. Available at: https://www.landesa.org/wp-content/uploads/Landesa-Issue-Brief-Land-Rights-and-Food-Security.pdf (retrieved May 30, 2021).

Latour, B. 1993. *We Have Never Been Modern.* Translated by Catherine Porter. Cambridge, MA: Harvard University Press.

La Via Campesina. 2017. *Struggles of La Via Campesina for Agrarian Reform and the Defense of Life, Land and Territories.* Harare, Zimbabwe: La Via Campesina.

La Via Campesina 2018. *Food Sovereignty Now! A Guide to Food Sovereignty.* Brussels, Belgium: European Coordination Via Campesina.

Law, J. 2011. What's wrong with a one-world world. Paper presented to the Center for the Humanities, Wesleyan University, Middletown, Connecticut, 19th September, 2011.

Lay, J., W. Anseeuw, S. Eckert, et al. 2021. *Taking Stock of the Global Land Rush. Analytical Report III.* Bern, Montpellier, Hamburg, Pretoria: CDE, University of Bern, CIRAD, German Institute for Global and Area Studies, University of Pretoria, Bern Open Publishing.

Le Heron, R. and M. Roche. 1995. A "fresh" place in food's space. *Area* 27(1): 23–33.

Lemke, T. 2002. Foucault, governmentality, and critique. *Rethinking Marxism* 14(3): 49–64.

Lentz, C. 2006. Indigenous theories of landownership. In: R. Kuba and C. Lentz (Eds.), *Land and the Politics of Belonging in West Africa*, 35–56. Leiden, Netherlands: Brill.

Lentz, C. 2007. Land and the politics of belonging in Africa. In: P. Chabal, U. Engel and L. de Haan (Eds.), *African Alternatives*, 37–58. Leiden, Netherlands: Brill.

Li, T. 2014. What is Land? Assembling a Resource for Global Investment. *Transactions of the Institute of British Geographers* 39(2014): 589–602.

Long, J.W. and F.K. Lake. 2018. Escaping social-ecological traps through tribal stewardship on national forest lands in the Pacific Northwest, United States of America. *Ecology and Society* 23(2):10.

MacKinnon, C.A. 1982. Feminism, Marxism, method, and the state: An agenda for theory. *Feminist Theory* 7(3): 515–544.

Maganga, F., K. Askew, R. Odgaard, and H. Stein. 2016. Dispossession through formalization: Tanzania and the G8 land agenda in Africa. *Asian Journal of African Studies* 40(August 2016): 3–49.

Maldonado-Torres, N. 2017. On the coloniality of human rights. *Revista Critica de Ciências Sociais* 114: 117–136.

Mandondo, A., L. German, H. Utila, and U.M. Nthenda. 2014. Assessing societal benefits and trade-offs of tobacco in the Miombo woodlands. *Human Ecology* 42(2014): 1–19.

Manji, A.S. 2006. *The Politics of Land Reform in Africa: From Communal Tenure to Free Markets.* London: Zed Books.

Marx, K. 1990. *Capital, Volume 1: A Critique of Political Economy.* Introduced by Ernest Mandel and Translated by Ben Fowkes. London: Penguin.

Mausch, K., D. Mithöfer, S. Asfaw, and H. Waibel. 2009. Export vegetable production in Kenya under the EurepGAP standard: Is large "more beautiful" than small? *Journal of Food Distribution Research* 40(3): 115–129.

Mbembe, A. 2017. *Critique of Black Reason*. Durham, NC: Duke University Press.

McMichael, P. 2005. Global development and the corporate food regime. In: F. Buttel, and P. McMichael (Eds.), *New Directions in the Sociology of Global Development*, 265–299. Amsterdam: Elsevier.

McMichael, P. 2009. A food regime analysis of the "world food crisis". *Agriculture and Human Values* 26(4): 281–295.

McMichael, P. 2012. The land grab and corporate food regime restructuring. *Journal of Peasant Studies* 39(3–4): 681–701.

McMichael, P. 2014. Rethinking land grab ontology. *Rural Sociology* 79(1): 34–55.

Merino Acuña, R. 2014. Descolonizando los derechos de propiedad: Derechos Indígenas comunales y el paradigma de la propiedad privada. *Boletín Mexicano de Derecho Comparado* XLVII(141): 935–964.

Mezzadra, S. and B. Neilson. 2013. Extraction, logistics, finance: Global crisis and the politics of operations. *Radical Philosophy* 178: 8–18.

Mignolo, W.M. 2012. *Local Histories/Global Designs: Coloniality, Subaltern Knowledges, and Border Thinking*. Princeton, NJ: Princeton University Press.

Mignolo, W. and C. Walsh. 2018. *On Decoloniality: Concepts, Analytics, Praxis*. Durham, NC: Duke University Press.

Moon, K. and D. Blackman. 2014. A guide to understanding social science research for natural scientists. *Conservation Biology* 28(5): 1167–1177.

Moore, D.S. 2005. *Suffering for Territory: Race, Place, and Power in Zimbabwe*. Durham, NC: Duke University Press.

Moore, J.W. 2011. Transcending the metabolic rift: A theory of crises in the capitalist world-ecology. *The Journal of Peasant Studies* 38(1): 1–46.

Moran, R.F. 1997. Neither black nor white. 2 *Harvard Latino Law Review* 61.

Moreton-Robinson, A. 2015. *The White Possessive: Property, Power, and Indigenous Sovereignty*. Minneapolis: University of Minnesota Press.

Morita, A. and C.B. Jensen. 2017. Delta ontologies: Infrastructural transformations in the Chao Phraya Delta, Thailand. *Social Analysis* 61(2): 118–133.

Motha, S. 2015. As if—Law, history, ontology. *UC Irvine Law Review* 5(2): 327–348.

Moyn, S. 2010. *The Last Utopia: Human Rights in History*. Cambridge, MA: Belknap Press.

Mujere, J. 2010. Land and the politics of belonging in Africa. *Africa* 80(3): 497–502.

Mwitwa, J., L. German, M. Ambayeba Kankolongo, and A. Puntodewo. 2012. Governance and sustainability challenges in landscapes shaped by mining: Mining-forestry linkages and impacts in the Copper Belt of Zambia and the DR Congo. *Forest Policy and Economics* 25(2012): 19–30.

Ndlovu-Gatsheni, S. 2012. Coloniality of power in development studies and the impact of global imperial designs on Africa. *ARAS* 33(2): 48–73.

Ndlovu-Gatsheni, S. 2013. *Coloniality of Power in Postcolonial Africa*. Oxford, UK: African Books Collective.

Ndlovu-Gatsheni, S. 2018. *Epistemic Freedom in Africa: Deprovincialization and Decolonization*. London and New York: Routledge.

Nolte, K., W. Chamberlain, and M. Giger. 2016. International Land Deals for Agriculture: Fresh Insights from the Land Matrix, Analytical Report II. Bern, Montpellier, Hamburg, Pretoria: Centre for Development and Environment, University of Bern; *Centre de Coopération Internationale en Recherche Agronomique pour le Développement*; German Institute of Global and Area Studies; University of Pretoria.

Okech, A. 2019. *Widow Inheritance and Contested Citizenship in Kenya*. London and New York: Routledge.

Ostrom, E. 1990. *Governing the Commons: The Evolution of Institutions for Collective Action*. Cambridge: Cambridge University Press.

Ouma, S. 2016. From financialization to operations of capital: Historicizing and disentangling the finance–farmland-nexus. *Geoforum* 72(2016): 82–93.

Oxfam. 2011. Land and power: The growing scandal surrounding the new wave of investments in land. *Oxfam Briefing Paper 151*. Oxfam International.

Oyewumi, O. 1997. *The Invention of Women: Making an African Sense of Western Gender Discourses*. Minneapolis: University of Minnesota Press.

Peet, R. and M. Watts. 2004. *Liberation Ecologies: Environment, Development, and Social Movements*. London and New York: Routledge.

Pellizzoni, L. 2015. *Ontological Politics in a Disposable World: The New Mastery of Nature*. Farnham and Burlington, UK: Ashgate.

Peluso, N. and C. Lund. 2011. New frontiers of land control: Introduction. *The Journal of Peasant Studies* 38(4): 667–681.

Postero, N. and E. Elinoff. 2019. Introduction: A return to politics. *Anthropological Theory* 19(1): 3–28.

Pritchard, W. 1998. The emerging contours of the third food regime: Evidence from Australian dairy and wheat sectors. *Economic Geography* 74(1): 64–74.

Quijano, A. 2007. Coloniality and modernity/rationality. *Cultural Studies* 21(2): 168–178.

Rocheleau, D., P.E. Steinberg, and P.A. Benjamin. 1995. Environment, development, crisis, and crusade: Ukambani, Kenya, 1890-l990. *World Development* 23(6): 1037–1051.

Rosset, P. 2013. Re-thinking agrarian reform, land and territory in La Via Campesina. *Journal of Peasant Studies* 40(4): 721–775.

Sachedina, H., J. Igoe, and D. Brockington. 2009. The spectacular growth of the African Wildlife Foundation and the paradoxes of neoliberal conservation. *Current Conservation* 3(3): 24–26.

Said, E. 1978. *Orientalism*. New York: Pantheon Books.

Sassen, S. 2013. Land grabs today: Feeding the disassembling of national territory. *Globalizations* 10(1): 25–46.

Schmid, U. 2001. Legal pluralism as a source of conflict in multi-ethnic societies: The case of Ghana. *The Journal of Legal Pluralism and Unofficial Law* 46(2001): 1–47.

Schmidt, E. 1990. Negotiated spaces and contested terrain: Men, women, and the law in colonial Zimbabwe, 1890–1939. *Journal of Southern African Studies* 16(4): 622–648.

Schoneveld, G.C. 2011. The anatomy of large-scale farmland acquisitions in sub-Saharan Africa. *CIFOR Working Paper* 85. Bogor, Indonesia: Center for International Forestry Research.

Scoones, I., R. Hall, S.M. Borras Jr, B. White, and W. Wolford. 2013. The politics of evidence: Methodologies for understanding the global land rush. *Journal of Peasant Studies* 40(3): 469–483.Scott, J. 1990. *Seeing Like a State: How Certain Schemes to Improve the Human Condition Have Failed.* New Haven: Yale University Press.

Selby, A. 2009. Institutional investment into agricultural activities: potential benefits and pitfalls. Paper presented at the conference "Land governance in support of the MDGs: responding to New Challenges". Washington, DC, 9–10 March, 2009.

Shipton, P.M. 2009. *Mortgaging the Ancestors: Ideologies of Attachment in Africa.* New Haven: Yale University Press.

Shore, C. and S. Wright. 1997. *Anthropology of Policy: Critical Perspectives on Governance and Power.* London and New York: Routledge.

Simpson, A. 2014. *Mohawk Interruptus: Political Life across the Borders of Settler States.* Durham, NC: Duke University Press.

Simpson, L.B. 2014. Land as pedagogy: Nishnaabeg intelligence and rebellious transformation. *Decolonization: Indigeneity, Education & Society* 3(3): 1–25.

Sivaramakrishnan, K. 1999. *Modern Forests: State-Making and Environmental Change in Colonial Eastern India.* Stanford, CA: Stanford University Press.

SNV and WBCSD 2008. *Negocios Inclusivos: Iniciativas Empresariales Rentables con Impacto en el Desarrollo.* The Hague and Geneva: SNV and World Business Council for Sustainable Development.

Sousa Santos, B. 2014. *Epistemologies of the South: Justice against Epistemicide.* London and New York: Routledge.

Spivak, G.C. 1993. "Can the subaltern speak?" In: L. Chrisman and P. Wiliams (Eds.), *Colonial Discourse and Post-Colonial Theory: A Reader*, New York: Harvester Wheatsheaf. 66–111.

Stevenson, M.L. 2000. Visions of certainty: Challenging assumptions. In: British Columbia Treaty Commission (Ed.), *Speaking Truth to Power: A Treaty Forum*, 113–133. Vancouver, BC: Minister of Public Works and Government Services Canada.

Stone, K. 1981. The structure of post-war labor relations. *Yale Law Journal* 90: 1509–1580.

Swyngedouw E. 2009. The antinomies of the postpolitical city: In search of a democratic politics of environmental production. *International Journal of Urban and Regional Research* 33(3): 601–620.

Terdiman, R. 1987. Translator's introduction: The force of law: Toward a sociology of the juridical field. *Hastings Law Journal* 38(1987): 805–853.

Thompson, E.J. 1963. *The Making of the English Working Class.* London: Victor Gollancz Ltd.

Tsing, A.L. 2003. Cultivating the wild: Honey-hunting and forest management in southeast Kalimantan. In: C. Zerner (Ed.), *Culture and the Question of Rights: Forests, Coasts, and Seas in Southeast Asia*, 24–55. Durham, NC: Duke University Press.

Tuck, E. and K.W. Yang. 2012. Decolonization is not a metaphor. *Decolonization: Indigeneity, Education and Society* 1(1): 1–40.

Tushnet, M. 1991. Critical legal studies: A political history. *Yale Law Journal* 100(5): 1515–1544.

Ubink, J.M. and K.S. Amanor, Eds. 2015. *Contesting Land and Custom in Ghana: State, Chief and the Citizen*. Leiden, Netherlands: Leiden University Press.

Unger, R.M. 1983. The Critical Legal Studies movement. *Harvard Law Review* 96: 561–675.

Valdes, F. 1997. Poised at the cusp: LatCrit Theory, outsider jurisprudence and Latina/o self-empowerment. *2 Harvard Latino Law Review 1*.

van der Ploeg, J.D. 2020. From biomedical to politico-economic crisis: The food system in times of Covid-19. *The Journal of Peasant Studies* 47(5): 944–972.

von Benda Beckmann, F. and K. von Benda Beckmann. 2006. Changing one is changing all: Dynamics in the Adat-Islam-State triangle. *Journal of Legal Pluralism* 53(2006): 239–270.

Voyles, T.B. 2015. *Wastelanding: Legacies of Uranium Mining in Navajo Country*. Minneapolis: University of Minnesota Press.

Wolfe, E. 2006. Settler colonialism and the elimination of the native. *Journal of Genocide Research* 8(4): 387–409.

Woodhill, J. 2016. *Inclusive Agribusiness: The State of Play*. Background working paper. Rome: Global Donor Platform for Rural Development.

World Bank. 2009. *Awakening Africa's Sleeping Giant: Prospects for Commercial Agriculture in the Guinea Savannah Zone and Beyond*. Washington, DC: World Bank.

Ye, J., J. D. van der Ploeg, S. Schneider, and T. Shanin. 2020. The incursions of extractivism: Moving from dispersed places to global capitalism. *The Journal of Peasant Studies* 47(1): 155–183.

Zhang, Y. 2011. *The Subjective Dimension of Marxist Historical Dialectics*. Berlin: CANut International Publishers.

PART I

Emergence of a Global Knowledge Regime

CHAPTER 1

Discursive Transformation

> What we might think of as "single reality" doctrines were: one, *worked up* in the North; two, *embedded* in Northern practices; three, *reproduced and re-enacted* in those practices; and . . . four, *transported* to the South and imposed on reluctant First Nations.
> —Law (2011: 2, emphasis in original)

This chapter traces the emergence of a global knowledge regime from the highly polarized debate surrounding "land grabbing" at the end of the 2000s to a somewhat fragile consensus within international development circles on what land is and how it should be governed today. After briefly sketching the trajectory of its emergence, I identify the core components of this emergent knowledge regime, from the problem spaces that define the targets of global concern and intervention, to a unified set of concepts and narrow set of instruments through which we come to think and enact these shared aims. While the problem spaces and global rule-making projects are in fact new, this chapter reveals a remarkable continuity in certain instruments through which they are deployed—and how the "global land grab" has become an opportunity for breathing new life and momentum into them. This is achieved, in part, through concerted efforts by key multilateral institutions to craft a new discursive space to channel the concerns of actors on both sides of the debate. Through this process, a narrowly conceived set of instruments are constructed as the natural mechanism for advancing an emergent set of concepts surrounding land—concepts whose force derives from their connection to widely held values and stereotypes in the Western imagination. While the discursive transformation is neither uncontested nor shared by all, it has taken center stage in international development circles—where a common set of concepts, practices, and theories of change have become stabilized.

THE GLOBAL LAND GRAB

The 2007–2008 spike in food and energy prices and the financial crisis which followed on its heels contributed to a "dramatic revaluation of land ownership" on a global scale (Borras et al. 2011), and a spike in both the pace and scale of farmland acquisition in the global South (Anseeuw et al. 2012). Concerns over "land grabbing" made headlines around the world. GRAIN, Sawit Watch, La Via Campesina, Friends of the Earth, FIAN, Oxfam, and others published reports with titles such as, "Seized!," "Losing Ground," "Our Land, Our Lives," and "Africa: Up for Grabs" (FoEE 2010; GRAIN 2008; Oxfam 2012). Reports expressed concerns that these trends would lead to the end of small-scale farming; highlighted human rights abuses associated with land grabs; and talked in terms of a new wave of colonialism in which Africa's agricultural land and natural resources were being exported with minimal benefit for local communities and national economies (FoEE 2010[1]). Soon after, critical agrarian scholars joined the chorus—calling attention to the contours of "large-scale (trans)national commercial land transactions" (Borras et al. 2011: 210); "new enclosures, property regimes, and territorializations" (Peluso and Lund 2011: 667); "rapid commodification and financialization of land on a world scale" (Margulis, McKeon, and Borras 2013: 6); and the implications of these trends for the generation of "massive structural holes in the tissue of national sovereign territory" (Sassen 2013: 26).

Actors as diverse as GRAIN (2008) and the World Bank (Deininger et al. 2011) attribute the growing pace and scale of land grabs to the intersection of the food and financial crises, drawing attention to rising food prices and their role in drawing countries heavily reliant on food imports to consider offshore production as a means to secure long-term food supplies, and to the role of the 2008 financial crisis in stimulating a search for alternative investments. Saturnino Borras et al. (2011) subsequently highlighted the intersection of four global crises (food, finance, energy, and environment/climate) while others explored the role of the "biofuel boom" linked to policy commitments to renewable energy (German, Schoneveld, and Pacheco 2011) and of "green grabs" (Fairhead, Leach, and Scoones 2012) in these dynamics. Growing financialization of land has also played a role, increasing the fungibility of land and opening up new frontiers for investment (Fairbairn 2014; McMichael 2012), as has the "rush" to secure control over water rights (Woodhouse 2012). Whatever its causes, it is clear that while the recent wave of farmland acquisitions shares continuities with the past, fundamental shifts also occurred in the pace and scale of land acquisitions (Anseeuw et al. 2012; Borras et al. 2011)[2] and in the economic and geopolitical relations involved (Cotula 2012; Hall 2011). The new wave is marked by new geographies of land, from the emergence of South-South dynamics, to the growth in land acquisitions by domestic elites and investments targeting domestic markets, as well as the blurring of the geographical origin(s) of investment. It also involves new players, new motivations, and new investment models brought by the emerging biofuel and biomass markets, growing participation by financial players, and the restructuring of global agri-food systems (Cotula 2012; Hall 2011).

Early stages of the land grab debate were marked by a high degree of polarization in perspective as actors from all walks of life sought to make sense of the phenomenon. In May 2009, *The Economist* published an article entitled, "Outsourcing's third wave: Buying farmland abroad,"[3] tracing the trend of wealthy food importing countries acquiring poor countries' farmland instead of buying food on the world market, and citing securities analyst Richard Ferguson in calling this the third wave of outsourcing.[4] The article asked whether this represented beneficial foreign investment or neocolonialism, crystalizing the stakes as follows:

> Early this year, the king of Saudi Arabia held a ceremony to receive a batch of rice, part of the first crop to be produced under something called the King Abdullah Initiative for Saudi agricultural investment abroad. It had been grown in Ethiopia, where a group of Saudi investors is spending $100m to raise wheat, barley and rice on land leased to them by the government. The investors are exempt from tax in the first few years and may export the entire crop back home. Meanwhile, the World Food Programme (WfP) is spending almost the same amount as the investors ($116m) providing 230,000 tonnes of food aid between 2007 and 2011 to the 4.6m Ethiopians it thinks are threatened by hunger and malnutrition.

The polarized nature of the debate at this point in time is then articulated:

> Supporters of such deals argue they provide new seeds, techniques and money for agriculture, the basis of poor countries' economies, which has suffered from disastrous underinvestment for decades. Opponents call the projects "land grabs," claim the farms will be insulated from host countries and argue

that poor farmers will be pushed off land they have farmed for generations. What is unquestionable is that the projects are large, risky and controversial. In Madagascar they contributed to the overthrow of a government.

The primary axis of this early polarization within the development establishment was between socially progressive NGOs and multilateral institutions. Yet even among the staunchest critics of land grabbing, a diversity of ideas emerged on how to define it and thus locate the boundary between ethical and unethical practice. The International Land Coalition (ILC) advanced one of the earliest definitions, for which land grabbing was defined as "acquisitions or concessions that are one or more of the following:

1. In violation of human rights, particularly the equal rights of women;
2. Not based on free, prior and informed consent of the affected land-users;
3. Not based on a thorough assessment, or are in disregard of social, economic and environmental impacts, including the way they are gendered;
4. Not based on transparent contracts that specify clear and binding commitments about activities, employment and benefits sharing; and
5. Not based on effective democratic planning, independent oversight and meaningful participation." (ILC 2011: 2)

It would seem that for the ILC and its member organizations, what distinguishes a land grab from acceptable forms of land transactions and use is largely a procedural matter rather than a question of substantive outcomes for customary land users. The Agrarian Justice Programme of the Transnational Institute questions this process-based definition on the basis of its focus on land rather than drivers of land grabs and the ambiguous threshold it sets up for distinguishing an illegitimate land acquisition from a proper one. "If companies or governments claim that the desirable formal principles and technical procedures were upheld, which many do, then is it no longer a land grab?" (TNI 2013). They instead advance a definition of land grabbing as "control grabbing," or "the capturing of power to control land and other associated resources like water, minerals or forests, in order to control the benefits of its use" (TNI 2013: 3). This definition situates the definition within a framing of power and influence, extending responsibility beyond those acquiring land to those with gate-keeper functions in government. FIAN, an international human rights organization working toward the realization of the right to adequate food and nutrition, also embraces this emphasis on control but take it a step further to include the distributive outcomes of land transactions. They define land grabs as "taking possession of and/or controlling a scale of land for commercial/industrial agricultural production which is disproportionate in size in comparison to the average landholding in the region" (FIAN 2010: 8), thereby extending the definition to substantive notions of justice. The definition advanced by Olivier De Schutter, former UN Rapporteur on the Right to Food, also centers on substantive outcomes, but sets the bar lowest in terms of what qualifies as a land grab—namely, "the acquisition or long-term lease of large areas of land by investors" (De Schutter 2011: 249). For FIAN and De Schutter, *how* land changes hands is not the crucial question—but the scale of the land being transacted and the very fact of its transfer.

How land grabs are defined matters—as it demarcates the boundary between acceptable and unacceptable practice. Yet while this conceptual diversity is notable, it is important to note the absence from this discussion of a suite of actors who are otherwise very vocal and influential in setting the terms of debate—as they refrain from use of the term "land grab" altogether. And we see in the alternative concepts advanced for engaging with this debate an effort to recast land grabs in other terms.

POWER/KNOWLEDGE: CONVERGENCE OF A GLOBAL KNOWLEDGE REGIME

Early Milestones in the Reframing Effort

Within a year of the 2008 outcry over the "global land grab," a number of key reports emerged that explored the potential benefits of the upsurge in interest in farmland in the global South, or entirely recast the terms of the debate. In January 2009, The World Bank and FAO published a report entitled, "Awakening Africa's Sleeping Giant: Prospects for Commercial Agriculture in the Guinea Savannah Zone and Beyond," in which they contrast the agricultural commercialization success stories of two "relatively backward and landlocked agricultural regions" (the Brazilian *Cerrado* and the Northeast Region of Thailand) and Africa's lagging agricultural sector, while drawing parallels between the agroclimatic conditions of these two regions and Africa's Guinea Savannah zone. In addition to framing a major chunk of the African continent as lagging behind and alluding to its backwardness, the report frames this 600 million-hectare agroecological zone stretching from West Africa to Mozambique as underutilized and available. Claiming that only 10% of the 400 million hectares suitable for agriculture is "cropped," the report states that, "the African Guinea Savannah is *one of the largest underused agricultural land reserves in the world*" (World Bank 2009: 2, emphasis added).

On the surface, the report does not explicitly support industrial-scale farming per se. Significant attention is given to the question of the "optimal farm size for driving rapid agricultural commercialization," and the authors find "little to suggest that the large-scale farming model is either necessary or even particularly promising for Africa" (World Bank 2009: 8). Yet the report goes on to identify three conditions under which large-scale farms are most appropriate—namely, where economies of scale are present; where markets have stringent quality standards demanding traceability; and "when relatively fertile land must be developed in very low population-density areas (*which include vast tracts of Guinea Savannah land*)" (World Bank 2009: 9, emphasis added). The last of these conditions is said to favor large-scale mechanized farming even for the production of staple foods. When exploring the alternative, smallholder-led commercialization, the report identifies how smallholder agriculture has driven agricultural growth and reduced poverty in many countries and family farms, but cautions on the risks of commercialization to intrahousehold distribution of income and women and child welfare. The report also claims that "at current productivity levels and farm size, agriculture is economically impoverishing and technically unsustainable" (World Bank 2009: 5). These discourses thus establish the conceptual canvas in which the transfer of large landholdings out of the customary domain and to private investors may be seen not as a threat to the continent, but the very basis for its advancement.

This report was followed by a World Bank report first launched in 2010 entitled, "Rising Global Interest in Farmland: Can It Yield Sustainable and Equitable Benefits?," where these arguments are deepened and bolstered with quantitative data. The report explores the desirability of so-called land expansion, identifying areas where investment could generate considerable benefits. Statistics on yield gaps, uncultivated land, and land availability are leveraged to bolster arguments about untapped potential, while projections of future market demand, potential value generated per hectare, employment generation by commodity, and land expectation values focus attention on prospects for wealth generation from investments in agriculture and land alienation to highly capitalized firms. The report highlights the centrality of new investment for poverty reduction, economic growth, environmental sustainability, and global food security, and positions large-scale farming as one of the "tools" for agricultural and rural development while downplaying its costs.

The report acknowledges concerns that have been raised about the risks that would accompany this expansion, yet dismisses the polarization by attributing it to an absence of empirical data. "Without reliable information on large-scale investment, it is difficult to determine which of these positions is right or to advise countries on how to minimize the risks associated with such investments while capitalizing on any opportunities" (World Bank 2009: ix). The report claims there are no inherent risks to such "investment," only inherent opportunities. National policy, legal, and institutional frameworks are positioned as the key to realizing this potential, enabling associated benefits to accrue to local populations, and ensuring that private sector decisions account for "potential external effects" (World Bank 2009: 68). "To make the most of these opportunities," claims Juergen Voegele, director of the Agriculture and Rural Development Department with the World Bank, "countries will need to better *secure local land rights* and *improve land governance*" (World Bank 2010: vii, emphasis added).

The burden of responsibility for global land grabs, in effect, is thus through creative discursive and statistical maneuvers, shifted onto developing countries. But not only that. Land governance emerges as a field of thought and action—not as an open cavass upon which all possible conceptions of *what land is*, *what it can do*, and *how humans should interact with it* (Li 2014: 590) may be cast, but involving very specific proscriptions for what it means—from "clearly defined rights to land and associated natural resources" to "voluntary and welfare-enhancing land transfers" (World Bank 2010: 70, 74). The preface to the final report, published in 2011, reinforces this framing:

> Institutional gaps at the country level can be immense. Too often, they have included a *lack of documented rights* claimed by local people and *weak consultation* processes that have led to *uncompensated loss of land rights*, especially by vulnerable groups; a limited capacity to assess a proposed project's technical and economic viability; and a *limited capacity to assess or enforce* environmental and social safeguards. (Deininger et al. 2011: xiv, emphasis added)

As this volume will argue, this advance specification of the relevant fields of thought and action proved crucial to the ability of the World Bank to harness early critiques of land grabs and the Western governments and corporations involved in them, to advance the interests of those very same actors.

In 2010, these aspirations were also codified in the form of the "Principles for Responsible Agricultural Investment that Respects Rights, Livelihoods and Resources" or PRAI, prepared by FAO, IFAD, UNCTAD, and the World Bank Group (2010). This document is purportedly advanced as a mere "contribution to an ongoing global dialogue," but is hugely influential as it begins to codify principles through which land loss to investors may be considered acceptable. As will be shown in the sections to follow, the principles that are advanced and how they are operationalized resonate with the longstanding interests and programming of the World Bank. The aspiration to advance "clearly defined rights to land and associated natural resources" in the document above (World Bank 2010: 70) becomes codified here as Principle 1—"Existing rights to land and associated natural resources are recognized and respected" (FAO et al. 2010: 2). This is said to require five specific things: (i) The identification of all rights holders; (ii) Legal recognition of all rights and uses, together with options for their demarcation and registration or recording; (iii) Negotiation with land holders/users, based on informed and free choice, in order to identify *the types of rights to be transferred* and modalities for doing so; (iv) Fair and prompt payment for all acquired rights; and (v) Independent avenues for resolving disputes or grievances (FAO et al. 2010: 2, emphasis added). Here, we see "rights" codified in the form of legal certainty of all rights holders, rights and uses, and the ability of rights holders to participate in the decision processes through which their land is to be alienated. The aspiration to advance "voluntary and welfare-enhancing land transfers" from the World Bank (2010: 74) also becomes codified in this document, primarily in Principle 4, which states, "All those materially affected are consulted, and agreements from consultations are recorded and enforced" (FAO et al. 2010: 3). The effectiveness of this consultation is said to rest on three specific elements:

1. Definitional and procedural requirements in terms of who represents local stakeholders and what is a quorum for local attendance need to be clarified;
2. The content of agreements reached in such consultations should be documented and signed off by all parties; and
3. Methods for enforcement and sanctions for non-compliance should be specified.

Once again, we see legal certainty emerge as an emphasis in defining who has the authority to transact in land; the substance of agreements reached; and the enforcement mechanisms to be applied. Good governance also appears here under Principle 3—"Transparency, good governance, and a proper enabling environment," in which a premium is placed on transparency and bringing the investment climate "into line with globally accepted best practices" (FAO et al. 2010: 2). For transparency, public availability of information on "land potential and availability, core aspects of prospective investments, and resource flows or tax revenues" are emphasized (FAO et al. 2010: 3). The need to develop institutional capacity to "handle investment selection, land transfers and incentives" is also emphasized under this principle. All of this seems to be geared toward a suite of conceptual and institutional conditions that enable land to be transferred out of the customary domain, while guaranteeing security of tenure and investment for those acquiring these rights. By 2012, this was further codified into a global Land Governance Assessment Framework that was advanced as a tool for identifying and monitoring "good practice" in the land sector (World Bank 2012). Indicators established for the optional module on large-scale land acquisition[5] normalize the transfer of land out of the customary domain—with "few conflicts addressed expeditiously," "direct and transparent negotiations" between rights holders and investors, and the definition and implementation of "social requirements" (in addition to short procedures for obtaining approval) now marking out in singular, unambiguous terms the meaning of "good land governance."

It is worth making mention of another report, published in June 2009 by a consortium of international organizations (FAO, IFAD, and IIED) and prepared by researchers at IIED in dialogue with FAO, IFAD, and World Bank staff (Cotula et al. 2009).[6] The report, entitled, "Land Grab or Development Opportunity? Agricultural Investment and Land Deals in Africa," analyzes the phenomenon using the more neutral language of "large-scale land acquisitions" and giving balanced attention to both opportunities and risks. Opportunities are said to include macro-level benefits and opportunities for economic development and rural livelihoods, and risks lost access to resources people depend on for their food security. Crucially, the report identifies the terms and conditions of land deals—how risks are assessed and mitigated, the business models deployed, and how costs and benefits are shared—as the key factor in determining which outcomes materialize (Cotula et al. 2009: 6). *Inclusive business* emerges through this and other early reports as a key object of the land governance agenda, and an additional means through which diverse interests in land—such as those of local land users and agribusiness firms—may be reconciled.

Thus, we see an impressive level of investment in knowledge production by key international development finance and research organizations on the heels of the outcry over the "global land grab." The analysis above suggests that the knowledge regime being constructed achieves at least four key things. First, it recasts land grabs using the more neutral language of "large-scale land acquisitions," "land expansion," and "land deals." This removes the stigma associated with it, and opens up the semantic field to other possible interpretations. In so doing, it also points the finger away from the "grabbers"—foreign corporations and governments. Second, it identifies a suite of potential benefits that large-scale investment can deliver. These discourses rest not only on "crisis narratives" of population growth and scarcity to express the urgency of these investments, but also seemingly hard facts and narratives of golden opportunities there to be captured if there is only the will to make it happen. Third, the new objects or targets of development intervention are established, with *land governance* hereby emerging as the crucial object of global and national rule-making (see, e.g., Margulis, McKeon, and Borras 2013) and *inclusive business* emerging as a secondary object of intervention that will run in parallel with and intersect in important ways with the land governance agenda. Finally, the very pathways to achieving these targets are codified in advance—thus narrowing the field of thought and action, and skillfully shifting the burden of responsibility onto host country governments. Legal certainty—in the "rights to land and associated natural resources" (including all rights holders, rights and uses), in the procedures for negotiating the transfer of land out of the customary domain, and in the investment climate—is advanced as a key pillar of good land governance. The foundation is now set for land to change hands not with a global outcry, but with some semblance of legitimacy as it is grounded in discourses of respecting and securing rights for local land users, and capturing opportunity.

Crisis Narratives, Mobilizing Metaphors, and Legitimation Tactics

Within these discourses, it is important to note the prevalence of strategic discursive techniques that are deployed to enhance the palatability of this alternative reality to "land grabs" that is being ushered into being. They include "crisis narratives" that construct one particular story of the problems demanding urgent attention while excluding others (Rocheleau, Steinberg, and Benjamin 1995); "mobilizing metaphors" or concepts that resonate with deeply held beliefs and values in society, and whose connections with previous associations are dropped as new meanings take hold (Shore and Wright 1997); and "legitimation tactics" that serve to legitimate actions that might otherwise be politically untenable. They are also rooted in prominent stereotypes and imagery of "the other" that are further reinforced through their ongoing deployment.

In land governance discourses, several prominent crisis narratives are worth highlighting. The first are Malthusian narratives of population growth, which are often used to justify interventions in the name of productivity enhancement or environmental management (Blewett 1995; Rocheleau 1995), and are used here in a call to expand agricultural production and increase yields to feed a growing population. At the start of the World Bank's annual Land and Poverty Conference in 2013, the Bank put out an official statement on land in response to a civil society campaign calling for a freeze on agricultural investments involving large land deals. The statement, titled "Access to Land is Critical for the Poor," starts with a crisis narrative to frame the urgency of increased investment and center the role of commercial firms:

> By 2050, the world will have two billion more people to feed. To do that, global agricultural production will need to increase by 70 percent. That calls for substantial new investment in agriculture—in smallholders and large farms—from both the public and private sectors. But investment alone will not be enough . . . Unless crop yields can be raised, many people will remain hungry, under-nourished, and unable to seize opportunities to improve their lives. (World Bank 2013)

The statement goes on to acknowledge the risks of large-scale land acquisitions, but to position weak land governance systems—a form of crisis narrative in itself—as the problem, and the World Bank as progressive ally:

> Usable land is in short supply, and there are too many instances of speculators and unscrupulous investors exploiting smallholder farmers, herders, and others who lack the power to stand up for their rights. This is particularly true in countries with *weak land governance systems* . . . The World Bank Group shares these concerns about the risks associated with large-scale land acquisitions. (World Bank 2013)

This notion of weak land governance resonates with wider narratives of "good governance" and "state failure" that have become so central to contemporary international discourse about African states. According to Branwen Gruffydd Jones, such concepts gain traction because they "mesh easily with a broader and long-entrenched Western imagination of chaos and anarchy in Africa: a general lack of capacity to develop, to rule or to be peaceful" (Gruffydd Jones 2013: 49). In tapping into such stereotypes, it reinforces them, and in so doing, strengthens the case for Western intervention.

A further discursive element is that of insecurity of tenure. Again, according to the World Bank:

> With the majority of the world's population lacking secure land and property rights, land is at the center of development challenges. Eliminating poverty and boosting shared prosperity; increasing food security; facilitating urbanization; addressing climate change; increasing resilience and reducing fragility; and reducing inequality and exclusion of vulnerable groups all depend on *secure land and property rights*.[7] (emphasis added)

As will be explored in Chapter 3, narratives of insecurity are more commonly advanced on the basis of threats purportedly posed to vulnerable groups by customary norms (and at times, by corrupt officials), than by those posed by large-scale land acquisitions. The *Gender in Agriculture Sourcebook* by the World Bank, FAO, and IFAD, for example, finds "local prohibitions against women's ownership of land . . . often more powerful than written laws that allow women to own land," and the attainment of gender equity is said to rest on "overcoming social and cultural constraints" (World Bank, FAO, and IFAD 2008: 127, 130). Such narratives are not new, forming the basis for the policy stance of influential development institutions such as the World Bank, IMF, and bilateral donor agencies since at least the 1960s (Kaarhus 2010; Stein 2020; World Bank 2011). A resolution passed in 1950 by the UN General Assembly called for an investigation into "the agrarian structures" that "impede economic development," resulting in a report in 1951 entitled, "Land Reform: Defects in Agrarian Structure as Obstacles to Economic Development" (UN 1951; see also Stein 2020). While the initial focus on redistributive reforms gave way to "a singular focus on formalizing individual private property rights" by the early 1980s (Stein 2020), the argument that "customary tenure did not provide the 'security' required for agricultural investment" has remained relatively constant (Peters 2018: 4). Similar arguments continue to be made today, with the World Bank declaring tenure security to be a fundamental precondition for investment:

> Reducing the number of poor living on less than $1.90 per day requires a focus on leveraging physical assets, by *improving security of private, customary, and common land rights*, so that more people can invest in and better manage their resources for future generations, start or grow a business, partner with the private sector, and improve their livelihoods.[8] (emphasis added)

Security thus doubles up as a crisis narrative (*in*security) and mobilizing metaphor through which the culturally and politically salient notion of security as an unquestionable good in the face of any number of perceived or real threats, is tapped into and redeployed. And while tenure security has longstanding roots in Western thought (Locke 1690; Macpherson 1978) and development policies and interventions, in the wake of the land rush it has increasingly featured in tandem with a narrative of women's unique vulnerability and insecurity and been mobilized in the name of gender equity. This coupling gives new weight to security discourses and the policy prescriptions and interventions which flow from them. A 2013 publication by the UN High Commission on Human Rights and UN Women entitled "Realizing Women's Rights to Land and Other Productive Resources" positions social norms as a key impediment to equity:

> In many communities gender disparities with regard to land and other productive resources are linked to assumptions that men, as heads of households, control and manage land—implicitly reflecting ideas that women are incapable of managing productive resources such as land effectively, that productive resources given to women are "lost to another family" in the event of marriage, divorce or (male) death, and that men will provide for women's financial security. Challenging these discriminatory ideas is critical. (UN 2013: 2)

Similar discourses were advanced in a March, 2019 with a World Bank press release entitled "Women in Half the World Still Denied Land, Property Rights Despite Laws" and announcing the launch of the "Stand for Her Land" campaign:

> "*Secure land rights* are essential for women's economic empowerment and creating incentives for investment, providing an asset that can be leveraged for agriculture or business development, and offering a solid foundation for

> financial stability," said Anna Wellenstein, Director, Social, Urban, Rural and Resilience Global Practice, World Bank . . . *Persistent discriminatory social norms and practices are among the strongest barriers standing between women and their land and property rights*. Weak implementation of policies, insufficient capacity to enforce laws, and a lack of political will further compound the problem.[9] (emphasis added)

It is ironic that women are mobilized to justify land programming in the name of tenure security, because early experiments to advance tenure security through titling were shown to disproportionately harm them (a theme explored in detail in Chapter 3). This discursive tactic thus works to both deflect attention to how tenure interventions have disempowered women in the past, and to tap into and mobilize longstanding concerns in Western society about gender equality in the call for Western intervention. This is not the first time the discursive framing of women as vulnerable has served to justify Western intervention. Such discourses resonated with earlier colonial and missionary rhetoric on the status of Muslim women used to justify colonial rule and, more recently, with how portrayals of Muslim women's use of the veil as a symptom of their oppression in the Western media were leveraged to justify Western military intervention in the "war on terror" (Abu Lughod 2002).

Perhaps the core mobilizing concept is that of rights, and "respect for land rights" in particular. Efforts by multilateral institutions, NGOs, and Indigenous rights advocates to ground land governance in international human rights principles (see, e.g., Kapstein 2018; UN 2013; UNPFII 2018), while having certain strategic benefits (see, e.g., Ruggie 2013), also lends the land governance agenda an unquestionable moral authority by grounding it in deeply entrenched moral precepts of the Western world. Here it is worth quoting extensively from Columbia University history professor Samuel Moyn:

> When people hear the phrase "human rights," they think of the highest moral precepts and political ideals . . . They have in mind a familiar set of indispensable liberal freedoms, and sometimes more expansive principles of social protection. But they also mean something more. The phrase implies an agenda of improving the world, and bringing about a new one in which the dignity of each individual will enjoy secure international protection. It is a recognizably utopian program: for the political standards it champions and the emotional passion it inspires, this program draws on the image of a place that has not yet

> been called into being . . . Human rights in this sense have come to define the most elevated aspirations of both social movements and political entities—state and interstate. They evoke hope and provoke action. (Moyn 2010: 1)

Mobilizing metaphors of rights, security, and gender equity or women's empowerment thus resonate with deeply held values of the Western world. Inherently desirable states to be achieved, it becomes inconceivable to question them. Together with the construction of "crisis narratives" that tell particular stories about the nature of problems demanding urgent attention, such as "tenure insecurity" and "poor land governance," they are part and parcel of the making of self-evident truths about the world. As will be explored in Chapter 2, they also form powerful mechanisms of actor enrollment.

Yet what about the objections that might be raised about the role of land markets, investments, or consultations in producing displacement? Here, a third set of discursive techniques have been deployed to deflect attention from the potential costs of the emergent land governance regime. These have included legitimation tactics that downplay the value of rural lifeways or work to erase their very existence. Discourses and statistics on yield gaps, uncultivated land and land availability in the World Bank's 2010 report "Rising Global Interest in Farmland," for example, are instrumental in framing current land uses and users as deficient and in need of intervention. Discourses calling the African Guinea Savannah "one of the largest underused agricultural land reserves in the world" (World Bank 2009: 2) also resonate with *terra nulius* doctrines long used by colonial superpowers to justify land takings based on the recognition of only certain forms of (sedentary, cultivated or "improved," and enclosed/privatized) land use as ownership (Samson 2008). Yet, as renowned legal scholar Liz Alden Wily points out, "It takes little investigation to see that virtually every inch of the continent is *owned* under indigenous/customary norms; *used* in accordance with custom . . . , and, where not settled or cultivated, is normally the *common property* of identifiable communities within whose customary territorial domains these assets fall" (Alden Wily 2010: 4).

While these crisis narratives are crucially important for what they bracket out, they are equally powerful for what they foretell, and thus the worlds they help to usher into being. Dianne Rocheleau notes how "the name of each crisis has carried with it the seeds of each solution" (Rocheleau 1995: 1038)—outcomes that can readily be achieved by specific development interventions. The same may be said about mobilizing metaphors and legitimation tactics. Thus, it is important to understand what is in the minds of the early framers of these narratives of crisis, deficiency, and utopian dreams. Perhaps unsurprisingly, for the World Bank and many of the multilateral agencies and bilateral "land donors" aligned with them, most arrows point in the same general direction. Tenure security and respect for land rights may be achieved through the formulas advanced in the "Principles for Responsible Agricultural Investment," which despite their provisional, voluntary and contested nature, have formed the bedrock for a vast array of subsequent rule-making projects centered on the normalization of land loss and state-backed titling of transferrable rights—both individual and collective (FAO et al. 2010; World Bank 2010).[10] The wide canvas of possible interpretations of rights, security, and women's empowerment is hereby reduced to the unambiguous codification of all rights holders, rights and uses, and procedures for the transfer and alienation of those rights. And as will be explored in Chapter 2, these discursive tactics become crucial for actor enrollment in the new regime of truth through their mobilizing effect (crisis = urgency), shifting the semantic referents of key concepts and enabling once divergent political projects to be brought under unifying labels.

Stabilization

Within a few years of the global scramble to discursively define the field of thought and action in the wake of the land rush, "good land governance" had become stabilized in a few key normative frameworks widely endorsed by actors across diverse political divides. And while "inclusive business" still lacks the widespread endorsement of shared norms that is seen for land governance, efforts have also been made to stabilize its meaning.

What has come to be seen as a global consensus on land governance was first codified in "The Voluntary Guidelines on Responsible Governance of Tenure of Land, Fisheries and Forests in the Context of National Food Security" (VGGTs), a globally negotiated and agreed framework endorsed by the Committee on World Food Security and FAO in 2012. The VGGTs has come to represent a "political agreement on the minimum standards for land governance," an "authoritative interpretation of international law," and a "global consensus on a set of norms" (Hall, Scoones, and Henley 2016: 10). This consensus is conceptually wide-ranging, encompassing concepts and principles that are often difficult to reconcile: recognition and respect for customary, Indigenous, women's, informal, undocumented, and subsidiary rights; self-governance of land for Indigenous peoples and other communities with customary tenure systems; equitable access for women; facilitation of the means of transfer of rights of use and ownership; state expropriation where rights are required for a public purpose; good faith consultation with Indigenous peoples before initiating any investment project; safeguards against the extinguishment of rights of others when states allocate tenure rights; and tenure governance for the benefit of all and with an emphasis on vulnerable and marginalized people (CFS and FAO 2012). Perhaps it is precisely because these guidelines promise to be everything for everyone that they are so widely upheld as a success story in international norm-setting for actors across a wide political and ideological spectrum.

Land governance concepts and instruments have also become stabilized within the 2030 Agenda for Sustainable Development and its Sustainable Development Goals—which are said to represent "an urgent call for action by all countries—developed and developing—in a global partnership."[11] Such benchmarks serve as powerful incentives for countries to align behavior with institutionally or globally recognized performance standards, highlighting the effectiveness of global standards but also raising concerns about mechanisms of social control (Berg and Cazes 2008; Shore 2008; Strathern 2000). In the case of the land rights indicators of the Sustainable Development Goals (SDGs), standardized methodologies for measurement (World Bank, FAO, and UN-Habitat 2019), global studies comparing country preparedness to report on their performance (Kumar, Quan, and Mboup 2017) and a proposed "State of Land Tenure and Governance" report by the Global Donor Working Group on Land[12] are helping to advance this alignment. The land indicators of concern here fall under two SDGs: Goal 1 (No Poverty) and Goal 5 (Gender Equality). The indicators are as follows:

- Indicator 1.4.2—Proportion of total adult population with secure tenure rights to land, with (a) legally recognized documentation; and (b) who perceive their rights to land as secure, by sex and by type of tenure.
- Indicator 5.a.1—(a) Proportion of total agricultural population with ownership or secure rights over agricultural land by sex; and (b) share of women among owners or rights-bearers of agricultural land, by type of tenure.
- Indicator 5.a.2—Proportion of countries where the legal framework (including customary law) guarantees women's equal rights to land ownership and/or control.

Indicator 1.4.2 is under the custodianship of the World Bank and UN Habitat. As may be seen here, legally recognized documentation is identified as a key indicator of tenure security but is placed on par with perceptions of tenure security irrespective of its formalization to capture both informal tenure rights and those with legally documented land rights who "still feel that their land rights are vulnerable to infringement by outsiders."[13] The indicator covers the entire adult population. Adults are classified as having legally recognized documentation for at least one parcel of land if, (a) they have access to the land under a tenure arrangement identified and legally recognized by the government, and (b) the document lists their name as a rights holder (FAO, The World Bank, and UN-Habitat 2019). Perceptions of tenure security measures the perceived likelihood that the owner/use right holder will involuntarily lose ownership or use rights to a given parcel in the next five years, on a scale of 1 to 7 (FAO et al. 2019). Indicator 5.a.1 is under the custodianship of FAO. This indicator focuses on all adults living in agricultural households—defined as "households who operated land for agricultural purposes and/or raised/tended livestock in the past 12 months." It would therefore seem to include pastoralists. Crucially, it considers not just a person's possession of legally recognized documentation (in the form of a document issued by a Land Registry/Cadastral Agency), but a person's right to bequeath or to sell the land (alienation rights), whether de jure or de facto. The presence of *any one* of three proxies—possession of a legally recognized document, the individual's right to sell, and the individual's right to bequeath—is considered sufficient to define a person as de-facto "owner" or "holder" of tenure rights over agricultural land (FAO et al. 2019: 17). Thus, *the right to alienate land can stand alone as a globally recognized indicator of tenure security*. While the right to bequeath is compatible with the widespread customary recognition of individual entitlements within African collective tenures, the right to sell—and thus alienate land from the collective (typically a descent group)—is not, suggesting some fundamental incompatibilities between the SDGs and African tenure relations.

Inclusive business has no similar globally agreed upon framework, yet the Land: Enhancing Governance for Economic Development (LEGEND) program of the UK's Department for International Development has been working to advance this aim. Their 2018 report entitled, "Land Governance and Inclusive Business in Agriculture: Advancing the Debate" is positioned to address the absence of any "global policy instrument that embodies international consensus on the criteria for evaluating inclusiveness in business relations" (German et al. 2018). The report identifies five "pillars of inclusive business" that emerged from the discourses of a sample of organizations from the private sector, non-governmental organizations, multilateral agencies, international financial institutions, donor agencies, and regional farmers' federations: (i) effective arrangements for voice and representation; (ii) inclusive and fair value chain relations; (iii) respect for land rights and inclusive tenure arrangements; (iv) employment creation and respect for labor rights; and (v) contribution to food security. Points of ongoing divergence of opinion on what each pillar means were highlighted, suggesting that a common understanding of what inclusive business or any of its constituent elements mean had yet to be stabilized.[14]

Dissenting Voices

The discursive and normative maneuvers to advance singular conceptions of land governance are not without their critics. Dissenting voices from within the international development arena have centered on the UN Rapporteur on the Right to Food, Olivier De Schutter, and the Civil Society and Indigenous Peoples Mechanism (CSM) of the UN Committee on World Food Security (CFS). As early as 2011, De Schutter challenged the centering of weak land governance as the central issue. In an article published in the *Journal of Peasant Studies*, he highlighted the enormous costs that would result from giving land to investors with greater access to capital—from forms of farming with much less powerful poverty-reducing impacts than ones centered on support to local farming communities, to increased vulnerability to price shocks from export-oriented agriculture, and an accelerated market for land rights with potentially destructive effects on the livelihoods of current land users and those reliant on the commons. He declared that what is needed instead, "is not to regulate land-grabbing as if this were inevitable, but to put forward an alternative program for agricultural investment" (De Schutter 2011: 250). He pointed to the Minimum Human Rights Principles for guidance in ensuring that investments leading to changes to rights over land are treated as a last resort.

Other dissenting voices have come from civil society, and in particular a food sovereignty movement calling for a restructuring of the global agri-food regime to reverse processes of displacement of family farms and restore Indigenous, peasant, and local sovereignty over land, germplasm, and agricultural production (Hamann 2020; La Via Campesina 2018; Wittman, Desmarais, and Wiebe 2010). Groups such as FIAN and La Via Campesina have worked tirelessly to raise awareness at the global level of the injustices of the current agri-food regime and to chart an alternative path. The Civil Society Mechanism, established as part of a wider suite of reforms in the CFS and in response to a specific invitation to establish a "facilitating body for CSO/NGO consultation and participation in the CFS,"[15] has become, for the actors involved, "the most important and inclusive platform" for addressing food security issues at the global level (CSM 2014: 6).

Other dissenting voices are found within academia, where early critiques of land grabbing coalesced surrounding academic conferences on global land grabbing in 2011 and 2012. These critiques, centered on critical agrarian studies and its flagship journals, have been sustained and deepened over time—shedding light on the contours of the phenomenon (Borras et al. 2012; Cotula 2012), while clarifying the relationship between land grabs and biofuels (Vermeulen and Cotula 2010); food regime restructuring (McMichael 2012); private equity capital (Daniel 2012); financialization (Fairbairn 2014); property law (Alden Wily 2012); and discourses linked to "green" agendas (Fairhead, Leach, and Scoones 2012) and empty and idle land (German, Gumbo and Schoneveld 2013a; White et al. 2012). Other papers have highlighted implications for land, labor and patterns of accumulation (White et al. 2012), and forms of resistance (Hall et al. 2015). Yet while academics have reinvigorated the debate over the meanings of "tenure security" (Burow, Brock, and Dove 2018; Chigbu, Paradza, and Dachaga 2019; Coulthard 2010; German and Braga 2019), the promise and constraints of smallholder "inclusion" (Chamberlain and Anseeuw 2019; Cramb et al. 2017; German et al. 2020), and the role of small, medium, and large-scale farming in rural futures (Jayne et al. 2016; Moyo, Jha, and Yeros 2013; Peters 2013), this has done little to expand the scope of discourse and policy action *within* international development circles, and therefore, how land governance is actually experienced by rural households.

KNOWLEDGE/PRACTICE: INSTRUMENTALITIES THROUGH WHICH SHARED CONCEPTS ARE ENCODED AND ENACTED

As one of the most direct illustrations of how the emergent knowledge regime is implicated in the making of the world, it is important to understand how land governance and its accompanying concepts (rights, security, gender equity) are being advanced on a global scale. I focus on two key instruments that have gained in popularity and acceptance in recent years: the formalization of property relations through land registration and titling (both individual and collective), and procedural guidelines for community consultation in the context of land acquisition and investment.

Land Titling

> Most of the poor already possess the assets they need to make a success of capitalism . . . But they hold these resources in defective forms . . . Because the rights to these possessions are not adequately documented, these assets cannot readily be turned into capital, cannot be traded outside of narrow local circles where people know and trust each other, cannot be used as collateral for a loan, and cannot be used as a share against investment.
>
> —de Soto (2000: 5–6)

> Improving tenure security for both men and women responds to the Sustainable Development Goals' (SDGs) target of "all men and women having equal rights to ownership and control over land by 2030." Reaching this goal will require investing in securing land and property rights through *systematic campaigns to record all land rights and issue land certificates.*
>
> —World Bank website[16] (emphasis added)

The first instrument through which customary land rights are to be respected and tenure security advanced is the formalization of property relations through government-issued land title. In much of the writing of the World Bank and other international donors, legally registered title is assumed to be equivalent to tenure security[17]—a "rare luxury for the majority of the world's poor."[18] This relationship should by no means be considered a given. As will be shown in Chapters 3 and 5, there is ample evidence of formalization *undermining* security and of conceptions of tenure security that stand in sharp contrast to these prescriptions. It is also important to note that it is not just the fact of state-sanctioned title, but the specific "rights" and exclusions attached to that formalization, that matter. Here, security is often equated by the custodians of international development with the ability to *alienate* those rights:

> Providing secure and *transferable land rights is critical to protecting the interests of local populations* while permitting entrepreneurial farmers to acquire unused land in regions of low population density, *allowing land to change*

> *hands* over time to those who can use it most productively, and providing incentives to invest in increasing land productivity. (World Bank 2009, emphasis added)

Such titling is purported to advance a host of benefits for local land users. These include enhanced tenure security, and the incentive this provides to farmers to work and to increase investments, output, and productivity (Deininger 2003; Deininger and Binswanger 1999; World Bank 1989); improved factor market functioning and access to credit (Deininger 2003; Deininger and Binswanger 1999; de Soto 2000; World Bank, FAO, and IFAD 2008); decreased conflict by addressing uncertain claims to resources (Feder and Feeny 1991); incentives to use the land sustainably (Deininger and Binswanger 1999, citing Baland and Platteau 1996); and the protection of women's access to and control of land (World Bank, FAO, and IFAD 2008). Titling is also positioned as a solution to a number of more contemporary problems. In a recent World Bank blog, it is said to be one of the key solutions to growing population and food demand:

> As populations and consumption continue to grow, the global demand for food will continue to increase as well . . . Research has shown that secure land titles provide incentives for farmers to invest in land, borrow money for agricultural inputs and improvements to their land, and enable land sale and rental markets to ensure full utilization of land. (Tuck and Zakout 2019)

It is also positioned as critical for climate change mitigation and adaptation:[19]

> If the world is to confront the challenges of mitigating and adapting to climate change while meeting the demands of a rapidly-growing global population, it is vital that we find the balance between conserving and regenerating forest areas with economic growth for poverty reduction . . . Good forest governance and strong institutions are core conditions for sustainably managed forests. Clear ownership, access, and management rights over forests are also vital to build forest-dependent communities' assets, create jobs and manage forest resources more sustainably.[20]

With the discursive anchoring of land titling in contemporary issues, it appears to be a response crafted to the unique needs of the present. Yet the argument that land titling provides tenure security, and that this serves as a necessary incentive for farmers to make on-farm investments, has been made by the World Bank for at least 45 years (Wachter and English 1992). The Bank has long advocated for a market-based system of property rights consisting of clear definition of (state-sanctioned) rights and the creation of land markets to enable land to be transferred to the most efficient uses and users (Binswanger, Deininger, and Feder 1993; Deininger and Binswanger 1999: 247, 250). These ideas are embedded in evolutionary theories of land rights that on the one hand assume that the global South will necessarily undergo an agrarian transition similar to what happened in Europe (Bromley personal communication; Li 2011: 293), and on the other that private claims to land will eventually replace those made on the basis of kinship (Yngstrom 2002; Vaughan 1996). Within these narratives, "traditional" landholding systems have long been seen as static and inflexible in the face of changing economic conditions, and titling has been advanced as a means of providing security of individualized rights in land (Yngstrom 2002; see also Platteau 1996; Williams 1994; World Bank 1989).

Peruvian economist Hernando de Soto has lent further credence to land titling, and has been key to popularizing these ideas among politicians, development agencies, and host countries (Askew and Odgaard 2019[21]). His theory of change, however, is distinct. He argues that so-called Third World countries could become more like the West if only they could unleash the potential of their existing assets, which represent substantial wealth but are currently in defective forms—representing "dead capital" that is financially and commercially invisible beyond localized spheres of customary interaction (de Soto 2000). The key to this transition is property law, a system of representation that allows the value of assets to travel beyond localized and familiar spheres. "With titles, shares and property laws," argues de Soto, "people could suddenly go beyond looking at their assets as they are (houses used only for shelter) to thinking about what they could be (security for credit to start or expand a business)" (de Soto 2003: 181). This process of "modernization" requires weaving the many extralegal property arrangements into a single system from which general principles of law can be drawn. This is envisioned not as a top-down process, but a process of discovering "the people's law"—obtaining documentary evidence of property representations in extralegal law, deconstructing them to identify the principles and rules that constitute the social contract underlying them, and codifying them to enable their comparison with formal law—a process which he terms the "representational ascent" (de Soto 2003: 183). This is rendered as a technical rather than political process in which extralegal relations are largely retained in a more codified and state-sanctioned form. While his theories have been critiqued by many (Kingwill et al. 2006; Musembi 2007; von Benda-Beckmann 2003), they have lent additional discursive-ideological weight to the longstanding interests of the World Bank and other multilateral agencies.

The World Bank, the G8, and many bilateral donors have supported national land titling programs across Africa, Asia, and Latin America (ActionAid 2015; Maganga et al. 2016[22]), often with the support of Hernando de Soto himself (Askew and Oedgaard 2019; Dubé 2015; Fernandes 2011). The World Bank has recently called for "a substantial new investment program on improving security of tenure on a mass scale in developing countries" under its Land 2030 Global Initiative.[23] The initial focus was on titling at individual or household level (co-titling in the name of spouses), yet recently formalization of collectively held rights has become prevalent. Formalization of collective rights is said to enable "a gradual and organic evolution from communal to more individual rights"; to reduce vulnerability to displacement emanating from the ambiguous legal status of local inhabitants; to establish an "accountable and representative structure" for local land administration (Deininger et al. 2011: 99, 101); and to put communities in a better bargaining position with outsiders who may wish to invest.[24]

Voluntary Codes of Conduct and Community Consultations

> If done well, consultation, both before project initiation and during implementation, can greatly increase the sustainability of investments by providing a space for seeking out mutually advantageous solutions.
>
> —World Bank (2010: 77)

A second key instrument through which "respect for land rights" is being operationalized at a global scale consists of procedural guidelines for community consultation in the context of land acquisition and investment. Following the early codification of "respect for land rights" as "negotiation with land holders/users, based on informed and free choice, in order *to identify the types of rights to be transferred* and modalities for doing so" in the Principles for Responsible Agricultural Investment (FAO et al. 2010: 2, emphasis added), procedural guidelines for responsible investment and land acquisition have proliferated in global rule-making projects surrounding land and its governance. In 2014, FAO published a technical guide entitled, "Respecting Free, Prior and Informed Consent: Practical Guidance for Governments, Companies, NGOs, Indigenous Peoples and Local Communities in Relation to Land Acquisition" (FAO 2014). And the following year saw a host of new voluntary guidelines on land-based investment, from the "Operational Guidelines for Responsible Land-Based Investment" (2015) of the United States Agency for International Development (USAID) to FAO's "Safeguarding Land Tenure Rights in the Context of Agricultural Investment" (2015); the "Analytical Framework for Land-Based Investments in African Agriculture" (2015) of the G8's New Alliance for Food Security and Nutrition in Africa; and The Interlaken Group and Rights and Resources Initiative's "Respecting Land and Forest Rights: A Guide for Companies" (2015).

While some guides give a nod to investments that do not require land acquisition, all outline a detailed set of steps for "responsibly" acquiring customary land. These guidelines thus endorse *transactional* views on land rights, in which a detailed set of steps for negotiating rights to be transferred and forms of compensation are laid out rather than how the existing suite of rights and entitlements should be safeguarded. The justification for pursuing voluntary codes of conduct rather than hard law instruments is seldom made explicit. Harold Liversage, Lead Technical Expert on Land Tenure at the International Fund for Agricultural Development, offers one set of rationales:

> Experience has shown that mandatory regulations, or other similar documents requiring obligatory compliance are more difficult to negotiate; take longer to agree; are sometimes diluted as a result; and are often more difficult to enforce. Hence, it is generally believed that "voluntary guidelines" or "principles" would be more appropriate, as they could be developed with greater multi-stakeholder engagement in a relatively short time, and with stronger statements. (Liversage 2010: 9)

In these and other guidelines, the consultation of "legitimate tenure rights holders" (a concept coined in the context of the VGGTs) has become a somewhat standardized process and language through which local land rights are to be respected. Procedural forms of rights recognition, and the variable forms of community consultation and engagement embedded in them, thus emerge as a second instrumentality through which "respect for land rights" and "tenure security" are enacted.

These guidelines do not just fall short in providing substantive protections. In endorsing variable forms of community *consultation*, most also fall short of endorsing even the best procedural standards. Free, prior, and informed consent (FPIC) certified by signed contracts—a process for obtaining the consent of customary rights holders to acquire rights to their land, and to specify the benefits or forms of compensation that are to accompany it—has emerged as the global gold standard for collective rights recognition in the context of investment (FAO 2014; ILO 1989; UN 2008). It differs from community consultation in several respects, but most importantly in enshrining the right to veto any legislative or administrative measures that may affect local lands, territories or resources.

Similar to titling, there is some continuity in World Bank Group endorsement of procedural interpretations of land rights. Prior to 2007, the Environmental and Social Safeguards[25] governing World Bank-funded projects endorsed the consultation of project-affected persons in the context of planning for and determining eligibility for compensation from involuntary resettlement for projects determined to be in the "public interest." In the event projects affected Indigenous Peoples (IP), the Safeguards endorse "free, prior and informed *consultation*" with affected IP,

> to ascertain their broad community support for projects affecting them and to solicit their participation: (a) in designing, implementing, and monitoring measures to avoid adverse impacts, or, when avoidance is not feasible, to minimize, mitigate, or compensate for such effects; and (b) in tailoring benefits in a culturally appropriate manner.

Thus, they fall short of endorsing consent and the right to veto displacement (displacement remains involuntary).

Despite these notable continuities in procedural interpretations of rights in the context of outside investment, it is possible to identify important discontinuities as well. In the first draft of the World Bank's *Rising Global Interest in Farmland: Can It Yield Sustainable and Equitable Benefits?*, for example, we see an endorsement of a more market-based version of land transactions between investors and customary land users as collectivities that alludes to (without explicitly endorsing) a more voluntary process. In a long-winded discourse about the relative merits of this approach, the Bank sets out its theory of change:

> Conceptually, expropriation is justified only as a last resort against moral hazard and holdouts by private owners where the public good is at stake and alternatives are not available (a planned road, for example, cannot be built just anywhere). Its use centralizes decision-making and may encourage corruption and rent-seeking. Moreover, even if it ensures the legality of land acquisitions, it cannot provide legitimacy for processes seen as contradicting local norms. Investors who acquire land that has been expropriated may see the viability of their investment jeopardized if they are unable to take possession of the land in question or find themselves exposed to a legacy of conflict due to long-standing disputes and unresolved claims . . . As long as land owners can be identified and a regulatory framework to guide the process and uphold basic standards is in place, the private sector will often be able to negotiate more flexibly and quickly than the government. This can provide advantages if delays in the ability to put the land to productive use are costly financially. It will be advantageous to focus public sector efforts on creating the basic institutional framework, and to inform those affected of their rights, ensure fairness of the process, and create a level playing field. (World Bank 2010: 75–76; see also the full explanation on pages 74–78)

Thus, a vision of land transactions unburdened by state mediation and mandatory compensation, and legitimated through participatory mechanisms of consultation, is hereby established as the desired means of acquiring communal land. Prior to the outcry over the global land grab, the International Finance Corporation had begun to advocate for forms of "stakeholder consultation" in the context of private investment, for the purpose of initiating and sustaining constructive external relationships surrounding investment projects (see, for example, IFC 2007). "Obtaining access to community land for survey work" had also been identified as one of several possible purposes of this consultation, alongside meeting regulatory requirements, negotiating compensation, building trust, or managing expectations (IFC 2007: 35–36). Yet this process was not specific to communities, involving any number of external parties identified by investors as being affected by—or capable of affecting—an investment project. And neither was land acquisition an explicit purpose. Thus, we see the "land grab" contributing to discursive and normative projects that provide moral cover for more rather than fewer land transactions in the global South, provided investors follow a set of procedural steps discursively rendered as equivalent to "respecting land rights."

Reasons for Skepticism

> Formalisation of property relations through the registration of land and the issuance of titles is but the latest in a long history of optimistic policy prescriptions imposed on the poor nations of the world . . . As with a long list of previous simple solutions to complex problems, this too shall pass.
>
> —Bromley (2008: 20)

It is worth reflecting on why the emergent land governance regime should not simply be taken at face value, as reflective of concrete global gains in stakeholder buy-in and endorsement of customary land rights protections, or simply as "truth." There are many possible answers to this question, but the one I will focus on here is the ambiguous if not downright discouraging evidence of the outcomes of the two instruments being advanced with such fervor on the global stage.

The decade or more prior to the 2008 financial crisis and outcry over the "global land grab" saw mounting evidence to question the benefits of land titling in the African context and elsewhere (Amanor 2001; Bromley 2008; Bruce and Mighot-Adholla 1994; Kerekes and Williamson 2010; Meinzen-Dick and Mwangi 2007). Daniel Bromley, Professor Emeritus of applied economics at the University of Wisconsin, reviewed the literature on titling back in 2008 and declared it, "the wrong prescription for the wrong malady." He concludes,

> As with the discredited Washington Consensus, the imperative of formalisation flows from the flawed inductive logic that says "rich countries have formalised tenure, therefore formalisation of tenure will help make you rich." Unfortunately, empirical research on formalisation of tenure as a stimulus to agricultural investment is unable to establish any robust and reliable connection between "more secure" tenure and enhanced agricultural productivity . . . Formalisation erodes and displaces existing social networks and arrangements that do offer security [and] offers little assurance that beneficial outcomes are inevitable. (Bromley 2008: 20)

He expresses surprise at the assumption that titles will magically create wealth, while highlighting all that this narrative of insecurity obscures—such as the securities already provided by social embeddedness in communities, villages, clans, and neighborhoods. He asks, "What arrogance is required to presume that titles will fix, rather than undermine, long-standing fundamental social and economic relations?," chalking up the push to formalize property relations to good old fashioned cultural imperialism. Other reviews of the evidence have provided equally robust critiques, from their faulty premises to the tendency of titling to encourage speculation by outsiders and to enhance not security, but poverty, inequality, and landlessness (Peters 2004; Stein 2020).

These arguments are not lost on the World Bank and other prominent advocates of land titling. A 1992 report on World Bank land titling programs concludes that, "of all the discussed land titling projects or project components, very few can be considered successful" (Wachter and English 1992: 7). And despite ample efforts by the World Bank's own land economists to review the counter-evidence of economists, anthropologists, and political scientists (e.g., World Bank, FAO, and IFAD 2008), the World Bank continues to equate tenure security with titling.[26] The World Bank's optimism about the "potentially large benefits" of titling (World Bank 2006: 165) in the face of mixed evidence leads Bromley to ask, "Is the World Bank advocating policy prescriptions that its own research staff cannot support?" (Bromley 2008: 21).

Yet it is not only titling that stands to be questioned rather taken at face value. The enthusiasm with "good process" in the context of land acquisitions comes on the heels of a proliferation of case studies profiling negative livelihood outcomes of land transactions involving consultations on communal lands (Nhantumbo and Salomão 2010; Obidzinski et al. 2012; Ribeiro and Matavel 2009; Schoneveld, German, and Nukator 2011), as well as a much deeper history of alienation of Indigenous lands through purportedly voluntary contracts and treaties (Banner 2005). A three-country project carried out by the World Resources Institute (WRI) finds that,

> In practice, community consultations are fraught with irregularities and seldom reflect genuine community consent. Consultations are often perfunctory, with government agents clearly on the side of investors. For their part, communities are barely in a position to participate meaningfully: power asymmetries and low levels of education hamper their ability to fully understand the process, their legal rights, and the nature and implications of the investment. Promises of job opportunities and other benefits induce community consent, but are often unfulfilled, leaving communities with no recourse. Likewise, many projects fail to get off the ground or founder soon after. (Salcedo-La Viña and Morarji 2016: 2)

Such deficiencies flow from a host of problems, both structural and agential. A four-country review of processes of large-scale land acquisition by myself, George Schoneveld, and Esther Mwangi (2013b) finds deficiencies in the law and in practice—giving consultations the character of symbolic gestures rather than procedures that can be expected to guarantee substantive safeguards or livelihood outcomes. This and other studies point to a litany of problems associated with consultation processes, from the duration of consultations (often limited to a single meeting) to the tendency for intermediaries to inflate benefits and obscure costs; coercion, intimidation, or higher-order directives that undermine the discretionary space of the consultation in favor of land alienation; circumvention of community consultations in favor of negotiations with district councils; limited awareness of local land users (e.g., low levels of legal literacy, lack of clarity on how much land is at stake, unrealistic/inflated expectations about future benefits); absence of downwardly accountable community representation (e.g. chiefs as the sole interlocutors, local elites dominating consultation deliberations, chiefs receiving bribes to acquiesce); incomplete or biased documentation of agreements reached verbally (e.g., lacking in detail, biased in favor of investors' interests, not time-bound, failure to provide affected communities copies of consultation records); and absence of compensation or irregularities in compensation mechanisms (e.g., compensation flowing to district councils rather than affected land users, low or symbolic compensation, undisclosed evaluation procedures, frequent failure of investors to comply with agreements) (see also Cleaver, Schram, and Wanga 2010; Habib-Mintz 2010; Manuel and Salomão 2009; Mkindi 2008; Nhantumbo and Salomão 2010; Nolte and Voget-Kleschin 2014; Overbeek 2010; Ribeiro and Matavel 2009; Sitoe 2009; Sulle and Nelson 2009). The scale and prevalence of such irregularities is of course suggestive of the wider power dynamics in which such deals are embedded, as elucidated by many authors (Alden Wily 2010; Fairbarn 2013; Nolte 2014; Vermeulen and Cotula 2010). As pointed out by Howard Stein and Samantha Cunningham, the notion of voluntarism "can deny the hegemonic forces that can be embedded in markets" (Stein and Cunningham 2015: 1). This is a far cry from the fairness and level playing field attributed to consultations by the World Bank and other prominent proponents.

As this book will show, the unqualified and widespread endorsement of land titling and community consultation stands in stark contrast with mounting evidence, both historical and contemporary, of their ambiguous and often harmful effects in practice. There is thus ample reason to take these discourses not as self-evident truths, but as rooted in particular historical circumstances, and both motivated by and constitutive of wider political economic relations.

DISCUSSION

This counter-evidence of the frequent failure of formalization and community consultations to advance customary rights or livelihoods calls for a more critical analysis of the knowledge/truth regime in which they are being advanced. This chapter has focused on crystalizing key facets of the emergent regime—from the core targets of development intervention ("land governance," "inclusive business"), to the crisis narratives, mobilizing metaphors and rationalization narratives that serve as a call to action while deflecting attention from the harm being done, and finally, the techniques through which they are enacted (formalization, community consultation). As this volume will attempt to show, this knowledge/truth regime is not a simple representation of the world as it is (the "truth" of its singular, universal essence), but embodies a very "provincialized" vision (Chakrabarty 2000) of what land is, what it can do and how humans should interact with it (Li 2014). Part II of the volume will attempt to hold key tenets of this regime to the test by exploring the extent to which their underlying assumptions hold up under scrutiny—whether in the published literature on gendered land relations, titling and value chain relations, or within other culturally situated ontologies of land and security. Divergences between theory and evidence, and between dominant and marginalized conceptions of land and security, will help to reveal this knowledge/truth regime not as a universal truth for all to apprehend and act upon, but as discourses that are deeply "situated" in particular times, places, actor constellations, and global economic interests (Chakrabarty 2000; see also Maldonado-Torres 2017; Mignolo and Walsh 2018) and which obscure as much as they reveal. But before embarking on this project, it is important to take a look at who has bought into these constructs, outside of the narrow confines of the multilateral agencies at the forefront of the emergent land governance orthodoxy.

REFERENCES

Abu-Lughod, L. 2002. Do Muslim women really need saving? Anthropological reflections on cultural relativism and its others. *American Anthropologist* 104(3): 783–790.

ActionAid. 2015. *New Alliance, New Risk of Land Grabs: Evidence from Malawi, Nigeria, Senegal and Tanzania*. Johannesburg: ActionAid International.

Alden Wily, L. 2010. "Whose land are you giving away, Mr. President?" Paper presented at the World Bank Conference on Land and Poverty, Washington, DC.

Alden Wily, L. 2012. Looking back to see forward: The legal niceties of land theft in land rushes. *The Journal of Peasant Studies* 39(3–4): 751–775.

Amanor, K. S. 2001. Land, labour and the family in southern Ghana: A critique of land policy under neo-liberalisation. *Research Report* No. 116. Uppsala: Nordiska Afrikainstitutet.

Anseeuw, W., M. Boche, T. Breu, M. Giger, J. Lay, P. Messerli, and K. Nolte. 2012.*Transnational Land Deals for Agriculture in the Global South: Analytical Report based on the Land Matrix Database*. Bern, Montpellier and Hamburg: Centre for Development and Environment, Agricultural Research Centre for International Development and German Institute of Global and Area Studies.

Askew, K. and R. Oedgaard. 2019. Deeds and misdeeds: Land titling and women's rights in Tanzania. *New Left Review* 118: 69–85.

Baland, J.-M. and J.-P. Platteau. 1996. *Halting Degradation of Natural Resources: Is There a Role for Rural Communities?* New York: Clarendon Press for the Food and Agriculture Organization.

Banner, S. 2005. *How the Indians Lost their Land*. Cambridge, MA: Harvard University Press.

Berg, J.M. and S. Cazes. 2008. Policymaking gone awry: The labor market regulations of the Doing Business Indicators. *Comparative Labor Law and Policy Journal* 29(4). Available at: https://ssrn.com/abstract=1177367.

Binswanger, H. P., K. Deininger, and G. Feder. 1993. Power, distortions, revolt, and reform in agricultural land relations. *Policy Research Working Papers* 1164. Washington, DC: The World Bank.

Blackman, A., L. Corral, E. Santos Lima, and G.P. Asner. 2017. Titling indigenous communities protects forests in the Peruvian Amazon. *Proceedings of the National Academy of Sciences* 114(16): 4123–4128.

Blewett, R.A. 1995. Property rights as a cause of the tragedy of the commons: Institutional change and the pastoral Maasai of Kenya. *Eastern Economic Journal* 21(4): 477–490.

Borras, S.M. Jr., R. Hall, I. Scoones, B. White, and W. Wolford. 2011. Towards a better understanding of global land grabbing: an editorial introduction. *The Journal of Peasant Studies* 38(2): 209–216, https://doi.org/10.1080/03066150.2011.559005.

Borras, S.M. Jr., J.C. Franco, S. Gómez, C. Kay and M. Spoor. 2012. Land grabbing in Latin America and the Caribbean. *The Journal of Peasant Studies* 39(3–4): 845–872.

Bromley, D.W. 2008. Formalising property relations in the developing world: The wrong prescription for the wrong malady. *Land Use Policy* 26(2008): 20–27.

Bruce, J. and S. E. Mighot-Adholla. 1994. *Searching for Land Tenure Security in Africa.* Washington, DC: World Bank.

Burow, P.B., S. Brock, and M.R. Dove. 2018. Unsettling the land: Indigeneity, ontology, and hybridity in settler colonialism. *Environment and Society: Advances in Research* 9 (2018): 57–74.

CFS. 2009. *Reform of the Committee on World Food Security, Final Version.* 35th Session of the Committee on World Food Security, October 2009. Rome: Committee on World Food Security.

CFS and FAO. 2012. *Voluntary Guidelines on the Responsible Governance of Tenure of Land, Fisheries and Forests in the Context of National Food Security.* Rome: Committee on World Food Security and the Food and Agriculture Organization of the United Nations.

Chakrabarty, D. 2000. *Provincializing Europe: Postcolonial Thought and Historical Difference.* Princeton, NJ: Princeton University Press.

Chamberlain, W. and W. Anseeuw. 2019. Inclusiveness revisited: Assessing inclusive businesses in South African agriculture. *Development Southern Africa* 36(5): 600–615.

Chigbu, U.E., G. Paradza, and W. Dachaga. 2019 Differentiations in women's land tenure experiences: Implications for women's land access and tenure security in Sub-Saharan Africa. *Land* 2019, 8(2), 22.

Cleaver, J., R. Schram, and G. Wanga. 2010. Bioenergy in Tanzania: The country context. In: *Bioenergy and Food Security in Tanzania.* Rome: Food and Agriculture Organization of the United Nations. Available at: http://www.fao.org/docrep/012/i1544e/i1544e.pdf/ (Accessed 22.03.11).

Cotula, L. 2012. The international political economy of the global land rush: A critical appraisal of trends, scale, geography and drivers. *The Journal of Peasant Studies* 39(3–4): 649–680.

Cotula, L., S. Vermeulen, R. Leonard, and J. Keeley. 2009. *Land Grab or Development Opportunity? Agricultural Investment and International Land Deals in Africa.* London: International Institute for Environment and Development.

Coulthard, G. 2010. Place against empire: Understanding Indigenous anti-colonialism. *Affinities: A Journal of Radical Theory, Culture, and Action* 4(2): 79–83.

Cramb, R., V. Manivong, J.C. Newby, K. Sothorn, and P.A. Sibat. 2017. Alternatives to land grabbing: Exploring conditions for smallholder inclusion in agricultural commodity chains in Southeast Asia. *The Journal of Peasant Studies* 44(4): 939–967.

CSM. 2014. *Civil Society at CFS: Contributions and Assessments of the Civil Society Mechanism (CSM) on the 41st Session of the UN Committee on World Food Security (CFS).* Rome: Food Security and Nutrition Civil Society Mechanism.

CSM. 2018. *Civil Society Report on the Use and Implementation of the Right to Food*

Guidelines. Rome: Working Group on Monitoring of the Civil Society Mechanism for relations with the Committee on World Food Security.

CSM. 2021. CSM opening statement on the negotiations of the guidelines on food security and nutrition. Available at: http://www.csm4cfs.org/csm-opening-statement-negotiations-voluntary-guidelines-food-systems-nutrition/ (accessed Jan. 31, 2021).

Daniel, S. 2012. Situating private equity capital in the land grab debate. *The Journal of Peasant Studies* 39(3–4): 703–729.

Deininger, K. 2003. *Land Policies for Growth and Poverty Reduction*. Washington, DC: The World Bank.

Deininger, K. and H. Binswanger. 1999. The evolution of the world bank's land policy: Principles, experience, and future challenges. *The World Bank Research Observer* 14(2): 247–276.

Deininger, K. and D. Byerlee with J. Lindsay, A. Norton, H. Selod and M. Stickler. 2011. *Rising Global Interest in Farmland: Can it Yield Sustainable and Equitable Benefits?* Washington, DC: The World Bank.

De Schutter, O. 2011. How not to think of land-grabbing: Three critiques of large-scale investments in farmland. *The Journal of Peasant Studies* 38(2): 249–279.

de Soto, H. 2000. *The Mystery of Capital: Why Capitalism Triumphs in the West and Fails Everywhere Else*. New York: Basic Books.

de Soto, H. 2003. Listening to the barking dogs: property law against poverty in the non-West. *Focaal—European Journal of Anthropology* 41(2003): 179–185.

Dubé, R. 2015. *To Have and To Hold: Property Titles at Risk in Peru*. Available at: https://www.lincolninst.edu/sites/default/files/pubfiles/2525_1864_To_Have_and_To_Hold_0415LL.pdf (accessed Oct. 21, 2019).

Fairbarn, M. 2013. Indirect dispossession: Domestic power imbalances and foreign access to land in Mozambique. *Development and Change* 44(2): 335–356.

Fairbairn, M. 2014. "Like gold with yield": Evolving intersections between farmland and finance. *The Journal of Peasant Studies* 41(5): 777–795. https://doi.org/10.1080/03066150.2013.873977.

Fairhead, J., M. Leach, and I. Scoones. 2012. Green grabbing: A new appropriation of nature? *The Journal of Peasant Studies* 39(2): 237–261.

FAO. 2014. Respecting free, prior and informed consent: Practical guidance for governments, companies, NGOs, indigenous peoples and local communities in relation to land acquisition. *Governance of Tenure Technical Guide* No. 3. Rome: Food and Agriculture Organization of the United Nations.

FAO. 2015. *Safeguarding Land Tenure Rights in the Context of Agricultural Investment*. Rome: Food and Agriculture Organization of the United Nations.

FAO, The World Bank, and UN-Habitat. 2019. *Measuring Individuals' Rights to Land: An Integrated Approach to Data Collection for SDG Indicators 1.4.2 and 5.a.1*. Washington, DC: World Bank. © FAO, The World Bank, and UN-Habitat.

FAO, IFAD, UNCTAD, and World Bank Group. 2010. *Principles for Responsible Agricultural Investment that Respects Rights, Livelihoods and Resources.* Rome and Washington, DC: Food and Agriculture Organization of the UN, International Fund for Agricultural Development, UN Conference on Trade and Development Secretariat and World Bank Group.

Feder, G. and D. Feeney. 1991. Land tenure and property rights: Theory and implications for development policy. *World Bank Economic Review* 5: 135–153.

Fernandes, E. 2011. *Regularization of Informal Settlements in Latin America.* Cambridge, MA: Lincoln Institute of Land Policy.

FIAN. 2010. *Land Grabbing in Kenya and Mozambique: A Report on Two Research Missions, and a Human Rights Analysis of Land Grabbing.* Heidelberg, Germany: FIAN International.

FoEE. 2010. *Africa: Up for Grabs, The Scale and Impact of Land Grabbing for Agrofuels.* Brussels: Friends of the Earth Europe.

Friis, C. and A. Reenberg. 2010. Land grab in Africa: Emerging land system drivers in a teleconnected world. *GLP Report* No. 1. GLP-IPO, Copenhagen.

G8. 2015. *Analytical Framework for Land-Based Investments in African Agriculture.* New Alliance for Food Security and Nutrition in Africa.

German, L. and C.M.T. Braga. 2019. Decentering emergent truths on tenure security: Archaeology of a global knowledge regime. *Journal of Peasant Studies*, https://doi.org/10.1080/03066150.2019.1682555.

German, L., D. Gumbo, and G. Schoneveld. 2013a. Large-scale land acquisitions: Exploring the marginal lands narrative in the Chitemene system of Zambia. *QA—Rivista dell'Associazione Rossi-Doria* 2(June): 109–135.

German, L., G.C. Schoneveld, and E. Mwangi. 2013b. "Contemporary processes of large-scale land acquisition in Sub-Saharan Africa: Legal deficiency or elite capture of the rule of law?" *World Development* 48(2013): 1–18.

German, L., G. Schoneveld, and P. Pacheco. 2011. The local social and environmental impacts of biofuels: A global comparative assessment and implications for governance. *Ecology & Society* 16(4): 29.

German, L.A., A.M. Bonanno, L.C. Foster, and L. Cotula. 2020. "Inclusive business" in agriculture: Evidence from the evolution of agricultural value chains. *World Development* 134(2020), 105018.

German, L., L. Cotula, K. Gibson, A. Locke, A. Bonanno, and J. Quan. 2018. *Land Governance and Inclusive Business in Agriculture: Advancing the Debate.* LEGEND State of the Debate Report 2. London: Overseas Development Institute.

GRAIN. 2008. SEIZED! The 2008 Land Grab for Food and Financial Security. *GRAIN Briefing*, October 2008.

Gruffydd Jones, B. 2013. "Good governance" and "state failure": Genealogies of imperial discourse. *Cambridge Review of International Affairs* 26(1): 49–70.

Habib-Mintz, N. 2010. Biofuel investment in Tanzania: Omissions in implementation. *Energy Policy* 38(8): 3985–3997.

Hall, R. 2011. Land grabbing in Southern Africa: The many faces of the investor rush. *Review of African Political Economy* 38(128): 193–214.

Hall, R., M. Edelman, S.M. Borras Jr., I. Scoones, B. White, and W. Wolford. 2015. Resistance, acquiescence or incorporation? An introduction to land grabbing and political reactions "from below." *The Journal of Peasant Studies* 42(3): 467–488.

Hall, R., I. Scoones, and G. Henley. 2016. *Strengthening Land Governance: Lessons from Implementing the Voluntary Guidelines*. London: Department of International Development.

Hamann, S. 2020. The global food system, agro-industrialization and governance: Alternative conceptions for sub-Saharan Africa. *Globalizations* 17(8): 1405–1420.

IFC. 2007. *Stakeholder Engagement: A Good Practice Handbook for Companies Doing Business in Emerging Markets*. Washington, DC: International Finance Corporation.

ILC. 2011. *Report of the ILC International Conference and Assembly of Members*. Tirana, Albania, 24–27 May 2011. International Land Coalition.

ILO. 1989. *C169—Indigenous and Tribal Peoples Convention*. Geneva: International Labor Organization.

Interlaken Group and RRI. 2015. *Respecting Land and Forest Rights: A Guide for Companies*. Washington, DC: The Interlaken Group and the Rights and Resources Initiative.

Jayne, T. S., Chamberlin, J., Traub, L., Sitko, N., Muyanga, M., Yeboah, F.K., W. Anseeuw, A. Chapoto, A. Wineman, C. Nkonde, and R. Kachule. 2016. Africa's changing farm size distribution patterns: The rise of medium-scale farms. *Agricultural Economics* 47(2016): 197–214.

Kaarhus, R. 2010. Women's land rights and land tenure reforms in Malawi: What difference does matriliny make? *Forum for Development Studies* 37(2): 171–192.

Kapstein, E.B. 2018. Governing the global land grab. *Global Policy* 9(2): 173–183.

Kerekes, C. and C. Williamson. 2010. Propertyless in Peru, even with a government land title. *The American Journal of Economics and Sociology* 69(3): 1011–1033.

Kingwill, R.A., B. Cousins, T. Cousins, D. Hornby, L. Royston, and W. Smit. 2006. Mysteries and myths: De Soto, property and poverty in South Africa. *Gatekeeper Series* No. 124. London: International Institute for Environment and Development.

Kumar, R., J. Quan, and G. Mboup. 2017. *A Multi-Country Capacity Assessment of National Statistical Offices Preparedness to Report on SDG Indicator 1.4.2*. UN Habitat, Ministry of Foreign Affairs of the Netherlands, Global Land Indicators Initiative and Global Land Tool Network.

La Via Campesina. 2018. *Food Sovereignty Now! A Guide to Food Sovereignty*. Brussels, Belgium: European Coordination Via Campesina.

Law, J. 2011. "What's wrong with a one-world world." Paper presented to the Center for the Humanities, Wesleyan University, Middletown, Connecticut, 19 September 2011.

Li, T. 2011. Centering labor in the land grab debate. *The Journal of Peasant Studies* 38(2): 281–298.

Li, T. 2014. What is land? Assembling a resource for global investment. *Transactions of the Institute of British Geographers* 39(2014): 589–602.

Liversage, H. 2010. Responding to "land grabbing" and promoting responsible investment in agriculture. *IFAD Occasional Paper* No. 2.

Locke, J. 1690. *The Second Treatise of Government* (T. Peardon, Ed. 1952). New York: The Liberal Arts Press.

Macpherson, C.B. 1978. *Property: Mainstream and Critical Positions*. Toronto: University of Toronto Press.

Maganga, F., K. Askew, R. Odgaard, and H. Stein. 2016. Dispossession through formalization: Tanzania and the G8 land agenda in Africa. *Asian Journal of African Studies* 40(August 2016): 3–49.

Maldonado-Torres, N. 2017. On the coloniality of human rights. *Revista Critica de Ciências Sociais* 114: 117–136.

Manuel, L. and A. Salomao. 2009. Biofuels and land rights in Mozambique: The Pro-Cana case. *Haramata* 54: 17–19.

Margulis, M.E., N. McKeon, and S.M. Borras Jr. 2013. Land grabbing and global governance: Critical perspectives. *Globalizations* 10(1): 1–23.

McMichael, P. 2012. The land grab and corporate food regime restructuring. *The Journal of Peasant Studies* 39(3–4): 681–701.

Meinzen-Dick, R. and E. Mwangi. 2007. Cutting the web of interests: Pitfalls of formalizing property rights. *Land Use Policy* 26(1): 36–43.

Mignolo, W. and C. Walsh. 2018. *On Decoloniality: Concepts, Analytics, Praxis*. Durham, NC: Duke University Press.

Mkindi, A. R. 2008. *Impact of Jatropha Trade in Tanzania*. Dar es Salaam: Environmental, Human Rights Care and Gender Organization.

Moyn, S. 2010. *The last Utopia: Human Rights in History*. Cambridge, MA: Belknap Press of Harvard University Press.

Moyo, S., P. Jha, and P. Yeros. 2013. The classical agrarian question: Myth, reality and relevance today. *Agrarian South: Journal of Political Economy* 2(1): 93–119.

Musembi, C.N. 2007. De Soto and land relations in rural Africa: Breathing life into dead theories about property rights. *Third World Quarterly* 28(8): 1457–1478.

Nhantumbo, I. and A. Salomão. 2010. *Biofuels, Land Access and Rural Livelihoods in Mozambique*. London: International Institute for Environment and Development.

Nolte, K. 2014. Large-scale agricultural investments under poor land governance in Zambia. *Land Use Policy* 38(2014): 698–706.

Nolte, K., W. Chamberlain, and M. Giger. 2016. International Land Deals for Agriculture: Fresh Insights from the Land Matrix, Analytical Report II. Bern, Montpellier, Hamburg, Pretoria: Centre for Development and Environment, University of Bern; *Centre de Coopération Internationale en Recherche Agronomique pour le Développement*; German Institute of Global and Area Studies; University of Pretoria.

Nolte, K., and L. Voget-Kleschin. 2014. Consultation in Large-Scale Land Acquisitions: An Evaluation of Three Cases in Mali. *World Development* 64 (2014): 654–668.

Obidzinski, K., R. Andriani, H. Komarudin, and A. Andrianto. 2012. Environmental and social impacts of oil palm plantations and their implications for biofuel production in Indonesia. *Ecology and Society* 17(1): 25. https://doi.org/10.5751/ES-04775-170125.

Overbeek, W. 2010. *The Expansion of Tree Monocultures in Mozambique: Impacts on Local Peasant Communities in the Province of Niassa*. Montevideo, Argentina: World Rainforest Movement.

Oxfam. 2012. Our land, our lives: Time out on the Global Land Rush. *OXFAM Briefing Note*, October 2012.

Peluso, N. and C. Lund. 2011. New frontiers of land control: Introduction. *Journal of Peasant Studies* 38(4): 667–681.

Peters, P.E. 2004. Inequality and social conflict over land in Africa. *Journal of Agrarian Change* 4(3): 269–314.

Peters, P.E. 2013. Land appropriation, surplus people and a battle over visions of agrarian futures in Africa. *The Journal of Peasant Studies* 40(3): 537–562.

Peters, P. 2018. Land grabs: The politics of the land rush across Africa. In: *Oxford Research Encyclopedia of Politics*. Oxford, UK: Oxford University Press. https://doi.org10.1093/acrefore/9780190228637.013.825.

Platteau, J.-P. 1996. The evolutionary theory of land rights as applied to sub-Saharan Africa: A critical assessment. *Development and Change* 27: 29–86.

Probst, B., A. BenYishay, A. Kontoleon, and T.N.P. dos Reis. 2020. Impacts of a large-scale titling initiative on deforestation in the Brazilian Amazon. *Nature Sustainability* 3(2020): 1019–1026.

Ribeiro, D. and N. Matavel. 2009. *Jatropha! A Socioeconomic Pitfall for Mozambique*. Maputo, Mozambique: Justiça Ambiental and União Nacional de Camponeses.

Rocheleau, D., P.E. Steinberg, and P.A. Benjamin. 1995. Environment, development, crisis, and crusade: Ukambani, Kenya, 1890-1990. *World Development* 23(6): 1037–1051.

Ruggie, J.G. 2013. *Just Business: Multinational Corporations and Human Rights*. New York: W.W. Norton & Company.

Salcedo-La Viña, C. and M. Morarji. 2016. Making women's voices count in community decision-making on land investments. *Working Paper*. Washington, DC: World Resources Institute.

Samson, C. 2008. The rule of *terra nullius* and the impotence of international human rights for Indigenous peoples. *Essex Human Rights Review* 5(1): 1–12.

Sassen, S. 2013. Land grabs today: Feeding the disassembling of national territory. *Globalizations* 10(1): 25–46.

Schoneveld, G., L. German, and E. Nukator. 2011. Land-based investments for rural development? A grounded analysis of the local impacts of biofuel feedstock plantations in Ghana. *Ecology and Society* 16(4): 10.

Shore, C. 2008. Audit culture and illiberal governance: Universities and the politics of accountability. *Anthropological Theory* 8 (3): 278–298.

Shore, C. and S. Wright. 1997. *Anthropology of Policy: Critical Perspectives on Governance and Power*. London and New York: Routledge.

Sitoe, A. 2009. *Governação Florestal em Niassa: O Caso de Muembe, Sanga, Lago e Cuamba*. Maputo, Mozambique: Associação Rural de Ajuda Mútua.

Stein, H. 2020. Institutional transformation and shifting policy paradigms: Reflections on land reform in Africa. In: C. Ochieng (Ed.), *Rethinking Land Reform in Africa: New Ideas, Opportunities and Challenges*, 85–110. Abidjan, Nigeria: African Development Bank.

Stein, H. and S. Cunningham. 2015. Land grabbing and formalization in Africa: A critical inquiry. *ASC Working Paper* 124/2015. Leiden, The Netherlands: African Studies Centre.

Strathern, M., Ed. 2000. *Audit Cultures: Anthropological Studies in Accountability, Ethics and the Academy*. London and New York: Routledge.

Sulle, E., and F. Nelson. 2009. Biofuels, Land Access and Rural Livelihoods in Tanzania. London: IIED.

TNI. 2013. *The Global Land Grab: A Primer*. Amsterdam: The Transnational Institute.

Tuck, L. and W. Zakout. 2019. 7 reasons for land and property rights to be at the top of the global agenda. *Voices* (World Bank blog), March 25, 2019. Available at: http://blogs.worldbank.org/voices/7-reasons-land-and-property-rights-be-top-global-agenda?CID=ECR_AL_BlogNotification_EN_EXT (Sept. 27, 2019).

UN. 1951. *Land Reform: Defects in Agrarian Structure as Obstacles to Economic Development*. New York: United Nations Department of Economic Affairs.

UN. 2008. *United Nations Declaration on the Rights of Indigenous Peoples*. New York: United Nations.

UN. 2013. *Realizing Women's Rights to Land and Other Productive Resources*. New York: UN Office of the High Commissioner for Human Rights and UN Women.

UNPFII. 2018. Indigenous Peoples' Collective Rights to Lands, Territories and Resources. Seventeenth Session of the United Nations Permanent Forum on Indigenous Issues, New York, 16–27 April 2018. Available at: https://www.un.org/en/ga/search/view_doc.asp?symbol=E/C.19/2018/5 (accessed Nov. 21, 2020).

USAID. 2015. *Operational Guidelines for Responsible Land-Based Investment*. Washington, DC: United States Agency for International Development.

Vaughan, M. 1996. The character of the market: social identities in colonial economies. *Oxford Development Studies* 24: 61–77.

Vermeulen, S. and L. Cotula. 2010. Over the heads of local people: Consultation, consent, and recompense in large-scale land deals for biofuels projects in Africa. *The Journal of Peasant Studies* 37(4): 899–916.

von Benda-Beckmann, F. 2003. Mysteries of capital or mystification of legal property? *Focaal—European Journal of Anthropology* 41(2003): 187–191.

Wachter, D. and J. English. 1992. The World Bank's Experience with Rural Land Titling. *Environment Department Divisional Working Paper* No. 1992-35. Washington, DC: The World Bank.

White, B., S.M. Borras Jr., R. Hall, I. Scoones, and W. Wolford. 2012. The new enclosures:

Critical perspectives on corporate land deals. *The Journal of Peasant Studies* 39(3–4): 619–647.
Williams, G. 1994. Modernizing Malthus: The World Bank, population control and the African environment. In: J. Crush (Ed.), *Power of Development*, 158–175. London and New York: Routledge.
Wittman, H., A. Desmarais and N. Wiebe. 2010. *Food Sovereignty: Reconnecting Food, Nature and Community*. Halifax, Nova Scotia: Fernwood.
Woodhouse, P. 2012. New investment, old challenges. Land deals and the water constraint in African agriculture. *The Journal of Peasant Studies* 39(3–4): 777–794.
World Bank. 1989. *Sub-Saharan Africa: From Crisis to Sustainable Growth*. Washington, DC: World Bank.
World Bank. 2006 *World Development Report 2006: Equity and Development*. Washington, DC: The World Bank.
World Bank. 2009. *Awakening Africa's Sleeping Giant: Prospects for Commercial Agriculture in the Guinea Savannah Zone and Beyond*. Washington, DC and Rome: The World Bank and Food and Agriculture Organization of the UN.
World Bank. 2010. *Rising Global Interest in Farmland: Can it Yield Sustainable and Equitable Benefits?* Washington, DC: The World Bank.
World Bank. 2011. *Land Policy: Securing Rights to Reduce Poverty and Promote Rural Growth*. Available at: https://documents1.worldbank.org/curated/pt/917391468268803373/pdf/933000BRI0P0710SB0update0LandPolicy.pdf (accessed May 27, 2021).
World Bank. 2012. *The Land Governance Assessment Framework: Identifying and Monitoring Good Practice in the Land Sector*. Washington, DC: The World Bank.
World Bank. 2013. Access to land is critical for the poor, April 8, 2013. Available at: https://www.worldbank.org/en/news/press-release/2013/04/08/world-bank-group-access-to-land-is-critical-for-the-poor (accessed Oct. 16, 2019).
World Bank, FAO, and IFAD. 2008. *Gender in Agriculture Sourcebook*. Washington, DC and Rome: World Bank, Food and Agriculture Organization (FAO) of the United Nations, and International Fund for Agricultural Development (IFAD).
World Bank, FAO, and UN-Habitat. 2019. Measuring Individuals' Rights to Land: An Integrated Approach to Data Collection for SDG Indicators 1.4.2 and 5.a.1. Washington, DC and Rome: The World Bank, Food and Agriculture Organization of the United Nations, and UN-Habitat.
Yngstrom, I. 2002. Women, wives and land rights in Africa: Situating gender beyond the household in the debate over land policy and changing tenure systems. *Oxford Development Studies* 30(1): 21–40.

CHAPTER 2

Enrollment

This chapter takes the emergent knowledge regime traced in Chapter 1 as its starting point, and profiles the extent to which different actor groups have enrolled in it, by coming to use its terminology or by engaging in discourses and actions supportive of it. The chapter is focused on those organizations most active in dialogues surrounding land governance *within the international development arena*. Thus, while the chapter takes a broad look across actors—from multilateral organizations and bilateral donors to international NGOs, development think tanks, and private firms or networks active in the land governance and inclusive business debates—it does not capture the views of academics, local NGOs, or private sector actors who have not chosen to invest in these debates.

The organizations selected for analysis are those who have been heavily involved in the discursive and programmatic spaces of land governance and inclusive business since the early days. For the multilateral agencies, this is identified by their role in hosting major fora on land governance and/or involvement in the codification of land governance and investment frameworks. In addition to the World Bank, I include the Food and Agriculture Organization of the United Nations and Committee on World Food Security. Select private firms were chosen for their active engagement in relevant international fora and initiatives, and for their representation of major commodity sectors that have been the focus of academic debates, activism, and normative frameworks on land and supply chain governance. These include Sime Darby (oil palm) and Illovo Group (sugarcane). It also includes the World Business Council for Sustainable Development, a CEO-led organization of over 200 leading businesses active in the debates on inclusive business (SNV and WBCSD 2010; WBCSD 2016), and OLAM International, a major food and agri-business company with a history of sourcing from small-scale farmers.

Four bilateral donor organizations were also included for having a substantial discursive engagement in land governance and inclusive business debates in addition to their sizeable portfolio of land-related programming: the Danish International Development Agency (DANIDA), the Foreign, Commonwealth and Development Office of the UK (FCDO), the Ministry of Foreign Affairs of the Netherlands (MoFA) and USAID.[1] Two development research organizations, the International Institute for Environment and Development and Overseas Development Institute, are also included in the analysis for their strong programmatic focus on land rights. The sample also includes La Via Campesina, the one grassroots organization that both aspires to represent the voice of "peasants, Indigenous people and rural workers" and has a sizeable web presence to enable such an analysis.

Among the non-governmental organizations selected for review are two that were among the most vocal early critics of land grabs, and have had an active and sustained presence at the annual World Bank Conference on Land and Poverty and in knowledge production on land governance, ActionAid and Oxfam. It also includes two membership organizations most active in research and advocacy on local land rights, the International Land Coalition and the Rights and Resources Initiative; and two international NGOs whose programming is strongly aligned around efforts to strengthen customary or Indigenous land rights, Landesa and Forest Peoples Programme.

The chapter begins with an exploration of the discursive alignments among these actors, and follows with a look at the degree to which shared discourses also reflect shared orientations toward the instrumentalities identified in Chapter 1 as key to land governance programming (land titling and community consultations or FPIC).

CONCEPTUAL ALIGNMENT

Given the growing recognition of the importance of the concepts we think through—whether in narrowing the conditions of possibility by embodying "basic commitments and assumptions about what things are, and what they could be" (Holbraad and Pederson 2017: 5), or by enabling new realities to come into being in the process of naming (Hacking 1986), I start with a look at the degree of actor enrollment in the concepts identified in Chapter 1. This was done through a search for key terms on the websites of each organization in the sample, to explore how the frequency of use varies prior to and following the outcry over the "global land grab."

A comparison of usage patterns in the 1999–2008 and 2009–2018 periods reveals a dramatic increase in the use of key terms associated with global land governance in the post-2008 period, with the exception of La Via Campesina and the negligible engagement with "women's land rights" discourses among private sector actors (Table 1)[2]. While this does not provide evidence for the convergence of meaning or of actor positionality vis-à-vis these terms, it does suggest both a rise in a shared conceptual space as well as convergence in the terminology used by differently positioned actors. The table also highlights those at the forefront of this global knowledge economy—namely, the World Bank and FAO—who have been instrumental in staking out the conceptual and semantic terrain of land governance, and to a lesser extent, the Foreign, Commonwealth and Development Office of the UK. Development think tanks and select NGOs are also seen to engage in these discourses early on in areas specific to their programmatic foci, with Forest Peoples Programme most engaged around the issue of tenure security and land rights, the International Land Coalition on land governance and women's land rights, and Rights and Resources Initiative on inclusive business. It is also interesting to note La Via Campesina's exclusive engagement with "land governance" and "land rights" and failure to engage with discourses emphasizing women's vulnerability or the inclusiveness of agribusiness.

While the actor categories in Table 1 should not be taken as internally coherent or clearly bounded from other categories, analyzing these data graphically according to these groupings does suggest some underlying patterns.[3] In the post-2008 period, NGOs emerge as a close second to multilateral financial institutions in their engagement with these key concepts (Figure 2). Equally revealing is the dominance of multilateral financial institutions, and to a lesser extent development think tanks, in advancing these concepts in the 10-year period preceding the financial crisis and outcry over land grabs.

Conceptual alignment by itself cannot be taken as sufficient evidence of semantic or political-ontological alignment surrounding the key questions of *what land is, what it can do* and *how humans should interact with it* (Li 2014). Different actors or organizations could be engaging with these concepts either to advance them or to call them into question, and the underlying meanings or semantic referents of these concepts may differ considerably. It is therefore important to ask, "What do these things mean, and how are they deployed, in the narratives from which they emanate?" and through this, to ask, "To what extent has the underlining meaning of these concepts also undergone increasing alignment across actor groups?"

Table 1. Prevalence of key land governance terminology on the websites of actors active in global land governance fora and debates[a]

Actor	"Land Governance" 1999–2008	"Land Governance" 2009–2018	"Tenure Security" 1999–2008	"Tenure Security" 2009–2018	"Land Rights" 1999–2008	"Land Rights" 2009–2018	"Women's Land Rights" 1999–2008	"Women's Land Rights" 2009–2018	"Inclusive Business" 1999–2008	"Inclusive Business" 2009–2018
Multilateral Institutions										
World Bank	23	551	482	1,080	1,140	2,340	75	445	3	211
FAO	13	425	290	410	795	1,440	67	252	5	185
CFS	0	11	0	4	0	10	0	2	0	27
Non-Governmental Organizations										
Oxfam	0	39	0	34	10	533	1	39	3	99
ILC	13	574	8	96	26	724	19	491	3	1
RRI	1	44	12	88	19	260	3	78	6	52
Landesa	0	65	0	86	4	529	3	319	0	0
ActionAid	0	14	0	16	21	758	1	6	0	0
FPP	10	602	121	827	660	4,710	2	7	0	0
Grassroots Peasants' Organizations										
Via Campesina	0	4	0	1	0	19	0	0	0	0
Private Sector										
WBCSD	0	4	0	4	2	21	0	1	2	79
Illovo	0	2	0	1	0	28	0	0	0	1
OLAM	0	0	0	0[b]	0	6	0	0[b]	0	2
Sime Darby	0	0	0	0	3	1	0	0	2	0
International Development Think Tanks										
IIED	6	99	75	83	172	397	38	78	1	54
ODI	2	59	40	70	156	236	9	59	3	24
Bilateral Donors										
DANIDA	0	2	1	4	9	78	2	2	0	6
FCDO[c]	1	86	64	201	299	891	36	64	0	88
MoFA[c]	0	3	0	6	4	77	0	2	0	59
USAID	0	35	1	78	9	351	0	59	0	27

[a] Adapted from German and Braga (2019). Searches carried out in April/May and November, 2019.

[b] Although there are 6 hits related to the tenure security of farmers and one related to their own security of tenure, and growing attention to women's economic empowerment.

[c] Added to table in March, 2021.

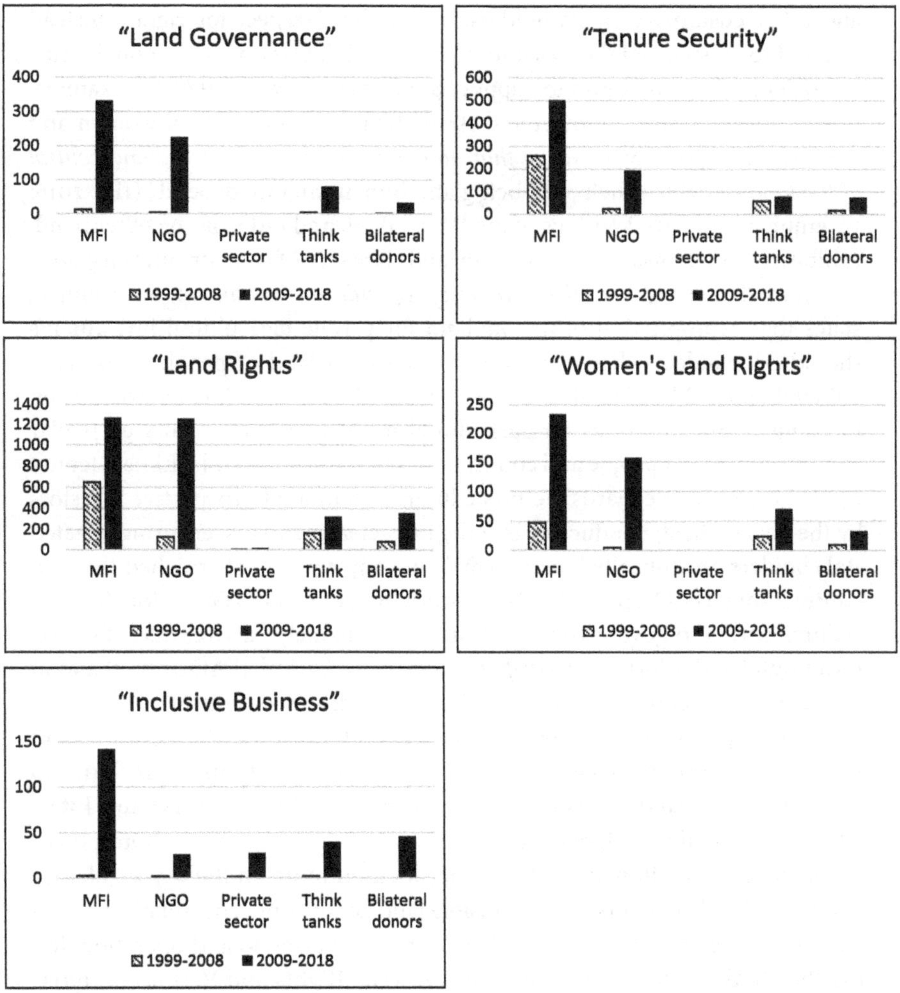

Figure 2. Level of discursive engagement with key land governance concepts, by category of actor

A review of global discourses on land governance and inclusive business that I carried out in 2017 in the context of a White Paper on inclusive business (German et al. 2018) highlighted the growing use of and support for these concepts, but also important differences in what they mean for different actors. One crucial distinction was whether land rights, use, and control were viewed as something that should be safeguarded for smallholders, Indigenous people, and other customary rights holders, or whether "respect for rights" instead referred to "responsible" transactions in land. ILC, Oxfam and regional farmers' federations were found to support the former view. For ILC, for example, this meant to "respect, protect and strengthen the land rights of women and men living in poverty, *ensuring that no one is deprived of the use and control of the land* on which their well-being and human dignity depend" (ILC 2016: 10, emphasis added). Writings of the World Bank and FAO, on the other hand, exhibited more transactional views on land rights. FAO's document, *Safeguarding Land Tenure Rights in the Context of Agricultural Investment*, for example, states that expropriation of *private* land for private agricultural investments should be avoided, whereas proposals for use of land of people considered vulnerable should be "carefully reviewed" (FAO 2015: 44). Furthermore, when focusing in on "proposals for agricultural investment that require particular scrutiny to prevent people and communities from losing their legitimate tenure rights," the only safeguards are procedural: screening of prospective investors by the government; conducting ex-ante impact assessments; ensuring affected stakeholders are consulted; and formalizing any agreements reached through consultations (FAO 2015: 48). Reference is made to the VGGTs for the procedural norms to govern these consultations—namely, "active, free, effective, meaningful and informed *participation and consultation*" (FAO 2015: 5) and in the case of Indigenous peoples, Free, Prior and Informed *Consent*.

This emphasis on procedural elements that constitute "respect for land rights"—as opposed to substantive outcomes or protections—was found to be uneven. The land rights discourses in the World Bank (2014) and Interlaken Group and the Rights and Resources Initiative (2015a) are both procedural and detailed in nature, the former focused more on the key regulatory and procedural elements for responsible land acquisition, consultation, resettlement, and compensation, and the latter on adhering to and operationalizing the VGGTs. The Interlaken Group and the Rights and Resources Initiative also take responsibilities further, emphasizing independent analysis, due diligence, and grievance processes applying to current and historic tenure rights and land-related corruption on existing company landholdings, new acquisitions and throughout the supply chain, followed by effective remedy in cases of past wrongs and adverse impacts. These interpretations stand in contrast with ILC (2016) and Oxfam (2014a, 2014b), which instead emphasize substantive outcomes such as the protection of diverse local tenure and production systems and equitable land distribution. For Oxfam, emphasis is placed on the effects of investments and supply chains relations on land concentration (Oxfam 2014b) and redistributive reforms where needed to counter excessive concentration (ILC 2016). Crucially, the ultimate aim of consultations were also found to differ in the narratives of different actors. While OLAM International was found to emphasize FPIC and ongoing dialogue *to secure a social license to operate* and ILC framed FPIC as a way *to center land users in decisions about land and ensure accountability to them* (ILC 2016), the World Bank (2014), FAO et al. (2010) and UNECA (2014) emphasize negotiations *to identify the rights to be transferred.* Once again, a crucial distinction in the meaning of land rights—between securing rights and access for customary land users, or enshrining the right to transact (and normalizing those transactions)—becomes apparent.

While such differences might undermine the argument for an emergent knowledge regime in international development circles, a few pieces of evidence do strengthen this claim. For at least some actors, it is possible to observe shifts in what respect for land rights means over time. Among socially progressive NGOs, for example, there is growing acknowledgement of the legitimacy of land transactions. The stance of Oxfam, one of the more active NGOs in global land rights fora and debates, has shifted at least in part from defensive to transactional conceptions of land rights, and from confrontation to engagement. In 2017, they put out a "Guide to Gender Sensitive Community Engagement in Large Scale Land-Based Investment in Agriculture" which provides a pathway for gender equitable land transfers through community input on the location of investment, procedures for community consent, community benefits agreements, and community engagement *to agree on the terms of their relocation.* A review of Oxfam contributions to the annual World Bank Conference on Land and Poverty also shows a spike in writing about land grabs in 2013, followed by direct engagement and shared panels with companies through their "Behind the Brands" campaign, in which attention shifted to (often favorable reviews of) corporate performance on land rights.

Rights and Resources Initiative has a longstanding interest in property rights to forest lands and resources, and has long provided the most updated information on global trends in forest tenure. Its mission, as articulated at its founding, was "to promote greater global commitment to pro-poor forest policy and market reforms to increase local household and community ownership, control, and benefits from forests and trees" (RRI 2005: 3–4). They also established as global goals poverty reduction in forested areas and a substantial increase in the forest area under local ownership and administration. And in their 2013–2017 framework proposal, they declared "an historic opportunity to mobilize action to secure lands in coming years and to improve livelihoods for hundreds of millions of forest dependent people" (RRI 2012). Yet in their 2015 guide with the Interlaken Group entitled, "Respecting Land and Forest Rights: A Guide for Companies" and its accompanying brief (Interlaken Group and RRI 2015a, 2015b), "actively respecting the land and forest rights of the communities" where a company operates consists of identifying and helping to legally secure local tenure rights, and ensuring *land acquisitions* are based on the FPIC of local communities and households (IG and RRI 2015b: 7). While a nod is given to the potential benefits of "innovative production models that rest upon the secure tenure rights of host communities" (investments that do not entail land alienation), the bulk of the guide is devoted to specifying procedural norms for bringing customary rights holders into the land acquisition process or addressing preexisting grievances. The alienation of customary land ("dispossession" in scholarly lingo) is thus considered acceptable, provided the company does not engage in corrupt practices or forced evictions; abides by the law; and follows a set of procedural guidelines for the acquisition of customary land centering on rights identification, consultation or FPIC, remedy and compensation—the formula set out early on by multilateral agencies five years prior (FAO et al. 2010). Here, infringements on legitimate land and forest rights are equated with *forced* evictions, not dispossession per se (IG and RRI 2015a: 13).

A June 4, 2018 posting on the Rights and Resources Initiative listserv on global deforestation commitments also demonstrates how secure rights for customary land users and corporations are now advanced in a single breath:

> Because communities have long protected the world's natural resources, inadequate recognition of their rights puts the forests and waters we all depend on for global environmental sustainability at risk. Without secure rights, conflict and deforestation often follow. Insecure rights also threaten companies' bottom lines and long-term financial success. Disputes over land between companies and local communities frequently lead to conflict, work stoppages, and stalled investments. These conflicts are of course detrimental to local peoples, but they are also costly to investors.[4]

While the argument that tenure security, consultations, and consent are also good for investors is made in part to secure widespread support for the recognition of customary land rights, representing these interests as synonymous obscures the role that titling may play in securing land for investors over local land users and alienating land from the customary domain.

It is important also to take note of the growing involvement of NGOs in the Global South in the land governance arena, and those chosen to represent those voices within international debates over land governance. In a July 2020 webinar to launch PRINDEX, a global survey intended to measure "how secure people feel in their land and property rights" hosted by the Land Portal Foundation, for example, the chosen voice of southern NGOs was the Founder and Executive Director of Ghanaian NGO COLANDEF.[5] With Ghana positioned as an outlier in the African context in terms of the strength of authority over land vested in neo-customary leaders, this choice is an odd one. Perhaps unsurprisingly, she chose to center traditional leaders as the core problem of tenure security in Ghana. While her presentation rightly centered tenure security concerns related to land transactions and how traditional authorities make decisions over land, the security of concern was for those acquiring land:

> If we want to acquire land for any investment, we are likely to transact with traditional leaders. And the Constitution recognizes them as custodians. That is the problem. At the point of that transaction, there has to be agreement between the one acquiring and the one giving away the parcel. So [the traditional leaders] are transacting land with unsuspecting people, not in a way that elicits tenure security. So it's a problem for those who want to transact land in Ghana, to know what they are acquiring. Once you've acquired the land, many unanswered questions remain. And so for us in Ghana, if you are discussing the land security challenge, it is right where land transactions are being done. So we are helping traditional leaders across the country to learn how to improve land transactions so the questions related to tenure security are addressed at the time of the transaction, before people move to actually use the land.

This perspective does not just obscure the consequences of these transactions for current land users, but aligns squarely with the transactional conceptions of land rights advocated for by the World Bank and other major land donors. The choice of whose voice to center is always a strategic one.

ENDORSEMENT OF INSTRUMENTALITIES

Perhaps the strongest evidence for an emergent knowledge regime lies in the degree of support given by diverse actors for the identified land governance instrumentalities. I pay particular attention to civil society and grassroots organizations, who might be expected to be the first to contest the emergent land governance orthodoxy.

If we look to the usage of related terms—from "land titling" to "community consultation" or "FPIC," we see an uptick in usage among most actors (Table 2). Yet a few actors stand out, among them the World Bank, FAO, NGOs, international development think tanks, and USAID. Multilateral Financial Institutions are again in the lead in advancing land titling and community consultation as core instrumentalities of land governance in the pre-2008 era, along with development think tanks and FCDO. Forest Peoples Programme also engages early on, yet is alone in advocating for the stronger procedural standard of FPIC. Yet in the decade to follow, everyone is fully engaged with these concepts, with the exception of La Via Campesina and the limited engagement of the private sector with land titling.[6]

A comparison of levels of discursive engagement with "community consultation" and "FPIC" shows other interesting patterns. For one, there is a huge uptick in engagement with these concepts from the decade prior to the global outcry over land grab to the decade following it—with the exception of La Via Campesina and to some extent the private sector. Yet there is also a patterning in choice of terminology—with NGOs, IIED, and FAO using the language of FPIC, and the World Bank, ODI, and USAID engaging more with the concept of consultations. Yet to understand how these patterns of use of relevant terminology map onto underlying visions for rural areas and the political orientations associated with these, it is again important to dig into what these concepts mean for different actors and how they discursively engage them.

A brief look at the links related to land titling, community consultations, and FPIC on the first page of each search from Table 1 suggests that the instruments themselves are widely endorsed by all actors, even prominent international NGOs active in land governance. While the ILC links point to mixed opinions on titling in line with its diverse membership, the links on the Oxfam and Landesa websites suggest a fairly uniform support for titling. It is worth quoting from Landesa's website at length:

> Most of the world's poor share three traits: they live in rural areas, rely on agriculture and forests to survive, and don't have legal control over the land on which they depend. We can help them escape this poverty trap. Stronger rights to land have the power to reduce poverty and conflict, increase economic activity, empower women, strengthen food security, and improve

Table 2. Prevalence of terminology related to prominent land governance instruments[a]

	"Land Titling"		"Community Consultation"		"FPIC"	
Actor	1999–2008	2009–2018	1999–2008	2009–2018	1999–2008	2009–2018
Multilateral Institutions						
World Bank	538	752	204	869	13	277
FAO	179	122	78	84	9	222
CFS	0	1 (mixed)	0	0	0	2
Non-Governmental Organizations						
Oxfam	0	24	1	57	3	88
ILC	6	39 (mixed)	0	7	2	78
RRI	0	0	0	6	5	137
Landesa	2	19	0	3	1	4
ActionAid	0	2	1	4	0	13
FPP	99	665	2	22	23	304
Grassroots Peasants' Organizations						
Via Campesina	0	1 (anti)	0	0	1	1
Private Sector						
WBCSD	0	1	1	3	0	6
Illovo	0	0	0	3	0	4
OLAM	0	0[b]	0	0[b]	0	42
Sime Darby	0	0	4	0	3	6
International Development Think Tanks						
IIED	57	49	29	31	5	91
ODI	77	57	19	18	2	6
Bilateral Donors						
DANIDA	0	3	0	3	0	8
FCDO[c]	29	118	798	4,850	0	36
MoFA[c]	0	3	0	2	0	2
USAID	3	351	0	28	1	9

a Adapted from German and Braga (2019). Searches carried out in April/May and November, 2019.
b Although there are 3 hits for "land titles" and 38 hits touching on themes related to community consultation.
c Added to table in March, 2021.

> environmental stewardship—for an individual, a family, a community, and an entire country . . . Strong, legal rights to land can provide the rural poor with the opportunity, security, and incentive they need to invest in their land to improve their harvests and their lives.[7]

Oxfam, ILC and RRI have also launched a global call to action to secure Indigenous and community land rights in 2016, with their "Land Rights Now" campaign—which at the time of writing boasted over 800 members.[8] Together with Landesa, they have also called for "full implementation of the SDGs land rights indicators,"[9] which strongly endorse titling. ActionAid also views the lack of legal recognition of land rights as part of the problem, claiming that, "Countries that maintain *ill-defined or weak land rights* for existing customary land users make it easier for powerful local and foreign interests to acquire land" (ActionAid 2014: 16). And a document put out in September, 2015 by ActionAid, FPP, GLTN, ILC, Landesa, Oxfam, and other prominent NGOs endorses a version of global land rights indicators that closely resembles those ultimately finalized under the SDGs (ActionAid et al. 2015). Even the Civil Society Mechanism, a body struggling to chart an independent path to the emergent land governance orthodoxy, has seemingly bought into dominant frameworks for rights protections. In reviewing instruments and interpretations that best support the livelihoods for small-scale producers, they highlight tenure systems "that ensure fair transfer of land, protection of tenure rights, respect for customary tenure, protection of the commons, non-discrimination, no forced evictions, and remedies for violations of tenure rights" (CSM 2018: 19).[10] This suggests an endorsement of the transactional conceptions of rights being advanced and normalized in the international arena. While some NGOs have specified alternative principles of tenure security, it is largely Indigenous and critical scholar-activists who are working to advance visions of land rights that are more empowering to the poor. These include a renewed focus on "territory" as a means to preserve or revitalize identity and community (Rosset 2013; Chapter 4, this volume); "property rights from below"[11] or "social tenures"[12] rooted in the norms and principles underlying customary tenures, and supportive of shared rights and mutual assistance (Cousins 2005); and a "land sovereignty" rooted in belonging and advancing "the right of working peoples to have effective access to, use of, and control over land and the benefits of its use and occupation" (Borras and Franco 2012: 6). It also includes "place-based ethics" (Coulthard 2010) or "grounded normativity" to center the ethics of Indigenous place-based practices—from reciprocity and solidarity, to "nonauthoritarian, nondominating, nonexploitive" relations to other people and nonhuman life forms (Coulthard and Simpson 2016: 254).[13]

Views on consultations and FPIC were also found to be almost uniformly positive among the organizations and sources reviewed. OLAM (2015, 2016) and Sime Darby (2014a, 2014b) emphasize FPIC for all land users and communities, while CFS (2014) and Interlaken Group (Interlaken Group and RRI 2015a) align these commitments to international law by emphasizing FPIC for Indigenous peoples. Community consultation and FPIC are also endorsed among NGOs, who tend to advocate for the stronger FPIC standard as a key means to operationalize land rights not just for Indigenous peoples, but for all project-affected communities (ActionAid 2015; Colchester 2010; Landesa 2019; Oxfam 2015). ActionAid, for example, equates the absence of FPIC as "land grabbing" and issues a strong endorsement of its application for all affected communities and all sub-groups therein (ActionAid 2015). Oxfam has developed a community engagement spectrum for extractive industry projects, in which FPIC is considered "the gold standard in terms of extractive industry community engagement practices" and "a critical tool for ensuring that [project-affected communities] have a say in whether and how extractive projects move forward" (Oxfam 2015: 3). And Forest Peoples Programme has been strongly involved in the development of guidelines for FPIC and in advocating for Indigenous peoples' rights to FPIC under international law (Colchester 2010; Colchester and MacKay 2004; Colchester and Farhan Ferrari 2007).

It is important to highlight that this alignment with the emergent knowledge regime is not absolute among socially progressive NGOs and grassroots organizations. Some NGOs, while supporting titling in principle, nevertheless raise concerns over the ways it has been deployed. ActionAid (2015), for example, notes the ambiguous nature of titling, capable of giving "small-scale food producers more security over their land" as well as helping governments "facilitate large-scale acquisitions of land" (ActionAid 2015: 7), and decries the growing risk of reduced access and control over land to investors under New Alliance-sponsored titling and land reform programs. Depending on how we view the evidence on land titling, this points to either a degree of naïveté surrounding the actual effects of instruments otherwise viewed as protective of customary rights, or simply an acknowledgement of their diverse and ambiguous effects. La Via Campesina, an international network of grassroots organizations that has maintained a more confrontational stance on land acquisitions and the "neoliberal agenda" (La Via Campesina 2017), is a clear outlier in opposing both land titling and transactional conceptions of rights in both principle and practice. With respect to titling, they state:

> By means of orchestrated land and seed laws, the common goods managed by the communities, land, water, seeds, and our territories, are turned into commodities under the dictate of land titling programmes and patents on life. Thus people are dispossessed of the very rights that guarantee the future of the planet and of humanity.[14]

They are similarly critical of voluntary guidelines enshrining the right to consultation and consent, and of the observed rapprochement of previously antagonistic actors and ideas:

> We, social movements, grassroots organizations and their allies, observe with concern that some states—together with some UN institutions and non-governmental organizations (NGOs)—are not focusing on the rights and needs of the most marginalized, but are concentrating their efforts on helping companies and private investors to use the Guidelines for their business interests.[15]

They go on to identify a large number of guidelines aimed not at helping states meet their commitments to customary rights holders under the VGGTs,[16] but at providing guidance to companies and private investors on how to use the guidelines in their business operations. Thus, while they were partners in an effort supported by FAO to translate the global norms crystalized in the VGGTs to grassroots organizations around the world,[17] their unique straddling of the discursive-ontological spaces of global policy fora and grassroots constituents helps lend their engagement the critical edge that has allowed for independence of thought from the emergent land governance orthodoxy. And together with FIAN, they have helped lead a call for ontological reimaginings of what land *is* and *should be*:

> The people—peasants, farmers, fisherfolk, pastoralists, men, women—who have lived in harmony on Earth for thousands of years, have been the guardians of the planet . . . Their worldview and relationship with the land they live on is built on the notion that human beings are not usurpers of Mother Earth,

> but rather protective sons and brothers to all living beings. There are many different ways of referring to nature across the world, and yet there is one common denominator: the inseparable relationship of all natural elements and the source of life they represent . . . Land, oceans, rivers, forests and nature as a whole, are not only a means of production, but also the foundation of life itself, of cultures and identities. They fulfil a social, environmental, cultural and spiritual function. (IPC 2016: 7)

MAKING SENSE OF ALIGNMENT

How do we make sense of the growing discursive, programmatic, and ontological alignment surrounding land and its governance? An obvious point of departure are the global rule-making projects surrounding land governance, which not only stabilize singular fields of thought concerning "land" and "land governance," but have created opportunities for the cross-fertilization and negotiation of ideas across actor groups. These efforts have included the overtly multi-stakeholder processes surrounding the PRAI, the VGGTs, the land indicators of the SDGs, and the *Framework and Guidelines on Land Policy in Africa* (AUC-ECA-AfDB Consortium 2010), as well as more one-sided efforts of multilateral and bilateral agencies to advance definitive codifications of "land governance" and "inclusive business."

The processes contributing to the formulation of the VGGTs, for example, was said to involve, "an inclusive consultation process started by the FAO in 2009, and finalized through intergovernmental negotiations" in which "no interest group—governments, CSOs, academia, private sector—felt left behind, and the States were engaged in word-by-word review of the guidelines."[18] This undoubtedly consolidated a common discursive space through the direct engagement of different interest groups in their formulation and endorsement.

The relative agency of differently situated actors within these fora is key to interpreting the significance of these processes. An archival and ethnographic study of the NGO strategy surrounding the VGGTs finds that "rather than boycott or attack the multinational firms with a stake in the VGGT process (mostly food companies), as they had often done in the past, NGOs instead reached out to them as potential allies" (Kapstein 2018: 174). Kapstein argues for the agency of NGOs in this process, who are said to have advanced a normative transformation in the context of deliberations occurring within the

Committee on World Food Security (CFS), in which the VGGTs shifted from a "technical" document intended to provide a framework for international land acquisitions to a multilateral agreement giving "at least equal weight to ensuring the rights of customary users to land that was the object of possible acquisition" (Kapstein 2018: 174). Yet this rapprochement also legitimated the codification and widespread endorsement of concepts such as "legitimate tenure rights";[19] "equal tenure rights" for women and men; and "consultation" and "active, free, effective, meaningful and informed participation" (but *not* consent) (CFS and FAO 2012: 5–6), while helping to normalize the voluntary nature of global norm-setting surrounding land, "the making of transactions" with identified rights, and—importantly—state sovereignty in matters pertaining to land (for example, by subsuming other rights to measures taken by states necessary for public purposes, and allowing states to unilaterally identify rights that are considered legitimate) (Art 2.1, 4.3 and 4.4). It was also palatable to governments due to the ability to "remain vague on the codification of tenure issues on the one hand while pledging their allegiance to human rights on the other," and the weak enforceability of human rights declarations (Kapstein 2018: 178; see also Moyn 2010).

A second example comes from the deliberations surrounding the Principles for Responsible Agricultural Investment. While civil society organizations used the CSM as a platform to engage intensively with the formulation of the Principles in 2009–2010, they were present alongside other key constituencies—from international financial institutions to representatives of UN agencies, private sector associations, philanthropic organizations, and international agricultural research organizations (CFS 2009). And in the twelve years since its founding, there has been growing frustration among members over the forum's influence, decision processes, and outcomes.[20] By 2014, the CSM had tried but failed to "redirect attention away from ensuring an environment for profitable external investments and toward responding to small-scale producers' stated needs and proposals" (CSM 2014: 14). In the deliberations surrounding the 41st Session of the UN Committee on World Food Security in 2014, they highlighted the "struggle of power in the international context" and the risks of the CFS becoming marginalized and "challenged by other global processes that follow different dynamics" (CSM 2014: 7)—such as the 2015 Agenda and the Sustainable Development Goals. They also pointed to the resistance of some governments within the CFS process to entertain debate surrounding their vision of "an alternative model of food production and consumption, based on peasant agriculture and local food systems" and raised concerns about the growing influence of the corporate sector in shaping public policies and UN standards (CSM 2014: 7).

They sharpened their critique of the process in 2018, decrying the effect of multi-stakeholder platforms in enabling the corporate capture of policy fora (CSM 2018),[21] and by 2021, they appear to have lost faith in the ability of the CSM to advance any of their collective aspirations. In the context of ongoing negotiations over the draft CFS Voluntary Guidelines on Food Systems for Nutrition, they noted:

> a clear inclination in the negotiations to avoid drawing attention to the responsibilities of the different actors, especially the responsibility of the agro-industrial model which is the one to blame both for the climate crisis and for nutritional deficiencies on a global scale . . . Who are these guidelines for? The reference to peasants' rights should be obvious in a document like this, yet today we see it in brackets, and it is being the subject of much debate in this process. For whom do we make food systems guidelines if we cannot name the pillar that underpins it? . . . It is unfortunate to see how a reformed CFS, whose prerogative is to put those most affected by hunger and malnutrition at the centre, is ignoring and side-lining these issues . . . Far from considering food and sustainable and healthy food systems as a public good, and seeking a broad approach to achieve them, what is being sought here is to preserve the interests of a few.[22]

Clearly, the politics are stacked against them and other visions of rural "development" are winning out. This account suggests that the multi-stakeholder consultations, interactions, and negotiations carried out in the process of formulating global normative frameworks surrounding land governance are instrumental not only in accommodating diverse visions, but in depoliticizing the policy process (see, for example, Duncan and Claeys 2018). They also seem key to legitimating the emergent normative frameworks through claims to inclusive process—*irrespective* of de facto actor buy-in. These processes of engagement also enable the codification of language that is more acceptable to a diverse array of actors, thereby giving the appearance of consensus while undermining prospects for meaningful shifts in the political economy of land.

Another set of examples concern normative frameworks advanced through less inclusive processes whose legitimacy and influence nevertheless stem from their purported relationship to these global frameworks. The Land Governance Assessment Framework, for example, was advanced as "a diagnostic tool to help evaluate the legal framework, policies, and practices regarding land governance and to monitor improvement over time" in countries around the world. Its authors are restricted to World Bank staff and consultants, yet the process is said to have benefited tremendously from interaction with the land governance initiatives of UN-Habitat, USAID, FAO (the VGGTs), and UNECA. A second example is the FAO Governance of Tenure technical guides,[23] developed in house but reportedly benefitting from "a wide range of representatives from the private sector, civil society and government" (FAO 2016: iii). The significance of such efforts to the consolidation of a global knowledge regime surrounding land and its governance is their advancement of technical guidelines representing singular interpretations of concepts pegged to globally negotiated norms. Here, once again, we see the "complex cultural work" involved in assembling land as a resource for global investment that Tania Li refers to (Li 2014).

While the technical guides are framed as instruments flowing from the VGGTs and the processes of stakeholder engagement leading to their formulation, it is worth noting their continuities with more longstanding political projects. In the Governance of Tenure Technical Guide No. 4 (*Safeguarding Land Tenure Rights in the Context of Agricultural Investment*), for instance, we see the clear endorsement of longstanding policy positions of the World Bank and Western donors. Features of good land administration, for instance, are those which guarantee ownership and security of tenure, and which support taxation, security of credit, land markets, and so on (FAO 2015: 35). These things are of clear value to governments, investors, and lending agencies yet, as will be shown in Part II of this volume, cannot be assumed to be evenly or always valued by the rural poor. As for tenure security, emphasis is placed not on safeguarding the resources on which rural livelihoods depend, but on "clear and unambiguous information on who holds what tenure rights to which parcels of land, and under what conditions"—thereby "making it easy for a potential investor to identify who holds the tenure rights to the land" (FAO 2015: 35–36). Emphasis on property valuation is also suggestive of an interest in taxation and land markets, longstanding policy prescriptions of the World Bank (Binswanger, Deininger, and Feder 1993; Deininger and Binswanger 1999). The effort to position these guides as *technical* documents which flow directly from the VGGTs, seems key to legitimating them and giving license to their authors to speak on behalf of other stakeholders in articulating a vision for what the VGGTs mean in practice.

Another key mechanism of this growing rapprochement of actors and ideas lies in a diverse array of collaborative and often multi-stakeholder partnerships surrounding land governance. The most notable is the Global Land Tools Network (GLTN), an influential broker of knowledge and tools related to land governance. The GLTN consists of a secretariat and 80 partners representing NGOs, academia, foundations, multilateral organizations, bilateral donors, and surveyor and law firms "who subscribe to a core set of values and principles and a shared work programme to improve tenure security" (GLTN 2018).[24] The GLTN coordinates the Global Land Indicators Initiative (GLII), established in 2012 by the Millenium Challenge Corporation, the World Bank, and UN-Habitat to "step up monitoring" of land governance. The GLII helped broker the inclusion of land targets and indicators under the SDGs; conducts regular trainings on land governance monitoring; and serves as a major knowledge broker and hub for the land governance community.

The efforts of the GLTN are supported by the Global Donor Working Group on Land (GDWGL), a network of 29 bilateral and multilateral donors that has collectively funded 853 programs on land (143 of which are still active) worth $ 2.3 billion USD.[25] Under the VGGTs, they classify their work into a few categories: legal recognition and allocation of tenure rights; administration of tenure; responses to emergencies; *transfers of tenure rights*; and promotion, implementation, and M&E. The global ecosystem of land governance programming shows not just the volume of financial flow going toward a unified vision for land in the global South, but is evidence of trends toward the standardization of uniform conceptions of what land is and how it should be governed. Not surprisingly, the GDWGL trace their origins not to the growing livelihood insecurity surrounding the 2008 outcry over global land grabbing, but to the "sharp and volatile increases in food prices that began in 2008"[26]—a narrative that rationalizes a particular version of rural futures involving agricultural intensification and the corporatization of agri-food regimes.

Other multi-stakeholder processes occur outside the scope of multilateral agencies. A partnership between Interlaken Group and the Rights and Resources Initiative (RRI), for example, has led to the development of guidelines for operationalizing the VGGTs in the forestry sector (Interlaken Group and RRI 2015a). The Interlaken Group brings together "leaders from influential companies, investors, CSOs, government and international organizations," while the Rights and Resources Initiative brings together research and development assistance organizations, grassroots and Indigenous organizations, and local and international advocacy and human rights groups. The joint development of a framework for operationalizing the VGGTs by such a diverse group of actors undoubtedly does important "cultural work" (Li 2014) in the world—in this case, enabling the translation of the vaguely defined concepts and seemingly contradictory aims enshrined in the VGGTs into specific operational formula. And it does this in the name of "community and indigenous organizations" worldwide—thereby legitimating these instruments and interpretations. The value of multi-stakeholder dialogue to the actors involved is captured on the RRI website as follows:

> It is our belief that when all key stakeholders with an interest in land and resources come together, greater cooperation, understanding, and respect lead to demonstrable progress on the recognition of rights of the local peoples who live and depend on these lands.[27]

It is also important to situate multi-stakeholder processes (and the related "business turn" in the NGO community[28]) and voluntary soft law instruments as symptoms and hallmarks of the neoliberal era, in which the shift from *government* to *governance* has involved the decoupling of social policy from the nation-state by outsourcing governance functions to non-state actors (Ferguson 2009; Ferguson and Gupta 2002; Lobao, Martin, and Rodríguez-Pose 2009). In this context, multi-stakeholder processes are not just mechanisms for democratization and empowerment, but may also help create the "conditions for the diffusion of markets and market-like mechanisms" (Collier 2012: 190) by helping to accommodate "potentially explosive political forces" (World Bank 2000: 107); bolstering popular legitimacy by discursively framing undemocratic policies as in the public interest (Ferguson 1990); or through the productive forms of power involved in the production of certain types of subjects (Barry, Osborne, and Rose 1996; Ferguson 2009; Miller and Rose 2008). The presumed multi-stakeholder endorsement of guidelines equating the notion of "safeguarding land tenure rights" with the specification of clear and unambiguous rights that may be transacted, collateralized and taxed is emblematic of how power may be working in and through these processes.

Yet it is important to also query the very assumption that the boundaries between these actors and actor categories are real and unblurred. There is the obvious case of entities like the Interlaken Group, a self-described informal network of leaders representing corporations, civil society, government and international organizations.[29] Yet recent scholarship has also highlighted how the boundaries between these categories are blurred through everyday practices. Boundaries between state and society, for example, are blurred in the tendency for local leaders to don symbols of state authority to legitimate their actions and bolster their own authority (Das and Poole 2004), and in the mixed identities and accountabilities faced by decentralized state authorities (Robbins et al. 2009). Others have watched with concern the volume of corporate funding flowing into non-governmental organizations (Sachedina, Igoe, and Brockington 2009). While it is beyond the scope of this volume to explore these questions in depth, a few examples highlight the need to question our assumptions that governmental, non-governmental, and corporate actors are by definition politically and financially independent. A look at the membership of the board of the nonprofit Landesa, for example, reveals partners, CEOs and directors of for-profit investment and financial services firms.[30] There is also a blurring of the boundary between governmental and non-governmental organizations in the volume of finance flowing from key Western "land donors" (DfID, Dutch Ministry of Foreign Affairs, Norway, USAID) to Cadasta Foundation, ILC, RRI and Oxfam, among others.[31] Here, multiple factors are observed to be contributing to the growing albeit incomplete alignment of formerly antagonistic actors in a shared land governance conceptual and operational space. Among these are the accommodation and consolidation of a shared conceptual-ontological space enabled through sustained dialogue; the flows of finance and collaborative projects that undo clear boundaries between actors; and discursive tactics which render certain operational interpretations of the VGGTs the definitive ones. And such dynamics mirror and reflect those of capitalism itself—an experimental, contingent, highly adaptive, and constantly mutating formation that is always unfinished and always in the making (Bear et al. 2015; Thrift 2005).

Yet the power dynamics surrounding these processes must also be located in knowledge production itself, from the heavy investment of funding in establishing the fields of thought and action in the wake of the outcry over global land grabs (or food price spikes) to how that knowledge continues to be brokered by powerful actors. The reports profiled as early milestones in the reframing effort in Chapter 1 were sponsored and authored by World Bank insiders and their partners (e.g., FAO, IFAD, UNCTAD). They emerged early on as "discussion notes to contribute to an ongoing dialogue" (in the case of the PRAI) or as drafts, enabling them to establish a boundary object against which debate would center while leaving room for accommodating critique. This is strategic from a politics of knowledge framing: by quickly staking out the field of thought and giving us a set of concepts to work with, these conceptions become naturalized while other realities are foreclosed. These constructs have since been sustained through heavy investment in knowledge brokerage. This takes a variety of forms: formal training of staff from line ministries and cadastral services around the world; multilateral and bilateral aid, in which donor agencies and their trusted consultants help to build the "technical" expertise and institutional and policy frameworks for advancing dominant ideas (Brown 2005; Daniel and Mittal 2010; Maganga et al. 2016); country-level piloting of land governance frameworks and performance monitoring (e.g., the World Bank, GLTN); annual land conferences that bring together development agencies, governments, civil society, and the private sector (e.g. the World Bank, the Dutch Land Academy);[32] the funding of country-level research institutes (e.g., Ethiolandnet) and research *agendas*, and their role in influencing government policy; and the funding and "technical" oversight provided by bilateral donors to the consultancy firms and think tanks they enlist to aid in knowledge brokerage.[33] Yet it has also manifested in the proliferation of NGOs working on knowledge production and training in the land governance arena—many of whom have either emerged or taken on new life in the context of these dynamics.[34]

SIGNIFICANCE

This chapter explored the levels and forms of multi-actor enrollment in the emergent land governance regime. The evidence points to a growing discursive alignment around a set of key terms (land rights, land governance, tenure security, women's land rights, and to some extent, inclusive business), as well as widespread endorsement of land titling and community consultations as key instrumentalities through which these concepts are to be enacted. While there may be notable gains for civil society, as argued by Kapstein (2018), there is also an unprecedented level of global political support and funding for longstanding political projects of the World Bank and Western donors. Titling is now squarely on the agenda and being advanced at an unprecedented pace and scale;[35] and community consultations or FPIC *in the context of land acquisitions* are widely endorsed by actors across the political spectrum as a means to operationalize land rights. Many view this as progress in customary rights recognition and protection, yet these ways of conceiving of land are fully compatible with the World Bank's longstanding endorsement of land markets as a way to advance narrow conceptions of efficiency in land use. This reality is not missed by organizations embedded in grassroots struggles for land and social justice. In the *People's Manual on the Guidelines on Governance of Land, Fisheries and Forests*, La Via Campesina notes that, "The Guidelines do not prohibit large-scale transactions in land tenure rights, in other words, land grabbing. . . . Unfortunately, power relations did not allow for social movements and other civil society participants to challenge land grabbing" (La Via Campesina 2017: 19). And in fact, as shown here, many NGOs are actually involved in the endorsement and codification of guidelines for land to change hands—albeit "responsibly."

From Chapter 1, we see the codification of certain truths in the global land governance arena—versions of reality that are advanced as self-evident through the discursive tactics involved, from crisis narratives to mobilizing metaphors and beyond. From this chapter, we see the level of enrollment of actors across the political spectrum in these narrow conceptions of "what land is, what it can do and how humans should interact with it" (Li 2014). But to what extent are these "truths" a reflection of underlying realities in the world, as opposed to deeply situated (historically, politically, ontologically) social constructs in need of questioning and provincialization (Chakrabarty 2000)? This is the question to which the manuscript now turns.

REFERENCES

ActionAid. 2014. *The Great Land Heist*. Johannesburg, South Africa: ActionAid International.

ActionAid. 2015. *Act on It: 4 Key Steps to Prevent Land Grabs*. Johannesburg, South Africa: ActionAid International.

ActionAid, IASS, Landesa, Habitat for Humanity, Columbia Center on Sustainable Investment, GLTN, ILC, Namati, Huairou Commission, Rights and Resources Initiative, IWGIA, Oxfam, and Forest Peoples Programme. 2015. *Land Rights: An Essential Global Indicator for the Post-2015 SDGs*. Available at: https://www.landcoalition.org/sites/default/files/documents/resources/land_rights_an_essential_global_indicator_-_sep_2_2015_0.pdf (accessed Nov. 24, 2020).

AUC-ECA-AfDB Consortium. 2010. *Framework and Guidelines on Land Policy in Africa*. Addis Ababa, Ethiopia: African Union Commission, Economic Commission for Africa and African Development Bank.

Barry, A., T. Osborne, and N. Rose, Eds. 1996. *Foucault and Political Reason: Liberalism, Neo-liberalism and Rationalities of Government*. Chicago: University of Chicago Press.

Bear, L., K. Ho, A.L. Tsing, and S. Yanagisako. 2015. Gens: A Feminist Manifesto for the Study of Capitalism. Theorizing the Contemporary, *Fieldsights*, Mar. 30. Available at: https://culanth.org/fieldsights/gens-a-feminist-manifesto-for-the-study-of-capitalism (accessed May 5, 2021).

Binswanger, H.P., K. Deininger, and G. Feder. 1993. Power, distortions, revolt, and reform in agricultural land relations. *Policy Research Working Papers* 1164. Washington, DC: The World Bank.

Borras, S.M. and J.C. Franco. 2012. A "land sovereignty" alternative? Towards a peoples' counter-enclosure. *TNI Agrarian Justice Programme Discussion Paper*.

Bromley, D. W. 2008. Formalising property relations in the developing world: The wrong prescription for the wrong malady. *Land Use Policy* 26(2008): 20–27.

Brown, T. 2005. Contestation, confusion and corruption: Market-based land reform in Zambia. In: S. Evers, M. Spierenburg and H. Wels (Eds.), *Competing Jurisdictions: Settling Land Claims in Africa*, 79–102. Leiden, Netherlands: Brill Academic Publishers.

CFS. 2009. *Reform of the Committee on World Food Security: Final Version*. Rome: Committee on World Food Security.

CFS. 2014. *Principles for Responsible Investment in Agriculture and Food Systems*. Rome: The Committee on World Food Security.

CFS and FAO. 2012. *Voluntary Guidelines on the Responsible Governance of Tenure of Land, Fisheries and Forests in the Context of National Food Security*. Rome: Committee on World Food Security and the Food and Agriculture Organization of the United Nations.

Chakrabarty, D. 2000. *Provincializing Europe: Postcolonial Thought and Historical Difference*. Princeton, NJ: Princeton University Press.

Chauveau, J.-P. 2003. Plans fonciers ruraux: Conditions de pertinence des systèms d'identification et d'enregistrement des droits coutumiers. *Dossier* no. 122. London: International Institute for Environment and Development.

Colchester, M. 2010. *Free, Prior and Informed Consent: Making FPIC Work for Forests and Peoples*. New Haven, CT: The Forests Dialogue.

Colchester, M. and F. MacKay. 2004. *In Search of Middle Ground: Indigenous Peoples, Collective Representation and the Right to Free, Prior and Informed Consent*.

Colchester, M. and M. Farhan Ferrari. 2007. *Making FPIC Work: Challenges and Prospects for Indigenous Peoples*. Moreton-in-Marsh: Forest Peoples Programme.

Collier, S.J. 2012. Neoliberalism as big Leviathan, or . . . ? A response to Wacquant and Hilgers. *Social Anthropology/Anthropologie Sociale* 20(2): 186–195.

Coulthard, G.S. 2010. Place against Empire: Understanding Indigenous Anti-Colonialism. *Affinities: A Journal of Radical Theory, Culture, and Action* 4(2): 79–83.

Coulthard, G. and L.B. Simpson. 2016. Grounded normativity/place-based solidarity. *American Quarterly* 68(2): 249–255.

Cousins, B. 2005. Tenure reform in South Africa: Titling versus social embeddedness. *Forum for Development Studies* 32(2): 415–442.

CSM. 2014. *Civil Society at CFS: Contributions and Assessments of the Civil Society Mechanism (CSM) on the 41st Session of the UN Committee on World Food Security (CFS).* Rome: Civil Society Mechanism for Relations with the UN Committee on World Food Security.

CSM. 2018. *Civil Society Report on the Use and Implementation of the Right to Food Guidelines.* Rome: Working Group on Monitoring of the Civil Society Mechanism (CSM) for relations with the Committee on World Food Security (CFS).

Daniel, S. and A. Mittal. 2010. *(Mis)Investment in Agriculture: The Role of the International Finance Corporation in Global Land Grabs.* Oakland, CA: The Oakland Institute.

Das, V. and D. Poole. 2004. *Anthropology in the Margins of the State.* Santa Fe, NM: The School for Advanced Research.

Deininger, K. and H. Binswanger. 1999. The evolution of the World Bank's land policy: Principles, experience, and future challenges. *The World Bank Research Observer* 14(2): 247–276.

Duncan, J. and P. Claeys. 2018. Politicizing food security governance through participation: Opportunities and opposition. *Food Security* 10(6): 1411–1424.

FAO. 2015. Safeguarding land tenure rights in the context of agricultural investment. *Governance of Tenure Technical Guide* No. 4. Rome: Food and Agriculture Organization of the United Nations.

FAO. 2016. Responsible governance of tenure: A technical guide for investors. *Governance of Tenure Technical Guide* No. 7. Rome: Food and Agriculture Organization of the United Nations.

FAO, IFAD, UNCTAD and World Bank Group. 2010. *Principles for Responsible Agricultural Investment that Respect Rights, Livelihoods and Resources.* Rome and Washington, DC: Food and Agriculture Organization of the UN, International Fund for Agricultural Development, UN Conference on Trade and Development Secretariat and World Bank Group.

Ferguson, J. 1990. *The Anti-Politics Machine: Development, Depoliticization, and Bureaucratic Power in Lesotho.* Cambridge, UK: Cambridge University Press.

Ferguson, J. 2009. The uses of neoliberalism. *Antipode* 41(S1): 166–184.

Ferguson, J. and A. Gupta. 2002. Spatializing states: Toward an ethnography of neoliberal governmentality. *American Ethnologist* 29(4): 981–1002.

German, L., L. Cotula, K. Gibson, A. Locke, A. Bonanno. and J. Quan. 2018. *Land Governance and Inclusive Business in Agriculture: Advancing the Debate.* State of the Debate Report 2018, Land: Enhancing Governance for Economic Development (LEGEND). London: Overseas Development Institute.

GLTN. 2018. *Global Land Tools Network Strategy 2018–2030.* Nairobi: Global Land Tool Network.

Hacking, I. 1986. Making up people. In: M. Baigioli (Ed.), *The Science Studies Reader,* 161–171. New York: Routledge.

Hall, R., I. Scoones and G. Henley. 2016. *Strengthening Land Governance: Lessons from Implementing the Voluntary Guidelines.* London: Department of International Development.

Holbraad, M. and M.A. Pederson. 2017. *The Ontological Turn: An Anthropological Exposition.* Cambridge, UK: Cambridge University Press.

ILC. 2016. *2016–2021.* Rome: International Land Coalition. Available at: http://www.landcoalition.org/sites/default/files/documents/resources/web_en_strategic_framework_2016-2021_spread.pdf (accessed Feb. 15, 2017).

Interlaken Group and RRI. 2015a. *Respecting Land and Forest Rights: A Guide for Companies.* Washington, DC: Rights and Resources Initiative.

Interlaken Group and RRI. 2015b. *Respecting Land and Forest Rights: Risks, Opportunities and A Guide for Companies.* Washington, DC: Rights and Resources Initiative.

IPC. 2016. *People's Manual on the Voluntary Guidelines on the Responsible Governance of Tenure of Land, Fisheries and Forests in the context of National Food Security: A Guide for Promotion, Implementation, Monitoring and Evaluation.* Rome: International Planning Committee for Food Sovereignty.

Kapstein, E.B. 2018. Governing the global land grab. *Global Policy* 9(2): 173–183.

La Via Campesina. 2017. *People's Manual on the Guidelines on Governance of Land, Fisheries and Forests: A Guide for Promotion, Implementation, Monitoring and Evaluation.* Harare, Zimbabwe: La Via Campesina.

Landesa. 2019. *Participating in Socially Responsible Land Investment: Model Guidebook for Communities Considering Agricultural Investment.* Seattle, WA: Landesa.

Land Portal. 2019. *Land Portal Annual Report 2019.* Groningen, Netherlands: Land Portal Foundation.

Lavigne-Delville, P. 1999. *Comment Articuler Droit Positif et Droits Fonciers Locaux: Expériences Récentes et Perspectives en Afrique de l'Ouest Francophone.* London: International Institute for Environment and Development.

Li, T. 2014. What is land? Assembling a resource for global investment. *Transactions of the Institute of British Geographers* 39(2014): 589–602.

Lobao, L., R. Martin, and A. Rodríguez-Pose. 2009. Editorial: Rescaling the state: new modes of institutional–territorial organization. *Cambridge Journal of Regions, Economy and Society* 2(2009): 3–12.

Maganga, F., K. Askew, R. Odgaard, and H. Stein. 2016. Dispossession through formalization: Tanzania and the G8 land agenda in Africa. *Asian Journal of African Studies* 40(Aug. 2016): 3–49.

Miller, P. and N. Rose. 2008. *Governing the Present.* Malden, MA: Polity Press.

Moyn, S. 2010. *The Last Utopia: Human Rights in History.* Cambridge, MA: Harvard University Press.

OLAM. 2015. *OLAM Livelihood Charter 2016.* Singapore: OLAM International.

OLAM. 2016. *The OLAM Code of Conduct.* Singapore: OLAM International.

OXFAM. 2014a. Moral hazard? "Mega" public–private partnerships in African agriculture. *Oxfam Briefing Paper* 188.

OXFAM. 2014b. Smallholders at risk: Monoculture expansion, land, food and livelihoods in Latin America. *OXFAM Briefing Paper* 180.

Oxfam. 2015. Community Consent Index 2015: Oil, gas, and mining company public positions on Free, Prior and Informed Consent. *Oxfam Briefing Paper* 207.

Oxfam. 2017. *Enabling Voices, Demanding Rights: A Guide to Gender Sensitive Community Engagement in Large Scale Land-Based Investment in Agriculture*. Oxfam International.

Ouédraogo, H.M.G. 2004. *Etude Comparative de la Mise en Oeuvre des Plans Fonciers Ruraux en Afrique de l'Ouest: Bénin, Burkina Faso, Côte d'Ivoire*. Ouagadougou, Burkina Faso: LandNet West Africa.

Robbins, P., K. McSweeney, A.K. Chhangani, and J.L. Rice. 2009. Conservation as it is: Illicit resource use in a wildlife reserve in India. *Human Ecology* 37(2009): 559–575.

Rosset, P. 2013. Re-thinking agrarian reform, land and territory in La Via Campesina. *Journal of Peasant Studies* 40(4): 721–775.

RRI. 2005. Rights and Resources Initiative: A New Global Initiative Advancing Forest Tenure, Policy and Market Reforms to Reduce Rural Poverty, Strengthen Forest Governance, Conserve Forest Ecosystems and Achieve Sustainable Forest-Based Economic Growth. Available at: https://www.forest-trends.org/wp-content/uploads/imported/global-initiative-pdf.pdf (accessed Nov. 24, 2019).

RRI. 2012. *Accelerating Reforms in Forest Rights, Governance, and Markets to Meet Global Challenges to Reduce Poverty, Conflict and Climate Change: A Framework proposal from the Rights and Resources Initiative, 2013–2017*. Washington, DC: Rights and Resources Initiative.

Sachedina, H., J. Igoe, and D. Brockington. 2009. The spectacular growth of the African Wildlife Foundation and the paradoxes of neoliberal conservation. *Current Conservation* 3(3): 24–26.

Scott, J. 1990. *Seeing Like a State: How Certain Schemes to Improve the Human Condition Have Failed*. New Haven: Yale University Press.

Sime Darby. 2014a. *Annual Report 2014*. Kuala Lumpur: Sime Darby.

Sime Darby. 2014b. *Sime Darby Plantation Sustainability Report 2014*. Kuala Lumpur: Sime Darby.

SNV and WBCSD. 2010. *Negocios Inclusivos: Creando Valor en América Latina*. Geneva and The Hague: World Business Council for Sustainable Development and Netherlands Development Organisation.

Thrift, N. 2005. *Knowing Capitalism*. London: Sage Publications.

UNECA. 2014. *Guiding Principles on Large Scale Land Based Investments in Africa*. Addis Ababa, Ethiopia: United Nations Economic Commission for Africa.

WBCSD. 2016. *Delivering on the Sustainable Development Goals: The Inclusive Business Approach*. Geneva: World Business Council for Sustainable Development.

World Bank. 2000. *Rising Global Interest in Farmland: Can it Yield Equitable and Sustainable Benefits?* (September 7, 2010 draft). Washington, DC: The World Bank.

World Bank. 2014. The practice of responsible investment principles in larger-scale agricultural investments: Implications for corporate performance and impact on local communities. *Agriculture and Environmental Services Discussion Paper* No. 8. Washington, DC: The World Bank.

PART II

Decentering Emergent Truths

CHAPTER 3

Women's Tenure Security and the False Promise of Titling

This chapter takes a deep dive into the politics of knowledge surrounding land titling, with a focus on women—a key focus of land governance discourse and programming. The formalization of land rights in the form of government-issued title has long been advocated for by the World Bank as a means to provide the security needed for land-based investments (Wachter and English 1992). In recent years, titling has been repurposed as a tool for addressing the threats posed by custom, as well as growing commercial interests in land. The primary discursive and programmatic focus of these efforts has been on the need for formalization to advance women's rights and tenure security. This has included, among other things, specific emphasis on women and girls in the VGGTs; the codification of women's tenure security and ownership of agricultural land in the SDGs; efforts to advance gender-responsive land tools;[1] and dedicated procedural guidelines, organizations, blogs, and media campaigns centered on women's land rights.[2] This is perhaps the arena of the current land governance era in which crisis narratives have bolstered the greatest number of new initiatives and some of the greatest missionary zeal. Highlighted in these accounts are the vulnerability of women's land rights; calls for action to safeguard these rights; and efforts to codify what this means in practice so as to measure and quantify progress toward specified aims.[3] In this chapter, claims related to the benefits of land titling are therefore explored through the interface of land tenure and the identities held by, and projected onto, women. With "the woman question" mobilized in support of interventionism and empire in histories of colonial rule as well as contemporary geopolitics (Abu-Lughod 2002: 784; see also Ahmed 1992;

Spivak 1988), such an analysis is likely to resonate well beyond the land governance arena.

This chapter begins by outlining the theories of change guiding donor interventions to strengthen women's tenure security, and follows with an in-depth look at the extent to which the key assumptions embedded therein are sustained by the evidence. A theory of change, or program theory, refers to "a structured set of assumptions regarding how an intervention works (or is expected to work) and how it influences (or is expected to influence) processes of change" (Vaessen 2016). Program theory is a phrase coined and popularized by Carol Weiss, who recognized it as a key component to program evaluation and an implicit component of any intervention (Weiss 1972, 1995). "Programmes are theories incarnate. They begin in the heads of policy architects, pass into the hands of practitioners and, sometimes, into the hearts and minds of programme subjects" (Pawson and Tilley 2004: 3). Yet not every program theory or core assumption underlying these theories holds up under scrutiny, which has led to a call to use theories of change as an explicit program evaluation strategy (Weiss 1995). This chapter is guided by the questions, "What theories of change related to women's property rights guide the interventions of key land donors?" and "To what extent are the key premises underlying these theories of change in land governance programming sustained by the evidence?"

The first section reviews the theories of change of a handful of organizations and initiatives observed to be highly influential in framing the debate: select donors active in framing and funding land programming interventions (World Bank,[4] USAID, the Ministry of Foreign Affairs of the Netherlands); select non-governmental organizations at the forefront of women's land rights efforts and campaigns (Landesa, Cadasta);[5] and multilateral efforts to codify land governance and women's land rights (SDGs, VGGTs). It is based on an analysis of material written or published by these organizations, including websites, formal publications, and requests for proposals, or of codified international norms. A number of key premises are distilled from this review, which are taken up in the subsequent section to guide the review of evidence. The latter is not meant to be a comprehensive review of the complex and multifaceted intersections of gender identities and land tenure, but rather an effort to explore whether the key premises underlying theories of change in land governance programming hold up in the face of the ethnographic and empirical evidence.[6] Given the nature of the evidence reviewed, the ontological question addressed in this chapter is not so much local conceptions of women's land rights and tenures, but rather the ontological assumptions underlying land governance discourses and programming centering on women (what *are* security, family, and marriage?), and the work that is done by them.

This chapter reveals how the push toward individualized title ignores the fundamentals of Africa's descent-based landholdings, undermining the effectiveness of these programs and all too often, women's rights and securities. This suggests that the theory of change surrounding women's tenure (in)security and the ontological assumptions underpinning it are rooted as much in the culturally-and historically-situated understandings of the Western development establishment, as they are a reflection of the lived experiences of women under customary (de facto) and state-sanctioned (de jure, or formalized) tenures.

THE THEORY OF CHANGE GUIDING GENDERED LAND PROGRAMMING

> Social programmes are regarded as products of the human imagination: they are hypotheses about social betterment. Programmes chart out a perceived course whereby wrongs might be put to rights, deficiencies of behaviour corrected, inequalities of condition alleviated. Programmes are thus shaped by a vision of change and they succeed or fail according to the veracity of that vision.
>
> —Pawson and Tilley (2004: 1)

In this section, I construct a theory of change out of the narratives of key organizations and initiatives involved in advancing women's land rights on the global stage. I proceed first by outlining the key narratives of each organization or initiative, and then use this to distill the theory of change (a simple narrative framing the problem and the nature of interventions seen to best address the problem) and the core assumptions or premises therein.

The World Bank

As articulated in Part I, the World Bank has long advocated for a market-based system of property rights consisting of clear definition of (state-sanctioned) rights and the creation of land markets to enable land to be transferred to the most efficient uses and users (Binswanger, Deininger, and Feder 1993; Deininger and Binswanger 1999: 247, 250). The World Bank's theory of change related to women's land rights is closely woven into their longstanding support for titling, which is said to lead to the protection of women's access to and control of land (World Bank, FAO, and IFAD 2008). The case for formalization has centered on the plight of women only recently, in the wake of criticism surrounding the gendered impacts of land titling.

A further review of documents produced by the World Bank with partner organizations reveals a number of perceived constraints to women's tenure security. Here, customary norms are prominent. The *Gender in Agriculture Sourcebook* of the World Bank, FAO, and IFAD, for example, frames cultural norms as a key impediment to land rights. It finds "local prohibitions against women's ownership of land . . . often more powerful than written laws that allow women to own land," and "overcoming social and cultural constraints" key to enhancing gender equity (World Bank, FAO, and IFAD 2008: 127, 130).[7] The text goes on to explain that "As secondary community members, [women's] rights to land are generally derived from a man relative or husband. In many countries, cultural if not legal norms dictate that men are the owners of land and that women have access to land only through their relationship with a man relative, such as a father, husband, brother, or even brother-in-law. Although *customary tenure systems* often do provide women with some basic security in situations when they are not living with a husband, this same system also *favors men when control over land is determined*" (World Bank, FAO, and IFAD 2008: 127, emphasis added). The solution to this is said to lie in addressing cultural constraints,[8] and in state-sanctioned rights (formal titling)—either through individual or joint titles (World Bank, FAO, and IFAD 2008: 133).

A second key constraint is said to be the absence of "women's independent property rights," both individual and communal, under customary or state-sanctioned property rights (World Bank, FAO, and IFAD 2008: 126). This independence is seen as key from the perspective of both conjugality and community. It is thus said that, "When land is acquired by a couple . . . the husband assumes sole ownership, excluding his wife from any ownership rights," and "women's rights to land and other resources may not be recognized" in community titling (World Bank, FAO, and IFAD 2008: 134). Tenure security for women is therefore believed to be advanced through the *independence of women's property rights* from male relatives and their civil status (World Bank, FAO, and IFAD 2008: 126). Women are also said to have limited ability to participate in land institutions and to claim legal rights due to their secondary status, lower socialization, undervalued productive work, and illiteracy

(World Bank, FAO, and IFAD 2008: 130). A final constraint to women's tenure security is said to lie in constraints to the "*transferability of rights.*"[9] Land transactions and land markets are said to contribute to increased productivity and reduced poverty by allowing "those who are productive, but either landless or own little land, to access land" and by facilitating the exchange of land as the off-farm economy develops, thereby "improving the allocation of land" (Deininger 2003: xxix, xix).

USAID

Key sources for USAID's theory of change on women's land rights are found on their website and requests for proposals under their Strengthening Tenure and Resource Rights (STARR) program. Their "Women's Empowerment" website has this to say about land rights:

> When they have more secure rights to land and resources through inheritance, joint or individual title, through marital property regimes, or through recognition and enforcement of their customary rights, women are better able to participate in household decision making, rent land and earn rental income, access credit and pursue off-farm entrepreneurial opportunities. Importantly, women smallholders who have increased tenure security may be more productive than women who face tenure insecurity. Increased productivity often leads to higher household incomes. With increased income, women may develop a greater voice in financial decision making within households.

The theory of change underlying the second phase of STARR (STARR II) also suggests that secure land rights for women will lead to investments to improve land and enhance productivity, greater participation in land rental markets, and higher income, and that this will in turn improve household food security and nutrition (USAID 2018a: 10). Access is said to be insufficient for women's tenure security, as "they might be able to use land for cultivation but cannot use it as collateral, rent or sell it"—thus highlighting the emphasis on transferability (USAID 2018a: 2). Tenure security is also implicitly or explicitly linked to formalization, as indicated in the statement that, "Insecure or uncertain property rights is one of the most limiting factors to achieving economic growth and democratic governance throughout the developing world, where an estimated 70 percent of land is *unregistered*" (USAID 2018a: 2, emphasis added). With statements such as, "addressing traditional, social and cultural norms that disadvantage women, such as land ownership, will take a long time to change" (USAID 2018b: 14), tenure security is also implicitly *not* linked to customary tenure. Women are also said to lack the ability to enforce the rights they do have "because of community pressure to keep them dispossessed, differences in how the laws are applied to men and women, lack of bargaining power, and/or a lack of access to unbiased forums to resolve land disputes and claim inheritance" (USAID 2018a: 2).

There is a remarkable coherence in the theories of change of the World Bank and USAID, both in the definition of the problem (*constraints associated with customary tenure, restrictions on collateralization and transfer, limited agency*), and in the solution proposed to address that problem—namely, formal state recognition in the form of *co-titling or individual titling* in the name of women. This is said to empower women socially and financially by conferring greater agency and autonomy at household and community levels (USAID 2013).

Cadasta Foundation

Cadasta Foundation is a Washington, DC-based nonprofit founded in 2015 with an aspiration to, "be the leading provider of technical tools and services to document land and resource rights and thus build stronger, more sustainable communities."[10] With this mission and a name derived from the word cadaster, their very *raison d'etre* is formalization. The theory of change behind this focus is laid out on their website:[11]

> It is estimated that 70 percent of land in the developing world is undocumented, leaving more than a fourth of the world's population vulnerable to conflict, evictions, and encroachment. Secure land rights are key to stability and prosperity. Without them, families and businesses lack the security they need to invest in their property. . . . By creating an accessible digital record of land, property, and resource rights, we help empower individuals, communities, organizations, governments, and businesses with the information they need to make data-driven decisions and put vulnerable communities and their needs on the map.

To ensure the use of their tools does not harm women's land rights, their Women's Land Rights guide also advocates for the following: education and awareness creation targeting men, women, local government officials, and community/customary leaders on the importance of documenting women's land rights; co-titling; ensuring leadership roles, balanced representation, and effective participation of women in teams working to document women's land rights; and providing gender-equitable access to Cadasta technology and the data it generates.[12]

Their theory of change thus identifies undocumented rights as the problem (and cause of conflict, evictions, and encroachment); and the *documentation* of women's land rights—whether within a process of formal state recognition, or part of an effort to strengthen women's ability to have their claims recognized as rights—as the solution. This is expected to reduce conflict, evictions, and encroachment; enhance investment; and therefore, to contribute to stability and prosperity.

Landesa

Landesa is a 501(c)(3) charitable organization registered in Washington State, USA. Women's land rights feature prominently on the main page of Landesa's website and of the Landesa Center for Women's Land Rights, where their theory of change is laid out for viewers:[13]

> Most of the world's poor share three traits: they live in rural areas, rely on agriculture and forests to survive, and don't have legal control over the land on which they depend. We can help them escape this poverty trap. Stronger rights to land have the power to reduce poverty and conflict, increase economic activity, empower women, strengthen food security, and improve environmental stewardship.
>
> Women in many of the poorest regions of the world are denied equal rights to access, use, inherit, control, and own land . . . The challenges are two-fold. First, laws and policies often dilute or deny women's rights to land. Second, even when laws enshrine such rights, legal loopholes, gaps in implementation, lax enforcement, and at times sex-discriminatory practices undercut these formal guarantees. As a result, often women's only claim to the land they rely on for food, income, and shelter is through their relationship to a male relative—a husband, father, or brother. They are susceptible to displacement and exploitation because they lack control over the land they depend on. That hampers women's ability to lift themselves and their families out of extreme poverty and impacts the way they farm in fundamental ways.

The site goes on to articulate the linkage between women's rights to land and productive assets, levels of participation in household decision-making, and a host of benefits to families—from health to food security and nutrition, education, access to micro-credit and formal loans, and reduced vulnerability to AIDS and domestic violence.

Thus, Landesa's theory of change articulates the problem as the lack of legal recognition of land rights (and its contribution to poverty traps), and lack of *equal rights* to access, use, inherit, control, and own land (resulting from failure of the legal framework and its implementation). While they do not explicitly blame formal laws or customary norms, they identify secondary rights in the form of *land access through male relatives as a source of vulnerability*. The solution lies in *formalizing rights*, which will incentivize economic activity, elevate women's status in the household and provide multi-faceted benefits to their families (in addition to improving environmental stewardship and reducing conflict).

Sustainable Development Goals

Tenure indicators are also enshrined in the No Poverty and Gender Equality Goals of the Sustainable Development Goals. As highlighted in Chapter 1, the relevant indicators are as follows:

- 1.4.2—Proportion of total adult population with secure tenure rights to land, with (a) legally recognized documentation and (b) who perceive their rights to land as secure, by sex, and by type of tenure.
- 5.a.1—(a) Percentage of people with ownership or secure rights over agricultural land (out of total agricultural population), by sex; and (b) share of women among owners or rights-bearers of agricultural land, by type of tenure.
- 5.a.2—Percentage of countries where the legal framework (including customary law) guarantees women's equal rights to land ownership and/or control.

The indicator focuses on all adults, irrespective of their livelihoods and place of residence (urban or rural). Their rights are considered legally recognized if they have access to land under a tenure arrangement legally recognized by the government (e.g., title, leasehold, use rights certificate, rental agreement) and the document lists their name as a rights holder. Perceptions of tenure security are based on fear of involuntary loss of the land within the next five years and the landholder's right to bequeath the land.

FAO is the custodian agency for indicators 5.a.1 and 5.a.2. The indicators focus only on those adults living in agricultural households (defined as those operating land for agricultural purposes or raising/tending livestock in the past 12 months). Tenure indicators under SDG 5 are intended to represent both a de facto (5.a.1) and de jure (5.a.2) measures of tenure security (FAO 2016: 3).[14] Indicator 5.a.1 relies on three proxies of tenure rights: presence of a legally recognized document in the name of the individual; the individual's right to sell; and the individual's right to bequeath the land (either alone or jointly with somebody else) (FAO 2016).

Six proxies have been identified for Indicator 5.a.2, which are evaluated through the presence or absence of the following within the legal and policy framework: joint registration of land (whether compulsory or incentivized); spousal consent for land transactions; women's and girls' equal inheritance rights; allocation of financial resources to increase women's ownership and control over land; explicit protection of the land rights of women under legal systems that recognize customary land tenure; and whether the legal framework mandates women's participation in land management and administration institutions.[15]

Here the *presence of legally recognized documentation (formalization)*, a measure of tenure security across all three indicators, is again presumed to advance tenure security for men and women. *Ability to transact in land* is also seen as enhancing security, as seen in the identification of the right to sell as one of three proxies of Indicator 5.a.1—which can stand by itself as an indicator of tenure security, even if the other two proxies do not hold true. Another core assumption implicit in indicator 5.a.2 proxies is that *equality enhances security*, from joint registration of spouses (co-titling), to consent to land transactions, and equality of inheritance rights. Women's *direct participation* in the institutions of land management and administration is also considered key to advancing tenure security.

Voluntary Guidelines on the Responsible Governance of Tenure

The VGGTs call on states to "recognize and respect all legitimate rights holders and their rights," whether or not these rights are formalized (CFS and FAO 2012: 3). Yet they also state that "States should provide legal recognition for legitimate tenure rights not currently protected by law" and equate tenure security with *legal protection* against forced evictions, harassment, and other threats (CFS and FAO 2012: 6). Another principle is that states should "take active measures to promote and facilitate the full realization of tenure rights or *the making of transactions* with the rights" (CFS and FAO 2012: 3), and protect against abuses of legitimate tenure rights by business enterprises. Key principles of implementation related to gender include "taking specific measures aimed at accelerating *de facto equality* when necessary" and ensuring that "women and girls have equal tenure rights and access . . . *independent of their civil and marital status*" (CFS and FAO 2012: 5). Responsibilities of states with respect to gender are to ensure "*equal tenure rights* for women and men, including *the right to inherit and bequeath* these rights" (CFS and FAO 2012: 6), and to "ensure that women and men enjoy *the same rights* in the newly recognized tenure rights, and that those rights are *reflected in records*" (CFS and FAO 2012: 11–12). Gender-sensitive policy frameworks are identified as those which ensure that "women can legally enter into contracts concerning tenure rights on the basis of equality with men"; "provide legal services and other assistance to enable women to defend their tenure interests"; and are developed through the participation of men and women (CFS and FAO 2012: 8). Regarding the interface of customary and statutory law, the VGGTs state that "where constitutional or legal reforms strengthen the rights of women and place them in conflict with custom, all parties should cooperate to *accommodate such changes in the customary tenure systems*" (CFS and FAO 2012: 15).

Core assumptions enshrined in these statements are that women's tenure security is advanced through formalization of rights; independence of rights; the ability to make transactions with rights; equality in tenure rights, access, and inheritance; and participation in the formulation of policy frameworks and legislation. Where customary and statutory law conflict, tenure security is also assumed to be advanced through changes in custom.

The Theory of Change

A review of these sources points to a strong consensus on the key elements of women's tenure security. The review also points to a high level of coordination of initiatives, with the World Bank, FAO, and UN-Habitat coordinating their efforts as custodian agencies for land tenure indicators in the SDGs; bilateral donors funding the work of non-governmental organizations;[16] conferences and policy fora bringing various actors to the same table (SDGs, VGGTs, Global Donor Platform on Rural Development, World Bank Land and Poverty Conference); and coordinated media campaigns (e.g., *Her Land,*

Her Story[17]). Thus, while financial flows between these entities are not apparent,[18] this level of consensus is not surprising.

The theory of change behind these actors and efforts may be summarized as follows:

> Women's land rights are under threat from customary tenure systems in which women are discriminated against and hold secondary rights through male relatives, as well as by limited recognition of their rights under statutory law. Women's tenure security may be advanced through individualized, independent rights backed up by the State; equality between women and men with respect to rights, access and inheritance; ability to transact in rights; direct participation of women in land governance institutions; and efforts to overcome social and cultural constraints so that they may exercise state-sanctioned rights.

Several key premises or assumptions underlying this theory of change may be identified from the above:

- Premise 1—Women's land rights are fragile under customary tenure systems.
  - Premise 1a: Women's land rights are undermined by their secondary status, acquired through their relationship with male relatives.
  - Premise 1b: Women have limited ability to claim and participate under customary arrangements.
- Premise 2—Tenure security is best advanced through formalization.
  - Premise 2a: Co-titling is an effective way to advance women's tenure security.
  - Premise 2b: Independent rights and individualized titles will advance women's tenure security.
- Premise 3—Transferability of title is key to tenure security and enhances women's economic empowerment.
- Premise 4—Formalization enhances women's welfare through enhanced productivity and empowerment in household economic decisions.

In the section which follows, I review the published literature in relation to each of these premises or assumptions to explore the extent to which they hold up under the evidence.

REVIEW OF THE EVIDENCE

It is worth reflecting first on the nature of the review and underlying evidence. This review was based on a literature search on Google Scholar using both "gender" and "women" as search terms, in combination with "land tenure" and terms related to specific premises—such as "customary tenure," "land titling," "formalization," "co-titling," and so on. The review of the evidence relied primarily on peer reviewed journal articles, with a preference given to papers that synthesize evidence nationally or across contexts. Where needed, non-peer reviewed works cited in these papers were drawn on to fill in gaps in the evidence. While the papers ultimately selected were driven by the search terms used, the review is not meant to be comprehensive. Rather, the search continued until enough relevant sources were found to provide evidence on the veracity of each premise across diverse contexts.

The evidence reviewed against each of the identified premises reveals outcomes shaped by unique historical, political, and cultural contexts, as well as by the particularity of tenure reforms themselves, and may thus be considered a fair reflection of the diverse realities on the ground. However, the patterning of the findings is also suggestive of differences in the researchers and the research itself. Research emanating from distinctive disciplinary backgrounds and theoretical lenses were observed to shape the questions asked (and not asked), the methods and variables chosen to answer these questions (and variables excluded from analysis), and thus the findings reached. This seems to have profoundly muddied the waters, in particular for those studies that stop at a surface level of analysis and aim to simply verify established theories of change (as opposed to achieving an open-ended and plural understanding of local tenure relations). Underneath these surface level understandings often lie more complex and nuanced realities that emerge only in those studies relying on more open-ended methodologies and a plurality of perspectives, including those of differently-situated women and their situated experiences with customary tenure and exogenous interventions. Rather than trying to prioritize some perspectives over others, I have taken these different sources and placed them on par—considering each a valid but also partial reflection of a more complex reality. The evidence presented below should be read with this in mind.

Premise 1—Women's Land Rights Are Fragile under Customary Tenure Systems

PREMISE 1A: WOMEN'S LAND RIGHTS ARE UNDERMINED BY THEIR SECONDARY STATUS, ACQUIRED THROUGH THEIR RELATIONSHIPS WITH MALE RELATIVES.

While these two premises are slightly different, many studies treat them in an integrated manner, making it difficult to tease them apart. The evidence here is therefore reviewed for both simultaneously.

Studies from a number of patrilineal African societies find women's access to land to be mediated through male entitlement and control through the institution of marriage, as well as the allocative powers of traditional authorities (see, e.g., Goebel 2005; Kapur 2011; Waterhouse 2001). A number of studies document the fragility of women's property rights following the death of their husbands, whether immediately afterward or as land values increase (Human Rights Watch 2003; Izumi 1999; Bikaako and Ssenkumba 2003). In Zimbabwe, for example, the post-independence government instituted the Legal Age of Minority Act giving women majority status at 18 years, yet "customary law" was said to prevail in practice—with titles to land assigned to men, and women keeping land in trust for male heirs upon the death of their husbands or "chased away" by the relatives of the deceased (Chimedza 1988; Goebel 2005).

Other authors profile how tenure security was once enjoyed by women under customary systems historically, yet highlight how land scarcity, population growth, restructuring programs, and growing commercialization of agriculture and land have undermined these functions (Davison 1988; Kapur 2011; Nhlapo 1987; Nukunya 1972; Pala Okeyo 1980). A review by Kapur finds that these changes have tended to release the family and community from their customary obligations to some of their members, and together with the actions of local elites, may allow discrimination and exclusion to be entrenched along the lines of gender, status, age, and ethnicity (Kapur 2011). In Tanzania, one study finds that widows were previously allowed to stay on the land after the death of their husbands; however, where market-based land ownership has taken root and conflicts over land have intensified, the protections provided by customary land tenure have rapidly eroded (Izumi 1999).

While some of the so-called customary systems undoubtedly embody inequities, it is important to view these through a deeper historical lens in which colonial regimes of rule and colonial and post-colonial land tenure interventions reinforced existing gender disparities or engendered new forms.

This has led some scholars of African land tenure to refer instead to *neo-*customary systems (Boone and Nyeme 2015). In precolonial times, women were found to exercise considerable control over land and agricultural production in some places (see, e.g., Crumley 1981 and Hoben 1975 on Ethiopia; and Mandala 1990 on Malawi). Studies profiling the erosion of women's land rights under colonialism include the Baganda in Uganda, where women's customary rights to land were stronger and more extensive in the precolonial era (Sebina-Zziwa 1995), and among the Anlo in Ghana, where the rights of daughters to inherit their father's property was recognized in the past, but by the 1970s there was a growing tendency to regard these claims as only a privilege and no longer a right (Nukunya 1972). The spread of Islamic culture and the gender ideology brought by colonial powers was found to reinforce male domination and encourage male control over land and labor (Davison 1988; Feder and Noronha 1987; Linares 1992). In some areas, contact with patrilineal systems of rule has resulted in men gradually increasing their sons' inheritance at the expense of their sisters' sons (see, e.g., Roden 1971 on Sudan). The combination of patriarchy and pressure on African men to grow cash crops under colonialism was said to be instrumental in some areas in eroding women's land rights, reinforcing male control over land and inducing a shift away from lineage and toward the nuclear family as the most important unit of economic cooperation (Awusabo-Asare 1990; Okali 1983). Karen Sacks (1982) argues that women's subordination began with the development of private property and the nation state, which were thought to have eroded kin corporations in which women in patrilineal societies remained members and cotenants of their natal lineage and its corporate resources. This erosion of corporate kin relations under processes of class formation was shown to have weakened women's roles as sisters relative to that of wives, undermining their status. Yet she argues that researchers themselves have also over-stated women's oppression by focusing on their roles as wives rather than sisters.

In Zimbabwe, women's lack of primary land rights was "underpinned historically by the definition of their legal status as minors, and the dual legal system that placed most African women under the dictates of customary law in the colonial period" (Goebel 2005: 154). This seems to have only worsened through interactions with the state following independence. Allison Goebel (2005) relates cases of the Zimbabwe Supreme Court in the late 1990s that successfully challenged women's legal equality.[19] The unequal status of men and women under the 1984 Citizenship Act in Zimbabwe is interpreted by some to reflect patrilineal patterns in Shona culture (Goebel 2005), but also to reinforce those tendencies by taking an androcentric interpretation of "culture" (with presumed allegiance only along patrilineal lines)—thus violating customary norms relating to ambilineal rights and obligations (Cheater and Gaidzanwa 1996). Representatives of the state frequently explain their failure to extend primary or even joint land rights to married women as reluctance to interfere with "culture" as read from the position of black male elites. In Malawi, a post-colonial program that titled land in matrilineal-matrilocal areas in the name of male relatives also reinforced patriarchy in land relations (Peters 2010). These examples show how the law and practices of the state may become mechanisms through which men may seek to capture or entrench patriarchal control, and how "custom" is itself contested and dynamically reconstituted along the lines of dominant interests and voices in society.

It is also important to nuance interpretations of gender discrimination with a deeper understanding of the dynamics involved in neo-customary systems that on the surface appear to pose a threat to women's land rights, but upon deeper analysis provide some crucial safeguards for women. As Carola Lentz (2006) points out, rights over and access to land are mediated by membership in specific communities—whether the nuclear or extended family, the clan, the ethnic group, or the nation-state, and claims are linked to group membership. Across Africa, that "community" in neo-customary agrarian societies is the descent group (clan or lineage), and as Pauline Peters has long argued, it is impossible to understand the inner workings of customary landholdings without an understanding of descent as the key organizing principle (Peters 2010, 2018). Most African societies are patrilineal, in which descent is traced through the male line and sons are the primary heirs of plots of land from fathers. Unmarried daughters may be given only temporary access to land which is revoked upon marriage when acquiring entitlements to land from her husband's descent group (see, e.g., Peters 2018). The reverse tends to hold in areas with matrilineal kinship, where land is accessed through the woman's lineage, typically through a woman's mother, older brother, or maternal uncle (Braga 2001; Kaarhus 2010; Peters 2010). Matrilineal societies tend to be further classified according to rules of post-marital residence—whether matrilocal (the minority) or virilocal, whereby the married couple takes up residence with or near either the wife's or husband's family. There is further variation within both patrilineal and matrilineal societies that turn on entitlements of women as daughters and sisters, wives and widows, making any generalization about the landholding status of "women in Africa" almost indefensible.

With decisions about land and its inheritance in both patrilineal and matrilineal kinship centered on the lineage, rules governing who is allowed to acquire which rights rest on a fundamental logic of keeping land within the lineage. Thus, even where exclusive residence and cultivation rights are held by households, as was true among Tswana agriculturalists of southern Africa for example, the tendency was for the land to be customarily inherited according to rules that *guaranteed its perpetual control and access by the social group* (e.g., lineage), and its alienation prohibited (Schapera 1970). This guaranteed ongoing tenure security for lineage members and residents through time, and is a key factor behind the so-called secondary status of women's rights in patrilineal societies (Lastarria-Cornhiel 1997). In patrilineal systems, if a woman's husband dies or the marriage ends in divorce, she either returns to her natal family or retains access in her husband's lineage. Rights within her husband's lineage may end at death or in the event she chooses to remarry outside her husband's lineage, which is a mechanism for avoiding the potential for land to be alienated from the lineage (Peters 2018). To say that this represents discrimination against women ignores the security this system provides for members of the entire lineage—men, women, and children alike. Here, land rights and interests break down not along gender lines, but along the lines of lineage—or lineal descent identities. To posit "that men are discriminating against women is to completely miss the logic of the landholding systems and the motivations of local actors" (Peters 2018: 46). Thus, women in the status of daughter or sister have completely different interests and rights than women in the status of wives and widows, and yet they continue to be treated as a coherent group with respect to interests and rights to land within international policy circles (Peters 2018). Thus, restrictions on the bundle of rights held by women that are interpreted as undermining their tenure security (e.g., alienation, inheritance) may exist to guarantee other, shared forms of security, while reforms designed to provide women the full bundle of rights may erode these systems. This is not to say that women are never discriminated against in patrilineal descent systems; rather, it is to highlight the risks of evaluating women's experiences through Western frameworks and ontologies that locate kin in the nuclear family, and security in the individual.

Studies from patrilineal societies reveal considerable diversity in practices. A comparative essay on patrilineal kinship in East Africa by Southall (1960) found wives to have a strong identification with their husbands' group and weak ties with their natal lineages among Nilotic speaking peoples, yet to maintain strong ties to their natal lineages throughout their lives among Bantu speaking peoples.[20] Married women in Bantu speaking communities of southern Uganda were found to often control property in their own right. Among the Nilotic Joluo of Kenya, women were found to be recognized as *wuon lowo*, "owners," by nature of their relationship as wife or daughter as well as *wuon puodho*, for whom use rights are derived from their labor investment. The latter could be traded without consulting the men from whom they received the plot, and thus acquired outside of the marital relationship (Pala Okeyo 1980). "Women thus exercised considerable leverage in matters relating to the use of land, particularly as long as it remained plentiful and security of tenure was vested in the patrilineage" (Pala Okeyo 1980: 37). Additional diversity in patrilineal societies is found within distinctive trajectories of change in women's and men's relative control over access to resources, which was found to depend on the flexibility of rules for group affiliation and perpetuation, and the role of marriage in defining the character of women's social identities (Hakansson 1994).

One of the best analyses of the property dynamics associated with matriliny is Pauline Peters' study of the matrilineal-matrilocal areas of the Shire Highlands of Malawi. Here, only "daughters" (younger female members of the matrilineage) were found to inherit their matrilineage's land, and sons to use the land of their wives or acquire temporary use rights of fields belonging to female matrikin (Peters 2010). In this region, the sibling bond between brother and sister—which is life-long—is often stronger than the conjugal bond between husband and wife, with most adults having several spouses over their lifetimes. While some have argued that these systems are no longer relevant due to the influence of markets and cultural change, the pattern of customary (female) inheritance documented by Peters has reportedly prevailed in spite of "a long and continuing history of prejudice against matriliny" (Peters 2010: 179). Peters documents several cases in two districts of Malawi in which brothers attempted to claim ownership over matrilineal land, were taken to customary courts, and all of the cases were ruled in favor of the sisters. In rare cases where men acquire fields in matrilineal areas (e.g., due to the absence of female heirs, or more recently, land purchase), they explained that the land was being acquired for their daughters. Male chiefs and elders were also found to rule in favor of sisters in cases involving efforts by brothers to claim ownership of their matrilineage's fields. Here, the presence of the *mwini mbumba* or elder brother customarily designated the caretaker or guardian of a group of sisters (*mbumba*) may give the impression that even women in these matrilineal-matrilocal societies are "secondary community members" whose rights are derived and access only secured from a male relative (see, e.g., World Bank, FAO, and IFAD 2008). Yet ethnographic findings often show otherwise. In this region, most adult brothers tend to live elsewhere (in their wives' villages or in town), and if their marital circumstances cause them to live with their matrikin, they depend on their "sisters" (in the Western sense, as well as matrilineal female cousins) for access to land. With the land in such circumstances typically received on loan and those receiving it considered borrowers rather than owners, their rights are also weaker than those of the female members of the matrilineage.

Characterizing informal property systems as defective also ignores their proven advantages. These are said to include increased land access for lower-income groups; the ability to access land without having to purchase it; the flexibility of access for those with secondary rights (e.g., pastoralists and migrant farmers in agricultural areas); and the fact that customary systems encompass not just rights, but duties of care, reciprocity, and connection (Lastarria-Cornhiel 1997; Mitchell 2007). Customary tenure systems are said to be structured to ensure that all members of the community have the means to sustain themselves, with rights of all households to access arable land for cultivation (Lastarria-Cornhiel 1997; see also Besteman 2014). In most areas, these land allocations were found to be both permanent and heritable. Thus, while the community or lineage may "own" the land, households often have secure rights to cultivate the land and pass it on to their heirs. Under optimal conditions of land abundance and peace, this is said to provide the means for women to access land to maintain themselves and their children through their husband's family or their birth family (Lastarria-Cornhiel 1997; Mackenzie 1995). The ability to access land without purchasing it is a clear advantage to poorer households (women, men, and children), and these benefits have been found to increase in cases where formal land markets unevenly disadvantage the poor (see, e.g., Chimhowu and Woodhouse 2006).

Finally, relationships with husbands and kin involve not just rights, but *responsibilities*, because land relations are embedded in and inseparable from social relations. One study from Uganda found women's customary use and decision-making rights to land to be widespread, with neither women nor men reporting independent rights to land (Doss, Meinzen-Dick, and Bomuhangi 2014). Thus, customary "ownership" was not associated with full rights to do anything one wants with the land independent from others—but rather a suite of social obligations in which rights and duties go hand in hand. Under this system, both men and women perceived their rights to be relatively secure. This finding was in stark contrast to documented (formalized) rights, which were found to rarely recognize women's rights to land—creating a host of vulnerabilities for women, relative to the suite of rights and obligations between spouses which tended to characterize the customary domain.

Even in Somalia, where customary tenure dictates that land should pass from father to son but never to daughters (in violation of both *shari'a* and state laws of inheritance), husbands are obligated to provide adequate land for women to feed themselves and their children and failure to do so was grounds for divorce (Bestman 2014). This is not to suggest that customary gender relations are always harmonious (see, e.g., the work of Geschiere and Nyamnjoh 1998 on witchcraft and the intensification of the politics of belonging under political liberalization). Rather, it is to acknowledge that even within customary regimes with the most inequitable norms of access to land and (female) labor, duties of care tend to safeguard land access for women and other secondary rights holders. This emphasis on responsibilities as much as rights in many customary systems, and the tendency for state law to emphasize exclusivity of rights and legal certainty (in who holds those rights), suggest that the social safety nets for women and vulnerable groups may be at stake in efforts to formalize.

PREMISE 1B: WOMEN HAVE LIMITED ABILITY TO CLAIM AND PARTICIPATE UNDER CUSTOMARY ARRANGEMENTS.

Evidence on women's ability to defend claims to land under customary tenure regimes points to a highly differentiated set of customs, capacities, and practices. Many studies now question the portrayal of women as having no voice within customary systems, illustrating that the symbolic power of male relatives within village and kinship domains observed by outsiders may mask the actual gender distribution of authority and capacity to claim (Peters 2010; see also Quisumbing et al. 2001; Rose 2004). In her 1997 review of the impact of privatization on gender and property rights, Lastarria-Cornhiel finds cultivation rights to be socially recognized under customary norms, and women to often insist on this recognition. And in the matrilineal-matrilocal areas studied by Peters (2010), women are by all measures fully empowered by "custom," shown to be capable of foiling the designs of colonial administrators, and considered today to be the "builders of the village," exercising considerable authority alongside their brothers. Within village and kinship domains, while brothers typically announce decisions made, actual decision-making occurs in consultation with his sisters. This stands in contrast to the strongly patriarchal structure of authority in society at large (government, civil service, Christian and Muslim religious hierarchies, private corporations) and the upper ranks of chiefs. As such, the authority of senior women in the matrilineage is usually invisible to outsiders.

Other authors support the notion that women are often marginalized in the customary domain, but highlight ongoing power struggles that play out during the imposition of land delimitation that intensify these challenges. This may occur, for example, when those in positions of power and authority in the area use community land delimitations as a means to assert their own knowledge and authority:

> As representatives of a state with an enacted non-discriminatory legal framework, local government officials did not in any way question male biases . . . , but rather used the delimitation process to assert and . . . strengthen their own positions and powers in relation to people and land. In practice, the process . . . did not provide a space for women to express their interests or put their concerns with access to—or exclusion from—land on the agenda. (Kaarhus and Dondeyne 2015: 213)

They conclude that delimited land presents the same challenges to securing women's access rights as customary arrangements.

Laurel Rose (2004), on the other hand, documents how women navigated the uncertain postwar legal context to assert their land rights, by accessing their birth home land or their deceased or ex-husband's land, and reinventing custom or applying new standards in anticipation of more equitable legislation. In so doing, they were shown to assert a wider suite of land rights than specified under either customary or formal law. Thus, notions of women's uniform victimization in the face of "custom" or statutory law must be taken as an empirical question rather than established fact. With few studies looking to the agency of women in asserting their right to occupation and use, such dynamics are poorly understood. One study from Ghana finds that women invest in social relationships to strengthen land claims, with tree planting representing an investment in the stability of the marriage and labor provisioning to her husband also guaranteeing her a share of the land should the marriage eventually end in divorce (Quisumbing et al. 2001). A study from the Gambia River Basin found women to repeatedly contest efforts by the colonial government and their husbands to control their land and labor in the context of agricultural intensification, efforts that repeatedly frustrated state projects (Carney and Watts 1991). This contestation rested on domestic entitlements women held to private *kamanyango* property under customary law, and forced a renegotiation of the conjugal contract as the growing season lengthened under the adoption of irrigated rice farming.

Premise 2—Tenure Security Is Best Advanced Through Formal State Recognition (Formalization)

The push for individual tenure dates back to the colonial era, and intensified during the final decade of colonial rule in an effort to stimulate agricultural development by overcoming the barriers to individual investment posed by "communal" tenures (Peters 2004). Independence did little to change these dynamics, with major aid agencies deepening the push for private, individual rights throughout the 1960s and 1970s, in a bid to enhance "security" through clearly defined and enforceable rights. Yet in practice, a large body of studies has shown:

> not only that such programmes failed to achieve the expected results of improving agricultural investment and productivity, but they also encouraged speculation in land by outsiders, thus displacing the very people—the local users of the land—who were supposed to acquire increased security through titling, and they facilitated practices of bribing, fraudulent titling and expropriation of land. (Peters 2004: 274)[21]

Tenure systems based on private property rights and a land market are often theorized as gender-neutral, given the assumed neutrality of access through the open market. Yet women's opportunities to acquire land and participate in the market system are often limited due to their limited access to capital, limited political power, a higher burden of care, and gender ideologies among government officials that discriminate against women (Lastarria-Cornhiel 1997; Nhlapo 1987). Furthermore, property rights are better understood as overlapping "bundles of rights" (Schlager and Ostrom 1992) or as a "web of interests" (Arnold 2002) than as ownership or the right to completely and exclusively control a resource (Meinzen-Dick and Mwangi 2008), and African property regimes are also said to be characterized by the multiplicity of interests and tenures on the same parcel of land (Lund, 2000). With land titling/privatization, most of these rights are brought together and claimed by one or two people, and the claims of subordinate right holders to conditional, partial, or common access tend to be neglected (Meinzen-Dick and Mwangi 2008; Shipton and Goheen 1992). It is therefore no surprise that titling tends to result in situations in which ownership "becomes concentrated in the hands of those persons (such as community leaders, male household heads) who are able to successfully claim their ownership right to land, while other persons (such as poor rural women, ethnic minorities) lose the few rights they had" (Lastarria-Cornhiel 1997: 1317; see also Bromley 2008; Meinzen-Dick and Mwangi 2008; Shipton and Goheen 1992). With titling discriminating *against* the interests of subordinate rights holders, women, elders, children, other dependent kin, and herders are more likely to be disadvantaged by their inability to claim ownership rights to land during the transition to state-sanctioned rights (Shipton and Goheen 1992; see also Davison 1988; Downs and Reyna 1988; Lastarria-Cornhiel 1997). Gender has also been found to intersect with class in shaping the outcomes of land allocations (Bloch 1989; see also Freudenberger 1994). Others marginalized in the titling process have tended to include migrants, pastoralists, marginalized ethnic groups, and transient users (Anaafo and Guba 2017; Meinzen-Dick and Mwangi 2008).

A key part of the problem is clearly the blindness (or disdain) of development agencies and the state to descent-based landholdings, and "the tendency to treat land tenure as solely an economic (rather than social) institution" (Besteman 1994). A study from Kenya found titling programs to shift corporate rights based on the patrilineage to "an almost exclusively male individualized tenure system" giving individual men the right to alienate land from which their female relatives once held considerable rights and continued to draw their livelihood (Pala Okeyo 1980). And Catherine Besteman's (2014) study from Somalia finds that the push toward individualized title, motivated in part by Mohammed Siad Barre's wish to eradicate the clan basis of authority over resources, was outright incompatible with (while rendering illegal) local farming strategies designed to spread risk, save labor, and maintain soil fertility and created a situation of absolute tenure insecurity. By allowing only one titleholder per household, it also jeopardized the rights of women and other household members.

Yet in order to provide nuance to this story, it is important to separate out the effects of formalization on women's tenure security under gender-blind policies, from its effects under land and inheritance policies explicitly designed to enhance gender equality. I start with a review of country case studies that highlight the consequences of gender-blind land titling programs for women. In the case of Ghana, rights and access for sharecroppers and pastoralists, and for women and their families, were once freely negotiated with chiefs. Following interventions by the Land Administration Project, commons are disappearing and land has been monetized such that earlier forms of secondary access (grants, sharecropping, political incorporation) have given way to rentals, leases, and purchases driven by the rent-seeking behaviors of chiefs. Women's rights of access are less predictable; chiefs can more easily alienate lands used by members of the land-owning community to other economic interests (thereby rendering people landless); and pastoralists have lost access due to the disappearance of the commons. Furthermore, women's ability to inherit land under matrilineal systems of inheritance has been undermined due to formalization, which has made it impossible for them to directly inherit their father's (now state-sanctioned) properties (Anaafo and Guba 2017; Tonah 2006).

In the case of Malawi, where customary tenure was seen as an obstacle to agricultural development, the Malawi Registered Land Act of 1967 was passed, with the support of international donors (Peters 2010). When the World Bank-funded Lilongwe Land and Development Programme sought to extend titling to rural areas in 1972, individual title was rejected by local inhabitants in the matrilineal Shire highlands. A sub-lineage unit called *ndunda* was then chosen as the relevant unit for registration, and land registered under the name of a single "proprietor"—usually the *mwini mbumba* (a senior male brother/uncle of the *mbumba*, a multigenerational descent group composed of female kin), who was taken by project proponents to be the owner (Holden, Kaarhus, and Lunduka 2006; Ng'ong'ola 1986). Ethnographic research shows tenure security to have decreased under the program "for many women who lost their customary rights under a matrilineal-matrilocal regime" (Peters 2010: 182). Land titled in the name of male "representatives" of matrilineal groups under this program (typically brothers or maternal uncles) was also often sold or mishandled to the detriment of women's rights and claims. Thus, not only did formalization erode women's rights in these areas, it also reinforced rather than mitigated the "secondary" status of women's rights (which tends to be interpreted as the product of timeless "custom" rather than the interaction with exogenous systems of authority).[22] Similar problems were found by Randi Kaarhus (2010) in other areas of Malawi.

In Zimbabwe, land titling under the resettlement policies of the 1980s and 1990s was found to create strategic spaces for widows, who were able to retain control of homesteads and fields following the death of a husband (Goebel 1999). However, permits were assigned to married couples in the husband's name only (Jacobs 1984), making divorce "a disaster" for women (Goebel 2002). The "fast-track" land reform initiated in 2000 to formalize occupations of commercial farms was also found to privilege men as primary recipients of resettlement land, and to prop up traditional authorities in ways that further marginalized women (Goebel 2005). It has also been seen as a takeover of land assets by the ZanuPF political elite (McFadden 2002 and Raftopolous 2002, cited by Goebel 2005), and contributed to growing (state-sanctioned) violence—which has taken the heaviest toll on women and children (Goebel 2005). Elite women have often been the beneficiaries of the fast-track reform process, suggesting that it is not just gender but also class and position within party politics that shape access. It is also important to view formalization from the perspective of how customary authorities are recognized in the law, and the effect this state sanctioning then has on women's land rights—in particular in light of research acknowledging how state and customary authority is co-constituted in ways that reflect and accommodate the interests of each (see, e.g., Ubink and Amanor 2015). In South Africa and Zimbabwe alike, the perceived threats to male authority under women's land rights movements have interacted with legal recognition of customary authority (e.g., the Traditional Leaders' Act of 1998 in Zimbabwe, which makes traditional leaders responsible for the allocation of land and land use and regulation) in ways that have caused patriarchal interests in land to become further entrenched—reconfiguring "custom" as well as the state's deployment of certain notions of "customary law," and their deference to it (Walker 2002), in the process.

Yet what about tenure reforms rooted in land and inheritance laws that have an explicit focus on gender equity? Other cases profile experiences under tenure reforms governed by laws aiming to redress gender inequities. In Mozambique, the 1997 Land Law includes provisions for guaranteeing women the right to access and use land and enables women to apply for individual title, while the 2004 Family Law gives equal rights to men and women to administer marital property and to inherit and bequeath property (including land and natural resources). The status of polygamy within these policies was hotly debated, yet the Family Law that was finally passed provides no legal recognition of inheritance rights for women in informal or polygamous unions (Kaarhus and Dondeyne 2015). Thus, despite the apparent gender neutrality of the land law, the estimated 33% of women living in polygamous unions and 55% of women living in informal unions remain unprotected by these laws.

Studies of Rwanda's national Land Tenure Regularization Programme (LTRP), which resulted in the issuance of 8.4 million titles, have produced mixed results. A study of the impact 2.5 years after the start of the LTRP by World Bank staffers (Ali, Deininger, and Goldstein 2014) finds that married women were 7% more likely to be regarded as joint land owners after LTR than before; and significant reduction in succession-related uncertainty—likely because registration required an explicit record of who will inherit a parcel. These achievements are due in large part to the statutory law on inheritance (*Law on Matrimonial Regimes, Liberalities and Successions* of 2000), which provides for widows to assume their husband's land rights, unmarried women to inherit land (if the sole surviving descendent of the patrilineal group), and married women who are only children to inherit their parents' land (Kapur 2011). On the other hand, the 1999 Inheritance Law abolished gender discrimination in land inheritance only for "legitimate" children, leaving the children of common law unions vulnerable (Pottier 2006). Under this legal regime, young women and girls are commonly labelled as illegitimate, and thereby disqualified from inheritance provisions (Newbury and Baldwin 2000; Pottier 2002). The laws also do not apply retroactively, undermining inheritance rights of the tens of thousands of women whose fathers and husbands died in the Rwandan genocide (Pottier 2006). Titling also resulted in a statistically significant *reduction* in the probability of having documented land ownership for women not legally married, since the law denies formal land rights to women in informal unions. The study by Daniel Ali, Deininger, and Goldstein (2014) also finds a large negative program impact on plans to bequeath land to girls in female-headed households. The authors speculate that this is due to the virilocal exogamous nature of society, for which "transferring land to females would imply putting one's old age support at risk" (Ali, Deininger, and Goldstein 2014: 273). Another study of formalization in Rwanda, Tanzania, and Uganda suggests the failure of property systems imported from the West rests on the resistance of local elites (Kapur 2011). The author identified a "Catch-22" of formalization of land rights in patriarchal societies, in which "local elites are sufficiently empowered to administer the formal titling regime that protects women's land rights, but are reluctant to do so because they perceive it as a system that will erode their land-based power base" (Kapur 2011: 91–92). Discretionary powers to grant or deny rights to housing for female-headed households under Rwanda's postwar *imidugudu* policy; discretionary powers extended to the Council of Succession to deny, limit, or rescind inheritance rights; and the reluctance of local authorities to enforce controversial decisions pose challenges to "true equality" despite the formal effort to guarantee equality under the law (Kapur 2011; Pottier 2006).

In Malawi, while the tenure reforms proposed in the new draft land policy had not yet been implemented at the time of study, some studies speculated on their likely implications for matrilineal-matrilocal/uxorilocal areas. The policy provides for all children, irrespective of sex, to inherit land from their parents. Kaarhus (2010) and Peters (2010) both anticipate the policy to erode women's rights by including sons as equal heirs; causing land to have to be further sub-divided (thus intensifying land pressure and competition); and eroding women's authority in lineage matters. In Ivory Coast, despite the formal intention to avoid simplification of customary rights in the context of registration by recording all interests in land, emphasis on mapping during registration undermined this aim (Chauveau, Bosc, and Pescay 1998) and women's rights to trees and grazing ended up being superseded in the records in favor of the right to cultivate (Lavigne Delville 1998)—reflecting a longstanding bias toward sedentary agriculture. Finally, legal requirements for new order rights in South Africa to be held jointly by all spouses undermines the tenure rights of divorcees and female household members who occupy and use land but are not wives (Cousins 2005).

These studies provide ample evidence to question the simplified theories of change underlying land titling programs. Even reforms carried out with an explicit gender equity imperative reveal biases in statutory law and its implementation, and uncertainties of outcome associated with the interface of statutory and customary law. It also becomes clear through these case studies how the specific ways in which rights are encoded under titling programs erode certain rights even as they protect others—creating unevenness of outcome not just for women and men, but for differently positioned women (rich and poor, monogamous and polygamous, with and without state-sanctioned marriage certificate). This points to the need to question the assumed dichotomy between customary tenures that discriminate against women, and the presumed neutrality of the "state." Far from a neutral arbiter of rights for all, the law and practices of the state are embedded in wider power relations and have become mechanisms through which men have sought to recapture patriarchal control (Cheater and Gaidzanwa 1996; Peters 2010). A rare study of the actual titling *process* (Kaarhus and Dondeyne 2015) found community land delimitation in Mozambique to provide a space for men to assert their power and authority, while women's voices and interests were marginalized—demonstrating how "a legally established opportunity to regulate and legitimize women's land rights was lost in a setting where traditional norms and male power positions were at stake" (Kaarhus and Dondeyne 2015: 195). The examples in the sections to follow raise questions about the purported separation of statutory and customary realms, as well as the ability of the formal state apparatus to serve as a neutral arbiter of women's equality.

PREMISE 2A: CO-TITLING IS AN EFFECTIVE WAY TO ADVANCE WOMEN'S TENURE SECURITY.

Here, the assumption is that where married women depend on land that is titled in their husband's name only, this will undermine their voice in household decision-making, undermine land access during marriage and enhance vulnerability to land loss following the husband's death or divorce. By placing a wife's name on the title, she will be empowered to play a role in any decisions related to land and related transactions and her tenure security strengthened. I draw on five studies covering six African countries to explore this assumption.

The outcomes of co-titling are relatively well-documented for Rwanda, where efforts to formalize women's land rights relied heavily on co-titling. The country's new land and inheritance legislation has formalized married women's co-ownership of land, and provided equal inheritance rights to daughters and sons. One study found 81% of the land owned jointly by men and their wives, 11% owned by women only, and 6% by men only (Gillingham and Buckle 2014). As for actual outcomes for those with title, one study found women to have a say on land use decisions requiring each of the spouses' legal consent—such as transfer, sale, leasing, and mortgaging (Bayisenge 2018). However, it was not found to shape the daily management of land and its produce, and women argued that men tend to have the final say on how women's property should be managed (Bayisenge 2018). Interviews with program implementers, who feel that the land certificate does not necessarily guarantee women's decision-making over land and has increased conflict due to the growing awareness of international gender norms, support this view (Bayisenge, Höjera, and Espling 2015). Challenges in getting co-titling to work for women's empowerment in Rwanda were said to include the "stickiness" of social norms and gender ideologies regulating access to land that make policies difficult to put into practice (Bayisenge 2015a, 2015b; Bayisenge, Höjera, and Espling 2015).

In Mozambique, while the Family Law (2003) extended inheritance rights to women married through informal unions and court verdicts were found to favor recognition of these rights, enforceability of these rulings was found to remain a challenge for both divorcees and widows (Kapur 2010). Comparative studies in South Africa and Uganda found limited evidence for the benefits of co-titling on women's ability to shape decisions about how to use or transact in property (Jacobs and Kes 2015; Swaminathan et al. 2007). These studies suggest that formalization does not necessarily overcome gender biases in land access and control, where they exist.

Several studies point to the weakness of co-titling as a mechanism for enhancing women's empowerment, given persistent gender bias within the formal institutions of the state. While the efforts of the Women and Land Lobby Group has led to formal commitment to co-titling for married women in Zimbabwe, in practice only the husband's name continued to be recorded on permits and title deeds (Goebel 2005). Furthermore, with most rural women not having registered marriages, no legal protections extended to them. This demonstrates the influence of wider political and gender dynamics in both the degree of protections extended in the law, and the ability to have co-titling translate into greater tenure security for women. Co-titling in Rwanda is also conditional on the matrimonial regime and whether marriage is registered or not. Thus, women living in informal marriages and in polygamous relationships continue to face challenges when attempting to actualize their rights (Bayisenge 2015b; Brown and Uvuza 2006; Pottier 2006; Vanhees 2014). In Mozambique, efforts to reconcile customary and statutory law following the war led to provisions permitting, but not requiring, co-titling and women's recognition as members of rural communities, perpetuating tenure insecurity faced by widows (Joireman 2007). For a country in which the majority of women are only married under customary law, women's ability to benefit from co-titling was also undermined by the recognition of only common-law (statutory) marriages (Lastarria-Cornhiel 1997). Studies from Rwanda have shown how informal relationships with husbands, extended families, or land officers enabled inequalities in the law to be overcome, enabling co-registration of women from unregistered marriages despite the absence of such protections in statutory law. This suggests that informal norms are not just an impediment to the recognition of women's rights, but can also help to advance them by overcoming constraints within statutory law.

These studies highlight the need to reconsider several assumptions within dominant theories of change, such as the locus of cultural biases against women's rights (presumed to be found in customary tenure rather than statutory law) and the ability of formalization to overcome these biases.

A final observation concerns the significance of marriage and post-marital residence for the shape of "the household" and its placement within the descent group, and how that shapes outcomes for women under co-titling. Under the matrilineal-matrilocal societies described by Peters (2010) in Malawi, co-titling would undermine women's already strong rights under customary law—and is likely to have effects opposite to those theorized. The structural basis of landholding and the variation therein clearly undermine the case for a one-size-fits-all approach.

PREMISE 2B: INDEPENDENT RIGHTS AND INDIVIDUALIZED TITLE WILL ADVANCE WOMEN'S TENURE SECURITY.

The absence of women's independent property rights is said to undermine tenure security and women's economic empowerment; therefore, individualized title in the name of women is said to advance women's tenure security. Where women are the sole caretakers of their families, independent access to land for women is said to be crucial (Lastarria-Cornhiel 1997). Yet whether this is best provided through customary channels or state law is unclear, based on the sources reviewed (which in general say little about this). A study from Rwanda found 77% of women prefer joint over independent titles as this would minimize conflict within families (Bayisenge 2018). A study from the southern African region questions the benefits of individualized title. Due to colonial histories of land alienation in the region, subsistence farming is often insupportable without remittances provided by husbands migrating for waged work. Women farmers therefore remain strongly dependent on husbands' contributions to farming investment, and a move to individualize title could undermine male commitments to the family farming enterprise (Goebel 2005). More importantly, emphasis on individualized title ignores the fundamentals of Africa's descent-based landholdings.

Premise 3—Transferability of Title Is Key to Tenure Security and Enhances Women's Economic Empowerment

Here, the assumptions that transferability of title *advances* tenure security, enhances women's economic empowerment and is best advanced through formalization will be explored. There is an ongoing debate in the literature about whether the transferability of titles following land titling exacerbates or alleviates poverty, for example by enabling "distress sales" or providing a means to achieve economic aspirations. The former concern is framed by Ali, Höjera, and Espling as follows: "by reducing transaction costs of transferring land, interventions to improve land tenure may make it easier for ill-informed households who lack access to credit and insurance to sell off their land in periods of distress well below its fair market value, [which could] make them enter a downward spiral of impoverishment" (Ali, Höjera and Espling 2014: 273). A Google Scholar search on "land market participation, effects on women" yields only two relevant studies, both co-authored by World Bank economist Klaus Deininger. A study from Rwanda (Ibid.) finds that land market activity declined 2.5 years after the start of land regularization, which leads them to conclude that the program did not cause "distress sales or widespread landlessness by vulnerable people." The second study (Holden, Deininger, and Ghebru 2011) finds that land certification initially enhanced land rental market participation of tenant and landlord households, with female landlords more willing to rent out their land following certification. However, the study does not look into the livelihood outcomes of this participation—undermining its usefulness to this review. A third study by Frank Place and Shem Migot-Adholla (1998), identified under other search terms, finds no evidence of increased land market activity following land titling in Kenya.

Other studies suggest that land tenure security is compromised under formalization *due to* the enhanced transferability of title in the form of land sales, in which land is permanently alienated. The processes involved, however, vary. In the case of Ghana, the breakdown of the trusteeship ethos of the chieftaincy institution has led to increased land sales, insecurity of land tenure for the poor and disappearing commons—factors which lead to adverse impacts on the ability of poor people to meet their livelihood needs (Anaafo and Guba 2017). A multiplicity of other causal processes has been identified, but largely from studies in urban areas. While relatively silent on gender, these studies may provide unique insights into the long-term consequences of titling. In many urban areas, expansion of freehold tenure has been shown to force existing low-income tenants out of their housing as they can no longer afford the rents, which often rise dramatically after titling (Payne 1997). Studies from Egypt and Rwanda profile the experiences of poor households who benefit at first from the allocation of titles, but are then vulnerable to forced evictions or market-driven displacement (Durand-Lasserve 2006; Sims 2002). Such evidence leads Geoffrey Payne, Durand-Lasserve, and Carole Rakodi (2009) to conclude that "the provision of titles may actually *reduce* security for both tenants and newly titled owners given the attraction of the suddenly enhanced value of their assets to higher-income groups or others with the motives and ability to take advantage of the changed tenure status" (Payne, Durand-Lasserve, and Rakodi 2009: 447, emphasis in original).

As to whether formalization is needed to overcome impediments to land markets under customary tenure, many studies of matrilineal and patrilineal systems alike have shown the presence of active land rental and transfer markets within customary tenure regimes (Berry 1975; Besteman 2014; Chimhowu and Woodhouse 2006; Colin 2005; Gyasi 1994; Hill 1963; Koné Ibo and Kouamé 2005; Lawry 1993; Peters 2010). Yet as evidenced by the West African *tutorat*, the institution governing reciprocal social relations between autochthons and strangers (Chauveau et al. 2006), these transfers often remain embedded within ongoing social relations. Here and elsewhere in West Africa, transfer of land to strangers is not a process of land alienation, but a process establishing economic obligations to landholding lineages, integrating strangers into village life and fulfilling long-lasting sociopolitical relationships (Bottazzi, Goguen, and Rist 2016; Tuboku-Metzger and Van der Laan 1981). Outright sales of land also occur, with increased frequency since the 1990s (Allott 1969; Bruce 1988; Besteman 2014; Cohen 1980; White 1963), and are often precipitated by wealthy landowners or the collusion of "traditional" leaders with politically powerful elites (Ng'ong'ola 1986). Thus, the claim that informality impedes land markets cannot be sustained by the evidence. What custom does seem to impede is land *alienation* from the social group, a feature which arguably does more to safeguard women's tenure security than undermine it.

Premise 4—Formalization Enhances Women's Welfare Through Enhanced Productivity and Empowerment in Household Economic Decisions

Here, the premise that women's land titling enhances welfare through a host of beneficial production factors and livelihood outcomes, such as increased access to credit, technology adoption, higher agricultural productivity, and higher incomes, will be explored. For this section, I draw exclusively from the review paper by Ruth Meinzen-Dick et al. (2019) on women's land rights as a pathway to poverty reduction. It should be noted that the papers reviewed in this study had highly variable definitions of what constitutes "rights" (e.g., formal title, reported ownership, use/management) and who holds them (e.g., individual women, households), and the authors erred on the side of inclusion—thus pointing to variability in how this was operationalized across studies.

The authors find strong evidence for the relationships between women's lands rights and bargaining power and decision-making on consumption, human capital investment, and intergenerational transfers. On the other hand, the paper finds limited evidence on associations between women's land rights and credit, technology adoption, or agricultural productivity. No papers were found that investigate the link between women's land rights and poverty writ large. Below, I quote directly from the paper on several of these outcome variables, and thus rely on the discriminations made by authors themselves on the validity of findings rather than a first-hand reading and evaluation of evidence.

Regarding the relationship between titling and access to credit, the review finds "little evidence supporting this, partly because it requires well-functioning credit markets, banking systems that accept land as collateral, and legal systems that effectively adjudicate cases where land is used as collateral" (Meinzen-Dick et al. 2019: 5). While few studies specifically assess the impact of *women's* land rights on credit, one study from Ethiopia finds that land certificates "may help" in obtaining microfinance or loans from informal sources by signaling that the holder is attached to a place and has capacity for repayment. The benefits were nevertheless found to be greater for male-headed households (Persha, Greif, and Huntington 2017). Here, it is worth quoting a study which finds that the postulated effect of land titling on access to credit in Hernando de Soto's home country of Peru had largely failed (Haldar and Stiglitz 2013)—with only 1.3% of families receiving title in Lima's informal settlements obtaining mortgages by 2002 (Calderon 2004). The authors acknowledge the flawed basis on which De Soto's theory rests as in part ontological: land is conceived of not as capital or a sellable asset, but "family assets" or "something almost sacred" (Haldar and Stiglitz 2013: 118).

Regarding the effects of titling on agricultural productivity, Meinzen-Dick et al. (2019) find mixed effects. They cite a quasi-experimental study from Ethiopia, which finds that the value of agricultural output increases in households with land certificates relative to those without, with the impact being greater for female headed households (Bezabih, Holden, and Mannberg 2016). A study by Mariapia Mendola and Franklin Simtowe (2015) on a land reform program in Malawi, on the other hand, failed to find significant improvements in agricultural productivity, agricultural income, food security, or access to social services for beneficiary households headed by women, while they did find an impact for male-headed households.

Findings related to technology and natural resource management, however, suggest more favorable outcomes. Land registration programs in Rwanda, Benin, and Ethiopia that have emphasized women's land rights were found to have "some impact" on technology adoption (Meinzen-Dick et al. 2019, citing Ali, Deininger, and Goldstein 2014; Goldstein et al. 2015; Deininger et al. 2008a, 2008b; Quisumbing and Kumar 2014). Similarly, Deininger, Ali, and Yamano (2008b) find that knowledge of land rights increases tree planting and soil conservation, with female-headed households significantly more likely to make such investments.

Other studies provide additional nuance on the relationship between formalization and environmental management. A study in Ghana (Awanyo 2009), for example, finds that tenure *in*security can prompt both women and men to invest in the resource base to strengthen land claims. Studies from Malawi highlight the importance of one's role within landholding lineages in shaping investment behavior; in areas where men move to live with their wives, they are less likely to invest in tree planting (Hansen and Luckert 2005; Lovo 2016), soil conservation, or hybrid maize (Lovo 2016). Similarly, when women move to live with their husbands, they invest less in soil improvements (Lovo 2016; Pircher, Almekinders, and Kamanga 2013). Thus, contextual nuances—from the way in which rights are conditioned by certain land uses, to inheritance and post-marital residence patterns—shape the nature and strength of the incentive facing land users to invest in technologies to enhance yields or sustain productivity.

DISCUSSION AND CONCLUSIONS

> Women's rights activists and lawyers in Africa have tended to treat the customary arena as inherently dangerous to women's interests, [with] customary entitlements to land vesting in women . . . rendered invisible to the formal legal system even in instances where women continue to use and occupy the land in question . . . Legal strategies that seek to avoid the customary arena may unwittingly remove the ground from under the feet of those women for whom customary entitlements are the best or only basis on which to assert or prove land rights.
>
> —Mnisi and Claasens (2009: 491–492)

This chapter sought to identify the theory of change associated with efforts to advance women's land rights, and to explore whether the key assumptions therein hold up against the evidence. For the select multilateral and bilateral aid agencies and non-profits reviewed for their prominence in this arena, and the emergent normative frameworks where women's land rights are codified, there is a remarkable consistency in that theory of change. Yet all too often, the key assumptions therein are not sustained by the evidence. While posing custom as a threat to women's land rights helps to bolster support for land titling interventions, it fails to take into account the social embeddedness and benefits of customary land relations or cater for consequences of formalization to women's customary entitlements. It also fails to acknowledge the diversity of women's experiences under distinctive systems of descent, inheritance, and conjugality; the diverse ways in which women participate in land use and governance or exercise their capacity to claim; or how the gender biases within so-called custom are often a by-product of longstanding relationships with the state or the culturally-situated ideologies and ontologies of the observer (see, e.g., Besteman 1994; Kaarhus 2010). The assumption that land titling will enhance tenure security for women in turn fails to acknowledge how titling simplifies the entitlement structure, dispossessing some as it recognizes the rights of others. Finally, assumptions that transferability of title advances tenure security and women's economic empowerment, and that it is best advanced through formalization, obscure the diverse ways in which tenure security may be *undermined* under formalization due to changing forms of transferability (from one that establishes and strengthens social relationships to one that severs them through permanent alienation), and the vibrancy of informal or "vernacular" land markets (Chimhowu and Woodhouse 2006; Colin and Woodhouse 2010). It is therefore no surprise that evidence on the economic and welfare benefits of land titling is so uneven, and that rights holders often resort to informality following titling (Ali et al. 2019; Marais et al. 2014).

This is not to say that there is no gender discrimination in African land tenure or inheritance systems; works documenting the lived experiences and voices of widows and the histories of (often radical) struggle from precolonial times show otherwise (see, for example, Ewelukwa 2002; Kolawole 1997; Okech 2019). The importance of this analysis is instead to render visible the highly contextualized, variable, and historically contingent circumstances faced by differently positioned women, and how this throws into question received wisdom on custom, kin, marriage, and security that suggest a uniformity of experiences and insecurities that does not exist. The analysis also reveals how the questions asked and metrics used to answer them may obscure more than they reveal, and how standardized interventions resting on these shaky analytical foundations may prove to erode more security than they generate. The chapter highlights realities that contradict those profiled in international development discourse not because gender discrimination in land and inheritance does not exist, but because productive forms of power have the effect of bracketing out from view other realities less aligned with dominant interests—naturalizing the realities that suit powerful actors and legitimate their actions.

A number of crucial lessons may be distilled from this literature review. The first, and perhaps most important, is *the insufficiency of simplified theories of change in understanding complex, situated realities of gendered land relations, as well as the ethical conundrums of defining interventions around them.* Insecurities tied to the secondary status of women's rights may exist for certain groups of women in some societies, yet this discourse masks other important realities—such as the inseparability of tenure from the social relations in which they are embedded, the web of responsibilities that exist within customary land relations, or the role that customary norms safeguarding land against alienation play in securing the rights of women and other vulnerable groups. In the context of growing land pressure and commercialization, and shifting and contested notions of custom, tenure security for women (and lower-class men and children, pastoralists and migrants) matters. However, this security is not necessarily best advanced by state-sanctioned (and individualized, alienable) rights. Neither is it self-evident that security is best delivered by exogenous interventions that reshape the rules of the game, and provide an opportunity for dominant interests to be asserted and further entrenched at the expense of marginalized groups and individuals (see, e.g., Benjaminsen et al. 2008; Cronkleton 2015; Lavigne Delville and Moalic 2019; Putzel et al. 2015).[23]

This highlights a second lesson that resonates with critical theories of rights and the law—namely that *the law and its enactment are inextricably embedded in wider gender, class, ethnic, and power dynamics which exist across a range of institutions* (state, market, community, descent group, household) that are likely to shape the way in which donor-supported reforms are interpreted, and the degree and character of their implementation. These power relations undermine the ability to predict outcomes associated with standardized interventions, and highlight the risks posed by interventions to rewrite the rules of the game on land tenure. With land tenure part of the fabric of social and power relations, "attempts at land tenure reform or changes in land tenure law are necessarily bound up with power structures" (Besteman 1994: 484). Where land registration "has been introduced in Africa, obtaining title to land has often worked to the benefit of urban elites and civil servants over rural dwellers, rural elites over rural commoners, men over women, and old over young" (Ibid: 484–485). The uncertainties and likely inequities of outcomes produced through the interplay of statutory and customary law, and through gender and class bias within statutory law and its implementation, thus raise questions about the ethics of titling programs—even for reforms explicitly designed to enhance gender equity.

Third, *treatment of "custom" in theories of change uncritically reinforces the call for state intervention, while failing to reflect the historical and contemporary co-constitution of "customary" and state authority or acknowledge gender bias within state institutions.* This is perhaps best illustrated by the resistance observed in recent legal reforms to extend land title and equal inheritance rights to women within informal or polygamous unions. Kaori Izumi suggests a more nuanced and grounded approach to the identification of women's land governance priorities which starts not by assuming fragility, or a fragility defined a priori in relation to kinship or custom, but by identifying "the ways in which land access and rights among women have been affected, negotiated, and contested by—and within—the institutions of the state, the market, and the social institutions of the community, the family, and the household" (Izumi 1999: 15). The current status of women's land rights and tenure security, and the outcomes of formalization, are shaped by the dynamic interface between customary and statutory authority systems. And as this review shows, women's vulnerability is not just derived from custom, but by legal reforms themselves—which curtail certain rights as they recognize others. Either system can place checks on the abuses of the other, and "at the end of the day women will be faced with negotiating those rights through the complex social field of formal and informal institutions (especially families), customary and general law practices and values" (Goebel 2005: 160–161).

A fourth lesson is that *it is crucially important to "disaggregate the customary," and to avoid the use of terminology that collapses a highly differentiated set of experiences into an implied uniformity ("women," "marginalization," etc.).* This review points to the differentiation of not just the interests and agency of women and men surrounding land and property, but also the differentiated interests of lineage members by birth and marriage, of customary authorities, and (male and female) non-elites, as well as those of longstanding residents and migrants, and diverse ethnic groups. If land governance interventions are to empower women and other marginalized groups and avoid dispossessing them of the rights they already enjoy, it will be important to go beyond conventional models of formalization and individualization. Innovation is instead needed in identifying and addressing the context-specific threats, concerns, and aspirations of vulnerable people—irrespective of how they are defined (gender, class, land use system, ethnicity, or personal experience, e.g., of hardship), while also maintaining the social safety net for all marginalized people (men and women) provided by customary property relations. This is not a technical task, but an inherently *political* one that is likely to run counter to the ideologies, interests, and commitments of power brokers at all levels of society. It is also important to recognize that women are not just women; they are also members of social groups defined by social class, ethnicity, and livelihood system (e.g., agriculturalist vs. pastoralist), among others, which also shape their rights, vulnerabilities, and agency. If land governance interventions are to empower women, they need to also consider the intersectional identities these women hold.

The studies reviewed here also reveal a crucial paradox of land titling/formalization—that inasmuch as it may provide certain safeguards against land takings vis-à-vis the state or other external threats for those whose names are put on the title, it also *enables land to be commoditized and alienated—thereby exacerbating the very forces undermining the security of women's (and men's) access to land in the first place.* Is formalization part of the problem, or part of the solution? While the diversity of local situations suggests there is no single answer, the weight of the evidence presented leans heavily toward the former—while titling itself leans in a direction that is heavily aligned with Western ideologies of land as both collateral and commodity, with longstanding interests of multilateral agencies in the strengthening of land markets, and with the contemporary political economy of African land.

Yet what about ontology? What are the ontological assumptions underlying land governance discourses and programming centering on women, and what work exactly are they doing in the world? Here, we must ask what family, conjugality, and security, or women for that matter, *are* for those advocating dominant theories of change surrounding women's tenure security. Clearly, the family is a nuclear household modelled on the West (rather than a landholding lineage), with conjugality consisting of a monogamous pair. Furthermore, we see that "the myth of households as composed of entirely separate individuals with opposed gender interests, in which marriage is predominantly a contract legitimating the exploitation of women" (Jackson 2007: 107) and the "celebrated image of African women as passive victims, marginalized without a voice" (Kolawole 2004: 253) are alive and well in land governance discourses. This is reminiscent of the tendency for "patriarchalizing interpretations of African societies" in which gender power relations are taken for granted and women are positioned as wives (Grassi and Vivet 2014:

8; Oyěwùmi 2003) rather than mothers, daughters, lineage members, household heads, or entrepreneurs. They also rest on processes of "othering" in which the liberated Western woman is constructed against universal images of the Third World woman (Mohanty 1988), creating "hierarchized binaries, where one is not only separate/different but also above/better than the other" (Arnfred 2004: 8). Oyeronke Oyěwùmi's work even shows that the category "woman," an essentialized grouping characterized by the social uniformity of its members, is often a Western construct projected on African societies rather than a meaningful organizing construct endogenous to African societies. Her work provides a powerful basis from which to question assumptions about women as universally subordinate.

What work do these ontological underpinnings *do* in the world? For one, they obscure the fact that the hierarchies of insiders/outsiders to a given lineage and of seniority defined by age are often more important than hierarchies of gender (Oyěwùmi 2003; see also Bottazzi, Goguen, and Rist 2016), and consanguinity more important than conjugality (Arnfred 2011). The focus on nuclear households thereby obscures not just the rights held and governed by lineages, but lineage-based responsibilities and securities—making it easier to foreground women's oppression as wives and widows (identities linked to marriage), as opposed to sisters and daughters or other securities engendered through forms of relationality that lie outside of marriage. They also obscure other forms of conjugality and relationality, from polygamy to same-sex marriage, extra-marital relationships and motherhood beyond marriage, and women's agency therein (Arnfred 2004; Kendall 1999). The construction of African societies as primitive, backward, and unchanging, and of African women as victims, have for too long legitimized Western efforts to come to the rescue (Arnfred 2004; Kolawole 2004). And with Western marriage constructs projected onto African societies, independent title or co-titling become naturalized as the instruments of choice for enhancing women's tenure security. Clearly, there is need to reconsider conceptions of custom, the state, the law, and gender that underlie the narrow suite of land programming interventions currently on offer—to reconsider whose interests are served by the current land governance orthodoxy.

The theories of change profiled herein appear to be as much a reflection of the interests and ideologies of outside actors as they are an account of local land relations and the concerns of rural women (or of migrants, pastoralists, marginalized ethnic groups, and lower-class men). If land governance interventions are to empower women and other marginalized groups and avoid dispossessing them of the rights they already enjoy, it will be important to look beyond simplified theories of change and standardized solutions and the ontological assumptions on which they rest. If intervention is the answer, more nuanced approaches attuned to the context-specific threats, concerns, and aspirations of differently-positioned women (poor, pastoralist, migrant, married, divorced, and widowed) and other marginalized peoples are needed. Yet the benefits of even the most nuanced and contextualized land governance programming must also be balanced against the risks involved, and the need to maintain whatever social safety nets currently exist for the most vulnerable (men, women, and children) under customary land relations (Bromley 2008). Here, the option of inaction may prove to do as much for women's land rights as the urgent interventionism that currently frames and curtails the field of vision and action in the land arena.

ACKNOWLEDGMENTS

An earlier version of this chapter was developed in 2018 under a consultancy agreement with Chemonics, who sponsored five days of my time to sketch out the theory of change on women's property rights; review the published evidence; and draft a final report.

REFERENCES

Abu-Lughod, L. 2002. Do Muslim women really need saving? Anthropological reflections on cultural relativism and its others. *American Anthropologist* 104(3): 783–790.

Ahmed, L. 1992. *Women and Gender in Islam*. New Haven: Yale University Press.

Ali, D.A., K. Deininger and M. Goldstein. 2014. Environmental and gender impacts of land tenure regularization in Africa: Pilot evidence from Rwanda. *Journal of Development Economics* 110: 262–275.

Ali, D.A., K. Deininger, G. Mahofa and R. Nyakulama. 2019. Sustaining land registration benefits by addressing the challenges of reversion to informality in Rwanda. *Land Use Policy*, 104317 [online].

Allott, A.N. 1969. Modern changes in African land tenure. In: E. Cotran and N.N. Rubin (Eds.), *Readings in African Law*, 236–242. London: Butterworths.

Anaafo, D. and B. Guba. 2017. Do land reforms have adverse impacts on the livelihoods of poor land users? Evidence from the Nkoranza South Municipality, Ghana. *Canadian Journal of African Studies* 51(2): 293–318.

Arnfred, S. 2004. Re-thinking sexualities in Africa: Introduction. In: S. Arnfred (Ed.), *Re-Thinking Sexualities in Africa*, 7–29. Stockholm: Almqvist & Wiksell.

Arnfred, S. 2011. *Sexuality and Gender Politics in Mozambique: Re-thinking Gender in Africa*. London: James Currey.

Arnold, C.A. 2002. The reconstitution of property: Property as a web of interests. *Harvard Environmental Law Review* 26: 281.

Attwood, D. 1990. Land registration in Africa: The impact on agricultural production. *World Development* 18(5): 659–671.

Awanyo, L. 2009. Exploring the connections: Land tenure, social identities, and agrobiodiversity practices in Ghana. *Geografiska Annaler* 91(2): 137–155.

Awusabo-Asare, K. 1990. Matriliny and the new intestate succession law of Ghana. *Canadian Journal of African Studies* 24: 1–16.

Bayisenge, J. 2015a. Women's experiences of land conflicts in the context of the Land Tenure Reform Program in Rwanda. *International Journal of Gender and Women's Studies* 3(1): 1–25.

Bayisenge, J. 2015b. Does the law work in their favor? The complexity of land rights of women living in polygamous relationships in Rwanda. *Journal of Culture and African Women Studies* 27.

Bayisenge, J. 2018. From male to joint land ownership: Women's experiences of the land tenure reform programme in Rwanda. *Journal of Agrarian Change* 18: 588–605.

Bayisenge, J., S. Höjera and M. Espling. 2015. Women's land rights in the context of the land tenure reform in Rwanda—the experiences of policy implementers. *Journal of Eastern African Studies* 9(1): 74–90.

Behnke, R.H. Jr, I. Scoones and C. Kerven, Eds. 1993. *Range Ecology at Disequilibrium: New Models of Natural Variability and Pastoral Adaptation in African Savannas.* London: Overseas Development Initiative.

Benjaminsen, T.A., S. Holden, C. Lund and E. Sjaastad. 2008. Formalisation of land rights: Some empirical evidence from Mali, Niger and South Africa. *Land Use Policy* 26(2008): 28–35.

Berry, S.S. 1975. *Cocoa, Custom and Socio-Economic Change in Rural Western Nigeria.* Oxford: Clarendon Press.

Besteman, C. 1994. Individualisation and the assault on customary tenure in Africa: Title registration programmes and the case of Somalia. *Africa* 64(4): 484–515.

Besteman, C. 1996. Local land use strategies and outsider politics: Title registration in the Middle Jubba Valley. In: C. Besteman and L.V. Cassanelli (Eds.), *The Struggle for Land in Southern Somalia: The War behind the War*, 29–46. Boulder, CO: Westview Press.

Besteman, C. 2014. *Unraveling Somalia: Race, Violence, and the Legacy of Slavery.* Philadelphia: University of Pennsylvania Press.

Bezabih, M., S. Holden and A. Mannberg. 2016 The role of land certification in reducing gaps in productivity between male- and female-owned farms in rural Ethiopia. *The Journal of Development Studies* 52(3): 360–376.

Bikaako, W. and J. Ssenkumba. 2003. Gender, land and rights: Contemporary contestations in law, policy and practice in Uganda. In: L. Muthoni Wanyeki (Ed.), *Women and Land in Africa: Culture, Religion and Realizing Women's Rights.* Zed Books. 232–277

Binswanger, H.P., K. Deininger and G. Feder. 1993. Power, distortions, revolt, and reform in agricultural land relations. *Policy Research Working Papers* 1164. Washington, DC: The World Bank.

Bloch, P.C. 1989. *The Dynamics of Land Tenure on the Bokel Small Irrigated Perimeters*. Madison, WI: Land Tenure Center, University of Wisconsin.

Boone, C. and L. Nyemi. 2015. Land institutions and political ethnicity in Africa: Evidence from Tanzania. *Comparative Politics* 48(1): 67–86.

Bottazzi, P., A. Goguen and S. Rist. 2016. Conflicts of customary land tenure in rural Africa: Is large-scale land acquisition a driver of "institutional innovation"? *Journal of Peasant Studies* 43(5): 971–988.

Braga, C. 2001. "They're squeezing us!" Matrilineal kinship, power and agricultural policies: Case study of Issa Malanga, Niassa Province. In: R. Waterhouse and C. Vijfhuizen (Eds.), *Strategic Women, Gainful Men: Gender, Land and Natural Resources in Different Rural Contexts in Mozambique*, 199–226. Maputo: UEM/Action Aid.

Bromley, D. W. 2008. Formalising property relations in the developing world: The wrong prescription for the wrong malady. *Land Use Policy* 26(2008): 20–27.

Brown, J. and J. Uvuza. 2006. *Women's Land Rights in Rwanda: How Can They Be Protected and Strengthened as The Land Law Is Implemented?* Seattle, WA: Rural Development Institute.

Bruce, J.W. 1988. A perspective on Indigenous land tenure systems and land concentration. In: R.E. Downs and S.P. Reyna (Eds.), *Land and Society in Contemporary Africa*, 23–52. Hanover, NH: University Press of New England.

Cadasta. 2019. *Covering New Terrain in the Fight for Land Rights: Cadasta 2019 Annual Report*. Available at: https://cadasta.org/wp-content/uploads/2020/05/Annual-Report_2019.5.13.Final_.pdf (accessed May 26, 2021).

Calderon, J. 2004 The formalization of property in Peru 2001–2: The Case of Lima. *Habitat International* 28(2): 289–300.

Carney, J. and M. Watts. 1991. Disciplining women? Rice, mechanization and the evolution of Mandinka gender relations in Senegambia. *Journal of Women in Culture and Society* 16(4): 651–681.

CFS and FAO. 2012. *Voluntary Guidelines on the Responsible Governance of Tenure of Land, Fisheries and Forests in the Context of National Food Security*. Rome: Committee on World Food Security and the Food and Agriculture Organization of the United Nations.

Chauveau, J.-P., P.M. Bosc and M. Pescay. 1998. Le plan foncier rural en Côte d'Ivoire. In: P. Lavigne Delville (Ed.), *Quelles Politiques Foncières en Afrique Rurale? Réconcilier Pratiques, Légitimité et Légalité*. Paris: Karthala and Ministère de la Coopération.553–582.

Chauveau, J.-P., J.-P. Colin, J.-P. Jacob, P. Lavigne Delville and P.-Y. Le Meur. 2006. *Changes in Land Access and Governance in West Africa: Markets, Social Mediations and Public Policies*. London: International Institute for Environment and Development.

Cheater, A. and R.B. Gaidzanwa. 1996. Citizenship in neo-patrilineal states: Gender and mobility in Southern Africa. *Journal of Southern African Studies* 22: 189–200.

Chimedza, R. 1988. Women's access to and control over land: The case of Zimbabwe. *Working Paper* AEE 10/88 (Department of Agricultural Economics and Extension, University of Zimbabwe).

Chimhowu, A. and P. Woodhouse. 2006. Customary vs private property rights? Dynamics and trajectories of vernacular land markets in Sub-Saharan Africa. *Journal of Agrarian Change* 6(3): 346–371.

Cohen, J.M. 1980. Land tenure and rural development in Africa. In: A.F. Bates and M.F. Lofchie (Eds.), *Agricultural Development in Africa*, 348–400. New York: Praeger.

Coldham, S.F.R. 1978. The effect of registration of title upon customary land rights in Kenya. *Journal of African Law* 22: 91–111.

Colin, J.-P. 2005. Le développement d'un marché foncier? Une perspective Ivoirienne. *Afrique Contemporaine* 213: 179–196.

Colin, J.-P. and P. Woodhouse 2010. Interpreting land markets in Africa. *Africa* 80(1): 1–13.

Cousins, B. 2005. Tenure reform in South Africa: Titling versus social embeddedness. *Forum for Development Studies* 32(2): 415–442.

Cronkleton, P. 2015. Formalization and collective appropriation of space on forest frontiers: Comparing communal and individual property systems in the Peruvian and Ecuadoran Amazon. *Society & Natural Resources* 28(5): 496–512.

Crummey, D. 1981. Women and landed property in Gondarine Ethiopia. *International Journal of African Historical Studies* 14: 444–465.

Davison, J. 1988. *Agriculture, Women, and Land: The African Experience*. Boulder: Westview Press.

Deininger, K. 2003. *Land Policies for Growth and Poverty Reduction*. Washington, DC: The World Bank.

Deininger, K., D.A. Ali, S. Holden, and J. Zevenbergen. 2008a. Rural land certification in Ethiopia: Process, initial impact, and implications. *World Development* 36(10): 1786–1812.

Deininger, K., D.A. Ali, and T. Yamano. 2008b. Legal knowledge and economic development: The case of land rights in Uganda. *Land Economics* 84(4): 593–619.

Deininger, K. and H. Binswanger. 1999. The evolution of the world bank's land policy: Principles, experience, and future challenges. *The World Bank Research Observer* 14 (2): 247–276.

Doss, C., R. Meinzen-Dick and A. Bomuhangi. 2014. Who owns the land? Perspectives from rural Ugandans and implications for large-scale land acquisitions. *Feminist Economics* 20(1): 76–100.

Downs, R.E. and S.P. Reyna, Eds. 1988. *Land and Society in Contemporary Africa*. Hanover, NH: University Press of New England.

Durand-Lasserve, A. 2006. Market-driven evictions and displacements: Implications for the perpetuation of informal settlements in developing cities. In: M. Huchzermeyer and A. Karam (Eds.), *Informal Settlements: A Perpetual Challenge?*, 202–227. Cape Town: University of Cape Town Press.

Ewelukwa, U.U. 2002. Post-colonialism, gender, customary injustice: Widows in African societies. *Human Rights Quarterly* 24(2): 424–486.

FAO. 2016. *Measuring SDG Indicator 5.a.1: Background Paper*. Rome: Food and Agriculture Organization of the United Nations.

FAO, The World Bank, and UN-Habitat. 2019. *Measuring Individuals' Rights to Land: An Integrated Approach to Data Collection for SDG Indicators 1.4.2 and 5.a.1*. Washington, DC: The World Bank.

Feder, G. and R. Noronha. 1987. Land rights systems and agricultural development in Sub-Saharan Africa. *World Bank Research Observer* 2: 143–169.

Freudenberger, M. S. 1994. Tenure and natural resources in The Gambia: Summary of research findings and policy options. LTC Manuscript. Madison, WI: Land Tenure Center, University of Wisconsin.

Galaty, J.G. 1992. "The land is yours": Social and economic factors in the privatization, sub-division and sale of Maasai ranches. *Nomadic Peoples* 30(1992): 26–40.

Galaty, J.G. 1994. Ha(l)ving land in common: The subdivision of Maasai group ranches in Kenya. *Commission on Nomadic Peoples* 34/35(1994): 109–122.

Galaty, J.G. 1999. Grounding pastoralists: law, politics, and dispossession in East Africa. *Nomadic Peoples* 3(2): 56–73.

Geschiere, P. and F. Nyamnjoh. 1998. Witchcraft as an issue in the "politics of belonging": Democratization and urban migrants' involvement with the home village. *African Studies Review* 41(3): 69–91.

Gillingham, P. and F. Buckle. 2014. *Rwanda Land Tenure Regularisation Case Study*. Surrey: HTSPE and DFID.

Goebel, A. 1999. 'Here it is our land, the two of us': Women, men and land in a Zimbabwean resettlement area. *Journal of Contemporary African Studies* 17: 75–96.

Goebel, A. 2002. Men these days they are a problem: Husband taming herbs and gender wars in rural Zimbabwe. *Canadian Journal of African Studies* 36: 460–489.

Goebel, A. 2005. Zimbabwe's "Fast Track" Land Reform: What about women? *Gender, Place & Culture* 12(2): 145–172.

Goldstein, M., K. Houngbedji, F. Kondylis, M. O'Sullivan and H. Selod. 2015. Formalizing rural land rights in West Africa: Early evidence from a randomized impact evaluation in Benin. *Policy Research Working Paper* No. WPS 7435. Washington, DC: World Bank Group.

Grassi, M. and J. Vivet. 2014. Fathering and conjugality in transnational patchwork families: The Angola/Portugal case. *TL Network e-Working Papers* No. 5. Lisbon: Transnational Lives Network.

Gyasi, E.A. 1994. The adaptability of African communal land tenure to economic opportunity: The example of land acquisition for oil palm farming in Ghana. *Africa* 64(3): 391–405.

Hakansson, N.T. 1994. The detachability of women: Gender and kinship in processes of socioeconomic change among the Gusii of Kenya. *American Ethnologist* 21(3): 516–538.

Haldar, A. and J.E. Stiglitz. 2013. Analyzing legal formality and informality: Lessons from land titling and microfinance programs. In: D. Kennedy and J.E. Stiglitz (Eds.), *Law and Economics with Chinese Characteristics: Institutions for Promoting Development in the Twenty-First Century*, 112–147. Oxford, UK: Oxford University Press.

Hansen, J.D. and M.K. Luckert. 2005. Tree planting under customary tenure systems in Malawi: Impacts of marriage and inheritance patterns. *Agricultural Systems* 84: 99–118.

Haugerud, A. 1989. Land tenure and agrarian change in Kenya. *Africa* 59(1): 61–90.

Hill, P. 1963. *The Migrant Cocoa Farmers of Southern Ghana: A Study in Rural Capitalism*. Cambridge: Cambridge University Press.

Hoben, A. 1975. *Land Tenure Among the Amhara of Ethiopia*. Chicago: University of Chicago Press.

Holden, S., R. Kaarhus and R. Lunduka. 2006. Land policy reform: The role of land markets and women's land rights in Malawi. *Noragric Report* No. 36. Norwegian University of Life Sciences.

Holden, S.T., K. Deininger and H. Ghebru. 2011. Tenure insecurity, gender, low-cost land certification and land rental market participation in Ethiopia. *The Journal of Development Studies* 47(1): 31–47.

Horowitz, M.M. 1986. Ideology, policy, and praxis in pastoral livestock development. In: M.M. Horowitz and T. Painter (Eds.), *The Anthropology of Rural Development in West Africa*, 251–272. Boulder, CO: Westview Press.

Human Rights Watch. 2003. Double standards: Women's property violations in Kenya. Available at: http://www.hrw.org/en/news/2003/04/29/womens-property-rights-violations-kenya.

Izumi, K. 1999. Liberalisation, gender, and the land question in sub-Saharan Africa. *Gender and Development* 7(3): 9–18.

Jackson, C. 2007. Marriage and creative conjugality. *Development and Change* 38(1): 107–129.

Jacobs, K. and A. Kes. 2015. The ambiguity of joint asset ownership: Cautionary tales from Uganda and South Africa. *Feminist Economics* 23–55.

Jacobs, S. 1984. Women and land resettlement in Zimbabwe. *Review of African Political Economy* 10(27–28): 33–50.

Joireman, S.F. 2007. The mystery of capital formation in Sub-Saharan Africa: Women, property rights and customary law. *World Development* 36: 1233–1241.

Kaarhus, R. 2010. Women's land rights and land tenure reforms in Malawi: What difference does matriliny make? *Forum for Development Studies* 37(2): 171–192.

Kaarhus, R. and S. Dondenye. 2015. Formalising land rights based on customary tenure: Community delimitation and women's access to land in central Mozambique. *Journal of Modern African Studies* 53(2): 193–216.

Kapur, A. 2010. Two faces of change: The need for a bi-directional approach to improve women's land rights in plural legal systems. *IDLO Customary Justice Working Paper Series* 2.

Kapur, A. 2011. Catch-22: The role of development institutions in promoting gender equality in land law—Lessons learned in post-conflict pluralist Africa. *Buffalo Human Rights Law Review* 17(11): 75–116.

Kendall, K. 1999. Women in Lesotho and the (Western) construction of homophobia. In E. Blackwood and S. Wieringa (Eds.), *Female Desires: Transgender Practices across Cultures*, 157–181. New York: Columbia University Press.

Kolawole, M.E.M. 1997. *Womanism and African Consciousness*. Trenton, NJ: Africa World Press.

Kolawole, M. 2004. Conceptualizing African gender theory: Feminism, womanism and the *arere* metaphor. In: S. Arnfred (Ed.), *Re-Thinking Sexualities in Africa*, 251–266. Stockholm: Almqvist & Wiksell.

Koné M., J. Ibo and N. Kouamé. 2005. *Marchés Fonciers et Intra-Familial / Intergénérational: Quelques de Données Empiriques pour une Approche des Processus*. Abidjan, Nigeria: CLAIMS.

Lastarria-Cornhiel, S. 1997 Impact of privatization on gender and property rights in Africa. *World Development* 25: 1317–1322.

Lavigne Delville, P., Ed. 1998. *Quelles Politiques Foncières pour l'Afrique Rurale? Réconcilier Pratiques, Légitimité et Légalité*. Paris: Karthala and Coopération Française.

Lavigne Delville, P. and A.-C. Moalic 2019. Territorialities, spatial inequalities and the formalization of land rights in Central Benin. *Africa* 89(2): 329–352.

Lawry, S.W. 1993. Transactions in cropland held under customary tenure in Lesotho. In: T.J. Bassett and D.E. Crummey (Eds.), *Land in African Agrarian Systems*, 57–74. Madison: University of Wisconsin Press.

Lentz, C. 2006. Indigenous theories of landownership. In: Kuba R and Lentz C (Eds.), *Land and the Politics of Belonging in West Africa*, 35–56. Leiden, Netherlands: Brill.

Linares, O.F. 1992. *Power, Prayer and Production*. Cambridge, UK: Cambridge University Press.

Lovo, S. 2016. Tenure insecurity and investment in soil conservation. Evidence from Malawi. *World Development* 78: 219–229.

Mackenzie, F. 1995. "A farm is like a child who cannot be left unguarded": Gender, land, and labour in Central Province, Kenya. *IDS Bulletin* 26: 17–23.

Mandala, E. 1990. *Work and Control in a Peasant Economy: A History of the Lower Tchiri Valley in Malawi, 1959–1960*. Madison, WI: University of Wisconsin Press.

Marais, L., J. Ntema, J. Cloete and A. Venter. 2014. From informality to formality to informality: Extralegal land transfers in an upgraded informal settlement of South Africa. *Urbani Izziv* 25: S148–S161.

McFadden, P. 2002. Post-coloniality in the Zimbabwean context: Implications for development studies. Public lecture, Seminar for National and International Development, Queen's University, Kingston, Ontario, Canada, 24 October, 2002.

Meinzen-Dick, R. and E. Mwangi. 2008. Cutting the web of interests: Pitfalls of formalizing property rights. *Land Use Policy* 26(1): 36–43.

Meinzen-Dick, R., A. Quisumbing, C. Doss and S. Theis. 2019. Women's land rights as a pathway to poverty reduction: Framework and review of available evidence. *Agricultural Systems* 172 (June 2019): 72–82.

Mendola, M. and F. Simtowe. 2015. The welfare impact of land redistribution: Evidence from a quasi-experimental initiative in Malawi. *World Development* 72: 53–69.

Mitchell, T. 2007. The Properties of Markets. In: D. MacKenzie, F. Muniesa and L. Siu (Eds.), *Do Economists Make Markets? On the Performativity of Economics*. Cambridge, UK: Cambridge University Press.

Mnisi, S. and A. Claassens. 2009. Rural women redefining land rights in the context of living customary law. *South African Journal on Human Rights* 25(3): 491–516.

Mohanty, C. 1988. Under Western eyes: Feminist scholarship and colonial discourses. *Feminist Review* 30(1): 61–88.

Mwangi, E. 2007. The puzzle of group ranch subdivision in Kenya's Maasailand. *Development and Change* 38(5): 889–910.

Newbury, C. and H. Baldwin. 2000. Aftermath: Women in Postgenocide Rwanda. Washington, DC: *CDIE/USAID Working Paper* 303.

Ng'ong'ola, C. 1986. Rural development and the reorganization of customary land in Malawi: Some lessons from the Lilongwe Land Development Programme. *University of Malawi Journal of Social Science* 13: 39–56.

Nhlapo, T. 1987. Law versus culture: Ownership of freehold land in Swaziland. In: A. Armstrong (Ed.), *Women and Law in Southern Africa*. Harare, Zimbabwe: Zimbabwe Publishing House.

Nukunya, G.K. 1972. *Land Tenure and Inheritance in Angola*. Legon, Ghana: Institute of Statistical, social and Economic Research, University of Ghana.

Okali, C. 1983. *Cocoa and Kinship in Ghana: The Matrilineal Akan of Ghana*. London: Kegan Paul International

Okech, A. 2019. *Widow Inheritance and Contested Citizenship in Kenya*. London: Routledge.

Okoth-Ogendo, H.W.O. 1976. African land tenure reform. In: J. Heyer, J.K. Maitha and W.M. Senga (Eds.), *Agricultural Development in Kenya*, 152–185. Nairobi: Oxford University Press.

Pala Okeyo, A. 1980. The Joluo Equation: Land reform = lower status for women. *Ceres* May–June: 37–42.

Parkin, D. 1980. Kind bridewealth and hard cash. In: J. Comaroff (Ed.), *The Meaning of Marriage Payments*, 197–220. New York: Academic Press.

Pawson, R. and N. Tilley. 2004. Realist evaluation. Available at: http://www.community-matters.com.au/RE_chapter.pdf (May 8, 2019).

Payne, G. 1997. *Urban Land Tenure and Property Rights in Developing Countries: A Review*. London: IT Publications/ODA.

Payne, G., A. Durand-Lasserve and C. Rakodi. 2009. The limits of land titling and home ownership. *Environment and Urbanization* 21(2): 443–462.

Persha, L., A. Greif and H. Huntington. 2017. Assessing the impact of second-level land certification in Ethiopia. Paper presented at the "World Bank Conference on Land and Poverty," March 20–24, 2017, Washington, DC.

Peters, P.E. 1994. *Dividing the Commons: Politics, Policy, and Culture in Botswana*. Charlottesville, VA: University of Virginia Press.

Peters, P.E. 2004. Inequality and social conflict over land in Africa. *Journal of Agrarian Change* 4(3): 269–314.

Peters, P.E. 2010. "Our daughters inherit our land, but our sons use their wives' fields": Matrilineal-matrilocal land tenure and the New Land Policy in Malawi. *Journal of Eastern African Studies* 4(1): 179–199.

Peters, P. 2018. Revisiting the social bedrock of kinship and descent in Africa. In: R. R. Grinker, S. C. Lubkemann, C. B. Steiner and E. Gonçalves (Eds.), *A Companion to the Anthropology of Africa*, 33–62. Oxford: John Wiley & Sons.

Pircher, T., C. Almekinders and B. Kamanga. 2013. Participatory trials and farmers' social realities: Understanding the adoption of legume technologies in a Malawian farmer community. *International Journal of Agricultural Sustainability* 11(3): 252–263.

Place, F. and S. Migot-Adholla. 1998. The economic effects of land registration on smallholder farms in Kenya: Evidence from Nyeri and Kakamega districts. *Land Economics* 74: 360–373.

Pottier, J. 2002. *Re-Imagining Rwanda: Conflict, Survival and Disinformation in the late 20th Century*. Cambridge: Cambridge University Press.

Pottier, J. 2006. Land reform for peace? Rwanda's 2005 land law in context. *Journal of Agrarian Change* 6(4): 509–537.

Putzel, L., A.B. Kelly, P.O. Cerutti and Y. Artati. 2015. Formalization as development in land and natural resource policy. *Society & Natural Resources* 28(5): 453–472.

Quisumbing, A.R. and N. Kumar. 2014. Land rights knowledge and conservation in rural Ethiopia: Mind the gender gap. *IFPRI Discussion Paper*. Washington, DC: International Food Policy Research Institute.

Quisumbing, A.R., E. Payongayong, J. B. Aidoo and K. Otsuka. 2001. Women's land rights in the transition to individualized ownership: Implications for tree-resource management in western Ghana. *Economic Development and Cultural Change* 50(1): 157–181.

Raftopolous, B. 2002. "The crisis in Zimbabwe". Keynote address, Canadian Association of African Studies Annual Conference, University of Toronto, Toronto, Canada, 29 May 2002.

Roden, D. 1971. Changing patterns of land tenure among the Nuba of central Sudan. *Journal of Administration Overseas* 10(4): 294–309.

Rose, L. 2004. Women's land access in post-conflict Rwanda: Bridging the gap between customary land law and pending land legislation. *Texas Journal of Women and Law* 13(2): 197–250.

Sacks, K. 1982. *Sisters and Wives: The Past and Future of Sexual Equality*. Champaign, IL: University of Illinois Press.

Schapera, I. 1970. *Tribal Innovators: Tswana Chiefs and Social Change 1795–1940*. London: Althone Press.

Schlager, E. and E. Ostrom 1992. Common property and natural resources: A conceptual analysis. *Land Economics* 68(3): 249–262.

Schmidt, E. 1990. Negotiated spaces and contested terrain: Men, women, and the law in colonial Zimbabwe, 1890–1939. *Journal of Southern African Studies* 16(4): 622–648.

Sebina-Zziwa, A. 1995. Impact of colonial land registration to women's land rights in Uganda. Kampala, Uganda: Makerere Institute for Social Research Manuscript, Makakere University.

Shipton, P. 1994. Land and culture in tropical Africa: Soils, symbols, and the metaphysics of the mundane. *Annual Review of Anthropology* 23: 347–377.

Shipton, P. 1988. The Kenyan land tenure reform: Misunderstandings in the public creation of private property. In: R.E. Downs and S.P. Reyna (Eds.), *Land and Society in Contemporary Africa*, 91–135. Hanover, NH: University Press of New England.

Shipton, P. and M. Goheen. 1992. Understanding African land-holding: Power, wealth, and meaning. *Africa* 62(3): 307–325.

Sims, D. 2002. What is secure tenure in Egypt? In: G Payne (Ed.), *Land, Rights and Innovation: Improving Tenure Security for the Urban Poor*. London: ITDG Publishing.

Southall, A.W. 1960. On chastity in Africa. *Uganda Journal* 24: 207–216.

Spivak, G.C. 1988. Can the subaltern speak? In: C. Nelson and L. Grossberg (Eds.), *Marxism and the Interpretation of Culture*, 271–313. Basingstoke: Macmillan Education.

Swaminathan, H., K. Ashburn, A. Kes and N. Duvvury. 2007. *Women's Property Rights, HIV and AIDS, and Domestic Violence*. Washington DC: ICRW.

Tonah, S. 2006. Migration and farmer-herder conflicts in Ghana's Volta Basin. *Canadian Journal of African Studies* 40(1): 152–178.

Tuboku-Metzger, F.C. and H.L. Van der Laan. 1981. A survey of leases granted under the protectorate land ordinance of 1927. *Research Reports* no. 12/1981. Leiden, Netherlands: African Studies Centre.

Ubink, J.M. and K. Amanor. 2015. *Contesting Land and Custom in Ghana: State, Chief and Citizen*. Leiden, Netherlands: Leiden University Press.

USAID. 2013. Land tenure, property rights, and gender: Challenges and approaches for strengthening women's land tenure and property rights. *USAID Issue Brief*.

USAID. 2018a. Integrated Land and Resource Governance Task Order, Solicitation No. SOL-OAA-17-00012. Washington, DC: USAID.

USAID. 2018b. USAID/Ethiopia Request for Task Order Proposal Number SOL-72066318R00024. Washington, DC: USAID.

Vaessen, J. 2016. Using "Theories of Change" in international development: Symptoms of sub-optimal use of program theory in the design and evaluation of policy interventions in international development. Available at: https://ieg.worldbankgroup.org/blog/using-theories-change-international-development (May 8, 2019).

Vanhees, K. 2014. Property rights for women in Rwanda: Access to land for women living in de facto unions. Masters' Thesis, Ghent University.

Wachter, D. and J. English. 1992 The World Bank's Experience with Rural Land Titling. *Divisional Working Paper* No. 1992–35. Washington, DC: The World Bank.

Walker, C. 2002. *Land Reform in Southern and Eastern Africa: Key Issues for Strengthening Women's Access to and Rights in Land*. Harare, Zimbabwe: FAO Sub-regional Office for Southern and Eastern Africa.

Waterhouse, R. 2001 Women's land rights in post-war Mozambique. In: A. Buregeya et al. (Eds.), *Women's Land and Property Rights in Situations of Conflict and Reconstruction*, 45–53. New York: United Nations Development Fund for Women. 45–53.

Weiss, C.H. 1972. *Evaluation Research: Methods of Assessing Program Effectiveness*. Englewood Cliffs, NJ: Prentice-Hall.

Weiss, C.H. 1995. Nothing as practical as good theory: Exploring theory-based evaluation for comprehensive community initiatives for children and families. In: J. Connell, A. Kubisch, L. B. Schorr, & C. H. Weiss (Eds.), *New Approaches to Evaluating Community Initiatives*, 65–92. New York: Aspen Institute.

White, C.M.N. 1963. Factors determining the content of African land-tenure systems in Northern Rhodesia. In: D. Biebuyck (Ed.), *African Agrarian Systems*, 364–373. London: Oxford University Press.

World Bank, FAO and IFAD. 2008. *Gender in Agriculture Sourcebook*. Washington, DC and Rome: World Bank, Food and Agriculture Organization (FAO) of the United Nations, and International Fund for Agricultural Development (IFAD).

CHAPTER 4

Collective Titling and Community Consultation

In presenting the main thesis of this book at the XVII biennial conference of the International Association for the Study of the Commons in Lima in July, 2019, a member of the audience asked rhetorically—as they believed the answer to be unambiguously clear, "If individual title yields questionable benefits, then surely collective title would address the problem?" Surely the massive enrollment of non-governmental organizations, the environmental community and civil society around collective titling—and the apparent buy-in of most of the scholars and students of customary rights present in that session—means something, and no doubt it does. But does it mean as much as we think it does? And is the work it does in the world exclusively part of a political project that we all wish to stand behind?

Since at least the 1980s, the environmental movement has called for greater recognition of Indigenous rights to land and forest resources (Arnt and Schwartzman 1992), with ideas of Indigenous peoples' symbiotic relationship to nature becoming key symbolic resources in the global environmental movement (Conklin and Graham 1995). Adoption of the Indigenous and Tribal Peoples Convention, 1989 by the International Labor Organization (ILO Convention 169) was a significant milestone in this struggle, recognizing the rights of ownership and possession over the lands traditionally occupied by Indigenous peoples and calling on governments to identify such lands and guarantee the effective protection of these rights (ILO 1989, Art. 14). The UN Declaration on the Rights of Indigenous Peoples of 2007 (UNDRIP) reaffirmed these rights while expanding upon them, recognizing rights to "lands, territories and resources which [Indigenous Peoples] have traditionally owned, occupied or otherwise used or acquired" and affirming rights to self-determination (UN 2007, Art. 3, 26). And in November, 2018, the UN General Assembly made a significant step in extending such rights to non-Indigenous communities by adopting the UN Declaration on the Rights of Peasants and Other People Working in Rural Areas.[1] These commitments have been amplified under global efforts to mitigate climate change, with stronger land and resource rights of Indigenous peoples and local communities whose well-being is tied to the forests advanced by the World Resources Institute as, "the best way to safeguard forests and mitigate climate change" (Stevens et al. 2014). And many socially progressive NGOs are also fully on board, equating collective rights with human rights; viewing collective rights as essential to the continuation of Indigenous peoples; and supporting efforts to secure land and territorial rights, often through mapping, demarcation and titling.[2]

Alongside this recognition of collective rights is the advancement of mechanisms to facilitate interactions with the state, whether it be forms of group registration as legal persons for purposes of registering land ownership; mechanisms for community consultation and consent in the context of laws, policies or projects affecting their lands; or means for Indigenous peoples to represent their own collectivities and interests vis-à-vis outsiders (Alden Wily 2018; Colchester 2004; FAO 2014). As noted by Marcus Colchester and Fergus MacKay, "recognition of collective rights, notably rights to common properties or territories, brings indigenous peoples' customary institutions into direct relations with outside interests" (Colchester and MacKay 2004: 1). Indigenous people are not only asking that their land and territorial rights be respected and defended, but that they be able to participate in lawmaking and to shape and derive fair benefits from projects affecting their territories (UNPFII 2018). This requires what has been called a "Middle Ground"[3] consisting of mutually agreed processes and points of contact to allow the parties to interact, backed by mutual recognition of one another's existence and rights (Colchester and MacKay 2004: 8). International human and Indigenous rights law widely recognizes the need for decisions affecting local rights, interests, land and resources to be conditional on processes of consultation and/or consent, and Free, Prior, and Informed Consent (FPIC) has emerged as the global gold standard for how this might be done (FAO 2014).

So, to what extent are these commitments being translated into law at the national level, and with what effect? In a 2018 review of collective land ownership in the twenty-first century, legal scholar Liz Alden Wily finds statutory recognition of rural communities as collective owners of their land to be substantial and a growing and increasingly accepted element of property relations (Alden Wily 2018). Alden Wily contrasts this with the trend over the preceding 2,000 years in Europe and its colonies, in which landed property only existed with the authorization and protection of the state; was by definition individual and private (and mostly male); and—with the thanks of Locke's labor theory of property— only recognized if "developed" (cultivated). Yet today, 73% of countries in her sample (n = 100) provide for collective tenure. She identifies a number of trends which provide a hopeful picture of the legal recognition of collective tenures—including the recognition that community property exists whether or not registered; provisions for its registration; and the recognition that this registration "formalizes rather than creates property" (Alden Wily 2018: 1). Do these trends represent a marked shift away from the "dominant strategy in the 20th century of extinguishing community-based and customary tenure in the name of progress" (Alden Wily 2018: 2), as Alden Wily suggests? Or might it be playing a part in the ongoing trend in the commodification of land and its transfer away from the customary domain?

This chapter explores these questions first through a look at idealized notions of what collective tenures and FPIC are designed to achieve among its advocates, and secondly through a look at how these commitments are operationalized in the context of growing pressure on customary land for agriculture and other extractive activities in two countries determined by Alden Wily to be among those in which collective land rights are strongest: Mozambique and Peru. The analysis demands close scrutiny of whether, and under what conditions, collective titling has become an instrument for securing customary land and resources *for customary users* or instead enabled its alienation.

THEORIZED BENEFITS OF COLLECTIVE TITLING AND COMMUNITY CONSULTATION/CONSENT

> Deficient processes for local consultation and unclear boundary descriptions create several problems: they reduce tenure security and investment incentives, increase the likelihood of conflict, and make it difficult for the public sector to collect land taxes and monitor whether investors comply with agreements they had entered into with local people.
>
> —Deininger et al. (2011: xxxii)

Communal Tenures and Collective Titling

There are at least three primary bodies of thought concerning the benefits of communal tenures and their formalization through collective title. The first view emanates from international law, and emphasizes Indigenous rights, identity and self-determination. These views are perhaps best exemplified by the deliberations of the UN Permanent Forum on Indigenous Issues, which in its 2018 meeting notes the inseparability of territory from Indigenous identity and cultural survival:

> Since the establishment, in 2000, of the Permanent Forum on Indigenous Issues by the Economic and Social Council, at each of its sessions indigenous peoples have emphasized the spiritual, social, cultural, economic and political significance of lands, territories and resources to their identity, well-being and survival. (UNPFII 2018: 4)

The report also notes,

> In the historic study of the problem of discrimination against indigenous populations prepared by the Special Rapporteur of the Subcommission on Prevention of Discrimination and Protection of Minorities, José R. Martínez Cobo, he noted that it was essential to know and understand the deeply spiritual, special relationship between indigenous peoples and their land as basic to their existence as such and to all their beliefs, customs, traditions and cultures. For such peoples, the land was not merely a possession and a means of production. *Their land was not a commodity which could be acquired, but a material element to be enjoyed freely.* (UNPFII 2018: 2, emphasis added)

Among the core principles emphasized by the Permanent Forum and supported by international law are the entitlement of Indigenous peoples to participate in drafting policies and laws related to resource management and development; to have a central role in decision-making and implementation of land- and resource-related projects; and to play a central role in dispute resolution involving their lands, territories and resources. They also include states' obligations to protect and enforce Indigenous peoples' rights to lands, territories and resources; and to identify these lands and provide specific legal protections for Indigenous rights of ownership over them. Article 14 of the Indigenous and Tribal Peoples Convention (1989) affirms such rights, while specifying that this includes not only lands traditionally occupied, but "lands not exclusively occupied by them, but to which they have traditionally had access for their subsistence and traditional activities. Particular attention shall be paid to the situation of nomadic peoples and shifting cultivators in this respect."

A second body of thought concerning communal tenures emanates from multilateral agencies, and places emphasis on the responsible governance of tenure in the context of growing pressures on land. Key proponents include the FAO and World Bank, who have been leading the effort to develop global standards for the responsible governance of tenure. The World Bank places emphasis on "clearly defined rights to land and associated natural resources," which is said to yield a host of benefits. The first is the increased social legitimacy and legal security of outside investment through the clarification of overlapping rights and claims. The second purported benefit is the clarity it provides in determining who to negotiate with, which is thought to limit fraudulent transactions:

> Recording rights provides outside investors with "somebody to talk to," a legitimate and authorized partner to negotiate on the nature of investments and on compensation. A formal record is also very much in investors' interest as it reduces the scope for fraudulent transactions and the need for costly inquiry to prevent the surfacing of possible undisclosed prior claims and overriding interests (such as land use restrictions). (Deininger et al. 2011: 98)

Finally, by clearly demarcating areas for cultivation and environmental protection, clearly defined rights are claimed to further facilitate strategies to prevent encroachment on protected areas. Formal registration of collective rights is also said to be necessary to enable "a gradual and organic evolution from communal to more individual rights," to reduce vulnerability to displacement emanating from the ambiguous legal status of local inhabitants, and to establish an "accountable and representative structure" for local land administration (Deininger et al. 2011: 99, 101).

FAO's position on communal tenures is perhaps best reflected in the Voluntary Guidelines on the Responsible Governance of Tenure (VGGTs), a document vetted by member nations (CFS and FAO 2012). For Indigenous peoples and others with customary tenure systems, the VGGTs endorse state recognition and protection of their "legitimate tenure rights," and the adaptation of national policy and legal and organizational frameworks to recognize these tenure systems. Among the responsibilities designated for states are the protection of Indigenous peoples and other communities with customary tenure systems against unauthorized use of their lands, and ensuring their full and effective participation in the development of laws and policies related to their tenure systems. In FAO's official statement to the UN Permanent Forum on Indigenous Issues in 2018, the lack of recognition of collective rights to land and the lack of Free, Prior, and Informed Consent was said to "push indigenous peoples into conditions of vulnerability," and respect for land rights were said to preserve biodiversity and enable Indigenous food systems to prosper.[4] Yet their views largely align with those of the World Bank in supporting investment and land transactions:

> The aim is not to discourage investment and prevent the development of new farmlands, but rather to ensure that such expansion occurs in ways that respect rights, secure favourable and sustainable livelihoods, and divert pressure away from areas that are crucial to local livelihoods and have high conservation value. (FAO 2014: iv)

The third body of thought is embedded in the international environmental movement, where a rethink of the exclusive focus on fortress conservation models is underway (Robinson et al. 2017) and support for communal tenures has also grown for the environmental services and values they provide (Colchester 2001).[5] Formalization of collective land and forest rights and government protection of these rights are said to reduce deforestation, lower carbon dioxide emissions, and maintain or increase forest carbon storage (Börner et al. 2020; Ding et al. 2016; Stevens et al. 2014). Lack of legal recognition of these rights is said to leave forests vulnerable to clearance for commercial logging, pasture, cropland, oil palm, or mining. In their 2021 report entitled, "Forest Governance by Indigenous and Tribal Peoples: An Opportunity for Climate Action in Latin America and the Caribbean" (FAO and FILAC 2021), FAO has now joined the chorus of actors calling for recognition that Indigenous and tribal peoples are part of the solution to deforestation rather than the cause, and for the recognition of collective rights as a solution to climate change by impeding encroachment by outsiders.

In these distinct views on collective tenures, it is possible to detect differences in the envisioned purpose of recognizing and formalizing collective rights—and on the crucial question of alienability. According to Marcus Colchester, founding member of the Forest Peoples Programme and long-time Indigenous rights advocate,

> Rather than accepting the given norms of national land tenure systems, which tend to parcel up land as the private property of individual land owners, the more progressive land tenure regimes applied to indigenous peoples recognize indigenous land ownership through *collective titles, which are inalienable*[6] (not transferable to third parties) and are vested in representative institutions of the people themselves. (Colchester and MacKay 2004: 8, emphasis added)

Such a view seems consistent with the views of conservation actors, who support Indigenous land tenures for the protective role this provides against environmentally harmful investment. Yet it stands in contrast with the views of the World Bank, which supports the titling of collectively held lands in part to enable their alienation. As framed by Deininger,

> Failure to map and record land rights, even if only at the community level, makes it difficult to identify boundaries and legitimate owners as a basis for engaging in mutually agreed land transfers. (Deininger et al 2011: 98)

This is a far cry from the so-called organic evolution from collective to individual rights advocated for by the World Bank. The international Indigenous rights community appears to occupy a middle ground, reaffirming the rights to self-determination and "the right to own, use, develop and control the lands, territories and resources" that Indigenous Peoples possess, and thus the freedom to conserve their forests or engage in partnerships for resource exploration with prospective investors. FPIC is seen as a crucial tool for enabling such engagements on terms that are respectful of local aspirations and compatible with the principle of self-determination (UN 2007; UNPFII 2018).

Community Consultation and Free, Prior, and Informed Consent

Free, Prior, and Informed Consent and weaker variants of it (e.g., community consultation) are procedural norms governing relationships between Indigenous peoples and other customary land users and outside actors (the state, corporations). In the context of land governance, it may come into play in a host of contexts: treaties and agreements between states and Indigenous peoples; development projects and finance; formulating policies and legislation shaping customary lands and resources; negotiating terms of access or collaboration between customary land users and corporations wishing to exploit, develop, or use customary land and resources; negotiating benefit sharing arrangements surrounding access to biological and genetic resources; negotiating terms under which protected areas will be established and managed; and, for some, specifying the terms of land alienation out of the customary domain (FAO 2014; Franco 2014; UNPFII 2005).

FPIC is grounded in the right to self-determination, which acknowledges "the sovereign right of Indigenous peoples to decide their own visions for development and political association" (Petkar 2017: 17).[7] In the specific context of efforts by corporations to acquire Indigenous lands and territories, FAO defines it more precisely as "a collective right of indigenous peoples to make decisions through their own freely chosen representatives and customary or other institutions and to give or withhold their consent prior to the approval by government, industry or other outside party of any project that may affect the lands, territories and resources that they customarily own, occupy or otherwise use" (Petkar 2017: 17). With the concept grounded in international Indigenous rights norms (e.g., sovereign-to-sovereign relations), these definitions restrict rights of FPIC to Indigenous people. Yet this need not be so, given that many customary rights holders are not formally recognized or do not self-identify as Indigenous yet have longstanding ties to place and are affected in similar ways by outside investments, land acquisitions, and conservation-driven land use restrictions. For example, the Principles for Responsible Agricultural Investment, or PRAI, an early milestone in the effort to codify community consultations as a principle of good land governance in the context of large-scale land acquisitions, advanced a vision to extend the right to be consulted beyond Indigenous peoples to "all of those materially affected" by investment projects. Yet the FPIC norm is weakened from consent to "meaningful consultation and representation" (FAO et al. 2010: 11), and the vision advanced falls far short of FPIC.

To understand this crucial distinction, FPIC needs to be understood in terms of its constituent elements and how these differentiate it from weaker procedural norms (e.g., prior consultation, community consultation, informed participation). A 2005 workshop held by the UN Permanent Forum on Indigenous Issues to deliberate methodological issues surrounding FPIC helped to codify these elements. "Free" was defined as "no coercion, intimidation or manipulation" during negotiations and deliberations, and "Prior" as consent being sought "sufficiently in advance of any authorization or commencement of activities," with respect shown "for time requirements of indigenous consultation/consensus processes" (UNPFII 2005: para. 46(i)). "Informed," in turn, was codified in the following terms: "information is provided, in a language and format that indigenous peoples will understand, that covers (at least) the following aspects" of any proposed project or activity:

(a) its nature, size, pace, reversibility and scope
(b) its purpose
(c) its duration
(d) the location of areas affected
(e) a preliminary assessment of the likely economic, social, cultural and environmental impact, including potential risks and fair and equitable benefit-sharing in a context that respects the precautionary principle
(f) personnel likely to be involved in its execution (e.g., Indigenous peoples, private sector, research institutions, government employees)
(g) procedures that the project may entail

"Consent" is the concept given most attention in the report. It was codified as consisting of dialogue in an atmosphere of mutual respect in good faith; full and equitable participation; an effective system for communication among interest-holders; participation of Indigenous peoples through their own freely chosen representatives; and the option of withholding consent (UNPFII 2005: para. 47). Further, consent should be interpreted "as indigenous peoples have reasonably understood it" (UNPFII 2005: para. 48). Participants emphasized as basic objectives of its application the improvement of living conditions of Indigenous peoples; the prevention of conflict, peace-building, and the establishment of a culture of respect and mutual understanding in the relations between Indigenous peoples, states, intergovernmental organizations, and the private sector; and the evolution of co-management by Indigenous peoples on programs and projects affecting them.[8] It was also interpreted as a procedural right linked to the more fundamental right to self-determination and other human rights, and to the achievement of the Millenium Development Goals.

Its application is also said to yield benefits to all parties,"reduc[ing] risk to tenure rights" (FAO 2015: 54), protecting the livelihoods of local communities, strengthening the viability and sustainability of business operations, and increasing investment potential and related benefits for host countries (FAO 2014: 10). By enabling both parties to reject efforts to "impose their will through violence or intimidation and agreeing on the need to maintain relations according to mutually agreed processes and norms," FPIC is thought to minimize the risk of disputes escalating into conflict (Colchester and MacKay 2004: 26). Even the weaker variants hinging on consultation over consent are said to protect local livelihoods and lead to positive socioeconomic impacts for local communities, while simultaneously strengthening local endorsement of planned operations, enhancing returns on investment, and improving the viability and sustainability of the business operation by avoiding operational delays linked to disputes and misunderstanding (USAID 2015; World Bank 2014).

The right to FPIC for Indigenous peoples is widely recognized in international human rights law. The UN Declaration on the Rights of Indigenous People of 2007 provides some of the strongest language on the rights to FPIC for Indigenous peoples, recognizing their rights to self-determination and requiring FPIC "prior to the approval of any project affecting their lands or territories and other resources, particularly in connection with the development, utilization or exploitation of mineral, water or other resources" (UN 2007, Art. 32.2); "before adopting and implementing legislative or administrative measures that may affect them" (UN 2007, Art. 19); and as a condition of their relocation (UN 2007, Art. 10). Where such rights have been violated, they also enshrine the right to redress in the form of restitution or "just, fair and equitable compensation" (UN 2007, Art. 28). Support for FPIC is also gaining traction with conservation bodies (Colchester 2004) and among market-based sectoral standards, such as the Forest Stewardship Council and the Roundtable for Sustainable Palm Oil.[9]

It should be noted that, despite efforts to embrace these ideas as key features of good land governance, support for the more stringent set of standards embodied in FPIC has been far from uniform. The wording of ILO 169, an instrument which is binding on ratifying countries, is suggestive of lukewarm support for the principle. It includes the right of Indigenous peoples to be *consulted* in good faith through their representative institutions with respect to legislative or administrative measures which may affect them, "with *the objective of* achieving agreement or consent" (ILO 1989, Art. 6, Items 1 and 2, emphasis added). It also recognizes their right to decide their own development priorities, and to exercise control, "to the extent possible," over their own economic, social, and cultural development (ILO 1989, Art. 7, Item 1). ILO 169 also stops short of FPIC in the case of exploitation of mineral or sub-service resources on Indigenous lands, requiring only consultation and fair compensation (ILO 1989, Art. 15, Item 2). "Free and informed consent" as a phrase is restricted to the decision to be relocated (ILO 1989, Art. 16, Item 2). While this more conservative language can be seen as a product of the times, failure to make the more ambitious UNDRIP binding is no doubt due to considerable resistance to the more ambitious standards for FPIC enshrined therein. Weaker variants of these processes ("free and informed participation," "community consultation," "effective and meaningful consultation") are also gaining in popularity not just within international legal instruments and national policies flowing from them, but in voluntary soft law instruments emerging to codify good land governance, industry standards, multi-stakeholder initiatives, and efforts by nongovernmental organizations to advance land rights protections (Colchester 2010; IG and RRI 2015; MacInnes, Colchester, and Whitmore 2017).

While the World Bank embraces the language of consultation, it too has shown considerable resistance to FPIC. Concerns expressed early on centered on the failure of the principle to be enshrined in international law, inconsistencies with national laws, and its impracticability (Colchester and MacKay 2004). In 2016, a briefing by the Forest Peoples Program strongly criticized the World Bank's Environmental and Social Framework (ESF) for its failure to endorse the FPIC standard in favor of "free, prior and informed consultation" and "broad community support" (FPP 2016). A revised ESF, published in 2017, suggests continued resistance to the full FPIC standard:

> The Bank will require the Borrower to engage with stakeholders, including communities, groups, or individuals affected by proposed projects, and with other interested parties, through information disclosure, *consultation, and informed participation* in a manner proportionate to the risks to and impacts on affected communities . . . Where Indigenous Peoples are present in, or have a collective attachment to, the proposed project area, the Bank will require the Borrower to undertake a process of *meaningful consultation* tailored to Indigenous Peoples. (World Bank 2017: 10, emphasis added)

Yet in a departure from the past, and in recognition of the "unique vulnerability" of Indigenous people and "Sub-Saharan African historically underserved traditional local communities" to the loss of, alienation from, or exploitation of their land and resources, the World Bank further requires its borrowers to obtain FPIC under specific conditions. These conditions include situations in which a proposed project is anticipated to have adverse impacts on land and natural resources subject to traditional ownership or under customary use or occupation; to cause relocation from such lands; or to have significant impacts on cultural heritage. Lest we think this battle won, they go on to weaken this commitment by claiming there is no universal definition of FPIC (in spite of the definition provided above), and declaring that FPIC "does not require unanimity and may be achieved even when individuals or groups within or among affected Indigenous Peoples explicitly disagree" (World Bank 2017: 10).

It is not just the form of the consultation that matters, but to whom it applies. Here, too, support for FPIC has been extended to (or better yet, fought for and demanded by) Indigenous peoples but not to other communities whose lands and territories are affected by policies and outside interventions. Formalized rights to FPIC lie exclusively in Indigenous rights law and jurisprudence—as shown above with ILO 169 and UNDRIP. Yet local communities not considered Indigenous are seldom afforded these same rights. In the VGGTs, the rights to FPIC are again restricted to Indigenous peoples, and to two specific contexts: project approval, and the adoption and implementation of "legislative or administrative measures affecting the resources" for which they hold rights (CFS and FAO 2012, Art. 12.7). For others, principles of *consultation* and *participation* apply, with the focus on land transactions or "investments involving all forms of transactions of tenure rights, including acquisitions and partnership agreements" (CFS and FAO 2012, Art. 12.9). Consultation and participation are defined in the VGGTs as, "engaging with and seeking the support of those who, having *legitimate tenure rights*, could be affected by decisions, prior to decisions being taken, and responding to their contributions." With states given the responsibility of defining the categories of rights that are considered legitimate (CFS and FAO 2012, Art. 4.4) and the VGGTs remaining voluntary, it is impossible to predict to whom these rights will apply or how these processes will play out in practice. The best source of evidence is perhaps in the documented processes and outcomes of consultations of customary land users in countries and contexts where hard international law on Indigenous rights does and does not apply.

From an ontological standpoint, at stake is the question of what collective rights and their recognition *are*. Are collective rights substantive protections against territorial encroachment, or socially recognized entitlements to be consulted in the context of land or resource alienation? And what does it mean for them to be recognized? To answer these questions, the next section moves beyond idealized notions of what collective tenures and FPIC are designed to achieve within prominent theories of change, to the everyday experiences of implementation in two countries identified by Alden Wily (2018) to be among those in which collective land rights are strongest and where the right to consultation is enshrined in law. While Peru falls outside of the core geographical focus of the volume, it is included here for the purpose of exploring the consequences of more widespread formal recognition of Indigenous identities to the traction of international legal protections surrounding the collective rights to self-determination, territorial sovereignty, and FPIC.

THE EVIDENCE: AN IN-DEPTH LOOK AT COUNTRIES WITH THE STRONGEST LEGAL PROTECTIONS FOR COLLECTIVE RIGHTS

This section explores legislation and practice associated with communal land rights recognition and community consultation/consent in Mozambique and Peru. Their designation as countries having strong legal provisions for community landholding by legal scholar Liz Alden Wily (2018) was determined by their formal recognition that collective landholding produces lawful property interests; the equal levels of protection afforded community and private lands; the extension of that protection not only to farms and houses, but to areas of communal use (rangelands, forests, etc.); the acceptance of self-governance of community lands; mechanisms for registration of community properties; and the acknowledgement of individual and family interests to specific parts of community property, nested under collective tenure as derivative rights (Alden Wily 2018: 7). Both countries also have legislation explicitly supporting processes of community consultation that pertain to areas under collective tenure, with Peru being the first country in Latin America to recognize the right to prior consultation through a national law.[10] Yet with the international Indigenous rights movement initially rooted in struggles among "first peoples" in white settler colonies, the resulting Indigenous rights laws have been more readily recognized to apply to Indigenous groups throughout Latin America (despite ongoing contestation of these rights and identities) than Africa (Hodgson 2009).[11] A comparison of experiences of collective land rights recognition from countries located in each region can therefore assist in distilling whether this distinction is a key factor in determining outcomes for Indigenous peoples.

Mozambique

Mozambique is recognized as having some of the most progressive land laws in the world, and has won praise for giving rural communities extensive rights over land and the role this may play in avoiding the landlessness that has occurred in other countries (Hanlon 2011). In an earlier comparative analysis of customary rights protections across sub-Saharan Africa by Alden Wily, Mozambique was identified as one of few countries "coming closest to overriding dispossessory norms" by "restoring admittance of real property rights" to customary landowners (Alden Wily 2011: 745, 744). Back in 2010, Mozambique was also singled out as "one country that has recently moved in the direction of more effective consultation" due to the introduction of standardized forms and procedures for structuring consultations (FAO et al. 2010: 12).

On the other hand, there is a strong political commitment to private investment as a means to increase production, generate tax dollars, minimize dependency on aid, and alleviate poverty (Republic of Mozambique 1995). In an effort to rebuild the economy following the end of the Mozambican Civil War in 1992, a legal framework was developed to encourage private investment by granting land use and benefit rights (DUATs) to foreign and domestic investors on a 50-year, renewable basis. The National Land Policy (*Resolução 10/95*, clause 14) thus has among its primary objectives "to create conditions for family farming to develop and grow . . . without lacking its primary resource, land" *and* "to promote private investment . . . without harming local interests." This balanced emphasis on customary rights protections and the stimulation of private investment begs the question of how these two sets of objectives can be achieved in parallel. Does commodification of customary land play a role, and if so, on what terms and to what effect? To answer these questions, it is important to explore the nuances and combined effects of both collective land rights recognition and community consultations.

FORMALIZATION OF COLLECTIVE RIGHTS

The General Peace Agreement signed in October 1992 ended 25 years of armed conflict in Mozambique, and competition for land surged as millions of refugees and internally displaced persons returned home; colonial-era landowners returned to claim abandoned farms; and investors were encouraged by the state to bring abandoned, empty land into production again (Hull and Whittal 2018). The land question was both complex and potentially explosive (Tanner 2002), and discussions leading up to (and since) the passage of the 1997 Land Law centered on these tensions between the recognition of customary rights and private investment. Prominent NGOs and academics argued against individual title as the only legal form of access to land due to its prohibitive cost and ineffectiveness, while others argued that legal recognition of (collective) customary rights would "'freeze' the rural population in systems which perpetuate gender discrimination" and conflict with the interests of investors wishing to acquire titles to use and develop land on parcels where customary rights apply (Kanji, Braga, and Mitullah 2002: 44). *União Nacional dos Camponeses* (UNAC), the national farmers' union, successfully lobbied for recognition of rights expressly obtained through customary law.

The 1997 Land Law and its accompanying regulations grant customary rights the same legal status as other land rights irrespective of their formalization, while providing mechanisms for their formalization (Alden Wily 2011; Norfolk and Tanner 2007). While the state continues to own the root title to land and to grant land use and benefit rights (*direito de uso e aproveitamento da terra* or DUAT) to land users, representing some continuity with early post-independence land law, the nature of the DUAT differs markedly from earlier legislation—providing private, exclusive, and inheritable rights to land and improvements (Norfolk and Tanner 2007). The law makes *de facto* customary rights (individual or collective), as well as informal rights obtained through good faith occupation for a period of at least ten years (individual rights), equivalent to the state-issued DUAT irrespective of their formalization (Norfolk and Tanner 2007). Testimony by male and female community members also stands alongside formal titles as legitimate proof of DUATs acquired through custom (Republic of Mozambique 1997, Art 15). Rights obtained through custom may be formalized in the name of the "community," resulting in a co-title governed by co-property principles specified in the Civil Code (Norfolk and Tanner 2007). A community's land is "defined very broadly to include farm areas, including fallow land, forests, sites of cultural importance, pasture, water sources, and areas for community expansion" (Hanlon 2011: 3). According to the Technical Annex to the Land Law Regulations, to ensure "representativeness of results and consensus," the process of delimiting community boundaries must also involve male and female neighbors representing diverse socio-economic and age groups, and be signed by 3–9 men and women selected in public meetings (Republic of Mozambique, 2000).

According to a 2007 report by FAO (Norfolk and Tanner 2007), while the process of delimitation has proven instrumental in strengthening local awareness of rights, community organization, and the capacity to engage with outside actors, the cards are stacked in favor of outside investment:

> Cadastral service attention to community consultations is driven by the need to secure new DUATs for investors, not to identify where local rights are and promote partnerships in which both sides gain and the poor can use the capital value of their land to break out of poverty. Contrary to the provisions of the Technical Annex, a new project is *not* preceded by delimitation or any other exercise to determine what land is already covered by customarily acquired and good faith DUATs. (Norfolk and Tanner 2007: 28, emphasis in original)

As a consequence, they find evidence of growing land concentration and enclosure. A 2017 study reaches similar conclusions:

> In Mozambique, changes in land access and use are shaping new landscapes, often at the expense of the poor. Despite progressive land legislation, elite groups and vested interests are consolidating land holdings while peasant producers are being dipossessed of their land and access to fertile plots is becoming increasingly difficult . . . Powerful interests are taking advantage of poor communities, who have limited access to information about the opportunities and safeguards that the law should provide. Meanwhile, peasants increasingly rely on smaller and fragmented plots and even face manipulation by those who are supposed to protect their interests . . . Meanwhile, socio-economic development has not provided local people with alternative sources of income. (Filipe and Norfolk 2017: 9, 12)

The first study concludes that local rights are "still extremely vulnerable to capture *in spite of the protection offered by the Land Law*" (Norfolk and Tanner 2007: 28, emphasis added), and the second blames the situation on competition for land and the state's weak capacity for implementing its legal land framework, while repeating the common refrain about Mozambique's exemplary protection of community-based land rights.[12] These assumptions that any problems stem not from the law but from poor implementation echo the widespread view that the limited coverage of "conventional registration" and formal community land delimitations are the problem, and land titling the solution to safeguarding customary land rights (Alden Wily 2011; De Wit and Norfolk 2010).[13] Yet I argue here that it is the very laws and regulations codifying formalization of communal tenures that create legal pathways for the alienation of customary land.

The clearest evidence for this is the mechanism established under the new Land Law to enable DUATs for land held under collective title—irrespective of their formalization—to pass out of the customary domain. First, DUATs may be administratively transferred between third parties when linked to the sale or transfer of standing assets and subject to state approval. This means that the mere recognition of collective rights in the form of DUATs acquired through customary use or formalized titling does little to guarantee local rights, access, or control. Secondly, the regulations to the Land Law recognize the rights of individual occupants holding land under permanent cultivation to an individual title over their land, as long as this does not impinge upon the rights of other community members—a logical and technical impossibility since the Technical Annex "provides for these rights to be individually registered and removed from the common-hold title of the community" (Norfolk and Tanner 2007: 26). Note that this is in line with the World Bank's vision of a "gradual and organic evolution from communal to individual rights" (Deininger et al. 2011: 99), but not the inalienable rights identified by Colchester and MacKay (2004) or the crucial importance of land to Indigenous peoples' existence and identities articulated by Martínez Cobo (UNPFII 2018: 2). A third mechanism for DUATs acquired through custom to be alienated from the customary domain is the mechanism provided by the Land Law for individual or corporate persons, foreign or national, to acquire DUATs through a request to the relevant authority, subject to the payment of land taxes and the implementation of a development plan (Norfolk and Tanner 2007). While a community consultation is needed to actually occupy the land in question, as will be explained below, this prior vetting and approval of DUATs at the national level has a powerful role in stacking the cards in favor of land alienation.

In addition to the alienability of DUATs acquired by custom, there are further ways in which either gaps and ambiguities in the law or actually codified laws are creatively interpreted to weaken customary rights in ways that are in fact legal. The first is an ongoing debate over the interpretation of Article 30 of the Land Law, which codifies who has the right to be consulted prior to land transactions. The ambiguity in the language of, "local communities' own mechanisms of representation and action," which are to govern matters pertaining to land use and benefit rights, has reportedly created room for wide discrepancies in interpretation. Chris Tanner, a tenure specialist with the UN's Food and Agriculture Organization with a long history of engagement in Mozambique's land policy reforms, explains it in the following way. Article 10 of the Land Law specifies that DUATs may be held individually or jointly by way of joint title—and that community DUATs therefore obey the principle of co-ownership. According to Article 12 of the Land Law Regulations, joint holding of DUATs by local communities is governed by Article 1403 et seq. of the Civil Code, which means that the rights of co-owners are qualitatively equal (in the absence of evidence to the contrary). This would suggest that all customary land users should be consulted. For other actors, including the national land director himself, it is instead Article 30 of the Land Law that governs who is to be consulted—which simply states that the mechanisms for representation of and action by local communities shall be established by law. Decree 15 of 2003, which instils the *régulo*[14] with public authority, is said to be the law in question, whereas Tanner insists that that the law governing Article 30 was never formulated (personal communication, 2017).

Another example concerns the practice of community titling. The absence of any statutory restrictions on the size of parcels that may be demarcated in the name of communities meant that in the early period following the passage of the new Land Law, demarcation of spatially extensive "communities" was carried out with the support of NGOs. Yet after some time, the government became concerned about the extent of the land area being titled in the name of communities, and approvals were stalled (Mucheio, personal communication[15]). The provincial cadastral services eventually stopped issuing definitive titles to larger communities, resorting instead to delimitation as the sole mechanism to formally register community boundaries. While prohibitive cost is often cited as the main impediment to the demarcation of entire communities,[16] this change and the backlog of approvals of community demarcations it has led to suggest an evolution in the interpretation of the Land Law which progressively restricts the customary rights recognized by law. According to the Technical Annex of the Land Law Regulations, the distinction between delimitation and demarcation is purely technical. Delimitation is a participatory process involving awareness creation, participatory mapping, and development of a sketch map with GPS coordinates, devolution of results to target and neighboring communities, and registration of the same in the National Land Cadaster. Communities having gone through this process are awarded a certificate or *certidão*. Demarcation is described as the next step in this process, involving a more rigorous survey process and resulting in the issue of a "definitive title."[17] The director of one of the provincial cadastral services of Nampula reiterated the view that this distinction is largely technical: "Delimitation is less precise. The rights are the same. The only difference is that DUATs are for 50 years, while certificates have no limit." His use of the term DUAT to refer exclusively to a definitive title rather than rights acquired through custom, and the practice of conferring a certificate to communities wishing to title their lands and stopping there, both diverge from the letter and spirit of the law.

This begs the question of what implication this distinction has to the lived experiences of collective rights recognition. Research I carried out with colleagues at Eduardo Mondlane University in 2013 highlighted how in both practice and public perception, the two had come to be seen not as different steps in a single technical process of formalizing collective rights, but as distinctive instruments in terms of their purpose, benefits and risks. Delimitation was understood as conferring *non-exclusive rights*, irrespective of existing land uses, to entire "communities" (territories of up to 10,000 hectares), whereas demarcation in the name of customary rights holders had come to mean the issue of more exclusive rights to small parcels (typically less than 50 or 100 ha) in the name of individuals or producer associations—subject to "effective use." The non-exclusivity of rights associated with community delimitation is said to have its origins in the deliberations leading up to the 1997 Land Law, when two proposals for community delimitation were proposed. One option focused on "closed boundaries," in which customary land would be strongly protected and not assigned to outside interests, and the other on "open boundaries," in which access to customary land and resources would be extended to outsiders (Chilundo et al. 2005). The second option was reportedly adopted into law to reduce the economic isolation of local communities; ensure local participation in economic development; and to enable good relations between outside parties and local communities (Tanner, de Wit, and Madureira 1998, cited in Chilundo et al. 2005). With the requirement that investors do a full demarcation to acquire a DUAT, and demarcation only permitted for land that is unoccupied (Hanlon 2004), the demarcation of entire communities would work at cross-purposes with the advancement of land markets.

A second example of efforts to further curtail customary rights recognition involved a proposed amendment to the Land Law Regulations issued by the Council of Ministers, which would have made community delimitations conditional on land use plans and political approval (Hanlon 2011). This move to further curtail the rights recognized by law was successfully rolled back through pressure from NGOs, who argued that delimitation "simply recognizes existing rights" and should not require permission from the Council of Ministers (Baleira and Buquine 2010; Hanlon 2011).

A final example is in the way the language surrounding the protection of existing livelihoods is watered down from the 1995 National Land Policy to the later Land Law and accompanying regulations. The former defines "local community" as "a grouping of families and individuals . . . which has as its objective *the safeguarding of common interests through the protection of* areas of habitation, agricultural areas, whether cultivated or in fallow, forests, sites of socio-cultural importance, grazing lands, water sources and areas for expansion" (Republic of Mozambique: 1995, emphasis added).[18] This language suggests that certain land uses will be safeguarded in the context of outside investment; however, no such restrictions are found in the 1998 Land Law Regulations specifying how the Land Law is to be implemented. The text of these regulations reads, "In the event other rights fall within the required area, the opinion [of the District Administrator] shall include the terms under which the partnership among the title holders of the DUAT acquired by occupation and the applicant shall be governed" (Regulations, Art 27). These terms are in turn determined through a community consultation.[19] This suggests that all customary land is up for negotiation, with the consultations preceding land acquisitions and any conditions set on those concessions serving as the primary mechanism for the exercise of customary land rights in the context of outside investment.

COMMUNITY CONSULTATION

Community consultations have been fully institutionalized in law and practice in Mozambique *in the context of the acquisition of customary land and resources* (see, e.g., Tanner and Baleira 2004). They represent the primary mechanism through which customary rights protections and the stimulation of private investment are to be achieved in parallel, and corresponding interests reconciled. According to Simon Norfolk and Christopher Tanner:

> The issue is more than whether or not investors can or should get access to local land. Most communities welcome them, knowing they can bring jobs

> and other benefits . . . The challenge is to use the 1997 Land Law to modernize the rural economy while gradually formalizing all legally recognized rights and regulating a process of controlled enclosures that can bring real benefits to the poor who are willing to cede or share their legal rights. (Norfolk and Tanner 2007: 28)

Given the crucial importance of the consultation in shaping the terms under which investors will gain rights to access, use, and control customary land, it is somewhat surprising that such limited detail is provided in the Regulations or Technical Annex of the 1997 Land Law on the procedures required for the consultation. The actual form used to verify that the consultation was carried out and to document the resulting agreements makes it clear that the primary focus of the consultation is a land transaction, that the specific location of the "required area" is fixed, and that the consultation is to take place in a single meeting.[20] It gives the impression that the process is a purely symbolic exercise designed not to produce mutual understanding (and much less deliberation), but to rubber stamp a land transaction.

The early empirical record was able to verify that despite some exceptions (e.g., Åkesson, Calengo, and Tanner 2009; Matável, Dolores, and Cabanelas 2011), in most cases, some form of meeting or consultation does occur prior to land acquisitions (Norfolk and Tanner 2007). Tanner and Sergio Baleira (2004) attribute this to their implementation by provincial cadastral services as an integral part of all new DUAT applications. Yet while the legislation has helped meetings to materialize, a 2004 study of the conduct of consultations and their livelihood implications found a host of weaknesses in the process (Tanner and Baleira 2004). The vast majority of consultations were found to take place in a single meeting that primarily involved local leaders. Women were rarely observed to participate actively or to sign the final agreement, and the voice of *régulos* was found to dominate—often to simply rubber stamp agreements already reached behind closed doors. Documentation was found to be inadequate in detail and standardization, with enormous variation in the type and quality of information provided, and often containing conflicting information concerning the crucial question of whether the land was already occupied. Conditions specified verbally or on other forms were found to be missing in the formal minutes, and none of the documentation was registered in a way that would give it legal validity in a court of law. The impression reached by the research team was that the provincial cadastral services personnel were "under great pressure from their superiors to carry it out as quickly as possible," and that the primary motive was not to educate the community or promote local development but to ensure the land request was not rejected by the local community (Tanner and Baleira 2004: 7). Despite the high value placed on the few employment opportunities that were observed to accrue from the national sample, the livelihood outcomes that were found to flow from these consultations reflected in large part the poor quality of the process that generated them.[21] Subsequent studies have found limited local awareness of the scale of proposed deals or the value of ceded land and resources, and limited ability to gauge questions of fairness; promises of benefits that were vague and not time-bound; formal documentation biased in favor of investors; failure of investors to comply with agreements; and consent forms signed by local residents at the behest of higher order directives, thereby undermining the aims and spirit of community consultations (Åkesson, Calengo, and Tanner 2009; Baleira and Buquine 2010; Manuel and Salomão 2009; Nhantumbo and Salomão 2010; Overbeek 2010; Ribeiro and Matável 2009). Chiefs have been observed to readily accede to land acquisitions, which has been variously explained in terms of bribes; their limited awareness of the option to refuse the deal; and their wariness of the consequences of opposition to projects endorsed by the government (Baleira and Buquine 2010; Borras, Fig, and Suárez 2011; Fairbairn 2013; Milgroom 2015). It is perhaps unsurprising, then, that a study on land and environmental conflict in the country found poorly conducted consultations to be a principal cause of acrimonious and long-lasting conflicts between affected people, the state, and outside investors (Baleira and Tanner 2004).

In 2011, a ministerial decree was issued to address some of these limitations; it specified that consultations should occur in at least two meetings held 30 days apart; that one copy of the minutes should be given to the community; and that the district authorities should state what consultative procedures were employed to safeguard the effective participation of community members (Porsani and Lalander 2018). Yet little appears to have changed. Studies published since this time have found various forms of manipulative influence over the consultation (Arnall 2019);[22] meetings held exclusively with the chief and individuals close to him (Fairbairn 2013) or with no women present (Porsani, Börjeson, and Lehtilä 2017); and the allocation of densely settled agricultural land to investors (Arnall 2019). Juliana Porsani and Rickard Lalander find that, "implementation remains limited by everyday practices that jeopardize deliberation," with power asymmetries between communities and outside actors and within communities resulting in consultations which "irremediably corroborate land concessions" (Porsani and Lalander 2018: 173). Unsurprisingly, consultations have not proven to be a mechanism to secure local livelihood benefits, as widely claimed (German et al. 2016; Mei and Alabrese 2013). One study summarizes this as follows:

> It has been hard to build effective partnerships between communities and investors, where communities (or community members) participate actively in investments and benefits are distributed in a fair manner. Examples of community-investor partnerships remain confined mainly to the forestry sector where investors have a very clear incentive to involve local communities and avoid conflict (as trees are a highly combustible resource). Power asymmetry in community-investor relations remains a major challenge. (Cabral and Norfolk 2016: 44)

With the unresolved debate at the national level over who has the right to be consulted—whether all community members, or only the *régulos*—it seems these irregularities are unlikely to be resolved anytime soon.

A case study from Nampula Province provides a more nuanced look at the dynamics of titling and the community consultation in plantation forestry—where Cabral and Norfolk indicate the best partnerships may be found. Findings are based on research I carried out in collaboration with Dr. Eunice Cavane from Eduardo Mondlane University in June, 2013 involving key informant interviews with iTC, an NGO hired to mediate community-investor conflict, and company representatives, as well as focus group discussions with community members involved in consultations, and subsequent email exchanges with NGO representatives.

Collective Rights in Practice: The Case of Mutapua

In 2012, a 28,406-hectare DUAT was issued in favor of a forestry company, Lúrio Green Resources (LGR), in Nampula Province. The DUAT encompassed the entire land area of at least 20 entire communities (Figure 1). A pseudo-consultation was carried out with the *régulo* and a handful of other community members, and the community of Mutapua ended up signing off on an agreement to cede land to the company in exchange for a verbal agreement to build a school and clinic and to provide 3 seedlings for each fruit tree destroyed during plantation establishment. With none of these conditions

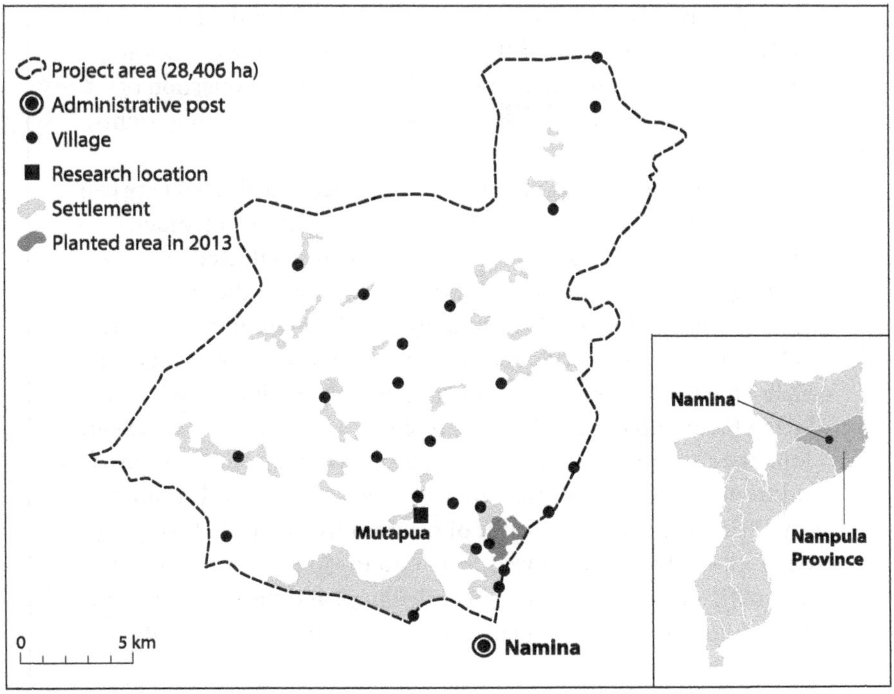

Figure 3. DUAT issued to Lúrio Green Resources for a forestry plantation in Nampula Province

documented in the official minutes of the consultation, which simply states that "this request of the area for the project to carry out its activities may be processed in conformity with the current Land Law," everything rested on the good faith of the investor. In practice, only seedlings were provided, all of which had died by the time of research. After the company had destroyed a number of fields during the early phase of expansion (area in dark green in Figure 1), conflict ensued.

Conflict stands out in the legislation (*Technical Annex of the Land Law Regulations*, Art. 7) as one of three criteria for prioritizing areas for community delimitation. The conflict surrounding the LGR investment made it a priority intervention area, and a service provider was contracted to delimit community land within the LGR concession and to support conflict resolution. Through this process, affected communities acquired formalized rights (in the form of a *certidão*) to customary land that was entirely encompassed *within* the DUAT already allocated to LGR. This begged the question of what purpose formalization had served, and how competing rights, interests and land uses were to be reconciled.

We found that the conflict resolution process facilitated between the community and LGR resulted in several concrete outcomes. First, residents of Mutapua (the community most affected by early plantings) were far more aware of their rights under the law than was true during the initial consultation. Both community members and company representatives saw compliance with agreements made during the initial consultation and additional conditions established during follow-up negotiations as pre-conditions of plantation expansion. The conflict resolution process also led to the identification of additional terms of agreement between the company and community. This included employment of community members (bringing the number of local employees from 0 to 10–30 permanent, and 20 seasonal); technical assistance in agriculture; and the establishment of an outgrower scheme. Finally, and perhaps most importantly, conflict had abated.

At the time of research, community members and leaders expressed ongoing concerns about the situation, saying that the initial terms of agreement associated with land loss had not yet been met. They also joked about the fact that while company employees receive a salary at the month's end, they are "cheap labor." Designated "focal points"—community members who provide technical assistance in agriculture to other community members, receive no compensation other than the equipment they use in their work for LGR (rubber boots, a bicycle and machete). The outgrower scheme was found to be of limited interest to community members, involving less than 20 households at the time of research. We were shown one outgrower contract that lacked any buy-back requirement for timber and was signed not by a LGR employee, but by a community member working as the local focal point to the project. The scheme seemed to be guided by a risk management logic rather than a productive one for the company. As expressed by a company representative:

> In the forest, we can put neither fence nor wall. We don't have the capacity to hire a battalion of rangers . . . Because the dry season lasts for 9 months. As part of us, as good neighbors, this has to be. This is our objective, to fight so that each community next to us is a good neighbor. When the neighbor is burning, I am also burning.*

By early 2014, an estimated 1,650 families were so disillusioned with the process that they saw no future for themselves in the concession area and were taking the initiative to relocate their families on their own accord. Neither delimitation nor procedural dimensions of customary rights protections (community consultation, conflict resolution) were observed to fundamentally alter the power dynamics involved, with households dispossessed of their formally recognized "land use and benefit rights."

Confused by what formalization actually means and its purported role in advancing tenure security, I posed this question to the Director of SPGC in Nampula Province. His immediate response was, "if there is no conflict, it implies there is security."** Yet in the LGR case, conflict had dissipated and tenure and livelihoods were in a condition of extreme precarity. After probing further, he was able to identify one additional dimension of security advanced by formalization—namely, the ability to guide, manage and control outside investment. "It is the district administrator accompanied by SPGC technical staff who define *some points of importance* to the community" (emphasis added). He went onto explain that, "Many times, . . . when an investor appears in a community to request a space, 'What will we gain with this?' is the first thing that is asked, because they already have a notion."

Yet far from being a crucial mechanism through which local communities can exercise their rights while achieving their development aspirations by leveraging land negotiations to their benefit, as framed at national and international levels, ethnographic observations suggest consultations systematically narrow the set of

*June 14, 2013 interview with LGR's Community Development Program Manager.

**June 28, 2013 interview with the Director of the *Serviço Provincial de Geografia e Cadastro* of Nampula Province.

options on the table, while disguising high-stakes impositions as freedom of choice. While this is only one case of many, it helps to expose the fallacies of both titling and consultation as mechanisms for advancing customary land rights and livelihood opportunity in Mozambique—exposing both as instruments which provide only symbolic benefits, while advancing the interests of corporations and political elites standing to benefit from the growing commodification of customary land. The precarity felt by rural households in the context of community-level rights and transactions has reportedly led many households to do what they can to self-finance the demarcation of tiny parcels (fractions of a hectare) to guarantee at least some security in the face of a growing land market.***

***July, 2012 interview with a representative of ORAM Sofala

Peru

> Despite the legal significance of a land title, collective titling alone does not assure the end of land/forest disputes with outsiders. The state needs to defend the property rights that it has recognized.
>
> —Larson, Monterroso, and Vigil (2019)

Peru is also one of the countries identified by Liz Alden Wily (2018) as among those where legal provision for community landholding is strongest, recognizing collective tenure for both Indigenous people and non-Indigenous communities; providing equivalent legal protection of community and private property; forbidding the sale of community property but permitting leasing; and "adopting the principle of Free, Prior and Informed Consent (FPIC) prior to intervention in community lands" (Alden Wily 2018: 16). Recognition of the legal existence of Indigenous communities and the imprescriptible nature of their property assets dates to the 1920 Constitution (Republic of Peru 1920). The Agrarian Reform of 1969 reaffirmed the "integrity of communal property rights," but did so in the name of peasant or *campesina* communities (Decree Law 17716, Art. 115)—shifting the legal designation from a racial to a socioeconomic term in line with the reform's broader goals of integrating rural communities into the national economy through enhanced agricultural productivity and commercialization (Nuñes Palomino 1985). In line with these broader goals, collective rights were seen as key to enhancing productivity by enabling the collectivization and "technification" of production and avoiding the inefficiencies of land fragmentation (Decree Law 17716, Art. 3, 115, and 117). A 1974 decree subsequently recognized the legal personhood of "Native Communities" in the eastern lowlands, yet similarly advanced this designation in the context of agricultural development goals. The decree aimed to sedentarize Indigenous communities and turn them into "development protagonists," while demarcating their lands according to "the area actually occupied" following sedentarization or an area corresponding to their needs (Decree Law 20653, Article 9). These distinctions between Native Communities in the lowlands and peasant communities in the highlands remain to this day.[23]

Today, approximately 35 million hectares of land are owned by Indigenous peoples and local communities in the country (RRI 2015), 12 million hectares of which are titled to the more than 1300 Native Communities in the Peruvian Amazon (Larson, Monterroso, and Vigil 2019). Furthermore, an estimated 7000 of the 10,000 native and peasant communities in the country hold formal collective titles to their lands (Smith 2020). In 2011, Peru also became the first country in Latin America to enact national legislation enshrining the right of Indigenous peoples to prior consultation for all sectors and policies prior to the approval of any legislative or administrative measures that may affect them, as established by ILO Convention 169 (Merino 2015).[24] There is therefore a solid legal basis for supporting Alden Wily's claims. Yet the wider trajectories of Indigenous rights recognition and the economic policies they reflect suggest ample reason for concern. The next two sections explore collective rights recognition and community consultation, respectively, with a focus on Indigenous peoples given the stronger protections for their collective rights in international law and Peru's formal endorsement of these international legal instruments.[25]

TRAJECTORIES OF INDIGENOUS RIGHTS RECOGNITION

Iliana Monterroso et al. (2017) trace a long historical arc of collective rights recognition in Peru from the 1960s, identifying three key periods: efforts to formalize collective rights in the Amazon during the 1970s; a marked shift over the next three decades (1980 to 2009) away from Indigenous rights protections as part of neoliberal reforms promoting private investment; and a renewed effort to reclaim collective rights from 2009 to the present. During the first phase, the Law of Native Communities and Agrarian Regional Promotion in the Lowland Forests and Valleys (Law 20653 of 1974) was passed to promote agricultural production and timber extraction through rural settlement schemes (Monterroso et al. 2017). The law restored the collective land rights of Amazonian Indigenous groups (*comunidades nativas*) (Greene 2006), establishing that lands of titled communities could not be alienated under any circumstances, nor subject to a lien for unpaid debts (Smith 2005). In other words, these rights were declared inalienable, imprescriptible (not subject to revocation or temporally bounded) and irreversible (Monterroso et al. 2017).[26]

The second phase witnessed large-scale infrastructure projects (roads, hydroelectric plants, oil pipelines) and an increase in the allocation of resource extraction rights to timber, mining, and hydrocarbons within territories customarily as well as formally recognized as Indigenous (Little 2014). Under the leadership of Alberto Fujimori, a host of reforms were undertaken to liberalize the economy and foster investment in the Amazon region and beyond—from the 1991 Law for the Promotion of Investment in the Agrarian Sector (Legislative Decree 653) and its associated efforts to provide legal security for investors, to a massive land titling program in 1992 (the Special Project on Land Titling, Law No. 25902). During this period, Indigenous federations at national and international levels mobilized to title more than 9 million hectares to 1,074 Native Communities. Yet the new Constitution of 1993 modified the communal tenure regime to allow communities to divide and sell their land, thereby rescinding their inalienable status and opening them up to foreign investment (Greene 2006),[27] and extraction continued on titled lands. With collective tenure viewed as an obstacle to land markets and agricultural investment (de Soto 2000, 2003; Plant and Hvalkof 2001), these reforms were further entrenched through the passage of a new land law in 1995, which provided additional pathways for peasant and Native Communities to sub-divide collective land into individual parcels (Monterroso et al. 2017).[28] The growth in infrastructure projects was further enabled through growing Pan-Amazonian political integration, and the passage of the Initiative for Integration of Regional Infrastructure of South America in 2000 (Monterroso et al. 2017; see also Little 2014). A study published in 2008 found oil blocks to cover more than two-thirds of the Peruvian Amazon (Finer et al. 2008)[29] and at the time of writing, at least 58 of the 64 blocks under contract with multinational companies or in final stages of negotiation overlaid lands titled to Indigenous peoples.

This upswing in infrastructure and extractive industries was met with opposition by Indigenous federations concerned about widespread contamination, as well as legal action by EarthRights International on behalf of Indigenous Achuar plaintiffs against U.S. oil company Occidental Petroleum in 2007 for widespread poisoning and destruction of their way of life (Finer et al. 2008; Hearn 2008).[30] Efforts were subsequently made by the Peruvian government to deepen neoliberal reforms through the negotiation of a free trade agreement with the United States in 2006.[31] President García publicly declared Indigenous people an obstacle to development, and in 2008 the executive branch issued a series of legislative decrees to bring Peruvian legislation in line with the accord (Larson, Monterroso, and Cronkleton 2017). This led to a sustained period of protests and civil disobedience from 2008 to 2009, when the Peruvian Congress agreed to repeal certain decrees and examine others in response to protests. The failure to follow through on these promises on the heels of a scandal involving members of the ruling party taking bribes from foreign oil companies in exchange for drilling rights in the Amazon, led to protests, road blockades, and the seizure of a petroleum facility by Indigenous people. This culminated in what is now called the *Baguazo*, two back-to-back massacres where the police force tried to break down a road blockade and attacked several thousand unarmed protesters with tear gas and live ammunition. Thirty-four police and civilians died, and at least 200 people were injured. Two weeks later, the decrees were repealed and the government entered into talks with Indigenous organizations to address their grievances (Larson, Monterroso, and Cronkleton 2017). The *Baguazo* was thus a turning point for efforts to reclaim Indigenous tenure rights, which, together with titling communities in Amazonian forestlands as part of the global climate mitigation agenda, has created renewed momentum for Indigenous rights recognition (Monterroso et al. 2017). It is also widely understood as the catalyst to Peru's formal recognition of ILO 169, in the form of the Prior Consultation Law (discussed in the section to follow).

While this trajectory might suggest all is nearly well with the recognition of collective territorial rights in the Peruvian Amazon, the struggle continues. There are several reasons for this that both predate and follow from the prior consultation law, from the multiple ways in which collective rights are curtailed both legally and administratively, to the nature of lands titled in the name of native communities. Cumbersome administrative and bureaucratic hurdles have served as a major constraint to land titling and resource rights. Søren Hvalkof (2002) identified 26 technical and legal stages involved in land titling at the regional level, and five additional stages at the national level. Furthermore, where communities inhabit forested areas, national legislation does not recognize their rights to property, instead limiting their rights to usufruct contracts or "assignment of the right to use" (*derechos de cessión de uso)* (Merino and Gustafsson 2021). To acquire usufruct contracts to forests falling within their territory, Native Communities must go through a series of costly and time-consuming bureaucratic steps, including the design of forest management plans (Larson, Monterroso, and Cronkleton 2017). The new Forest and Wildlife Law of 2000 introduced an even more onerous bureaucratic process for the approval of management and annual operational plans, while failing to clarify procedures for Indigenous groups in communal lands to access or manage forest resources (Monterroso et al. 2017). Furthermore, delays in forest zoning on land undergoing titling on behalf of Native Communities has meant Indigenous communities are often unable to complete the titling process before third parties register contesting claims (Monterroso et al. 2017). Overlaps in areas granted to timber concessionaires and claimed by Indigenous groups has held back the titling process for Native Communities, and brought communal titling to a virtual stand-still by the turn of the millennium (Larson, Monterroso, and Cronkleton 2017).

Rights have also been curtailed legally in multiple ways. The first is the requirement that land held by Native Communities be titled to be legally recognized (Alden Wily 2018). This has enabled the allocation of concessions prior to formalization, and held up land titling processes as overlapping claims are resolved (Monterroso et al. 2017). Peru is also notable for its retention of state ownership of forests in its recognition of collective tenure (Alden Wily 2018). In 1975, a year after collective territorial rights were recognized, Peru passed its first regulations targeting forest resources (Forest and Wildlife Law, Decree 21147), centralizing control over forest resources and declaring them state property. Any individual, community, or company interested in gaining access could only do so through a contract and forest management plan. As such, gaining title to land has historically not ensured rights to use forest resources, because these rights are controlled by the state and gaining access is costly and complex (Alden Wily 2018; Monterroso et al. 2017). Data from the Center for International Forestry Research indicates that 79% of Peru's forests are either government owned and administered or government owned and designated for private use, while only 1% are owned by Indigenous peoples (Monterroso et al. 2017). The 17% of forests under Native Communities in the Amazon are government owned. An additional decree issued in 1975 (Supreme Decree 0062/75-AG) specified that land suitability for different uses, based on soil chemical analyses, must be established to determine the proper uses of titled lands as either agriculture, pasture, or forestry. Land is only titled to Native Communities for areas classified as agricultural (Monterroso et al. 2017). A Ministerial Resolution in 2015 (No. 0355–2015-MINAGRI) further entrenches this system by issuing guidelines for soil analyses to categorize the best use of land as a prerequisite for titling of Native Communities (Monterroso et al. 2017).

Even greater restrictions apply to sub-surface resources. Since 1969, the Peruvian state has held exclusive rights to grant mineral and oil concessions (Smith 2005). Article 29 in the same law that affirmed collective rights in the Amazon (Law 20653 of 1974) allowed for free passage for oil and gas pipelines and installations for mineral and petroleum exploration, while declaring that no payment of indemnity to the property owner is required (Smith 2005). While Article 7 of the 1995 Land Law and accompanying procedural codes make the extraction of subsoil resources conditional on an agreement with the land owner, and Peru's ratification of ILO 169 requires Indigenous people to share in the benefits of extraction and be paid compensation for any damages occurring to their homeland, Peruvian jurisprudence has not recognized rights to subsoil resources found in Indigenous territories (Smith 2005). By 2015, approximately 48 million hectares of oil and gas concessions had been issued that overlapped with four territorial reserves, five communal reserves, and at least 70% of Native Communities' land (RRI 2015: 184).

Indigenous rights following the Bagua massacre have been further curtailed legislatively through a series of laws passed by congress since 2013 called *paquetazos*, which have weakened protections against the expropriation of land held by native and *campesino* communities to facilitate commercial concessions (Mendez 2015; RRI 2015). Justified by the economic slowdown, these decrees weaken the normative framework guaranteeing respect for human rights, environmental protections, and the land rights of Indigenous and peasant communities. Decree 1192 of 2015 normalized processes of involuntary expropriation, removing its exceptional character and enabling a private investor or public-private partnership to expropriate land through an expedited process (Mendez 2015). Decree 1210, passed three weeks later, had a single article which modified Article 10 of Decree 1192, which had excluded the lands and territories of Indigenous people from these expedited procedures. Additional decrees that same year created conflicts of interest in the environmental approval process for large-scale investments by transferring responsibilities for approvals to relevant sectoral authorities whose interests align with those of investors.

In addition to contesting the various ways in which rights are curtailed *within lands formally titled in the name of Native Communities*, Indigenous peoples have, since at least the 1980s, contested the territorial reach of titling (Chirif Tirado, Hierro, and Smith 1991; Smith 2002). In the first decade after passage of the 1974 law, government officials recognized and titled only individual Indigenous settlements, irrespective of their small size, resulting in the legal fragmentation of Indigenous territories. According to Richard Chase Smith,

> Most Amazon peoples were broken up into archipelagos of small, often isolated, communities; the lands between were opened for colonization and extractive activities by nonindigenous peoples. Many of these individual communities were too small and densely populated to permit traditional practices of extensive resource use and management. (Smith 2005: 234–235)

Yet this fragmentation of Indigenous territories had one silver lining in helping to foster collective identity through the high levels of participation required to formalize the patchwork of smaller self-governing units (Smith 2005). In the 1980s, the Coordinating Body for Indigenous Organizations of the Amazon Basin (COICA) brought international discourse on Indigenous land rights emphasizing rights not to land, but to contiguous Indigenous territories—including all forest, aquatic, and subsoil resources, to national Indigenous land rights struggles in the Amazon region (Chirif Tirado, Hierro, and Smith 1991; Smith 2002). This early shift in the idiom of land claims from "land" to Indigenous "territory" forms part of a political strategy of Indigenous self-determination, breaking with liberal conceptions of land as a means of production (Hvalkof 2002: 93). Hvalkof elaborates on the conceptual significance of territory as related to nationhood—connoting spatial integrity and collective rights for inhabitants; control over resources and development in the spirit of self-determination; and collective responsibility and accountability. Since then, this demand for the recognition of the "integral territory" of Indigenous peoples, and the related demand for their recognition as self-determining Indigenous nations rather than isolated communities, has been part of the Indigenous land rights struggle in Peru (Merino 2021a), yet has faced ongoing resistance by the government which has sought to translate these struggles into "limited institutional arrangements" (Merino 2019).

The latest milestone in this struggle to "disrupt the legal framework of property titling" and create "a new relationship with the state in such a way that we exert self-government" (Wrays Perez, cited by Merino 2019: 521) was the proclamation by the 65 Indigenous Wampis communities, in November 2015, of their own autonomous territorial government and their autonomy within the Peruvian state based on their right to self-determination—representing the first Indigenous autonomous government in Peru.[32] With this, they are seeking to gain recognition of, and regain control over, the 1.3 million hectares of territory that correspond with the lands historically occupied by Indigenous peoples, as a means to defend their livelihood from growing pressure from extractive industries and to preserve their cultural identity. Representatives of the 27 registered communities formally signed onto the *Statute of the Autonomous Territorial Government of the Wampis Nation*, "a form of political constitution defining rights and duties for the nation, communities and individuals, and establishing government structures, electoral processes and a vision for development" (Merino 2019: 520), following a multi-year process of internal deliberation. Insisting on the recognition of the *totality* of the territory they have historically occupied, they agreed to resist further titling of isolated communities and affirm within their statute their full rights within international law—including the need for any activity that could affect Wampis territory to have the Free, Prior and Informed Consent of the Wampis Nation. In May, 2017 a delegation delivered a declaration of the constitution to the National Congress. While the Peruvian government remains reluctant to recognize the Wampis Nation formally, the Wampis have strengthened their rights to the territory by speaking with a single voice and emphasizing their rights as an Indigenous Wampis people rather than as isolated communities. These dynamics echo other works finding forms of property enactment and the webs of social relations reinforcing collective norms to be more important than the legal title in shaping tenure security (Blomley 2014; Cronkleton and Larson 2015; Hvalkof 2002). Eight other Amazonian peoples working with the Wampis since 1995 under the umbrella of the "Regional Coordinator of Indigenous Peoples from San Lorenzo" (CORPI) are currently in the process of formulating their own statutes (Merino 2019).

COMMUNITY CONSULTATION

Research published prior to 2009 highlights the ways in which decisions regarding investments in Indigenous lands were taken between Peru's ratification of ILO 169 in 1994 and the passage of national legislation to back up this commitment in 2011. Smith (2005), for example, describes the social and environmental impact of and consultation processes surrounding the Shell-Mobil Consortium in the context of new oil drilling in the Camisea gas fields following a decades-long process of territorial and community consolidation and an ongoing process of territorial zoning and resource management among the Indigenous Machiguenga. The Consortium's efforts to address the social and environmental impacts of the project reportedly ignored this historical process, which had included a biodiversity study by the Smithsonian, an Oxfam-Woods Hole study of vegetative cover with GIS database, and a diagnostic study for long-term development. None of the organizations involved in this long-term planning were informed, and the studies conducted by the Consortium were carried out by outsiders, none of whom had any experience working with the Machiguenga. Several consultations were carried out, some of which led to compensation. However, Smith declares these compensations to be mostly symbolic. In one case, Chevron compensated a community for exploratory rights on the lower Urubamba in the form of t-shirts, soccer balls and school supplies (notebooks, pencils). Even the 100,000 USD to be paid to one community for the establishment of the Shell-Mobil Consortium base camp and the 20,000 USD to be paid to another for the digging of test wells were deemed negligible when considering the scale of the total investment and its long-term consequences. Furthermore, and in adherence with the land law at the time, Shell-HSE focused on resolving issues with selected communities directly affected by their operations, leaving aside wider impacts affecting the Machiguenga as a whole—such as right of way, environmental use and protection, or any long-term benefits to the Machiguenga in exchange for resources extracted from their homelands. "Because they have no rights to subsoil resources, the local population was viewed by both state officials and by those involved in the Shell-Mobil Consortium as an obstacle rather than a partner in the business deal" (Smith 2002: 248). This led to conflict over the forms and pace of the consultation between project advocates and local communities. The compensation was never paid out as the project was cancelled due to disputes with the Peruvian government over the terms of the deal, and the deal was awarded to two conglomerations of smaller companies, none of whom are well-known internationally. It is unclear whether these companies acquired the duties to compensate, with levels of international recognition being key to the reputational risks faced by companies, but the Camisea pipeline had five major spills in its first 18 months of operation (Griffiths 2007).

It was not until 2011, on the heels of the Bagua massacre, that Peru's commitment to community consultation at the international level gained traction within national law. The *Law of the Right to Prior Consultation of Indigenous or Original Peoples, Recognized in Convention 169 of the International Labor Organization* (Law No. 29785) requires that Indigenous peoples should be consulted prior to taking any administrative or legislative action that directly affects their collective rights, physical existence, cultural identity, quality of life, or development (Law No. 29785, Art. 2), but notably falls short of requiring consent or recognizing the right to self-determination. The legislation further states that this consultation should take place prior to the adoption of the legislative or administrative measure by state entities (Law No. 29785, Art. 4). Additional principles include "good faith" (consultations to be taken in a climate of trust, collaboration, and mutual respect, with each party acting in good faith); "reasonable timeframe" (to permit representative organizations to understand, reflect, and formulate concrete proposals relevant to the measure in question); "absence of coercion or conditions"; and "timely information" (the right to receive all the information necessary for them to be duly informed about the measure in question from state actors) (Law No. 29785, Art. 4). The information provided should include the "motives, implications, impacts and consequences" of the proposed legislative or administrative measure (Law No. 29785, Art. 12). It states that such consultation is only obligatory for the state (Law No. 29785, Art. 2), and that Indigenous people should participate through their own representative organizations chosen according to custom (Law No. 29785, Art. 6). To what extent has this changed the prevalence and quality of community consultations in the context of legislative measures and investment projects?

While Indigenous people have expressed concern[33] over the separation of steps 6 (dialogue between representatives of the state and Indigenous people) and 7 (decision), and in the language associated with step 7 giving the state the final decision to approve the measure in question (Law No. 29785, Art. 15), it is seen as a significant legislative achievement for the recognition of Indigenous rights. The government also initiated the first consultation in the context of a new forest law and its accompanying regulations from 2011–2015. As a consequence of this consultation, the law recognized the exclusive rights of peasant and Native Communities to use forest resources within their territories, whether forestlands are found on land titled in the name of Native Communities or held under usufruct, and confirms rights of Native Communities to prior informed *consultation* (Monterroso et al. 2017).

On the other hand, the reforms advanced by President Humala (known in Peru as *paquetazos*) to expand foreign investment were adopted with neither open debate nor consultation of affected communities, in violation of the prior consultation law (IBC 2016, cited by Monterroso et al. 2017). Furthermore, a special decree by the Ministry of Mining in 2015 (001–2015-EM) states that resolutions from community leaders were sufficient proof of consent to authorize the use of communal land for mining, contradicting provisions for participation through "representative institutions and organizations" in the prior consultation law (Monterroso et al. 2017). Implementation of the consultation process has reportedly been uneven, with consultation in some cases occurring after a concession is granted and in others Indigenous organizations saying they received insufficient information about the potential impacts of proposed investments (Larson, Monterroso, and Cronkleton 2017). Other critics of Peru's prior consultation law suggest the legislation is unlikely to transform conflicts as long as the normative framework itself is contested and the preconditions for participatory governance—such as state institutions capable of (or motivated to) justly balancing diverse interests, reduction of power imbalances within consultations, and joint decision-making processes with binding agreements—are lacking (Schilling-Vacaflor and Flemmer 2015). Roger Merino (2018), on the other hand, critiques the law for how it reinforces the mediating role of the state between social groups and channels and binds Indigenous politics, transforming demands for institutional transformation (such as territorial protection, self-determination, and social and economic rights) into "merely participatory provisions of specific projects" (Merino 2018: 75). He calls it a "form of liberal legality embedded in coloniality" by failing to recognize Indigenous peoples as nations with territorial rights (Merino 2015: 1). While the *consultation standard* enshrined in the binding ILO Convention and to a large extent Peruvian law is recognized as being inferior to the *consent standard* within UNDRIP and international jurisprudence, Merino (2017) also points out how far both are to *consent as an expression of self-determination* that is advocated by Indigenous peoples and recognized in neither national nor international law. Merino thus calls for "re-politicizing the current governance that defines in advance the boundaries and scope of any demand mediated through participatory channels" (Merino 2018: 82).

While the state is still resisting its duties to duly consult directly affected Indigenous communities according to the guidelines established in the prior consultation law, Indigenous communities have begun demanding its recognition through the courts. In 2017, the Wampis Nation won a major legal victory, with the Fourth Constitutional Court of Lima ruling that an oil company granted permission from the Peruvian government to run assessments on Wampis land could not continue their work without the approval of the Wampis government and were forced to halt their work.[34]

Those studying collective land rights and community consultation in Peru in recent years tend to reach a similar conclusion: that despite all of the gains on paper, collective rights continue to be threatened by economic development policies and the everyday practices of lawmakers and bureaucrats, both of which favor foreign investment in extractive industries (Larson, Monterroso, and Vigil 2019; Merino 2015, 2018). Optimistic views expressed by some authors at the turn of the century (Hvalkof 2002)[35] are in sharp contrast with recent explanations for the ambiguous roles of contemporary rights frameworks in both democratizing and perpetuating long-standing inequalities. According to Anne Larsen:

> While this ambiguity is often explained as a consequence of poor implementation and the 'birth defects' of compromised standards, . . . the new jungle law is characterised by judicial, administrative and regulatory assaults on the emancipatory potential of rights. Rights, under the new jungle law, are not simply a response to frontier injustices, extrajudicial punishment and violence . . . Instruments like ILO Convention 169 are no longer being ignored. Rather, they are . . . instrumentalised and adjusted to business realities and national development priorities. (Larsen 2016, para 42)

Once again, the observed shortcomings in the recognition of collective rights are not attributable to extralegal practices or even poor implementation, but to the instrumentalization of property rights and prior consultation to align them with dominant interests. For Peru, where once progressive laws enshrining collective rights that were *inalienable* were eroded even as the international Indigenous rights regime took root, the future of collective rights seems to rest less on the legal regime than on ongoing efforts of Indigenous peoples to defend their rights to territory, to self-determination, and to consent. To echo the words of Hvalkof (and Bateson 1972, from whom he takes inspiration), "a territory is a living social entity, which only exists as part of the social enactment by its inhabitants" (Hvalkof 2002: 94–95).

RECOGNITION OF COLLECTIVE RIGHTS IN MOZAMBIQUE AND PERU: OUTLIER OR NORM?

To address the likelihood that some readers might dismiss these findings outright for representing isolated cases not reflective of wider trends, I would like to start by placing the Mozambican and Peruvian experience in a wider context. In terms of collective land rights, back in 2007 the United Nations Permanent Forum on Indigenous Issues recognized the false promise of collective titling in safeguarding the crucial relationship between Indigenous territory and identity:

> *Land-titling* procedures have been slow and complex and, in many cases, the titles awarded to the communities are not respected in practice. At the same time, privatization of traditional lands is on the increase. This measure *is claimed to benefit indigenous owners in that it provides legal certainty. The Special Rapporteur has, however, observed that in the long run the indigenous communities tend to lose their traditional lands and territories* to the various private economic interests of either firms or individual invaders and settlers who have managed to install themselves in traditional indigenous areas. (A/HRC/4/32, para. 14, emphasis added) (see UNPFII 2018)

The 17th Session of the UN Permanent Forum on Indigenous Issues, which met in April 2018 and had as its central theme "Indigenous People's Collective Rights to Lands, Territories and Resources," highlights ongoing challenges to Indigenous land rights recognition—from the failure to demarcate Indigenous lands to the powers of the state to extinguish collective rights; legal, political, and administrative barriers; limited recourse to courts and other legal remedies; vulnerability to violence, intimidation, and corruption; armed conflict and militarization of Indigenous lands; and ongoing removal of Indigenous peoples when exploitation of their lands is linked to national interests such as mining, logging, conservation, infrastructure, or industrial agriculture. The closing remarks painted a rather dismal picture of, "tremendous pressure from extractive industries, infrastructure projects, large-scale agriculture, hydroelectric dams and even conservations efforts that have led to the dispossession and displacement of Indigenous peoples."[36] Alden Wily adds to this list failure to enact implementing regulations; coerced subdivision of already titled lands; state sanctioning of major encroachments through expanding definitions of public property; and attempts to do away with recently enacted protections. Yet as these case studies show, it is not just through extralegal maneuverings that customary rights are eroded. Evidence in this chapter that the very laws and regulations advanced to recognize and protect customary tenures are in fact creating legal pathways for the alienation of customary land finds support in the work of legal scholars. In a study of land law reforms taking place over a 50-year period in seven Eastern African countries, for example, Patrick McAuslan's (2013) found that "however dressed up and hedged about with controls and regulations, all the reforms embrace and facilitate the development and operation of a modern statute law-based land market" (McAuslan 2013: 229). In noting the alignment of his findings with the longstanding push from the international community to support the "homogenisation of national land laws based on the Anglo-American legal model to facilitate an international land market"—a set of relationships also explored by Ambreena Manji in *The Politics of Land Reform in Africa*—he concludes that, "the World Bank has, quite simply, won" (Manji 2006.). Here, it is the World Bank's vision of collective titling that has gained traction within national land laws, and it has done so at a time of growing demand for commodities, and the opening of new frontiers of extraction and land control in Amazonia, sub-Saharan Africa, and beyond (de Jong, Knippenberg, and Bakker 2017; Little 2014; Peluso and Lund 2011).

As for collective rights to consultation and content, countless studies of consultation processes find widespread evidence that these processes are riddled with irregularities that ultimately undermine the spirit of supporting norms—whether domestic or international law, voluntary codes of conduct or industry standards (Andrew and Van Vlaenderen 2011; Cleaver, Schram, and Wanga 2010; Habib-Mintz 2010; Manuel and Salomão 2009; Mkindi 2008; Nhantumbo and Salomão 2010; Nolte and Voget-Kleschin 2014; Overbeek 2010; Ribeiro and Matável 2009; Sitoe 2009; Sulle and Nelson 2009; Waterhouse, Lauriciano, and Norfolk 2010). A rare comparative study across Mozambique, Tanzania, and the Philippines finds that:

> In practice, community consultations are fraught with irregularities and seldom reflect genuine community consent. Consultations are often perfunctory, with government agents clearly on the side of investors. For their part, communities are barely in a position to participate meaningfully: power asymmetries and low levels of education hamper their ability to fully understand the process, their legal rights, and the nature and implications of the investment. Promises of job opportunities and other benefits induce com-

> munity consent, but are often unfulfilled, leaving communities with no recourse. Likewise, many projects fail to get off the ground or founder soon after. (Salcedo-La Viña and Morarji 2016: 2)

And reflecting on the literature and the long-term work of Forest Peoples Programme in supporting the rights of Indigenous peoples to FPIC, Marcus Colchester and Fergus MacKay wrote:

> Case studies show that consent is frequently engineered and indigenous institutions are out-maneuvered by competing interests seeking access to indigenous peoples' common resources . . . Two of the main challenges of the Middle Ground [include] the need for indigenous societies to agree means to represent their own collectivities and, secondly, for *mutually* agreed negotiating processes so that indigenous peoples can treat with industrial societies without being divided and ruled. (Colchester and MacKay 2004: 1, emphasis in original)

They identified as key constraints to the realization of the FPIC principle the engineering of consent through the militarization of isolated communities; the manipulation of communities, "introducing factionalism, dividing communities and promoting individuals, who may have no traditional authority as leaders, to represent communities"; and widespread use of bribes and unregulated patronage over prominent decision-makers (Colchester and MacKay 2004: 26).

A four-country review of processes of large-scale land acquisition in Africa I took part in (German, Schoneveld, and Mwangi 2013) found common shortcomings to include the limited duration of consultations (often limited to a single meeting); the tendency for intermediaries to inflate benefits and obscure costs; coercion, intimidation, or higher-order directives that undermine the discretionary space of the consultation in favor of land alienation; circumvention of community consultations in favor of negotiations with local government; limited awareness of local land users (e.g., low levels of legal literature, lack of clarity on how much land is at stake, unrealistic/inflated expectations about future benefits); absence of downwardly accountable community representation (e.g., chiefs as the sole interlocutors, local elites dominating consultation deliberations, chiefs receiving bribes to acquiesce); incomplete or biased documentation of agreements reached verbally (e.g., lacking in detail, biased in favor of investors' interests, not time-bound, failure to provide affected communities copies of consultation records); and absence of compensation or irregularities in compensation mechanisms (compensation flowing to district councils rather than affected land users, low or symbolic compensation, undisclosed evaluation procedures, frequent failure of investors to comply with agreements). Together, these shortcomings give consultations the character of symbolic gestures rather than procedures that can be expected to guarantee substantive safeguards or livelihood outcomes. The latest report from the Land Matrix further reinforces these findings, finding "scant consultation" with affected communities to be common and the "non-consensual and uncompensated loss of land" to often come with limited benefit (Lay et al. 2021: 8). It is clear that the experiences profiled in Mozambique and Peru are far from unique.

THE DISPOSSESSORY LOGICS OF COLLECTIVE RIGHTS RECOGNITION

Here I return to the question posed at the beginning of this chapter, namely, whether the renewed commitment to collective titling represents a marked shift away from the dominant twentieth-century strategy of extinguishing communal and customary tenure in the name of progress, or is instead playing a part in the ongoing trend in the commodification of land and its transfer away from the customary domain. While the views expressed by different constituencies are decidedly mixed, in practice, for both Mozambique and Peru, evidence points to the latter. Rights are being formalized in the name of collective rights holders and consultations are being carried out in the context of new investment and land or resource acquisition, but collective rights to territory and to shape the trajectories of development and resource extraction on customary land are as precarious as ever.

This situation is in no small part due to the fact that the form of collective rights recognition being codified within national legal orders and enacted within local landscapes is not that which sanctifies the "three I's" advocated by Indigenous rights defenders in Peru (territorial rights that are inalienable, imprescriptible, and irreversible), as formerly recognized by law, but rather rights that may be reversed legislatively, are curtailed substantively and spatially, and are readily subdivided and alienated. These practices resonate most with the more transactional conception of collective rights recognition advocated for by the World Bank. This alignment is undoubtedly linked to a suite of interrelated factors, from the World Bank's financial and technical leverage over national legal reform processes, to the political economic forces profiled in the Introduction to this volume, and the articulation of these forces with the aligned interests of economic and political elites in Mozambique and Peru and in countries positioned as their "development partners" in North America and Europe. What insights does this provide about the international land governance orthodoxy? Perhaps, it reveals how distinct conceptions about the work being done with formalization of collective (and perhaps also individual) rights helps to create a sense of collective purpose that is in fact a chimera, yet which allows for their uneven implementation on the ground to go unnoticed.

These findings resonate with critical theories of law and property, whereby the architecture of collective rights recognition may be defined as much by rights that are bracketed away in the course of formalization as those that are recognized through it. In both countries, this is seen in the failure to codify consent, and in the legal provisions for the subdivision and commodification of communal lands and their de jure or de facto transfer out of the customary domain. In Peru, it is further seen in the restriction of collective rights to the land surface (soil, not aboveground or belowground resources) and only to those lands formally designated as agricultural. It is also visible in the ongoing resistance to recognize customary rights that are undocumented or the vast Indigenous territories lying in the interstices of isolated settlements. In Mozambique, additional evidence is found in the non-exclusivity of rights to collective lands formally recognized. Such a rights regime does less to recognize and safeguard communal and customary rights than it does to guarantee ongoing access by outsiders and foster the movement of land and resources to land users deemed "more efficient" by the powers that be.

Yet the ongoing precarity of collective rights under such a legal regime also stems from how the institutional architecture and political economy of land place customary rights holders in the impossible position of being fully and exclusively responsible for their own fate—expected to fight a battle stacked heavily against them. With collective title excluding forestry and sub-surface resources (Peru), non-exclusive (Mozambique), subdivisible, and alienable (both countries), consultation stands as the only mechanism to mediate outside access to customary land and resources. The World Bank's declaration that FPIC "does not require unanimity and may be achieved even when individuals or groups within or among affected Indigenous Peoples explicitly disagree" (World Bank 2017: 10) opens the door to a divide and rule strategy for opening collective lands and territories to outside interests, and reveals the World Bank's ongoing commitment to the alienation of collective lands and territory. Community consultation and FPIC are further undermined by the narrow conceptual and administrative space of their application—namely, investment projects, land acquisition, or predrafted legislative instruments (German and Braga 2019; see also Merino 2018). The review of international land rights discourses by German and Braga (2019) finds a growing emphasis on procedural over substantive forms of rights recognition in which the process of consultation or consent is circumscribed to the context of investment approval and land acquisitions. Distinct from the more protective positions on land rights advocated by civil society, such as the International Land Coalition's emphasis on no one being "deprived of the use and control of the land on which their well-being and human dignity depend" (ILC 2016: 10), the paper finds that "respect for land rights" is coming to mean adherence to key procedural elements for "responsible" land acquisition. This stands in sharp contrast to notions of self-determination embodied in UNDRIP principles of the freedom to pursue one's economic, social, and cultural development; to define those development priorities and strategies; and to choose whether or not to participate in the political, economic, social, and cultural life of the nation-state. The emphasis on personal responsibility[37] and freedom of choice, alongside the narrowing of that choice and the active role of governments in creating the conditions for the commodification of rural land and life, is reflective of prominent academic critiques of neoliberal ideology (Dean 2010; Gordon 1991; Miller and Rose 2008). Far from establishing "the sovereign right of Indigenous peoples to decide their own visions for development and political association" (Petkar 2017) or even protecting local livelihoods and ensuring positive socioeconomic impacts for local communities (USAID 2015; World Bank 2014), consultations appear to confer a license to operate (and appropriate) irrespective of the social outcomes. Recognizing collective title while conferring rights to watered down standards for consultation in the context of alienation of titled land thus emerges as a remarkably efficient strategy for dispossessing large numbers of land users while securing land for investors and legitimating the same.

These findings also resonate with key tenets of critical race theory, from the tendency for rights to be framed in procedural rather than substantive terms; to be rolled back when conflicting with the interests of the powerful; to be alienating, separating people from one another and from collective life; and to be gradually "cut back by narrow interpretation, administrative obstruction or delay" (Delgado and Stefancic 2017: 29). And they also resonate with insights on settler colonialism—from the territoriality of the state ("settler colonialism's specific, irreducible element," Wolfe 2006: 388) to the tendency for land rights to be circumscribed by the imperative to reinscribe colonial power relations on the ground, and the reinforcement of the sovereignty of the state in its exclusive authority to define exactly which procedural and substantive rights are recognized and curtailed (Blomley 2014).

With Peru's greatest gains in collective rights recognition occurring prior to the advent of international Indigenous rights law and the continuing precarity of collective rights under this law, what separates the dynamics of customary rights recognition in Mozambique and Peru is not so much the question of Indigeneity and the protections afforded in international law, as hypothesized at the outset. Rather, it is the level of self-organization of Indigenous peoples in Peru and their sophisticated efforts to draw on every resource at their disposal (international allies, international law, domestic courts, raw protest) to defend their lands against outsiders and enact alternative visions of themselves and their territory as self-determined Indigenous nations.

CONCLUDING REMARKS

The widespread call from within civil society for more formal state recognition of collective rights[38] and more consultation is unlikely to substantially enhance the security of customary rights holders with collective tenures under the current political economic landscape. While these forces will continue to undermine prospects for collective tenure security and self-determination, it is worth reflecting on alternative forms of collective rights recognition more empowering of customary rights holders. Perhaps the best place to start is to listen to customary rights holders themselves. In Mozambique, communities seem to be longing for rights that truly defend land and resources that are crucial to rural livelihoods against takings, and to enable rural households to continue to sustain their livelihoods. Formal employment in new agribusiness ventures are undoubtedly valued, yet not at the expense of the livelihoods of the majority (although affected households are often asked to bear the burden of displacement for the sake of job creation, irrespective of their ability to access those jobs). In Peru and elsewhere in Latin America, where collective aspirations are more clearly articulated from Indigenous peoples themselves, the answer is perhaps easier. Rights should be formalized not in the name of communities but rather Indigenous nations, and not at the level of isolated settlements but rather contiguous Indigenous territories. These rights should be inalienable, imprescriptible, and irreversible. They should include not just rights to the topsoil and to areas designated by outsiders as suitable to specific land uses, but to the entire territory. How that territory and those resources are to be governed should be decided not through instrumental approaches to consultation or consent led by outsiders that have proven to "significantly risk narrowing down the claim space" (Larsen 2016), but by grassroots decision-making processes governed by the principle of collective self-determination.[39]

Yet as Merino (2021b) points out, the challenges to achieving this vision are enormous.[40] With the most robust forms of FPIC falling short of "consent as an expression of self-determination" (Merino 2017), procedural rights are clearly inadequate. And while strong and representative Indigenous organizations capable of ensuring decisions made reflect and balance the interests of all are essential to navigating both of these challenges and for defending collective territorial rights,[41] Indigenous political representation remains contested (Bauman and Williams 2004; Larson 2008; Valdivia 2005, 2007) and localized process is a poor match to the powerful interests and historical momentum behind Indigenous dispossession. Under such circumstances, customary rights holders are easily divided, and efforts to enact rather than seek state recognition of self-determination are easily ignored (Merino 2021a). Legal safeguards against alienation are thus needed to ensure lands with crucial livelihood functions are safeguarded (as alluded to in Mozambique's Land Policy) and that ongoing access, use, and control are firmly in the hands of customary users. To achieve this, the World Bank, G8,[42] and other prominent "development partners" in the land sector would have to change their ways.

Navigating these visions will also require efforts to address interests within the collective that are at odds with the vision of territorial integrity, such as those embracing transactional conceptions of land-as-commodity. Here, principles of Indigenous property law that have proven effective in holding onto tribal lands in the context of centuries of past land speculation are instructive. While representing a distinct geography and history, the Cherokee conception of "common property" denoting not equal shares of a commonly held parcel as is common in Anglo-American property law, but reflecting an interest in preserving tribal territorial and political integrity (Leeds 2000), is instructive. Here, "relentless recognition of individual Cherokee rights to the lands [Cherokee families] were already occupying," together with restriction on property transactions to non-Cherokees and "a right of first refusal to other Cherokees, with a secondary priority to the nation itself" have allowed for the Eastern Band of Cherokees to sustain and subsequently expand their collective landholdings—and thus their cultural and political identity—in the wake of aggressive and often violent settler colonial expropriation (Leeds 2000: 495). With descent-based African land tenures integrating individual and heritable rights to parcels with areas of communal access, and safeguarding both collective and individual interests in land in the face of informal and formal land markets, such an approach would be a far better solution to the "representational ascent"[43] than those currently on offer.

REFERENCES

Åkesson, G., A. Calengo and C. Tanner. 2009. *Study on Community Land Rights in Niassa Province, Mozambique*. Department of Urban and Rural Development Reports, Swedish University of Agricultural Sciences. Available at: https://issuu.com/durd/docs/2009_6 (accessed May 17, 2020).

Alden Wily, L. 2011. 'The law is to blame': The vulnerable status of common property rights in Sub-Saharan Africa. *Development and Change* 42(3): 733–757.

Alden Wily, L. 2018. Collective land ownership in the 21st Century: Overview of global trends. *Land* 7(68), https://www.doi.org/10.3390/land7020068.

Andrew, M. and H. Van Vlaenderen. 2011 Commercial biofuel land deals and environment and social impact assessments in Africa: Three case studies in Mozambique and Sierra Leone. *Land Deal Politics Initiative Working Paper* No. 1. Available at: https://assets.publishing.service.gov.uk/media/57a08adae5274a31e00007f0/LDPI-WP-01.pdf (accessed May 17, 2020).

Arnall, A. 2019. "Employment until the end of the world": Exploring the role of manipulation in a Mozambican land deal. *Land Use Policy* 81(2019): 862–870.

Arnt, R.A. and S. Schwartznian. 1992. *Um Artifício Orgânico: Transição na Amazônia e Ambientalismo (1985–1990)*. Rio de Janeiro: Rocco.

Bateson, G. 1972. *Steps to an Ecology of Minds*. New York: Balantine.

Baleira, S. and E. Buquine. 2010. *Estudo sobre Conflito de Interesses na Gestão e Exploração da Terra em Mocambique: Os Casos dos Distritos de Massinga, Zavala, Macomia e Mecufi*. Maputo, Mozambique: Associação Rural de Ajuda Mútua. Available at: https://landportal.org/pt/library/resources/estudo-sobre-conflito-de-interesses-na-gestão-e-exploração-da-terra-em-moçambique (accessed May 17, 2020).

Baleira, S. and C. Tanner. 2004. *Relatorio Final da Pesquisa sobre os Conflitos de Terra, Ambiente e Florestas e Fauna Bravia*. Maputo: Centro de Formação Jurídica e Judiciária.

Bauman, T. and R. Williams. 2004. The business of process: Research issues in managing indigenous decision-making and disputes in land. *AIATSIS Research Discussion Paper* No. 13. Canberra: Australian Institute of Aboriginal and Torres Strait Islander Studies.

Bebbington, T. 2009. *The New Extraction: Rewriting the Political Ecology of the Andes*. NACLA Report on the Americas. New York: North American Congress on Latin America.

Blomley, N. 2014. Making space for property. *Annals of the Association of American Geographers* 104(6): 1291–1306.

Börner, J., D. Schulz, S. Wunder and A. Pfaff. 2020. The effectiveness of forest conservation policies and programs. *Annual Review of Resource Economics* 12 (Oct 2020): 45–64.

Borras, S.M., D. Fig, and S.M. Suárez. 2011. The politics of agrofuels and mega-land and water deals: Insights from the ProCana case, Mozambique. *Review of African Political Economy* 38(138): 215–234.

Cabral, L. and S. Norfolk. 2016. Inclusive land governance in Mozambique: Good law, bad politics? *IDS Working Paper* No. 478. Available at: https://opendocs.ids.ac.uk/opendocs/bitstream/handle/20.500.12413/12187/Wp478.pdf?sequence=1 (accessed May 20, 2020).

CFS and FAO. 2012. *Voluntary Guidelines on the Responsible Governance of Tenure of Land, Fisheries and Forests in the Context of National Food Security*. Rome: Committee on World Food Security and the Food and Agriculture Organization of the United Nations.

Chilundo, A., B. Cau, M. Mubai, D. Malauene and V. Muchanga. 2005. *Research Report 6: Land Registration in Nampula and Zambezia Provinces, Mozambique*. London: International Institute for Environment and Development.

Chirif Tirado, A. and P. García Hierro. 2007. *Marcando Territorio: Progresos y Limitaciones de la Titulación de Territorios Indígenas en la Amazonía*. Copenhagen: International Work Group for Indigenous Affairs.

Chirif Tirado, A., P.G. Hierro, and R.C. Smith. 1991. *El Indígena y Su Territorio Son Uno Solo: Estrategias para la Defensa de Los Pueblos y Territorios Indígenas en la Cuenca Amazonica*. Lima: Oxfam America and COICA.

Cleaver, J., R. Schram, and G. Wanga. 2010. Bioenergy in Tanzania: The country context. In *Bioenergy and Food Security: The BEFS Analysis for Tanzania*, 23–45. *Environment and Natural Resources Management Working Paper* No. 35. Rome: FAO. Available at: http://www.fao.org/bioenergy/21031-02ea135adb6370b32c694cc820c6fdbd5.pdf (accessed Nov. 25, 2020).

Colchester, M. 2001. *A Survey of Indigenous Land Tenure*. Rome: Food and Agriculture Organization of the United Nations.

Colchester, M. 2004. Conservation policy and indigenous peoples. *Environmental Science and Policy* 7(3): 145–153.

Colchester, M. 2010. *Free, Prior and Informed Consent: Making FPIC Work for Forests and Peoples*. New Haven, CT: The Forests Dialogue.

Colchester, M. and F. MacKay. 2004. *In Search of Middle Ground: Indigenous Peoples, Collective Representation and the Right to Free, Prior and Informed Consent*. Moreton-in-Marsh, UK: Forest Peoples Programme.

Conklin, B.A. and L.R. Graham. 1995 The shifting middle ground: Amazonian Indians and eco-politics. *American Anthropologist* 97(4): 695–710.

Cronkleton, P. and A. Larson. 2015. Formalization and collective appropriation of space on forest frontiers: Comparing communal and individual property systems in the Peruvian and Ecuadoran Amazon. *Society and Natural Resources* 28(5): 496–512.

Dean, M. 2010. *Governmentality: Power and Rule in Modern Society*, 2nd Ed. London: Sage.

Deininger, K., D. Byerlee, J. Lindsay, A. Norton, H. Selod and M. Stickler. 2011. *Rising Global Interest in Farmland: Can it Yield Sustainable and Equitable Benefits?* Washington, DC: World Bank.

de Jong, E.B.P., L. Knippenberg and L. Bakker. 2017. New frontiers: An enriched perspective on extraction frontiers in Indonesia. *Critical Asian Studies* 49(3): 330–348.

Delgado, R. and J. Stefancic. 2017. *Critical Race Theory: An Introduction*. New York: New York University Press.

de Soto, H. 2000. *The Mystery of Capital: Why Capitalism Triumphs in the West and Fails Everywhere Else*. London: Basic Books.

de Soto, H. 2003. Listening to the barking dogs: property law against poverty in the non-West. *Focaal—European Journal of Anthropology* 41(2003): 179–185.

De Wit, P. and S. Norfolk. 2010. *Recognizing Rights to Natural Resources in Mozambique*. Washington, DC: Rights and Resources Initiative.

Ding, H., P. Veit, A. Blackman, E. Gray, K. Reytar, J.C. Altamirano and B. Hodgdon. 2016. *Climate Benefits, Tenure Costs: The Economic Case for Securing Indigenous Land Rights in the Amazon*. Washington, DC: World Resources Institute.

Fairbairn, M. 2013. Indirect dispossession: Domestic power imbalances and foreign access to land in Mozambique. *Development and Change* 44(2): 335–356.

FAO. 2014. *Respecting Free, Prior and Informed Consent: Practical Guidance for Governments, Companies, NGOs, Indigenous Peoples and Local Communities in Relation to Land Acquisition*. Rome: Food and Agriculture Organization of the United Nations.

FAO. 2015. *Safeguarding Land Tenure Rights in the Context of Agricultural Investment*. Rome: Food and Agriculture Organization of the United Nations.

FAO and FILAC. 2021. *Forest Governance by Indigenous and Tribal Peoples: An Opportunity for Climate Action in Latin America and the Caribbean*. Santiago, Chile: FAO.

FAO, IFAD, UNCTAD, and the World Bank Group. 2010. *Principles for Responsible Agricultural Investment that Respects Rights, Livelihoods and Resources (Extended Version)*. Rome, New York and Washington, DC: FAO, IFAD, UNCTAD and the World Bank Group.

Filipe, E. and S. Norfolk. 2017. *Understanding Changing Land Issues for the Rural Poor in Mozambique*. London: International Institute for Environment and Development.

Finer, M., C.N. Jenkins, S.L. Pimm, B. Keane, and C. Ross. 2008. Oil and gas projects in the western Amazon: Threats to wilderness, biodiversity, and indigenous peoples. *PLOS One* 3(8): e2932.

FPP. 2016. Effective participation and Free, Prior and Informed Consent. Moreton-in-Marsh, UK: Forest Peoples Programme. Available at: https://www.forestpeoples.org/sites/fpp/files/publication/2016/03/fpp-fpic-not-fpicon-final.pdf (accessed Apr. 12, 2022).

Franco, J. 2014. *Reclaiming Free, Prior and Informed Consent (FPIC) in the Context of Global Land Grabs*. London: The Transnational Institute.

German, L. and C.M.T. Braga. 2019. Decentering emergent truths on tenure security: Archaeology of a global knowledge regime. *Journal of Peasant Studies* 48(6): 1228–1259.

German, L., E. Cavane, A. Sitoe, and C. Braga. 2016. Private investment as an engine of rural development: A confrontation of theory and practice for the case of Mozambique. *Land Use Policy* 51(2016): 1–14.

German, L., G.C. Schoneveld, and E. Mwangi. 2013. "Contemporary processes of large-scale land acquisition in Sub-Saharan Africa: Legal deficiency or elite capture of the rule of law?" *World Development* 48(2013): 1–18.

Gordon, C. 1991. Governmental rationality: An introduction. In: G. Burchell, C. Gordon and P. Miller (Eds.), *The Foucault Effect: Studies in Governmentality*, 1–51. Chicago: University of Chicago Press.

Greene, S. 2006. Getting over the Andes: The geo-eco-politics of indigenous movements in Peru's twenty-first century Inca Empire. *Journal of Latin American Studies* 38(2): 327–354.

Griffiths, T. 2007. *Exigiendo Responsabilidad al BID y la CFI en Camisea II: Una Revisión de Estándares Internacionales Aplicables, y Diligencia y Conformidad Debidas*. San Francisco: Amazon Watch.

Habib-Mintz, N. 2010. Biofuel investment in Tanzania: Omissions in implementation. *Energy Policy* 38(2010): 3985–3997.

Hanlon, J. 2004. Renewed land debate and the 'cargo cult' in Mozambique. *Journal of Southern African Studies* 30(3): 603–626.

Hanlon, J. 2011. *Mozambique Political Process Bulletin* 48(February 22, 2011). Available at: http://www.open.ac.uk/technology/mozambique/sites/www.open.ac.uk.technology.mozambique/files/pics/d128132.pdf (accessed May 17, 2020).

Hearn, K. 2008. 'For Peru's Indians, Lawsuit Against Big Oil Reflects a New Era'. *Washington Post* January 31, 2008. Available at: http://www.washingtonpost.com/wp-dyn/content/article/2008/01/30/AR2008013003744.html (accessed Sept. 6, 2018).

Hilgers, M. 2010. The three anthropological approaches to neoliberalism. *International Social Science Journal* 61(202): 351–364.

Hodgson, D.L. 2009. Becoming Indigenous in Africa. *African Studies Review* 52(3): 1–32.

Hull, S. and J. Whittal. 2018. Filling the gap: Customary land tenure reform in Mozambique and South Africa. *South African Journal of Geomatics* 7(2): 102–117.

Hvalkof, S. 2002. Beyond indigenous land titling: Democratizing civil society in the Peruvian Amazon. In: J. Chase (Ed.), *The Spaces of Neoliberalism: Land, Place and Family in Latin America*, 87–116. Bloomfield, CT: Kumarian Press.

IBC. 2016. *Tierras Comunales: Más que Preservar el Pasado es Asegurar el Futuro, El Estado de las Comunidades Indígenas en el Perú (Informe 2016).* Lima: Instituto del Bien Común.

IG and RRI. 2015. *Respecting Land and Forest Rights: A Guide for Companies.* Washington, DC: The Interlaken Group and the Rights and Resources Initiative.

ILC. 2012. *ILC's Approach to Indigenous Peoples' Issues.* Rome: International Land Coalition. Available at: https://www.landcoalition.org/en/resources/ILCs_Approach_to_Indigenous_Peoples_Issues/ (accessed Nov. 25, 2020).

ILC. 2016. *2016–2021.* Rome: International Land Coalition. Available at: http://www.landcoalition.org/sites/default/files/documents/resources/web_en_strategic_framework_2016-2021_spread.pdf (accessed Feb. 15, 2017).

ILO. 1989. *Indigenous and Tribal Peoples Convention, 1989.* Geneva, Switzerland: International Labor Organization.

Kanji, N., C. Braga and W. Mitullah. 2002. *Promoting land rights in Africa: How do NGOs Make a Difference?* London: International Institute for Environment and Development.

Larsen, P.B. 2016. The 'New Jungle Law': Development, indigenous rights and ILO Convention 169 in Latin America. *International Development Policy / Revue Internationale de Politique de Développement* (Online) 7.1.

Larson, A.M. 2008. Indigenous peoples, representation and citizenship in Guatemalan forestry. *Conservation and Society* 6(1): 35–48.

Larson, A.M., I. Monterroso, and P. Cronkleton. 2017. *Collective Titling in the Peruvian Amazon: A History in Three Acts.* Bogor, Indonesia: Center for International Forestry Research.

Larson, A.M., I. Monterroso, and N.H. Vigil. 2019. Conflict in collective forest tenure: Lessons for Peru from a comparative study. *CIFOR Infobrief* No. 243.

Lay, J., W. Anseeuw, S. Eckert, et al. 2021. *Taking Stock of the Global Land Rush. Analytical Report III.* Bern, Montpellier, Hamburg, Pretoria: CDE, University of Bern, CIRAD, German Institute for Global and Area Studies, University of Pretoria, Bern Open Publishing.

Leeds, S. 2000. The burning of Blackacre: A step toward reclaiming tribal property law. *Kansas Journal of Law and Public Policy* 10(3): 491–504.

Little, P. 2014. *Megaprojects in the Amazon Region: A Geopolitical and Socio-environmental Analysis with Proposals of Better Government for the Amazon.* Lima: DAR.

MacInnes, A., M. Colchester, and A. Whitmore. 2017. Free, Prior and Informed Consent: How to rectify the devastating consequences of harmful mining for Indigenous peoples. *Perspectives in Ecology and Conservation* 15(3): 152–160.

Manji, A.S. (2006.) *The Politics of Land Reform in Africa: From Communal Tenure to Free Markets.* London: Zed Books.

Manuel, L. and A. Salomão. 2009. Biofuels and land rights in Mozambique: The Pro-Cana case. *Haramata* 54: 17–19.

Matável, N., S. Dolores, and V. Cabanelas. 2011. *Lords of the Land: Preliminary Analysis of the Phenomenon of Land Grabbing in Mozambique.* Maputo, Mozambique:

Justiça Ambiental and União Nacional dos CamponesesMcAuslan, P. 2013. *Land Law Reform in Eastern Africa: Traditional or Transformative? A Critical Review of 50 Years of Land Law Reform in Eastern Africa, 1961–2011*. London : Routledge.

Mei, G. and M. Alabrese. 2013. Communities' Ability in Consultations and Land Transactions: Improving the "Empowering Effect" of Tenure Security Initiatives in Rural Mozambique. Paper presented at the World Bank Conference on Land and Poverty, Washington, DC, Apr. 8–11, 2013. Available at: https://namati.org/wp-content/uploads/2017/04/Mei-2013_Mozamb-Comm-land-CaseSts.pdf (accessed May 20, 2020).

Mendez, L.H. 2015. 'Quinto paquetazo normativo o la expropriación sin límites'. America Latina en Movimiento, July 10, 2015. Available at: https://www.alainet.org/es/articulo/172876 (accessed Sept. 6, 2019).

Merino, R. 2015. Coloniality and indigenous territorial rights in the Peruvian Amazon: A critique of the Prior Consultation Law. *Bath Papers in International Development and Wellbeing* No. 38. Bath, UK: The Centre for Development Studies.

Merino, R. 2017. Law and politics of indigenous self-determination: The meaning of the right to prior consultation. In: I. Watson (Ed.), *Indigenous Peoples as Subjects of International Law*, 120–140. London: Routledge.

Merino, R. 2018. Re-politicizing participation or reframing environmental governance? Beyond indigenous prior consultation and citizen participation. *World Development* 111(2018): 75–83.

Merino, R. 2019. Rethinking Indigenous politics: The unnoticed struggle for self-determination in Peru. *Bulletin of Latin American Research* 39(4): 513–528.

Merino, R. 2020. Rethinking Indigenous politics: The unnoticed struggle for self-determination in Peru. *Bulletin of Latin American Research* 39(4): 513–528.

Merino, R. 2021a. *Buen vivir* and the making of Indigenous territories in the Peruvian Amazon. *Latin American Perspectives* 238(48, 3): 136–151.

Merino, R. 2021b. *Socio-Legal Struggles for Self-Determination: Reimagining the Nation, Reinventing the State*. London: Routledge.

Merino, R. and M.-T. Gustafsson. 2021. Localizing the indigenous environmental steward norm: The making of conservation and territorial rights in Peru. *Environmental Science and Policy* 124 (2021): 627–634.

Milgroom, J. 2015. Policy processes of a land grab: At the interface of politics "in the air" and politics "on the ground" in Massingir, Mozambique. *The Journal of Peasant Studies* 42(3–4): 585–606.

Miller, P. and N. Rose. 2008. *Governing the Present*. Malden, MA: Polity Press.

Mkindi, A.R. 2008. Impact of jatropha trade in Tanzania. Dar es Salaam, Tanzania: Environmental, Human Rights Care and Gender Organization.

Monterroso, I., P. Cronkleton, D. Pinedo, and A.M. Larson. 2017. Reclaiming collective rights: Land and forest tenure reforms in Peru (1960–2016). *Working Paper #224*. Bogor, Indonesia: Center for International Forestry Research.

Nhantumbo, I. and A. Salomão. 2010. *Biofuels, Land Access and Rural Livelihoods in Mozambique*. London and Maputo: IIED and CTV.

Nolte, K. and L. Voget-Kleschin. 2014. Consultation in large-scale land acquisitions: An evaluation of three cases in Mali. *World Development* 64(2014): 654–668.

Norfolk, S. and C. Tanner. 2007. Improving tenure security for the rural poor, Mozambique. *Legal Empowerment of the Poor Working Paper* No. 5. Rome: Food and Agriculture Organization of the United Nations. Available at: http://www.fao.org/nr/lten/abst/lten_080601_en.htm (accessed May 17, 2020).

Nuñes Palomino, P.D. 1985. *Law and Peasant Communities in Peru (1969–1988)*. Doctoral dissertation, Wageningen University.

Overbeek, W. 2010. *The Expansion of Tree Monocultures in Mozambique: Impacts on Local Peasant Communities in the Province of Niassa*. Montevideo, Argentina: World Rainforest Movement. Available at: https://wrm.org.uy/wp/wp-content/uploads/2013/01/Book_Mozambique.pdf (accessed May 17, 2020).

Peluso, N. and C. Lund. 2011. New frontiers of land control: Introduction. *The Journal of Peasant Studies* 38(4): 667–681.

Petkar, I. 2017. *Conceptualizing Free, Prior and Informed Consent: Interpreting Interpretations of FPIC*. Thesis submitted in partial fulfillment of the requirements of a Master of Arts, Colombia University.

Plant, R. and S. Hvalkof. 2001. *Land Titling and Indigenous Peoples*. Washington, DC: Inter-American Development Bank.

Porsani, J. and R. Lalander. 2018. Why does deliberative community consultation in large-scale land acquisitions fail? A critical analysis of Mozambican experiences. *Iberoamerican Journal of Development Studies* 7(2): 164–193.

Porsani, J., L. Börjeson and K. Lehtilä. 2017. Land concessions and rural livelihoods in Mozambique: The gap between anticipated and real benefits of Chinese investment in the Limpopo Valley. *Journal of Southern African Studies* 43(6): 1181–1198.

Republic of Mozambique. 1995. *National Land Policy, Resolution 10/95*. Maputo, Mozambique: Boletím da República.Republic of Mozambique. 1997. *Lei de Terras (Lei no 19/97)*. Maputo, Mozambique: Boletím da República.

Republic of Mozambique. 1998. *Regulamento da Lei de Terras (Decreto 66/98)*. Maputo, Mozambique: Boletím da República.

Republic of Mozambique. 2000. *Anexo Técnico ao Regulamento da Lei de Terras (Diploma Ministerial 29-A/2000)*. Maputo, Mozambique: Boletím da República.

Republic of Peru. 1920. *Constitución para la República del Perú*. Lima: Republic of Peru.

Ribeiro, D. and N. Matável. 2009. *Jatropha! A Socioeconomic Pitfall for Mozambique*. Maputo, Mozambique: Justiça Ambiental and União Nacional de Camponeses.

Robinson, B.E., Y.J. Masuda, A. Kelly, et al. 2017. Incorporating land tenure security into conservation. *Conservation Letters* 11(2): 1–12.

RRI. 2015. *Who Owns the World's Land? A Global Baseline of Formally Recognized Indigenous and Community Land Rights*. Washington, DC: Rights and Resources Initiative.

Salcedo-La Viña, C. and M. Morarji. 2016. Making women's voices count in community decision-making on land investments. *Working Paper*. Washington, DC: World

Resources Institute. Available at: https://www.issuelab.org/resources/25829/25829.pdf (accessed Nov. 25, 2020).

Schilling-Vacaflor, A. and R. Flemmer. 2015. Conflict transformation through prior consultation? Lessons from Peru. *Journal of Latin American Studies* 47(4): 811–839.

Sitoe, A. 2009. Governação florestal em Niassa: O caso de muembe, sanga, lago e cuamba. Maputo, Mozambique: Associação Rural de Ajuda Mútua.

Smith, R. 2002. Los indígenas Amazónicos suben al scenario internacional: Reflexiones sobre el accidentado camino recorrido. In: F. Morin and R. Santana (Eds.), *Lo Transnacional: Instrumental y Desafio para los Pueblos Indigenas*, 203–242. Quito, Ecuador: Abya Yala.

Smith, R. 2005. Can David and Goliath have a happy marriage? The Machiguenga people and the Camisea Gas Project in the Peruvian Amazon. In: P.J. Brosius, A.L. Tsing, and C. Zerner (Eds.), *Communities and Conservation: Histories and Politics of Community-Based Natural Resource Management*, 231–255. Walnut Creek, CA: AltaMira Press.

Smith, R. 2020. We are here: The state of community-based landscapes in Peru. In: N. Robins and B. Fraser (Eds.), *Landscapes of Inequity: Environmental Justice in the Andes-Amazon Region*, 229–264. Lincoln, NE: University of Nebraska Press.

Stevens, C., R. Winterbottom, J. Springer and K. Reytar. 2014. *Securing Rights, Combating Climate Change: How Strengthening Community Forest Rights Mitigates Climate Change*. Washington, DC: World Resources Institute.

Sulle, E. and F. Nelson. 2009. *Biofuels, Land Access and Rural Livelihoods in Tanzania*. London: International Institute for Environment and Development.

Tanner, C. 2002. Land rights and enclosures: Implementing the Mozambican Land Law in practice. In: W. Anseeuw and C. Alden (Eds.), *The Struggle Over Land in Africa: Conflict, Politics and* Change, 105–130. Cape Town: HSRC Press.

Tanner, C. and S. Baleira. 2004. *A Legislação Sobre o Acesso aos Recursos Naturais em Moçambique: O Impacto das Novas Leis e das Consultas Comunitárias Sobre o Bem-Estar a Nível Local*. Matola, Mozambique: Centro de Formação Jurídica Judiciária and FAO.

Tanner, C., P. de Wit and S. Madureira. 1998. Proposta para um programa de delineação das comunidades locais. FAO Project GCP/MOZ/059/NET. Document presented on the National Seminar on Community Land Delimitation and Management, Beira, Sofala Province, 12–14 August 1998.

UN. 2007. *United Nations Declaration on the Rights of Indigenous Peoples*. New York: United Nations.

UN. 2018. *United Nations Declaration on the Rights of Peasants and Other People Working in Rural Areas*. Geneva: United Nations Human Rights Council.

UNPFII. 2005. *Report of the International Workshop on Methodologies regarding Free, Prior and Informed Consent and Indigenous Peoples*. Fourth Session of the United Nations Permanent Forum on Indigenous Issues, New York, 16–27 May, 2005. https://undocs.org/E/C.19/2005/3.

UNPFII. 2018. Indigenous Peoples' Collective Rights to Lands, Territories and Resources. Seventeenth Session of the United Nations Permanent Forum on Indigenous Issues, New York, 16–27 April, 2018. Available at: https://www.un.org/en/ga/search/view_doc.asp?symbol=E/C.19/2018/5 (accessed Nov. 21, 2020).

USAID. 2015. *Operational Guidelines for Responsible Land-Based Investment.* Washington, DC: United States Agency for International Development.

Valdivia, G. 2005. On indigeneity, change, and representation in the northeastern Ecuadorian Amazon. *Environment and Planning A: Society and Space* 37(2): 285–303.

Valdivia, G. 2007. The "Amazonian trial of the century": Indigenous identities, transnational networks, and petroleum in Ecuador. *Alternatives* 32(2007): 41–72.

Wacquant, L. 2012. Three steps to a historical anthropology of actually existing neoliberalism. *Social Anthropology / Anthropologie Sociale* 20(2012): 166–79.

Waterhouse, R., G. Lauriciano and S. Norfolk. 2010. Social analysis of selected projects: Large-scale land acquisition for agricultural production, Mozambique. Background study for the World Bank. Available at: https://www.open.ac.uk/technology/mozambique/sites/www.open.ac.uk.technology.mozambique/files/pics/d128185.pdf (accessed May 17, 2020).

White, R. 1991. *The Middle Ground: Indians, Empires, and Republics in the Great Lakes Region, 1650–1815.* Cambridge: Cambridge University Press.

Wolfe, P. 2006. Settler colonialism and the elimination of the native. *Journal of Genocide Research* 8(4): 387–409.

World Bank. 2014. The practice of responsible investment principles in larger-scale agricultural investments: Implications for corporate performance and impact on local communities. *Agriculture and Environmental Services Discussion Paper* 08. Washington, DC: World Bank.

World Bank. 2017. *The World Bank Environmental and Social Framework.* Washington, DC: The World Bank.

CHAPTER 5

Contested Ontologies of Security

> Thinking about land has been and remains largely ethnocentric . . . Rarely has anyone gone as far as to ask what we mean by the terms "land", "tenure" and "rights." The notion of "land tenure" may have distorted as much as it has clarified . . . Only by asking "what is land" can a reasonable cross-cultural comparison of land practices be begun . . . "Tenure" presents even more difficulty because it contains a more tangled ambiguity than does "land." It assumes that "land" . . . can be "held."
>
> —Bohannan (1963: 1)

The centrality of "tenure security" as a conceptual underpinning of land governance discourse and practice is evident just about anywhere one looks, from the Voluntary Guidelines on the Responsible Governance of Tenure of Land, Fisheries and Forests in the Context of National Food Security (CFS and FAO 2012) to the Framework and Guidelines on Land Policy in Africa (AUC-ECA-AfDB Consortium 2010) and the discursive and programmatic engagements of the donor community with land governance.[1] The African Union's Declaration on Land Issues and Challenges in Africa identifies strengthening security of land tenure for women as one of two key aims of land governance on the continent, and the global community is moving quickly, not just to codify tenure security through a narrow set of indicators, but to have these indicators taken up and used to evaluate tenure security and the impact of land governance interventions globally.[2] But what exactly does it mean, and to whom? And what is the consequence of codifying it in specific ways and having land policies and programs align to advance these conceptions? This chapter draws on social theory, dominant land governance discourses, and ethnographic evidence from across Africa to explore these questions.

Anthropologists have long sought to relativize and challenge Eurocentric perspectives by bringing emic or "insider" perspectives to bear on "assumptions that may seem self-evident, even absolute" (Holbraad and

Pedersen 2017: 2). Recent social scientific scholarship takes this a step further by calling into question "one's assumptions about what any given object or term of inquiry might *be*" (Holbraad and Pedersen 2017: 2). This is not just an academic exercise. Social scientists have long shown how ideas we hold about the world—whether categories of people ("poor," "unproductive," "oppressed"), environmental conditions ("degraded," "pristine") or notions of progress ("developed," "modern")—make the world by shaping our engagements with it, and by normalizing the actions of the powerful (Abu-Lughod 2002; Chakrabarty 1992; Escobar 1988; Fairhead and Leach 1996; Spivak 1993). Efforts to get ahead of the game and establish a semantic field through which the world is brought to think about things in certain ways (and thus foreclosing other ways)—establishing the concepts through which the world is thought, defining those concepts in certain ways, codifying them for their measurement—is thus just as much an exercise of power as any other. The amount of money flowing into land governance discourses, dialogue, evidence and tools, and the proliferation of cooperative and multi-stakeholder initiatives in the land sector, suggests there is indeed interest in defining the field of thought and action. The best way for those operating from inside those knowledge practices to "see" them is to relativize them—to explore alternative conceptions and worlds that are bracketed out by them. For this, the call for reflexivity (to question our very assumptions about "what is x?" in acts of interpretation and translation) in ontological anthropology (Holbraad and Pedersen 2017: 11), combined with ethnographic data to contrast dominant concepts and ontological assumptions with marginalized ones (from global Norths and Souths), provide a powerful set of tools to step outside of the concepts we think with. I say "we" because I, too, lived in that world for a time.

ONTOLOGIES OF TENURE SECURITY IN THE INTERNATIONAL DEVELOPMENT COMMUNITY

The Land Portal Foundation, a public benefit organization registered in the Netherlands whose mission is "to create, curate and disseminate land governance information,"[3] defines "security of tenure" as the certainty that a person's rights to land will be recognized by others and protected in cases of specific challenges.[4] A review of selected websites and publications from the international development community points to a number of assumptions that flow from this idea which border on the ontological—or questions of what *is*.

First, social relations tend to be seen as a factor undermining security of tenure, with both customary tenure and gender norms viewed or portrayed as threats. This appears to stem from the priority of the individual as opposed to a social person, and the corresponding emphasis by the World Bank and others on *private*, ideally *individualized* and *alienable*, rights to land as the basis for tenure security. This may also be seen within evolutionary theories of land rights, which have long framed "traditional" landholding systems as static and inflexible in the face of changing economic conditions (Yngstrom 2002; see also Platteau 1996; Williams 1994; World Bank 1989). In a more recent example, the Gender in Agriculture Sourcebook of the World Bank, FAO, and IFAD (2008) frames cultural norms as a key impediment to land rights, finding "local prohibitions against women's ownership of land . . . often more powerful than written laws that allow women to own land" (127). The text goes on to explain that,

> As secondary community members, [women's] rights to land are generally derived from a man relative or husband. In many countries, cultural if not legal norms dictate that men are the owners of land and that women have access to land only through their relationship with a man relative, such as a father, husband, brother, or even brother-in-law. Although customary tenure systems often do provide women with some basic security in situations when they are not living with a husband, this same system also favors men when control over land is determined. (127)

It is not just relations with the "customary," but also marital relations and communal ownership which are posed as threats. The text states that, "When land is acquired by a couple, . . . the husband assumes sole ownership, excluding his wife from any ownership rights" (World Bank et al. 2008: 126) and "women's rights to land and other resources may not be recognized" in community titling (Bank et al. 2008: 134).

This narrative is widespread in the international development arena, and often based on questionable evidence. Landesa, for example, has sought to quantify the problem by drawing on an OECD database of countries with "*some* customary, traditional or religious practices that discriminate against women," using this evidence to declare that there are 90 countries where "*customs inhibit women's access to land*" (emphasis added).[5] This narrative has been picked up by a host of organizations on the front lines of efforts to advance tenure security worldwide, with *Her Land, Her Story*—a campaign organized by the Cadasta Foundation and the Land Portal—framing women's vulnerability as a problem of "laws or customs [that] undermine or block women's rights to own, manage, or inherit land or property."[6] The attainment of gender equity is said to rest on "overcoming social and cultural constraints" (World Bank, FAO, and IFAD 2008: 130); "independent and transferable rights to land;"[7] and "secure access to land and other natural resources for women, *independent of men relatives* and independent of their civil status" (World Bank, FAO, and IFAD 2008: 126, emphasis added). Such prescriptions say more about Western values (of individualism) than the needs of women, and suggests that nothing less than the break-up of customary tenures at the level of the descent group and even the household.

Secondly, tenure security in these narratives is seen as best advanced through formal state recognition. Embedded in this idea are ontologies of the "state"—conceived of as a neutral arbiter of rights and thus superior to "custom" in guaranteeing security. Security is equated with state-sanctioned rights not just for the World Bank,[8] but for top land donors and the UN system at large. The linkage between tenure security and state sanctioning of rights was recently codified in the indicators advanced for measuring progress against the Sustainable Development Goals, for example, in which "legally recognized documentation" is identified as a key indicator of tenure security. The Global Donor Working Group on Land has been lobbying to move these indicators to "Tier I status" (GDWGL 2018),[9] which would have entrenched this stance through the systematic collection of information on tenure security indicators for at least 50% of the population in at least 50% of countries globally by 2020.[10]

A third ontological orientation in land discourses conceives of land as a discrete entity, abstracted from the social and ecological relations in which it is embedded (Bonanno, Foster, and German 2019). Flowing from this, alienability of land is seen as a feature capable of enhancing tenure security. Let me say that again: land alienability as *advancing* security. The crucial question here is, "whose security of tenure, exactly, is of concern?" With a full 25% of the VGGT text dedicated to transfers and changes to tenure rights, it is clear that it is not just customary land users.[11] Here it is easy to see how narratives of tenure security can be advanced in the same historical moment, and often in the same breath, alongside land markets and codes of conduct for "responsible" land transactions via mechanisms for investors to negotiate long-term, exclusive rights to customary land via consultations and contracts with local land users or their presumed representatives (AUC-ECA-AfDB Consortium 2010; FAO 2015; FAO et al. 2010; IG and RRI 2015; New Alliance for Food Security and Nutrition in Africa and Grow Africa 2015; USAID 2015). Thus, the link between "tenure security," the low-cost transfer of land through rentals and sales markets, and "improved land allocation" as articulated by the World Bank's leading land economist nearly 20 years ago (Deininger 2003: xix), has now gained traction in global land governance instruments, from the VGGTs to the SDGs.

ALTERNATIVE ONTOLOGIES OF SECURITY

> The existence of a right is best understood in terms of a power which society allocates to its various members to execute a particular range or quantum of functions in respect of any given subject matter. Where that power coincides with or amounts to exclusive control of that subject matter it is normal or ordinary to talk of the existence of ownership (Honoré 1961) and that subject matter as property. And yet it would appear to be self-evident . . . that it is not essential to or even prudent in all human relationships that a coincidence of power and exclusivity of control in any individual or group of individuals in respect of all contexts, things or objects should exist. . . . Nowhere is this more clearly the case than in respect of land in Africa.
>
> —Okoth-Ogendo (1989: 7–8)

This section draws on ethnographies of land in Africa to explore how land and tenure security are conceived of otherwise, and to provincialize the narrow conceptions advanced within dominant framings. Given the distinctive logics of land use and occupation under different livelihood systems, I explore ontologies of land and security in ethnographies of both agricultural and pastoralist societies before looking across them at elements that connect them. With the ontological evidence decidedly patchy, I turn to those sources that provide the clearest evidence irrespective of publication date. While this brings in somewhat dated evidence and may suggest an assumption that what was true in the past remains true today, I triangulate with contemporary sources to interrogate such assumptions. It is also important to acknowledge that customary land relations (and the ontologies attached to them) are not just a product of "historical and political factors associated with the post-colonial style of governance" (Chauveau and Colin 2010: 99), but the affordances of local ecologies and the land use systems that are viable therein. This may lend to them a certain character of stability borne out of necessity, or multifaceted unravelings, contestations, and counter-mobilizations in the face of rapid economic and political change (e.g., Blewett 1995; Bollig and Lesorogol 2016; Galaty 2016).

Ontologies of Land and Security among Agriculturalists

A number of rich ethnographic studies provide insights into ontologies of land and security among Africa's horticultural and agricultural societies. Max Gluckman's research in the 1930s among Lozi agriculturalists living on the margins of the Upper Zambezi River, while more normative than ontological, is one of the most widely known accounts. Lozi farmers were found to hold conceptions of land tenure akin to ownership at the time of his research, and considered all land and its products the property of the nation through the king. Gluckman found Lozi citizenship to confer the rights to build, to arable land, and to the use of public lands for grazing and fishing, yet for it to be "by the king's bounty that his subjects live on and by the land" (Gluckman 1965: 37). Lozi commoners thus thought of themselves as permanently indebted to the king for the land and resources that sustained them, and often refused payment for goods he acquired from them. The king's rights entitled him to demand allegiance from those who settled on Lozi land; to distribute any land that had not been previously allocated; to expropriate land for public services, provided he asked permission and replacement land was provided; and to claim land that had been abandoned or for which heirs could not be traced. Yet in exchange, he held a number of corresponding duties: to give every subject land to live on and to cultivate; to bestow the rights to fish, hunt and gather natural resources; and to protect people's land against trespass and forced expropriation. This system of landholding propagated downward to lower levels of the hierarchy of kinship relations, through the granting of rights of administration to heads of villages—with landholding an inherent attribute of citizenship and each social position in the hierarchy. Ironically, Gluckman's analysis leaned toward the ontological only when he zoomed out to "tribal society" writ large. Here, he generalized in saying that ownership is not absolute, due to the role that property plays in,

> a nexus of specific relationships . . . Property law . . . defines *not so much rights of persons over things, as obligations owed between persons in respect of things* . . . Correspondingly, if new relationships are being established, this is done through transfers of property, which create and define these relationships . . . Material culture may be regarded as part of social relations, for ma-

> terial objects are chains along which social relationships run . . . Thus people not only create their material culture and attach themselves to it, but also build up their relationships through it and see them in terms of it. (Gluckman 1965: 45–46, emphasis added)

This example, while somewhat dated, helps to illustrate how conceptions of ownership over land, where they exist, may not be absolute, but rather part of the representation and constitution of social relationships, symbolic of membership in wider social groups, and reflective of social history. Research among other patrilineal groups reaffirm this emphasis on social relationships surrounding land. Paul Bohannan's research among Tiv shifting agriculturalists of West Africa, for example, suggests Tiv conceptions of geography are seen through the lens of genealogy (Bohannan 1963). Lineage members hold permanent rights in the genealogical map of their agnatic lineage, but the association of that social map with specific pieces of ground is only brief in duration. Tiv concepts of "land" include the layers *tar* (which holds people, their compounds and farms) and *nya* (earth); the former shifts locations with respect to *nya*, which is immutable. People hold permanent rights to *some* farm in the *tar*, and may be said to hold "farm tenure" but not "land tenure" (Bohannan 1963: 4). Tenure security is therefore anchored firmly in genealogical relations. And among the patrilineal Joluo of Kenya, *wuon lowo* ("owner") refers to those with rights to allocate land as well as those whose rights to land are guaranteed for an extended period of time, or "as long as the individual maintains the recognized relationship, for *it is this relationship that carries a proprietary right*" (Pala Okeyo 1980: 37, emphasis added).

More recent ethnographic accounts help to counter any assumption that alternative ontologies of land and security are purely a relic of the past. West and East African ethnographies continue to find land and place to be part and parcel of social identity. The first set of examples come from West Africa, where contemporary ethnographic accounts of ontologies of land and security are particularly rich. In the Dagara and Sisala villages in northwestern Ghana and neighboring Burkina Faso studied by Carola Lentz, settlement histories are used by horticulturalists to establish claims over territory (Lentz 2006b), and "the strongest claims of ownership are those that can be traced to the deep past"—with first-comer status conferring the most comprehensive rights over land (Lentz 2013: 2). These claims are not uncontested, with latecomers instead basing their claims on continuous use of the land. Yet spiritual relations tend to uphold the claims of firstcomers, who are "believed to have established a special relationship with the spirits of the land, thus playing a crucial role in 'opening up' the wild bush or forest for human settlement" (Lentz 2013: 49). First-comers established shrines for the spirits of the earth, bush, hills, and rivers, with the earth shrines regarded as the most powerful. Lentz summarizes their meaning and significance as follows:

> Earth shrines simultaneously constitute territorial cults and economic, social and political institutions. In a literal sense, they are containers for the earth deity and the spirits of the pioneers' ancestors that need to be regularly appealed to for blessing. And they are symbolic vessels that embody the local community's inextricable link with the land. (Lentz 2006b: 83)

This inextricable link to the land suggests that rights are vested first and foremost in the lineage of first-comers and inalienable. This interpretation is supported by the fact that the office of the earth priests—the designated custodians of these shrines—tends to be vested in the lineage of the first-comers. It is also supported by the inextricable relationship between place and belonging, in which land and community are inseparable (Lentz 2006b). Furthermore, some respondents were said to believe that rights to *use* the land can be ceded, but not full property rights, which would include the right to spiritual control over shrines. This suggests that it is the shrines and the ritual control over these shrines that are inalienable, and that the inalienability of property from the first-comer lineage is an artefact of these relationships (Lentz 2013). Ritual politics are therefore essential to defending, challenging, or redefining land tenure (Lentz 2006b).

It is also worth exploring the nature of the relationship between land users on the one hand, and earth shrines and priests and the spiritual realm mediated by them on the other. The earth shrines and their custodians are thought to provide spiritual protection and fertility to local residents; "in exchange for sacrifices that the earth priest offered on behalf of the community, the earth god was believed to grant the local community permission to exploit the natural resources and guarantee its material and spiritual well-being" (Lentz 2006b: 82). The spiritual realm is therefore not passive but agential, capable of intervening in human affairs; local residents, in turn, must behave in certain ways to appease the spirits and thereby ensure their own well-being. Similar relationships are found in Kissi and Kuranko-speaking farming communities of Guinea, where land spirits (*nina*) have their own parallel society with villages and settlements, and can make "unexpected physical attacks or outrageous demands" on humans (Fairhead and Leach 1996: 91, 106). Establishing territorial control, ensuring the success of farming and other productive activities, and securing human health and well-being requires establishing a "productive relationship" with these spirits through offerings, rituals, and abiding by established social-ecological norms. Within these ontologies, land has agency, with human fate tied to human relations to the land and the spirit world attached to it.

John Unruh's work in Sierra Leone addresses the ontological underpinnings of the "strong notion of the fundamental inalienability of land" in West Africa:

> The belief that land exists for the dead, the living, and the unborn (within the lineages), and so cannot be permanently alienated, is a significant feature of landholding in rural Sierra Leone—as it is elsewhere in West Africa—and strongly influences current land tenure. As a result, land transfers are problematic, although they are attempted, and the idea that most or all members of a lineage need to agree to any transfer is strong. In its extreme form . . . , it is impossible to get all family members together to agree to a transfer, because most of them are not yet born. In such a situation, any transfers that are made can easily be cast as illegitimate and the land reclaimed. (Unruh 2008: 103)

While transfers can occur and individualized rights to land are a growing phenomenon in the region, this tends to be the case primarily within the lineage rather than with outsiders. And in cases where such individualization becomes increasingly common within lineages, "it is here where sanctions against the rights of individuals to transfer land to outsiders without consulting holders of allodial title or lineage heads, are most strongly evoked" (Unruh 2008: 104, with reference to Hagberg 2006; Lentz 2006b; Lund 2006). This finding resonates with the work of Rosalie Kingwill from the Eastern Cape, South Africa, where those holding freehold title continue to regard the land as family property held by the unilineal descent group (Kingwill 2013).

On the other hand, it is possible to see how customary land relations are increasingly strained through interactions with the wider political economy of land. Unruh documents how land sales to outsiders are seen as a process of excluding youth from their customary entitlements and a feature of the less than legitimate formal system of land tenure. He interprets this attachment of youth to customary tenure constructs as a positive development for a segment of the population that comprises a potential source of instability in postwar Sierra Leone. Unruh also touches briefly on the ontological dimensions of the asset itself, which is implicated in both the inalienability of land and conceptions of security. Land is thought to keep on giving over time, and to outlive all owners and occupants. "Thus, regardless of how poor the agricultural season, or the occupants, there is an important 'element of continuation' regarding how land functions over generations, that is fundamental to food and personal security, livelihood, and identity" (Unruh 2008: 103).

Parker Shipton's 2009 book *Mortgaging the Ancestors: Ideologies of Attachment in Africa* profiles conceptions of land, security, and belonging for Nilotic Luo agriculturalists of western Kenya and their Bantu-speaking neighbors. Here, despite over a century of changes brought by colonial rule, population growth and land titling, conceptions of property remain closer to belonging or attachment than ownership. Here, "people do not just own or inherit land . . . ; they also belong to it. Belonging to land is part and parcel of belonging to other people—in groups, networks and open categories" (Shipton 2009: 111). Luo settlement in the region is naturalized in a myth of a giant serpent who led them up the Nile and appears from time to time to confirm to them that their home is the proper one (Whisson 1962). Graves, homestead sites, and clearings of ancestors are sacred sites and place markers for those who can claim descent from them, serving as "the very anchors of social identity" (Shipton 2009: 87). There is a multigenerational dimension to this anchoring, with graves and the land around them considered a sacred heritage belonging not just to the dead and the living but also the unborn. In Luoland and other parts of East Africa, "a family's land is entrusted to the living by their ancestors, with the understanding that it must be passed on to future generations" (Meinert, Willerslev, and Seebach 2017: 40); here, rights to the land are reaffirmed by a lineage's continued occupation of it. With the dead buried outside the doorways of homes, ancestors remain present, active forces in people's homes and lives, and are often thought to look after the unborn. These places on the landscape anchor people's membership in families and in larger groups, and Luo people "look upon graves and the old homestead sites of their forebears as their anchors—in time, in space, and in culture and society" (Shipton 2009: 14). Said somewhat differently, in "Luo country you *are* your land" (Shipton 2009: xii). Even social signifiers such as genealogical order and order of marriage (for wives) are written into the landscape in the form of homestead sites, with positions on the ground corresponding to a position in a genealogy (Shipton 2009: 91). Divisions between land and identity, the social and material, and the material and the mystical are thus blurred.

This does not mean that land transfers are not a feature of customary land relations. On the contrary, "swapping and long-term entrustment of land are customs as old as any in Luoland" (Shipton 2009: 124), and "land transfers between families, and invitations to live among the people on that land and their kind, are powerful ways of defining social identities" throughout the region (Shipton 2009: x). It is, rather, freehold tenure and its ties to alienability (through mortgage or permanent sale) that "challenges the attachments of rural-dwelling people to their kin, to ancestral lands, and through ancestors to divinity" (Shipton 2009: xi). When land is lost to lenders, these attachments to ancestors and place are lost, a process Luo people think of as raiding (Shipton 2009: 5). Yet in spite of the challenges formal alienability poses to customary land relations, these are not outdated conceptions eroding under modernizing influences. Rather, Shipton demonstrates a *heightened* importance of kinship and descent in the reckoning and defending of land claims under growing competition for land, and the ongoing use of graves as "tools of territoriality, and anchors of being" (Shipton 2009: 96).

A final example comes from a rare comparative study of local institutions and ontologies of land across five countries and six floodplains in Africa (Haller 2010, 2019), where predominant conceptions of land are embedded in notions akin to an area or territory inhabited by spiritual beings that influence human production and consumption. Here, land is not a discrete entity disconnected from other resources, but one element within concepts embodying multiple closely interconnected resources. This resonates with Hastings Okoth-Ogendo's observation that, "In Africa, . . . the soil per se often was and remains shrouded in mystery and ritual, the subject of a vocabulary that made very little distinction between it and the creatures which live upon it" (Okoth-Ogendo 1989: 8). Dominant notions of ownership were found to be absent, with the first-comers to an area seeing themselves not as owners of the land but rather those who first established contact with supernatural powers that could, if not respected, transform elements of the environment in ways harmful to people—such as illness, drought, or wildlife attack (Haller 2010). Security for these groups was found to be conceived not in purely economic terms, but also in political and supernatural terms. People were found to be concerned with a secure livelihood as well as the political security that an area, with all its resources, provided and reciprocal resource use within and between those occupying different territories was seen as a means of mitigating economic and political risks alike. For these floodplain societies, human relationships with the land are,

> seen as a kind of reciprocal arrangement of give and take based on the notion that spirits are the actual owners and that one is not alone in the territory. Another level is made up of the ancestral spirits who grant the use of the landscapes with their multiple interrelated resources. The interaction with these powers controlling the landscapes is organized via rituals and related offerings in order to make and renew spiritual contracts on the landscape. (Haller 2019: 8)

Here, once again, conceptions of land and tenure are wrapped up in the spiritual realm and deeply relational (to spirits and neighboring groups). Land is not a discrete entity but part of a complex of resources whose use is mediated by the spiritual realm and part of complex, overlapping claims and entitlements among first-comer (often hunter-gatherer and fishing communities) and late-comer (agricultural and pastoralist) groups.

Ecologies and Ontologies of Tenure Security among Pastoralists

For pastoralists, the spatial and temporal uncertainties of rainfall and forage resources demand an orientation to land use, and to tenure and livelihood security, that reflects the unique constraints this poses to human and livestock survival. Developed in symbiotic relationship to marginal ecological zones, pastoralism is evidence of the great capacity of humans to adapt to even the harshest of environments (Fratkin 1997; Galvin 2009; Scoones 1994). In the arid and semi-arid lands where pastoralism is found, rainfall is limited and highly variable across space and time. Availability of water and forage is shaped by these climatic patterns, and access to large territories is therefore essential to livestock survival and range rehabilitation. Tenure security can therefore only meaningfully be conceived of as processes through which that access is secured. Cultural behaviors observed to be widespread among pastoralists, including flexibility, mobility, and diversity of livestock species (Coughenour et al. 1985; Ellis and Swift 1988; Hjort 1981; Homewood and Rodgers 1991), must therefore be seen as environmental adaptations geared toward securing that access and buffering risks related to drought and livestock disease (Fratkin 1997). Yet mobility is not just good for pastoralists; it is also essential for rangeland regeneration (Kerven et al. 2008; Niamir-

Fuller 1999). And contrary to equilibrium perspectives in ecology which view pastoralists as disturbances to an otherwise pristine environment, there is a growing understanding of how rangeland ecology and pastoralism have co-evolved, with pastoralism a functional part of these ecosystems and necessary for their maintenance (Lambin et al. 2001; Oba, Stenseth, and Lusigi 2000).

Two examples from African rangelands help to illustrate the unique ways in which these environmental adaptations play out. Maasai pastoralists of eastern Africa traditionally coupled small, mobile herding units with the maintenance of far-reaching social relations throughout pastoralist society and beyond as means of adapting to the vagaries of semi-arid environments (Spear 1993). They have a "a multilevel governance structure at multiple and nested spatial scales" providing for flexible negotiation of access to water and pasture based on norms of reciprocity (Mwangi and Ostrom 2009: 202), and flexible mechanisms for livestock and household movement which occurs "within a framework of political relationships . . . by which shared exigencies are defined cooperatively . . . ; competitively . . . ; or both" (Spear and Waller 1993: 79). Age sets also unite men of a given age into a single social institution, with major ceremonies linked to the age-set system uniting all Maasai sections throughout their territory (Spencer 1993)—helping to cement a sense of shared social identity across units of residential organization and providing an additional framework for cooperation. Furthermore, a system of gerontocracy, which has been described as "the dominant premise of Maasai society" (Spencer 1993: 141), helps to cement the authority of elders and their grazing decisions (including, crucially, the designation and enforcement of "drought reserves") and thereby ensures the cooperation necessary for collective survival. Economic interdependencies with those practicing complementary modes of subsistence (farmers, hunter-gatherers) through individual networks of exchange and obligation; the tendency for language, culture, and institutions (e.g., clans and age-sets) to cut across ethnic boundaries; and ethnic mobility and fluidity serve as additional adaptive strategies which mitigate drought, disease, and warfare (Galaty 1993; Sobania 1993; Spear 1993; Waller 1984, 1993). Evidence of explicit ontologies of land are harder to find, outside of notions of land as "communal territory containing resources rather than as a resource which could be appropriated by individuals" (Spear and Waller 1993: 258). Yet it is clear that notions of ownership apply far more to livestock than land.

The Nuer, who reside in the swamps and open savanna along the Nile River within the current boundaries of South Sudan and Ethiopia, also rely on mobility over large areas to ensure the viability of their livelihoods and rangeland regeneration. Sir Edward Evans-Pritchard's 1940 ethnography of the Nuer reads as an iconic example of culture as environmental adaptation, in which livelihood activities and mobility are tightly coupled with environmental constraints and opportunities, and in turn supported by systems of social organization, institutions, and ideology. The Nuer migrate not just in search of water and pasture, but in response to annual flooding which drives them and their herds to seek higher ground in the rainy season and to flee this higher ground during drought. This migration is also essential to their diet, with the millet grown inland on slightly higher ground complementing the fish found in rivers distant from these areas. While war-related dislocations, the spread of the market economy, and Christianity have disrupted Nuer society and contributed to the growth of individualism, mobility continues to be essential to the viability of agropastoralism across Nuerland—buffering against the vagaries of pastoralism, such as livestock losses due to disease, conflict, and drought (Abdalla 2013; Hutchinson 1996).

Their social organization, like that of the Maasai, reflects this mobility imperative. "The vulnerability of cattle coupled with the large living space required for them are compatible only with . . . the existence of a tribal organization embracing a large territory, and some feeling of community over yet larger areas" (Evans-Pritchard 1940: 50). The largest political unit is the tribe, representing a unit with shared identity who at the time of Evans Pritchard's research affirmed "their obligation to combine in warfare against outsiders and acknowledge the rights of their members to compensation for injury" (Evans-Pritchard 1940: 5). This is also the primary unit around which notions of land tenure are centered—with each tribe having "its particular territory and owning and defending its own building sites, grazing, water supplies, and fishing-pools" (Evans-Pritchard 1940: 119), and a name which refers to both its members and to their territory. While opposition to neighboring tribes and "their feeling of superiority and the contempt they show for all foreigners and their readiness to fight them" (Evans-Pritchard 1940: 123) might suggest the tribal territory sets an upper limit on mobility, people often journey to visit kin in other tribes, receive hospitality and protection through diverse forms of kinship and affinity, and at times becoming permanently incorporated into them—often by becoming incorporated into the age-set system of the new tribe. Thus, while the borders of tribal belonging and territory are perhaps more strongly evident among the Nuer, the observed porosity of territory and identity is remarkably similar to the Maasai.

Within tribal boundaries, while each household owns its own food and provides independently for the needs of its members, land, its products, and economic life have long been characterized by sharing and reciprocity. The rights of homesteads to cultivate the land behind their homesteads is secondary to existing users, and newcomers may select a plot of land to farm through their relations to village members. At the time of Evans-Pritchard's study, meat was widely distributed, people were obliged to give part of their catch of fish to those who asked for it, and there was widespread assistance during times of shortage of milk or grain. "This habit of share and share alike is easily understandable in a community where everyone is likely to find himself in difficulties from time to time, for it is scarcity and not sufficiency that makes people generous, since everybody is thereby insured against hunger" (Evans-Pritchard 1940: 85). These relationships to land and its products suggest that property itself had a different meaning for the Nuer. "People not only create their material culture and attach themselves to it, but also build up their relationships through it and see them in terms of it" (Evans-Pritchard 1940: 89). For the Nuer, land and identity were thus inseparable; duties toward others tended to be elevated over rights; and land tenure and relationality were not just collective, but permeable in terms of both who belongs and to whom entitlements were extended. Furthermore, tenure and livelihood security were historically not enhanced through the hoarding of land and its products, but through emphasis on collective well-being and on material belongings as vehicles for strengthening social relations. While subsequent accounts of the Nuer emphasize the growing differentiation in identities, values, and livelihood strategies across Nuerland in interaction with the state and market economy (e.g., Hutchinson 1996), they lack the ethnographic and ontological depth to enable a more contemporary account of these notions of land and property.

These examples demonstrate how conceptions of tenure security grounded in bounded territorial units and social identities, and exclusive rights, can only be conceived of as undermining pastoralist tenure and livelihood security. "The centrality of mobility and the need to access resources flexibly in different places at different times according to the vagaries of the climate create a situation in which access is more important than ownership and in which hard territorial boundaries would be a constraint to survival" (Robinson 2019: 5). It is therefore not surprising that the move to sedentarize pastoralists, fix boundaries, and establish unambiguous and exclusive rights to discrete units of territory have undermined pastoralist livelihoods, exacerbated inequality, undermined human health, and led to rangeland degradation (Berihun 2014; Blewett 1995; Fekadu 2014; Fratkin and Roth 2006; Galaty 1992, 1994, 1999; Ntiati 2002). While in certain circumstances pastoralists have embraced land titling and subdivision of the commons, this has often occurred under duress—whether from the dominance of elite interests supported by the state (Mwangi 2007; see also Ensminger and Rutten 1991); land markets and the pro-private bias of land adjudication officers (Lesorogol 2008); perceived threats of expropriation by the government and elites (Galaty 1992, 1994); or fear of being left out of range sub-division (Galaty 1994, Mwangi 2007).

Relational Ontologies of Land and Security

While each of these examples must be understood on their own terms, as unique manifestations of human relationships to land, it is worth reflecting on whether any commonalities emerge in these conceptions of land, property, and security across livelihood systems and geographies. Whether due to the contrast with dominant ontologies of land or to their prominence in the reviewed ontological orientations themselves, *relational dimensions of security* stand out as a dominant theme across the ethnographic accounts reviewed. This takes many forms, from the absence of a term for land as an entity disconnected from other resources in local languages and cognition, to diverse forms of relationality between human communities and with spirits and ancestors. The absence of the concept *land* in local lexicons is suggestive of the embeddedness of land in a web of relationships with other resources rather than a discrete entity in its own right. Forms of human relationality concerning land and property include the nature of property itself (with social relations built up through property, and property as a reflection of those relationships); the importance of obligations over, or on par with, rights; the embeddedness of individual or household rights within descent-based landholdings that ensure the continuity of both social identity and territory for the descent group; and complex institutional mechanisms for securing access to water and forage among pastoralists.

Security-through-reciprocity also emerges as another dimension of relational conceptions of land, a feature not just of pastoralist societies, but of hunter-gatherers and settled agriculturalists in both drylands and floodplains. Among !Kung hunter-gatherers, for example, "access to land is collective and non-exclusive and, like so much else in !Kung life, flexible: most people live as visitors or residents in a number of different areas during their lives, and establishing short-term residence at one watering hole does not jeopardize one's claim to residence at another" (Shostak 1981: 9). Visitors are expected to ask permission before making use of an area's resources, and accepting this favor brings with it an obligation to reciprocate at a later date. Similar patterns are found among pastoralist societies, for whom security-through-reciprocity is observed not just between adjacent pastoralists surrounding access to watering points and forage, but historically with those practicing complementary modes of subsistence (farmers, hunter-gatherers) which provided a defense against drought, disease, and warfare (Galaty 1993; Sobania 1993; Waller 1993). Thus, security is not just about the rights that one can claim for oneself and one's kin, but about social obligations and duties—and thus sociality/relationality. This finding should not be interpreted as part of a primitive past, or otherwise reify "us/them" notions of social difference (and the hierarchies that flow from that). These findings resonate with the work of Appadurai in contemporary Western contexts, where "persons and things are not radically distinct categories" and "the transactions that surround things are invested with the properties of social relations" (Appadurai 2006: 15). More importantly, while the draw of market individualism is real, security through sociality persists in part due to staunch and at times violent social resistance to changes that threaten these relations—some of which emanate from development interventions themselves (Chauveau and Richards 2008; Peters 2010).

And as was evident among West African horticulturalists, security-through-reciprocity, sociality and relationality is not just restricted to the living or to the human realm, but extended by some societies to the supernatural realm and to ancestors—a feature widely documented in the ethnographic literature from diverse regions of the world (Clay 1991; Dove 1988; Jorgenson 1989). With spirits and ancestors capable of intervening in human affairs as agents, this relationality is neither inert nor unidirectional. Since abiding by established norms helps both to restore the ecological order and to reaffirm the social order, this relationality with non-humans and its physical manifestation on the landscape in the form of shrines helps to blur boundaries (human-nonhuman, material-spiritual) and to connect social identities to place.

In an ambitious attempt to derive "the dimensions of power over land in all of its social, cultural and political complexity" from an evaluation of anthropological and agronomic data on African land relations, Okoth-Ogendo (1989) identifies a set of emergent features that stand in contrast to Western conceptions of property. Within African land relations, property in land does not involve vesting the full complement of power that it is possible to exercise to particular individuals or groups. Secondly, powers over land originate in social adhesion or membership in a production unit rather than through market operations, and are thus necessarily transgenerational rather than inherited—with "the rules of transmission implied in the power of control guaranteeing the vital link between the past, the present and the future" (Okoth-Ogendo 1989: 11). Control is thus exercised through the permanent members of the particular production unit. With "the primary obligation of those in whom the power of control is vested being to guarantee access to present members and to preserve the land resources of the unit for the benefit of future generations, the outright disposal of land to persons external to a given unit of production is therefore alien to African land law" (Okoth-Ogendo 1989: 11).

It is important here not to gloss over how the focus on ontologies tends to obscure the internal struggles over the meaning and use of land among members of lineages and other collectivities, and the conflict that has ensued from the same, in the context of growing land scarcity and land markets. Ethnographic accounts from across the region provide evidence for the growing pace and contestation of enclosures and subdivision of communal land, monetization of land and grazing rights, land expropriation by local elites, and narrowing conceptions of belonging—often implicated in growing inequality (Amanor 1999; Bassett 2009; Berry 1993; Lentz 2006a; Lesorogol 2008; Mwangi 2007; Peters 2004, 2013; Peters and Richards 2011; Sikor and Lund 2010; Turner and Moumouni 2019; Ubink and Amanor 2008). This points to the likelihood that the ontologies profiled in this chapter are contested or at odds with certain interests in land among customary land users themselves.

Yet with historical accounts from across the continent pointing to long histories of (largely informal) land rentals and sales (e.g., Berry 1993; Chauveau et al. 2006; Chimhowu and Woodhouse 2006; Kuba and Lentz 2006); substantial ambiguity and ongoing contestation over what such transfers mean[12] (Chauveau and Colin 2010; Colin and Woodhouse 2010; Lentz 2006b); and recollectivizations (Colin and Ayouz 2006; Galaty 2016), the question of what exactly has changed becomes blurred. What does seem clear is that authority, belonging, and property are contested, and that the ontologies of security profiled herein have served as a basis for contesting land transactions seen as a threat to collective well-being of specific local constituencies (Chauveau and Richards 2008; Galaty 2016; Lesorogol 2008)—a function that is likely to have a much longer history than the latest wave of enclosures.

THE WORK BEING DONE THROUGH DOMINANT ONTOLOGIES OF LAND AND SECURITY

> Assembling land as a resource available for some purposes to the exclusion of others requires a great deal of complex cultural work.
>
> —Li (2011: 592)

This chapter sought to provincialize notions of tenure security being advanced by the international development establishment by drawing on dominant land governance discourses and ethnographic evidence from across Africa to ask, "What exactly does tenure security mean, and to whom?" If we contrast the ontological assumptions behind development discourses on land and tenure security with the ethnographic evidence reviewed here, one contrast stands out as the most salient. Dominant conceptions of land tenure conceive of restrictions on rights as threats to security, and the severance of relationships—both social (of marriage, kin and community) and ecological (land from water, forests, wildlife)—as the pathway through which rights are to be advanced by discretely bounding parcels of land from the networks of relations in which they are embedded. The ethnographic evidence, on the other hand, points to social relationships, duties toward others in respect to land, and enduring ties to place as the very elements through which social identities are maintained and tenure and livelihood security advanced. This relationality is not restricted to the human realm, but extends agency to—and thus human responsibility toward—ancestors, spirits, and future generations. Ontologies of land and security are also marked by relations of belonging rather than ownership, with people belonging to the land as much as land to people.

Relational ontologies are not restricted to remote areas of Africa, but are observed throughout Asia, Latin America, North America, and beyond, in areas well within the grasp of globalizing influences and having undergone profound cultural change (DePuy et al. 2021). How then, did *an ontology of security as severance, independence, and exclusivity* come to occupy center stage within global land governance discourses? And to what extent does this remake the world through our habits of thought, our practices, or the behaviors which have become normalized?

If we agree with the knowledge-power arguments in the social sciences, a disembodied conceptualization of land and security in which land and rights holders are removed from the web of social, symbolic, and ecological relations in which they are embedded undoubtedly does work in the world. But what kind of work, exactly? Here, I draw on a theoretical framework articulated by Noel Castree (2003) as conceptual scaffolding to illustrate the core work being done as the commodification of customary land. Drawing on the work of others that came before him (Dant 1999; Kopytoff 1986; Thomas 1991), he highlights how the commodity status of an object, idea or creature "is not intrinsic to it but, rather, assigned" (Castree 2003: 277). And with that recognition that the identity of things is not fixed but socially constructed, he asks, "What kind of characteristics do things take-on when they become commodities?" (Castree 2003: 277). Based on a review of contemporary Marxist theorists, he identifies six such characteristics, all of which resonate to some degree with the constructed wisdoms of the land governance orthodoxy: privatization, alienability, individuation, abstraction, valuation, and displacement. Here, I focus on two that are highly relevant yet not immediately obvious to all: abstraction and individuation.

For Castree, abstraction refers to the "process whereby the qualitative specificity of any individualized thing (a person, a seed, a gene, or what-have-you) is assimilated to the qualitative homogeneity of a broader type or process" (Castree 2003: 281). Is this abstraction not part and parcel of the process through which land loses all of its relational-historical-cultural-symbolic particularities to become a disembodied and generic unit of territory that can move between similarly abstracted and bounded actors? And is individuation, "the representational and physical act of separating a specific thing or entity from its supporting context," not the same representational work as the ontologies of severance profiled in dominant land governance discourses and practices, and which stand in such stark contrast to the relational ontologies of land and inseparability of social groups, identities, and place so prevalent in the ethnographies reviewed here? Individuation further involves,

> putting legal and material boundaries around phenomena so that they can be bought, sold and used by equally "bounded" individuals, groups or institutions (like a firm). As with privatization, capitalist commodity exchange is simply not possible unless commodities can be separated out as discrete ontological entities with their own qualitative specificities. (Castree 2003: 280)

And yet these specificities have nothing to do with land's inherent qualities or materiality; as Tania Li points out,

> Land is not like a mat. You cannot roll it up and take it away. It has presence and location . . . To turn it to productive use requires regimes of exclusion that distinguish legitimate from illegitimate uses and users, and the inscribing of boundaries through devices such as fences, title deeds, laws, zones, regulations, landmarks and story-lines. (Li 2011: 589)

As a long history of scholarship from across the social sciences has shown, the work being done here—and in economic and property theory more broadly—is deeply cultural and situated, "freighted with particular historical meanings" that are always deeply political (Peters 1994: 1; see also Bhandar 2018; Blomley 2007, 2014; Li 2014; Moreton-Robinson 2015). The most relevant are critiques of the methodological individualism in neoclassical economics and rational choice theory that serves as the theoretical bedrock of the "freehold/security/investment" model, and its role in casting individual rights as the ideal and social relations as development constraints while obscuring the wider social, cultural, and political processes in which land relations are embedded (Granovetter 1985; Peters 1993; Stein 1995). Other bodies of scholarship offering relevant critiques of individuation include the work of common property scholars demonstrating that land and resources held in common are not destined to produce tragedies, but assume crucial social and ecological functions (Blewett 1995; Ostrom 1990), and the work of anthropologists and relational contract theorists on the sociality, relationality, and moral calculus of gifts and exchange (Macneil 1978; Mauss 1966; Perry 1989; Sahlins 1972). Echoing the second side of Karl Polanyi's "double movement," Jonathan Parry (1989) shows how across historical and cultural contexts, the moral objections to exchange are often leveraged on the grounds of equity and efforts to safeguard social life.

Scholarship exploring the complex cultural work involved in abstraction include writings on the social construction of seemingly stable and uniform entities such as commodities, markets, money, and property (Appadurai 1986, 2006; Callon 2017; Hart 2005, 2007; Mitchell 2008). The core of economic abstraction is the process that Polanyi's describes as "dis-embedding," the policy-driven process through which markets and other aspects of economic life shifted from being embedded in social relations (aligned with social norms and regulated by social institutions) to their dis-embeddedness from social life (Polanyi 1944). While Polanyi traces this process to the late eighteenth and early nineteenth century, this process has accelerated globally since World War II as a function of Western power (Carrier and Miller 2020). As James Carrier and Daniel Miller point out, this process has both substantive and conceptual dimensions to it—working through "the ways that people, firms and other agents organize and carry out their activities of the production and circulation of objects and services," as well as in "the concepts and models of economic abstraction, which are taken to be the fundamental reality" (Carrier and Miller 2020: 2). Where these models become prescriptive of what the world ought to be, a process they call "virtualism," it manifests as "a practical effort to make the world conform to the structures of the conceptual" (Carrier and Miller 2020: 2). Thus, the cultural and situated economic concepts from the West—from abstraction and individuation to (neo)liberal political ideology and methodological individualism of neoclassical economics and rational choice—take their hold on the world through the power of ideas.

In the context of farmland, abstraction has been studied by Stephan Ouma, most notably in the "collective yet contested practices of classification, valuation and valorization" through which farmland has been constructed as an asset class in the post-2008 era (Ouma 2018: 66). Here, abstraction may be seen most clearly in the complex maneuverings[13] required to imbue the geographically and technologically distinctive features of a specific unit of farmland with the qualities required for it to be recognized as an asset "in the relational investment universe of the world of money management" (Ouma 2018: 69). Collectively these works critique not just the "made-up" character of private property[14] and the economic individualism of markets (and atomistic economic analysis and ideology underpinning it), but the dehumanizing, impersonal, and alienating premise of an individual rather than a social person.

With other identified elements of commodification (privatization, alienability, and valuation) also resonating with the *non-relational ontology of security* being forged by the World Bank and others active in the international land governance debate, the underlying work being done in tenure security discourses points clearly to that of commodification. This resonates with the longstanding emphasis of the World Bank on the creation of land markets to enable land to be transferred to the most efficient uses and users (Binswanger, Deininger, and Feder 1993; Deininger 2003; Deininger and Binswanger 1999: 247, 250). As David Westbrook points out, the construction of markets is not just about "the creation and alienation of property rights," but also involves "the destruction of meaning" (Westbrook 2004: 164). And lest we believe this commodification is being advanced for the benefit of customary rights holders as the discourse would have us believe, it is worth reflecting on the *longue durée* of discourses in support of customary land rights recognition. In Africa, efforts dating from the late colonial period to convert customary tenure into private property have exacerbated conflict over land, encouraged speculation, and frequently displaced the intended beneficiaries (Peters 2019). And to dispel notions that the U.S. and Europe are any different, legal and discursive moves to recognize Native American land rights were found by historian Stuart Banner to correspond with those moments in time when outside interests in land acquisition was most intense and these very same rights were most rapidly extinguished

(Banner 2005). A rich scholarship on the enclosures of the English commons also profiles growing land concentration; livelihood precarity and dispossession for the majority; and declines in employment, job security, and real wages (Neeson 1989; Peters 1994; Snell 1985).

It is worth asking whether the absence of such an ontology or "regime of truth" surrounding land governance would undermine the work being done under its legitimating influence—such as titling in the name of individuals, and land enclosures, transfers, and acquisitions. With the *alienability* of land passing as tenure *security* and large-scale land acquisitions not subsiding despite the growth in "land governance" and reduced media attention on the issue (Nolte, Chamberlain, and Giger 2016), surely this cultural work is yielding results. Non-relational ontologies of security are therefore a prime example of the productive forms of power through which the world is made, shaping not just the concepts we think with (land, rights, security), but what those concepts mean and how they are enacted and in so doing, remake the world. Here, they are undoubtedly key to mobilizing the international development establishment behind the progressive language of tenure security, while naturalizing the commodification and alienation of customary land.

REFERENCES CITED

Abdalla, A.J. 2013. People to people diplomacy in a pastoral system: A case from Sudan and South Sudan. *Pastoralism: Research, Policy and Practice* 3(12), https://doi.org/10.1186/2041-7136-3-12

Abu-Lughod, L. 2002. Do Muslim women really need saving? Anthropological reflections on cultural relativism and its others. *American Anthropologist* 104(3): 783–790.

Amanor, K. 1999. Global restructuring and land rights in Ghana: Forest food chains, timber and rural livelihoods. *Research Report* No. 108. Uppsala, Sweden: Nordiska Afrikainstitutet.

Appadurai, A. 1986. *The Social Life of Things: Commodities in Cultural Perspective.* Cambridge, UK: Cambridge University Press.

Appadurai, A. 2006. The thing itself. *Public Culture* 18(1): 15–21.

AUC-ECA-AfDB Consortium. 2010. *Framework and Guidelines on Land Policy in Africa.* Addis Ababa, Ethiopia and Abidjan, Nigeria: African Union Commission, Economic Commission for Africa and the African Development Bank.

Banner, S. 2005. *How the Indians Lost their Land.* Cambridge, MA: Harvard University Press.

Bassett, T.J. 2009. Mobile pastoralism on the brink of land privatization in Northern Côte d'Ivoire. *Geoforum* 40(5): 756–766.

Berihun A.G. 2014. Unsustain the sustainable: An evaluation of the legal and policy interventions for pastoral development in Ethiopia. *Pastoralism* 6(2): 1-14. https://doi.org/10.1186/s13570-016-0049-x.

Berry, S. 1993. *No Condition is Permanent: The Social Dynamics of Agrarian Change in Sub-Saharan Africa*. Madison, WI: University of Wisconsin Press.

Bhandar, B. 2018. *Colonial Lives of Property: Law, Land and Racial Regimes of Ownership*. Durham, NC: Duke University Press.

Binswanger, H.P., K. Deininger, and G. Feder. 1993. Power, distortions, revolt, and reform in agricultural land relations. *Policy Research Working Papers* 1164. Washington, DC: The World Bank.

Blewett, R.A. 1995. Property rights as a cause of the tragedy of the commons: Institutional change and the pastoral Maasai of Kenya. *Eastern Economic Journal* 21(4): 477–490.

Blomley, N. 2007. Making private property: Enclosure, common right and the work of hedges. *Rural History* 1(1): 1–21.

Blomley, N. 2014. Making space for property. *Annals of the Association of American Geographers* 2014 (6): 1291–1306.

Bohannan, P. 1963. 'Land', 'tenure' and land-tenure. In: D. Biebuyck (Ed.), *African Agrarian Systems*, 101–115. Oxford University Press.

Bollig, M. and C. Lesorogol. 2016. The "new pastoral commons" of Eastern and Southern Africa. *International Journal of the Commons* 10(2): 665–687.

Bonanno, A., L.C. Foster, and L. German. 2019. Land as an object of 'good governance': Beyond rights and property. Paper presented at the 'Workshop on the Ostrom Workshop,' Boomington, IN, June 19, 2019.

Callon, M. 2017. Afterword: The devices of attachment. In: F. Cochoy, J. Deville and L. McFall (Eds.), *Markets and the Arts of Attachment*, 180–195. London: Routledge.

Carrier, J.G. and D. Miller. 2020. *Virtualism: A New Political Economy*. London: Routledge.

Castree, N. 2003. Commodifying what nature? *Progress in Human Geography* 27(3): 273–297.

CFS and FAO. 2012. *Voluntary Guidelines on the Responsible Governance of Tenure of Land, Fisheries and Forests in the Context of National Food Security*. Rome: Committee on World Food Security and the Food and Agriculture Organization of the United Nations.

Chakrabarty, D. 1992. Provincializing Europe: Postcoloniality and the critique of history. *Cultural Studies* 6(3): 337–357.

Chauveau, J.-P. and P. Richards. 2008. West African insurgencies in agrarian perspective: Côte d'Ivoire and Sierra Leone compared. *Journal of Agrarian Change* 8(4): 515–552.

Chauveau, J.-P. and J.-P. Colin. 2010. Customary transfers and land sales in Côte D'Ivoire: Re-visiting the embeddedness issue. *Africa* 80(1): 81–103.

Chauveau, J.-P., J.-P. Colin, J.-P. Jacob, P. Lavigne Delville, and P.-Y. Le Meur. 2006. *Changes in Land Access and Governance in West Africa: Markets, Social Mediations and Public Policies*. London: International Institute for Environment and Development.

Chimhowu, A. and P. Woodhouse. 2006. Customary vs private property rights? Dynamics and trajectories of vernacular land markets in Sub-Saharan Africa. *Journal of Agrarian Change* 6(3): 346–371.

Clay, J. 1991. Cultural survival and conservation: Lessons from the past twenty years. In: M.L. Oldfield and J.B. Alcorn (Eds.), *Biodiversity: Culture, Conservation and Ecodevelopment*, 248–273. Boulder: Westview Press.

Colin, J.-P. and M. Ayouz. 2006. The development of a land market? Insights from Côte d'Ivoire. *Land Economics* 82(3): 404–423.

Colin, J.-P. and P. Woodhouse. 2010. Introduction: Interpreting land markets in Africa. *Africa* 80(1): 1–10.

Coughenour, M.B., J.E. Ellis, D.M. Swift, D.L. Coppock, K. Galvin, et al. 1985. Energy extraction and use in a nomadic pastoral ecosystem. *Science* 230:619–625.

Dant, T. 1999. *Material Culture in the Social World*. Buckingham, UK: Open University Press.

Deininger, K. 2003. *Land Policies for Growth and Poverty Reduction*. Washington, DC: The World Bank.

Deininger, K. and H. Binswanger. 1999. The evolution of the World Bank's land policy: Principles, experience, and future challenges. *The World Bank Research Observer* 14(2): 247–276.

DePuy, W., J. Weger, K. Foster, A. Bonanno, S. Kumar, K. Lear, R. Basilio, and L. German. 2021. Environmental governance: Broadening ontological spaces for a more livable world. *Global Environmental Change*, https://doi.org/10.1177/25148486211018565.

Dove, M. 1988. Living rubber, dead land, and persisting systems in Borneo: Indigenous representations of sustainability. *Bijdragen tot de Taal-, Land- en Volkenkunde* (Journal of the Humanities and Social Sciences of Southeast Asia) 154(1): 20–54.

Ellis, J. and D.M. Swift. 1988. Stability of African pastoral ecosystems. *Journal of Range Management* 41: 450–459.

Ensminger, J. and A. Rutten. 1991. The political economy of changing property rights: Dismantling a pastoral commons. *American Ethnology* 18: 683–699.

Evans-Pritchard, E.E. 1940. *The Nuer: A Description of the Modes of Livelihood and Political Institutions of a Nilotic People*. Oxford, UK: Oxford University Press.

Fairhead, J. and M. Leach. 1996. *Misreading the African Landscape: Society and Ecology in a Forest-Savanna Mosaic*. Cambridge, UK: Cambridge University Press.

FAO. 2015. *Safeguarding Land Tenure Rights in the Context of Agricultural Investment*. Rome: Food and Agriculture Organization of the United Nations.

FAO, IFAD, UNCTAD, and the World Bank Group. 2010. *Principles for Responsible Agricultural Investment that Respects Rights, Livelihoods and Resources*. Rome and Washington, DC: FAO, IFAD, UNCTAD, World Bank Group.

Fekadu B. 2014. The challenges to pastoral transformation to sedentary farming: The case of Karrayyu pastoralists. In: Mulugeta Gebrehiwot Berhe (Ed.), *A Delicate Balance: Land Use, Minority Rights and Social Stability in the Horn of Africa*, 66–91. Addis Ababa, Ethiopia: Institute for Peace and Security Studies, Addis Ababa University.

Fratkin, E. 1997. Pastoralism: Governance and development issues. *Annual Review of Anthropology* 26: 235–261.

Fratkin, E. and E.A. Roth. 2006. *As Pastoralists Settle: Social, Health, and Economic Consequences of the Pastoral Sedentarization in Marsabit District, Kenya*. New York: Kluwer.

Galaty, J.G. 1992. "The land is yours": Social and economic factors in the privatization, sub-division and sale of Maasai ranches. *Nomadic Peoples* 30(1992): 26–40.

Galaty, J.G. 1993. Maasai expansion and the new east African pastoralism. In T. Spear and R. Waller (Eds.), *Being Maasai*, 61–86. London: James Currey.

Galaty, J.G. 1994. Ha(l)ving land in common: The subdivision of Maasai group ranches in Kenya. *Nomadic Peoples* 34/35(1994): 109–122.

Galaty, J.G. 1999. Grounding pastoralists: Law, politics, and dispossession in East Africa. *Nomadic Peoples* 3(2): 56–73.

Galaty, J. 2016. Reasserting the commons: Pastoral contestations of private and state lands in East Africa. *International Journal of the Commons* 10(2): 709–727.

Galvin, K.A. 2009. Transitions: Pastoralists living with change. *Annual Review of Anthropology* 38(2009): 185–198.

GDWGL. 2018. Minutes, 12th Physical Meeting of the Global Donor Working Group on Land. Rome, 18 October, 2018.

Gluckman, M. 1965. *Politics, Law and Ritual in Tribal Society*. Chicago: Aldine.

Granovetter, M. 1985. Economic action and social structure: The problem of embeddedness. *American Journal of Sociology* 91: 481–510.

Hagberg, S. 2006. Money, ritual and the politics of belonging in land transactions in western Burkina Faso. In: R. Kuba and C. Lentz (Eds.), *Land and the Politics of Belonging in West Africa*, 99–118. Boston: Brill Press.

Haller, T., Ed. 2010. *Disputing the Floodplains: Institutional Change and the Politics of Resource Management in African Wetlands*. African Social Studies Series. Brill: Leiden.

Haller, T. 2019. The different meanings of land in the age of neoliberalism: Theoretical reflections on commons and resilience grabbing from a social anthropological perspective. *Land* 8(7): 104.

Hart, K. 2005. *The Hit Man's Dilemma: Or, Business, Personal and Impersonal*. Chicago: Pricky Paradigm Press.

Hart, K. 2007. Money is always personal and impersonal. *Anthropology Today* 23(5): 12–16.

Hjort, A. 1981. A critique of "ecological" models of pastoral land use. *Ethnos* 46(3–4): 171–189.

Holbraad, M. and M.A. Pederson. 2017. *The Ontological Turn: An Anthropological Exposition*. Cambridge, UK: Cambridge University Press.

Homewood, K.M. and W.A. Rodgers. 1991. *Maasailand Ecology: Pastoralist Development and Wildlife Conservation*. Cambridge, UK: Cambridge University Press.

Honoré, A.M. 1961. Ownership. In: A.G. Guest (Ed.), *Oxford Essays in Jurisprudence*, 108–147. London: Oxford University Press.

Hutchinson, S.E. 1998. *Nuer Dilemmas: Coping with Money, War, and the State*. Berkeley: University of California Press.

IG and RRI. 2015. *Respecting Land and Forest Rights: A Guide for Companies*. The Interlaken Group and Rights and Resources Initiative.

Jorgenson, A.B. 1989. A natural view: Pwo Karen notions of plants, landscapes, and people. *Folk* 31: 21–51.

Kerven, C., K. Shanbaev, I. Alimaev, A. Smailov, and K. Smailov. 2008. Livestock mobility and degradation in Kazakhstan's semi-arid rangelands: Scale of livestock mobility in Kazakhstan. In: R. Behnke (Ed.), *The Socio-Economic Causes and Consequences of Desertification in Central Asia*, 113–140. Basel: Springer.

Kingwill, R.A. 2013. *The Map is Not the Territory: Law and Custom in 'African Freehold', a South African Case Study*. Doctoral Thesis, University of the Western Cape.

Kopytoff, I. 1986. The cultural biography of things. In: A. Appadurai (Ed.), *The Social Life of Things*, 64–91. Cambridge, UK: Cambridge University Press.

Kuba, R. and C. Lentz, Eds. 2006. *Land and the Politics of Belonging in West Africa*. Boston : Brill.

Lambin, E.G., B.L. Turner, H.J. Geist, et al. 2001. The causes of land-use and land-cover change: Moving beyond the myths. *Global Environmental Change* 11(2001): 261–269.

Lentz, C. 2006a. Decentralization, the state and conflicts over local boundaries in northern Ghana. *Development and Change* 37(4): 901–919.

Lentz, C. 2006b. Indigenous theories of landownership. In: R. Kuba and C. Lentz (Eds.), *Land and the Politics of Belonging in West Africa*, 35–56. Leiden: Brill.

Lentz, C. 2013. *Land, Mobility and Belonging in West Africa: Natives and Strangers*. Bloomington, IN: Indiana University Press.

Lesorogol, C. 2008. *Contesting the Commons: Privatizing Pastoral Lands in Kenya*. Ann Arbor, MI: University of Michigan Press.

Li, T. 2011. Centering labor in the land grab debate. *The Journal of Peasant Studies* 38(2): 281–298.

Li, T. 2014. *Land's End: Capitalist Relations on an Indigenous Frontier*. Durham, NC: Duke University Press.

Lund, C. 2006. Who owns Bolgatanga? A story of inconclusive encounters. In: R. Kuba and C. Lentz (Eds.), *Land and the Politics of Belonging in West Africa*, 77–98. Boston: Brill Press.

Macneil, I.R. 1978. Contracts: Adjustment of long-term economic relations under classical, neoclassical, and relational contract law. In: E.G. Furubotn and R. Richter (Eds.), *The New Institutional Economics of Markets*, 854–901. Cheltenham: Edward Elgar.

Mauss, M. 1966. *The Gift*. London: Routledge and Kegan Paul.

Meinert, L., R. Willerslev, and S.H. Seebach. 2017. Cement, graves, and pillars in land disputes in northern Uganda. *African Studies Review* 60(3): 37–57.

Mitchell, T. 2008 Rethinking economy. *Geoforum* 39(2008): 1116–1121.

Moreton-Robinson, A. 2015. *The White Possessive: Property, Power, and Indigenous Sovereignty*. Minneapolis: University of Minnesota Press.

Mwangi, E. 2007. The puzzle of group ranch subdivision in Kenya's Maasailand. *Development and Change* 38(5): 889–910.

Mwangi, E. and E. Ostrom. 2009. A century of institutions and ecology in East Africa's rangelands: Linking institutional robustness with the ecological resilience of Kenya's Maasailand. In: V. Beckmann and M. Padmanabhan (Eds.), *Institutions and Sustainability*, 195–221. Berlin and Heidelberg, Germany: Springer.

Neeson, J.M. 1989. Parliamentary enclosure and the disappearance of the English peasantry, revisited. In: G. Grantham and C.S. Leonard (Eds.), *Agrarian Organization in the Century of Industrialization: Europe, Russia and North America*, 89–120. Research in Economic History Supplement 5A. Copenhagen: JAI Press.

New Alliance for Food Security and Nutrition in Africa and Growth Africa. 2015. *Analytical Framework for Land-Based Investments in African Agriculture*. Johannesburg: New Alliance for Food Security and Nutrition and Grow Africa.

Niamir-Fuller, M., Ed. 1999. *Managing Mobility in African Rangelands: The Legitimization of Transhumance*. London: Intermediate Technology Publications.

Nolte, K., W. Chamberlain, and M. Giger. 2016. *International Land Deals for Agriculture: Fresh insights from the Land Matrix, Analytical Report II*. Bern, Germany, Montpellier, France, Hamburg, Germany and Pretoria, South Africa: Centre for Development and Environment, University of Bern: *Centre de Coopération Internationale en Recherche Agronomique pour le Développement*, German Institute of Global and Area Studies and University of Pretoria.

Ntiati, P. 2002. Group Ranches Subdivision Study in Loitokitok Division of Kajiado District, Kenya. *LUCID Working Paper Series* no. 7., Nairobi, Kenya: International Livestock Research Institute.

Oba, G., N.C. Stenseth, and W.J. Lusigi. 2000. New perspectives on sustainable grazing management in arid zones of sub-Saharan Africa. *BioScience* 50: 35–51.

Okoth-Ogendo, H.W.O. 1989. Some issues of theory in the study of tenure relations in Africa agriculture. *Africa* 59(1): 6–17.

Ostrom, E. 1990. *Governing the Commons: The Evolution of Institutions for Collective Action*. Cambridge, UK: Cambridge University Press.

Ouma, S. 2018. This can('t) be an asset class: The world of money management, "society," and the contested morality of farmland investments. *Environment and Planning A: Economy and Space* 52(1): 66–87.

Pala Okeyo, A. 1980. The Joluo Equation: Land reform = lower status for women. *Ceres* May–June: 37–42.

Parry, J. 1989. On the moral perils of exchange. In: J. Parry and M. Bloch (Eds.), *Money and the Morality of Exchange*, 64–93. Cambridge, UK: Cambridge University Press.

Peters, K. and P. Richards. 2011. Rebellion and agrarian tensions in Sierra Leone. *Journal of Agrarian Change* 11(3): 377–395.

Peters, P.E. 1993. Is "rational choice" the best choice for Robert Bates? An anthropologist's reading of Bates' work. *World Development* 21(6): 1063–1076.

Peters, P.E. 1994. Common property, property and social analysis. Paper presented at the 'Meeting of the Society for Economic Anthropology,' March 1994. Available at: http://dlc.dlib.indiana.edu/dlc/bitstream/handle/10535/8224/Common%20Property,%20Property%20and%20Social%20Analysispdf.pdf?sequence=1 (retrieved May 12, 2021).

Peters, P.E. 2004. Inequality and social conflict over land in Africa. *Journal of Agrarian Change* 4(3): 269–314.

Peters, P.E. 2010. "Our daughters inherit our land, but our sons use their wives' fields": Matrilineal-matrilocal land tenure and the New Land Policy in Malawi. *Journal of Eastern African Studies* 4(1): 179–199.

Peters, P.E. 2013. Conflicts over land and threats to customary tenure in Africa. *African Affairs* 112(449): 543–562.

Peters, P.E. 2019. The significance of descent-based 'customary' land management for land reform and agricultural futures in Africa. Paper presented at the '2019 Conference on Land Policy for Africa,' November 25–29, 2019, Abidjan, Côte d'Ivoire.

Platteau, J.-P. 1996. The evolutionary theory of land rights as applied to Sub-Saharan Africa: A critical assessment. Development and Change 27(1996): 29–86.

Polanyi, K. 1944. *The Great Transformation: The Political and Economic Origins of Our Time*. Boston: Beacon.

Robinson, L.W. 2019. Open property and complex mosaics: Variants in tenure regimes across pastoralist social-ecological systems. *International Journal of the Commons* 13(1): 1–23.

Sahlins, M. 1972. *Stone Age Economics*. Chicago: Aldine.

Scoones, I. 1994. *Living with Uncertainty: New Directions in Pastoral Development in Africa*. London: Intermediate Technology Publications.

Shostak, M. 1981. *Nisa: The Life and Words of a !Kung Woman*. London: Earthscan.

Sikor, T. and C. Lund. 2010. *The Power of Possession: Property, Authority and Access to Natural Resources*. Hoboken, NJ: Blackwell Publishing.

Snell, K.D.M. 1985. *Annals of the Labouring Poor: Social Change and Agrarian England, 1660–1900*. Cambride, UK: Cambridge University Press.

Sobania, N. 1993. Defeat and dispersal: The Laikipiak and their neighbors at the end of the nineteenth century. In: T. Spear and R. Waller (Eds.), *Being Maasai: Ethnicity and Identity in East Africa*, 105–119. London: James Currey.

Spear, T. 1993. Introduction. In: T. Spear and R. Waller (Eds.), *Being Maasai: Ethnicity and Identity in East Africa*, 1–24. London: James Currey.

Spear, T., and R. Waller. 1993. *Being Maasai: Ethnicity and Identity in East Africa*. London: James Currey.

Spencer, P. 1993. Becoming Maasai, being in time. In: T. Spear and R. Waller (Eds.), *Being Maasai: Ethnicity and Identity in East Africa*, 140–156. London: James Currey.

Spivak, G.C. 1993. Can the subaltern speak? In L. Chrisman and P. Williams (Eds.), *Colonial Discourse and Post-Colonial Theory: A Reader*, 66–111. New York: Harvester Wheatsheaf.

Stein, H. 1995. Institutional theories and structural adjustement in Africa. In: J. Harriss, J. Hunter and C. Lewis (Eds.), *The New Institutional Economics and Third World Development*, 109–132. London: Routledge.

Tarim, E. (2012) Storytelling and structural incoherence in financial markets. *Journal of Interdisciplinary Economics* 24(2): 115–144.

Thomas, N. 1991. *Entangled Objects*. Cambridge, MA: Harvard University Press.

Turner, M.D. and O. Moumouni. 2019 Mosaics of property: Control of village land in West Africa. *The Journal of Peasant Studies* 46(6): 1167–1191.

Ubink, J.M. and K.S. Amanor. 2008. *Contesting Land and Custom in Ghana: State, Chief and the Citizen*. Leiden, Netherlands: Leiden University Press.

Unruh, J. 2008. Land policy reform, customary rule of law and the peace process in Sierra Leone. *African Journal of Legal Studies* 2(2): 94–117.

USAID. 2015. *Operational Guidelines for Responsible Land-Based Investment*. Washington, DC: US Agency for International Development.

Waller, R.D. 1984. Interaction and identity on the periphery: The trans-Mara Maasai. *The International Journal of African Historical Studies* 17(2): 243–284.

Waller, R.D. 1993. Acceptees and aliens: Kikuyu settlement in Maasailand. In: T. Spear and R. Waller (Eds.), *Being Maasai*, 226–257. London: James Currey.

Westbrook, D.A. 2004. *City of Gold: An Apology for Global Capitalism in a Time of Discontent*. New York and London: Routledge.

Whisson, M.G. 1962. The journeys of the JaRamogi. *Conference Papers*, East African Institute of Social Research. Kampala, Uganda: Makerere University.

Williams, G. 1994. Modernizing Malthus: The World Bank, population control and the African environment. In: J. Crush (Ed.), *Power of Development*, 158–175. London and New York: Routledge.

Williams, J.W. (2014) Feeding finance: A critical account of the shifting relationships between finance, food and farming. *Economy and Society* 43(3): 401–431.

World Bank. 1989. *Sub-Saharan Africa: From Crisis to Sustainable Growth*. Washington, DC: The World Bank.

World Bank, FAO, and IFAD. 2008. *Gender in Agriculture Sourcebook*. Washington, DC and Rome: World Bank, Food and Agriculture Organization of the United Nations, and International Fund for Agricultural Development.

Yngstrom, I. 2002. Women, wives and land rights in Africa: Situating gender beyond the household in the debate over land policy and changing tenure systems. *Oxford Development Studies* 30(1): 21–40.

CHAPTER 6

The Strategic Importance of "Inclusive Business" to Land Governance

The "complex cultural work" involved in assembling land as a resource available for commercial investment (Li 2014: 592) involves not just efforts to frame women's tenure security as under threat and titling as the silver bullet to address these insecurities, or efforts to extract land and its users from the web of relations in which they are embedded. These moves are indeed essential to efforts to commodify land through the establishment of conceptual-ontological and axiological pathways to legitimate the alienation of land from the customary domain. Yet this cultural work must also, by necessity, include efforts to frame the incoming investment itself as an opportunity for those customary land users whose relationship to that investment-based displacement would otherwise be known through the lens of dispossession or land grabbing. This necessity came into being precisely by the impossibility of imagining local land users could be anything *but* dispossessed back in 2008:

> It's *hard to imagine* how conceding farmland to other countries, or to private investors, so that they can produce food to be shipped off to other people, can do anything but take us in the opposite direction and strike a blow at so many movements' struggles for genuine agrarian reform and indigenous peoples' rights. (GRAIN 2008: 10, emphasis added)

And yet this is precisely what the "inclusive business" concept does for our imaginings. This work of rendering investment as a grand opportunity for smallholders and rural communities enables investors to be seen not as "land grabbers," but as the very source of opportunity in rural areas.

The call for private investment as a driver of rural development is not new, and in fact is as old as the neoliberal project itself. As public development finance has been scaled back in the context of free market reforms and official development assistance has declined, developing countries have increasingly looked to the private sector for the required investment in rural development. From the New Partnership for Africa's Development (NEPAD) Declaration to the Addis Ababa Action Agenda and the Sustainable Development Goals, private sector investment, expertise, and innovation have been advanced as crucial to alleviating poverty and achieving the Sustainable Development Goals (NEPAD 2002; UN 2015). Private investment and "particularly foreign direct investment" are now considered "vital complements to national development efforts" (UN 2015: 17)—capable of producing "triple wins" for business, national economies and the rural inhabitants. Eager to capitalize on the opportunities presented by private sector finance or held hostage by the conditionalities of aid, host countries have enacted reforms crucial to attracting foreign investment into priority sectors: rewriting their land laws to facilitate market transactions while providing pathways for foreigners to acquire secure access to land; engaging in business climate reforms to streamline investment procedures; establishing "land banks" by negotiating with customary land owners; and establishing "one-stop shops" to attract and support private investment (Brown 2005; German and Schoneveld 2012; IEG 2015; Maganga et al. 2016). Ontologically, the "inclusive business" concept was key to the making of a world in which the alienation of land out of the customary domain is not an act of dispossession, but a generator of long-awaited economic opportunity. And thus, for many operating in the international development arena, private investment in rural land is no longer the boogeyman of the "land grab" era, but a more benign presence with the potential to advance the interests and aspirations of the rural poor.

This chapter profiles the growing prominence of "inclusive business" as a twin conceptual-programmatic scaffolding to "land governance" following the late-2000s outcry surrounding the global land grab. The chapter provides a brief historical overview of inclusive business debates within international development circles. This is followed by a review of alternative framings from academia and beyond, as a means to open our field of vision to both the critiques of inclusionary discourses and to the options that are foreclosed by dominant framings. Evidence from published reviews and comparative studies on inclusive business in agriculture are then reviewed to locate the realities of actual inclusive business (IB) practices within this conceptual canvas. The chapter concludes with a discussion to distil what is foregrounded and silenced in dominant discourses, as revealed once again from the often stark contrasts between theories of change and lived realities.

THE CONSTRUCTION OF "INCLUSIVE BUSINESS" AS AN OBJECT OF DEVELOPMENT FINANCE AND INTERVENTION

Global development debates surrounding inclusive business consolidated and then grew rapidly in the wake of the financial crisis. In 2008, when a number of actors were engaged with efforts to enhance smallholder participation in global value chains, the terminology had not yet coalesced around this concept—with "responsible procurement schemes" (Bienabe and Vermeulen 2007; CIPS and Tradecraft 2008), "equitable partnerships" (FAO and CIFOR 2002), "inclusive agrifood markets" (Vermeulen et al. 2008), "mutually beneficial partnerships" (FAO and CIFOR, 2002), and "inclusive capitalism" (Hart, 2007) as just some of the diverse referents for similar ideas (Vorley, Lundy, and MacGregor 2008). Following the food price crisis of 2008 and the outcry over global land grabs, inclusive business has taken off as a topic of debate and organizing concept for global development interventions (German et al. 2018; Woodhill 2016). A recent stock-taking identified thousands of projects working to link small-scale producers with markets;[1] at least seven significant practitioner knowledge hubs or networks; and greater than USD 3 billion in annual funding (Woodhill 2016).

Inclusive businesses are said to be those which benefit "poor producers and/or consumers by providing access to markets, services and products in ways that improve their livelihoods, while at the same time being a profitable commercial venture" (Woodhill 2016), and "those which do not leave behind small-scale farmers and in which the voices and needs of those actors in rural areas in developing countries are recognized" (Vorley, Lundy, and MacGregor 2008). A common refrain poses business-led solutions as inherently superior, representing "a philosophy of economic empowerment rather than charity" (Woodhill 2016: 5; see also UNDP 2013: 8).

Debates surrounding inclusive business have helped to define the terms, establish aspirations and enshrine these commitments within relevant policy documents; and identify a global division of roles and responsibilities for action. While early initiatives to address the interests of smallholders and rural communities in the context of growing investment and related land acquisitions focused on "doing no harm," ambitions have expanded to "shared growth" and smallholder inclusion. This is perhaps seen most clearly in the language and aspirations separating the Principles for Responsible Agricultural Investment (FAO et al. 2010), from the later Principles for Responsible Investment in Agriculture and Food Systems of the Committee on World Food Security (CFS 2014). The latter establishes aspirations for agricultural investment that go far beyond "no harm" aspirations to include:

> a significant contribution to enhancing sustainable livelihoods, in particular for smallholders, and members of marginalized and vulnerable groups, creating decent work for all agricultural and food workers, eradicating poverty, fostering social and gender equality, eliminating the worst forms of child labour, promoting social participation and inclusiveness, increasing economic growth, and therefore achieving sustainable development. (CFS 2014: 3)

This shift reflects the growing awareness and concerns associated with the risks of letting the logic of large-scale land-based investments (LSLBI) and free markets dictate outcomes for smallholders:

> Experience has shown investors in LSLBI involved in primary production tend to vertically integrate into the entire chain of agriculture-related business, including seed supply, agro-chemicals, processing, machinery, storage, transport, marketing, etc. This has led to fewer inclusive agricultural development models for local farmers, and, simultaneously, new "enclaves" and "closed value-chains" which exclude smallholder producers and processors. (AU, AfDB, and UNECA 2014: 21)

> Sub-Saharan Africa is today among the fastest-growing regions in the world . . . However, many people remain excluded from the benefits of this growth, without access to basic goods and services or opportunities for employment and regular income . . . Inclusive businesses integrate low-income individuals into value chains in various capacities, be it as consumers, producers, employees and entrepreneurs. Thus, they bring the benefits of growth directly to low-income communities. This is not charity. Inclusive businesses create a strong foundation for profit and long-term growth by bringing previously excluded people into the marketplace. (UNDP 2013: 8)

The concept now has many reference points within global and regional normative frameworks. One of the core ideas advanced by the Guiding

Principles on Large-Scale Land Based Investments in Africa (AU, AfDB, and UNECA 2014) is that investments should not just represent commercially viable and profitable businesses, but also be structured to benefit the national economy and improve the livelihoods of local communities. Observing the failure of Africa's "tremendous growth" to "trickle down into poverty reduction and achievement of the MDGs" (UNECA and AU 2016: 1), the African Union Commission has also proposed the creation of an African Inclusive Markets Excellence Center "as a direct contribution to reconciling growth with inclusive development." The Center is being established to promote regional economic integration through transformative regional value chains which support more inclusive markets and businesses, measured in terms of job creation, income generation, and poverty reduction. "Inclusive business" has thus emerged as the magic bullet that will bring the interests of smallholders and global capital into alignment.

As with collective land rights, there are multiple visions for what this might mean. Early discourses focused on "business models" or "the way in which a company structures its resources, partnerships and customer relationships to create, capture and distribute value" (Cotula and Leonard 2010: 6). This framing around models tended to draw a sharp line between business arrangements involving land acquisition ("plantations") and more inclusive alternatives "that support family farming and that benefit local communities" (Cotula and Leonard 2010: 3), such as contract farming, joint ventures, management contracts, community leases, farmer-owned business, and upstream/downstream business linkages (Vemeulen and Cotula 2010). The emphasis was on how to structure agricultural investments in ways that do not involve large land acquisitions. Yet more recent writing in the international development arena has moved away from this dichotomy between "inclusive" and "exclusionary" business models to emphasize the diversity of arrangements and experiences within each model (German et al. 2018; Mujenja and Wonani 2012; Potter 2015; Prowse 2012; World Bank 2014). Yet the discursive shift from business models to "pillars of inclusiveness," a shift I did not personally advocate but played a key role in advancing[2] (German et al. 2018), and selective evidence on "good practices" in large-scale agricultural investments (World Bank 2014), have obscured the *inherent* features of industrial-scale plantations that position them not just as more exclusionary, but as posing unique risks to rural livelihoods.

Another discursive shift has resulted in the centering of agribusiness within definitions of inclusiveness. In 2015, the G20 advanced a typology of inclusive business forms: (i) IB Models, relying primarily on commercial financing and integrating marginalized actors (so-called Base of the Pyramid[3]) into core business operations; (ii) IB Activities, with social inclusion being somewhat ancillary to core business operations, and involving mixed sources of finance; and (iii) Social Enterprise Initiatives, in which the pursuit of social objectives are at the forefront, profits are reinvested to strengthen this mission rather than diverted to shareholders, and finance is external (G20 2015). The same year, FAO (2015) similarly distinguished between inclusive business models based on the drivers—whether small-scale producers, corporate buyers, public procurement initiatives, or intermediaries aiming to foster economic development and farmer empowerment. Yet this nuance has progressively given way to a more singular conception positioning agribusiness firms in the lead, with various forms of public support (Kelly, Vergara, and Bammann 2015; Woodhill 2016; World Bank 2014). A report written for the Global Donor Platform for Rural Development states, "it is businesses who implement inclusive strategies and . . . the whole idea only works if it is commercially viable for them" (Woodhill 2016: 5). Commercial viability, profitability, and scalability are increasingly advanced as features marking the boundaries of inclusive business (FAO 2015; Woodhill 2016; World Bank 2014). While this suggests a move to marginalize social enterprise-type programs from the concept's semantic domain, there have also been efforts to center private firms in the definition of "social enterprise" (Tinsley and Agapitova 2018).

A final discursive move has involved efforts to expand the scope of the value chain actors being "included" beyond smallholders and rural communities, to consumers. By framing inclusion as benefits accruing to consumers through the provision of affordable goods and services (World Bank 2014; WBCSD 2016), the central role of highly capitalized firms in the inclusive business arena is further naturalized.

While the inclusive business concept and related initiatives have been strongly advanced by international financial institutions, multilateral organizations, and donor programs, there has also been significant buy-in from socially-conscious NGOs. Woodhill's 2016 mind map of "illustrative" inclusive agribusiness initiatives profiles nine major initiatives being pioneered by international NGOs such as Mercy Corp, Oxfam, SNV, WWF, World Vision, and others.

ALTERNATIVE FRAMINGS

Perspectives advanced from within the critical agrarian studies tradition in academia and neo-populist social movements provide insights into other possible conceptualizations of the inclusive business concept that are worth keeping in mind in our efforts to make sense of the evidence. Marxist-inspired critiques, for example, have explored foreign investment as processes of "primitive accumulation" (Hall 2013; Mehta, Veldwisch, and Franco 2012; Moyo, Yeros, and Jha 2012), in which investment-induced land loss and job creation are seen not as opportunities, but as a process of proletarianization through which those dispossessed of their means of production (land) are forced to sell their labor on unfavorable terms. Evidence highlighting the labor-displacing character of much of the investment (Li 2011; see also Schoneveld, German, and Nukator 2011) also reveals these processes not as net employment generators, but as processes of marginalization of the rural labor force. Drawing on David Harvey's (2003) notion of "accumulation by dispossession," this scholarship has also highlighted how market liberalization and commodification may also enable local assets to be released at minimum cost and appropriated by outsiders—with wealth creation directly intertwined with processes of dispossession of rural people (Amanor 2018; Borras and Franco 2012; Chinsinga 2016; Hall 2013; Wolford et al. 2013). Writings on "competitive exclusion," "selective marginalization," and land and resource enclosures, for example, highlight how the competition induced by new investment, value chain features, or land markets, and unequal representation in decision-making, may result in the progressive exclusion of certain classes of land users from their land, jobs, value chains, or output markets (Oberlack et al. 2016; Mamonova 2015; Plank 2013). Other writers have highlighted the presence of "enclave economies" in which investments establish few linkages to the local economy, thereby limiting local benefits capture (Ferguson 2006; Matenga and Hichaambwa 2017). And many authors have highlighted the so-called unanticipated effects for those practicing other livelihood systems in areas impacted by investments (Indigenous peoples, pastoralists, shifting agriculturalists), and for secondary rights holders facing enclosures of livelihood assets as rights are formalized in the name of value chain participants (Fairhead, Leach, and Scoones 2012; Obidzinski et al. 2012; White et al. 2012).

Another body of work has highlighted how smallholder engagement within global value chains may not always contribute to beneficial outcomes for those families involved, with adverse forms of incorporation that do little to improve a household's welfare or actually deepen poverty (McCarthy 2010; Hickey and du Toit 2007) and growing social differentiation in the context of heightened competition (Sulle 2016). Smallholder incorporation may lead to low or diminishing returns to families due to unfavorable terms of engagement of land and labor, whether due to forced/coerced entry, low bargaining power under conditions of monopsony,[4] limited transparency in compensation mechanisms, transfer of excess business risk to smallholders, or chronic indebtedness (Cooke 2012; Cooke, Toh, and Vaz 2011; Herrmann and Grote 2015; Taruvinga 2011; Wendimu, Henningsen, and Gibbon 2016). It may also undermine household food security or gender equity as households reallocate limited land, labor, or capital to cash crops (Carney 1988; Dancer and Sulle 2015; McKersie and Hichaambwa 2011; Van den Broeck and Maertens 2016); result in smallholders shouldering excess risk (Dolan and Humphrey 2004; Mausch et al. 2009; Monson 2009; Smalley, Sulle, and Malale 2014); or undermine tenure security through "control grabs," whereby smallholders lose the freedom to reallocate land and labor as they deem most beneficial (White et al. 2012), or outright land loss under growing pressure on land and co-optation of traditional leaders (Chinsinga 2016).

These narratives of growing inequity, loss of control, and increasing rural instability due to involvement in global capitalist agribusiness production are in sharp contrast with narratives of mutual benefit in international development circles. How can we make sense of this polarization?

EVIDENCE OF THE INCLUSIVENESS OF AGRICULTURAL VALUE CHAINS

The bulk of the evidence surrounding the actual livelihood impacts of inclusive business in agriculture consists of publications from international financial institutions and other development actors touting the virtues of inclusive business and drawing mostly on cases selected for their success (Hystra 2015; IFC 2011, 2014, 2016; Vermeulen and Cotula 2010; World Bank 2014) or emphasizing lessons learning for programmatic purposes rather than evaluation of impacts (Technoserve and IFAD 2011; IFC 2011, 2014, 2016; World Bank 2014). Given the sheer volume of writings from within the international development community on the topic, it is interesting to note the shaky evidence base on which these concepts stood. According to a 2016 paper written for the Global Donor Platform for Rural Development on the state of play of inclusive agribusiness:

> There is *remarkably little evidence* to date on the scale of impact or the depth of the inclusive benefits for the poor. There have been very few cross case study analyses done, and very little synthesis of what evidence does exist. For practitioners involved in the inclusive agribusiness space . . . there appears to be plenty of anecdotal evidence of successful examples which keeps driving faith in the inclusive agribusiness effort. There are a limited number of collations of case studies that reinforce this view. However, from all quarters of the inclusive agribusiness field there are calls for a much greater focus on scaling up inclusive agribusiness efforts. This widespread demand from involved businesses and practitioners in itself suggests that at this stage the impacts are more limited than might be hoped for. (Woodhill 2016: 20, emphasis added)

Peer reviewed literature provides one avenue for going beyond success cases and "lessons learned". Yet, with a highly diverse set of experiences emanating from different commodities, business models, and contexts, sampling is an ongoing challenge. Here, I rely exclusively on comparative analyses and wider reviews in an attempt to reach beyond the specificity of individual cases.

The first set of papers are comparative analyses of a sample of businesses selected for their inclusion of smallholders and local communities, providing insights into how these businesses function but not the overall trends in inclusiveness for the sector as a whole. The first set of papers, by Wytske Chamberlain and Ward Anseeuw, are from South Africa, where the policy context may be characterized by efforts to (at least nominally) redress historical inequities in landownership through land reform and Black ownership and control over agribusinesses. Here, partnerships with commercial entities are a precondition for land restitution to Black farmers to ensure the continuity of commercial land use, and conditionalities on public finance to agribusiness provide incentives for private firms to partner with new Black landowners (Chamberlain and Anseeuw 2019). Thus, structural conditions are in place to encourage the proliferation of such partnerships. Their analysis compares fourteen "inclusive businesses" selected for their organizational uniqueness and relative stability, and excludes poorly performing and failed ventures—with cases thereby reflecting a diversity of experiences within functional partnerships rather than the general state of play per se. They found that whereas the structural goals of "land reform, project development and market integration are generally achieved, the transformation and beneficiary development objectives are compromised" (Chamberlain and Anseeuw 2018: 1). Commercial firms were found to contribute to investment needs in the sector and smallholder market integration, and most case studies showed either sustained performance or growth at project level (in the form of an increase in land under production, the accumulation of assets and infrastructure, and/or the accrual of income at project level). However, these partnerships enabled these firms to control smallholder assets, and financial or material rewards for beneficiaries were very low or non-existent (Chamberlain and Anseeuw 2018). Heavy debt loads, limited opportunities for employment or skills transfer, reinvestment needs to make newly acquired lands productive, and non-transparent use of funds by organizational leadership were each found to have undermined returns to individual participants. While land ownership was key to the negotiating power of smallholders (and the reason for their engagement in the first place), the power imbalance engendered through corporate partners' established market integration and financial and capacity advantages hindered the ability to turn the land asset to their advantage (Chamberlain and Anseeuw 2018, 2019). Rather, smallholders in many cases were found to be passive participants, with control over their land and operations left fully in the hands of the commercial partner through land leases or management contracts. The dominant position of commercial farmers led to disproportionate risk related to the farming operation to be transferred to smallholders.

The authors identified a set of structural limitations to the inclusiveness of the partnerships studied. First, the policy environment was found to induce dependency relationships between actors in which partnerships with smallholders were not key to the business logic, but rather "a necessary cog" in profit-driven business strategies. Financial contributions to the business were also skewed toward the commercial partners, resulting in governance structures benefiting them rather than smallholders. They also found pricing decisions to lie exclusively with the commercial partners as owners of the crops, directly countering distributive objectives. The authors conclude that "the structural differences of objectives and the overarching knowledge gap, both during design and implementation, makes any true inclusiveness in the short term a serious challenge, certainly for the individual beneficiaries involved, regardless of how the IB is structured and operated" (Chamberlain and Anseeuw 2018: 11–12). They concluded by refuting the assumption that "inclusive businesses and their leading agri-businesses, as sole stakeholders, are effective for achieving inclusive agricultural development" (2019: 321), and suggest support and investment by the state or other third parties are needed for safeguarding smallholder assets, mediating between partners and balancing power relations, monitoring compliance with agreements, exploring more flexible options for land use, and for legal support. The authors suggest consideration of "development approaches focusing more on smallholder farmers and on their endogenous growth" (Chamberlain and Anseeuw 2018: 14).

In a second comparative study financed by the Community Lands Initiative (*Iniciativa de Terras Comunitarias*, or iTC), I worked with collaborators from Eduardo Mondlane University to analyze 16 community-investor partnerships spread across six Mozambican provinces (German et al. 2016). These partnerships were purposively selected by the iTC from among communities where community land delimitations or demarcations had been carried out. While partnership building was not an explicit intervention strategy, community-investor partnerships are an envisioned program outcome according to the iTC theory of change—whether by strengthening existing partnerships through land titling or establishing enabling conditions for partnerships to emerge (e.g., legal literacy, community organizing, participatory planning). The sample included corporate social responsibility-type activities in addition to partnerships characterized by value chain integration in line with dominant conceptions of partnership in the country, and were purposively sampled to capture some of the best practices in iTC focal villages rather than a random sample of either community-investor partnerships or iTC focal villages (German et al. 2016). For each case study, research explored partnership quality, local benefits, and factors shaping each.

Criteria employed as proxies for partnership quality set the bar rather low: terms of agreement are formalized in a written contract—"even if ambiguous, incomplete, or departing from verbalized understandings"; partnerships have a basic level of functionality (they are operational and generating "some kind of local benefit"); and partnership arrangements share risks and rewards equitably. Each criterion was found in roughly half of the cases, and only four of the partnerships (25% of the sample) met all quality criteria. Despite a few notable exceptions (e.g., a horticultural contract farming scheme and a community-led business for seed multiplication benefiting from a long history of NGO support), the study found partnerships to have generated limited benefits for local communities, with many generating no benefits, and others being mostly symbolic or having very limited social reach. Partnerships with community entities was part of the core business logic in only half of the cases; in others, it was driven by conflict, political pressure, or other external factors and simply a hoop that had to be jumped through to get on with core business activities. A second crucial factor was the weakness of community consultation as a mechanism to leverage meaningful benefits—often despite iTC investments in local land titling, awareness creation, and capacity building. Key points of negotiation such as the business model, contractual terms and patterns of land occupation were not subject to negotiation; benefits were often paltry in comparison to the land ceded to investors; and community partners struggled to hold investors accountable. While the legal framework provides the opportunity for communities to leverage their customary rights to secure benefits from investment, it is not a requirement of either investment or land acquisition—and intermediaries are often found to be on the side of investors. Consultations are therefore high-stakes events on a highly uneven playing field. While examples of successful partnerships do exist, they are again rare—in spite of the skewed project sample from which the cases were drawn.

Other studies employ methodological designs that provide a better glimpse of the broader dynamics at play. A 2017 Forum published in *The Journal of Peasant Studies* examines investment dynamics, processes of change, expansion and contraction in farm sizes, and patterns of accumulation across three models of agricultural commercialization: plantations, commercial farming, and outgrower and contract farming (Hall, Scoones, and Tsikata 2017). The sample covers one example of each in each of three countries, Ghana, Kenya, and Zambia, and was selected for crop diversity—thereby representing "a series of cases, rather than a systematic comparative assessment" (Hall, Scoones, and Tsikata 2017: 521). They found that "for certain crops in certain areas where land is extensive and water is available, large-scale agriculture can have benefits"—such as wage employment and flexible temporary employment that can be beneficially combined with other sources of livelihood (Hall, Scoones, and Tsikata 2017: 531). However, these investments tend to take the form of "enclave" investments with few linkages to the local economy and lead to displacement and dispossession of existing farming communities. While most of the jobs generated were temporary and with poor employment conditions, these jobs were found to be valued by youth where other opportunities were limited due to land constraints or limited rainfall, and by women valuing a more flexible employment arrangement given other demands on their time. Opportunities for livelihood improvement and accumulation were found for some outgrower cases, especially if combined with other livelihood options. Commercial farms were found to generate the most forward and backward linkages with the local economy, yet also led to the greatest competitive exclusion—squeezing out opportunities for others and exacerbating inequality and landlessness. Yet the particularities of the cases exert a strong influence on findings, limiting the study's utility in gaining a broader picture of agrarian change or its implications for social inclusion.

In a subsequent analysis of trends in a sample of agricultural value chains published as a *World Development* review, my co-authors and I provided an analysis of the overall trends in inclusiveness for the agricultural sector as a whole (German et al. 2020). With much of the published work at the end of the 2010s pointing to the contingency and context-specificity of livelihood outcomes of smallholder-agribusiness partnerships, the academic gaze seemed to be squarely focused on the behaviors of individual businesses as the key to social inclusion. We sought to complement this focus by identifying key structural factors shaping value chain evolution (such as crop features, market dynamics, or policy drivers) and their implications for inclusiveness, and thus to identify underlying drivers shaping the performance of specific investments. The review centered on a typology of seven value chain types selected for their uniqueness and diversity, with one crop selected from each as an illustration. The review focused on one or more regions where each crop is prevalent and where there is abundant published research on the structuring of value chains and their implications for inclusiveness. Our findings pointed to an overall trend toward "more *ex*clusive agribusiness as governments scale back support to smallholders, more stringent standards raise barriers to entry, and firms streamline operations to enhance competitiveness" (German et al. 2020: 1). Some of the identified trends were cross-cutting across value chains, linked to market liberalization and structural adjustment reforms either directly or indirectly. These included government roll-back of earlier forms of support to smallholders, and the enhanced competition and price volatility induced through market liberalization—each of which has disadvantaged smallholders. These wider political economic trends also serve as the backdrop to two interrelated trends in global agribusiness value chains that have restructured production and processing in the global South: the growing importance of product and process standards, and increasing concentration along value chains—trends which were also found to be "working at cross-purposes with the logics of social inclusion" (Humphrey and Memedovic 2016: 14).

Yet other factors specific to particular crops and value chains were also found to have a bearing on inclusiveness, creating particular vulnerabilities for smallholders that made the actual livelihood outcomes conditional on the presence and quality of systems in place to support their integration on favorable terms, or to buffer them from risk. Monopsony, coerced entry (e.g., where farmers participate in outgrower schemes as a condition of land retention or titling), loss of freedom of choice over land use decisions, off-loading excess risk on smallholders, and poor labor conditions were found across value chains to contribute to adverse forms of incorporation. Where real gains to employees, outgrowers, and independent smallholders were found, these were typically islands of success or achieved through considerable *public* finance and support rather than business-led strategies of inclusion. The study drew on the identified shortcomings of observed value chain relations to identify the qualities of value chains that might be deemed most inclusive—namely, those that "enable synergies of land and labor with other economic activities; are versatile in end use (e.g., consumption and sale); are low risk (limited capital outlay, low risk credit, low agronomic risk); and leave control over land and labor in the hands of rural households" (German et al. 2020: 15).

PRODUCTIVE FORMS OF POWER IN THE INCLUSIVE BUSINESS DEBATE

What emerges from this analysis are not just highly polarized narratives about what it means to invest in land-intensive enterprises in rural areas and to include local land and labor in global supply chains, but (once again, and not surprisingly) an arguable disconnect between dominant narratives of inclusiveness and realities on the ground. Here, I want to take some time to crystalize what "inclusive business" centers in our imagination, and the corresponding silences this produces. This is a question addressed in our *World Development* review (German et al. 2020) and the nuanced evidence therein. This discussion draws from those observations and expands upon them based on the evidence laid out in this chapter and elsewhere.

The inclusive business concept and related discourses tend to center in the social (and in particular, international development) imaginary agribusiness firms as the key to rural opportunity and much-needed finance, technical expertise, and markets. The very notion of "inclusion" suggests there is someone outside of rural areas extending a hand to rural communities. This, in turn, invokes long-held stereotypes about "subsistence farmers" operating outside the market, and corresponding calls within the development establishment to modernize them. These are not endogenous visions of rural futures being advanced, or the values, expertise, and productivity of rural communities being centered. The centrality of agribusiness firms to rural futures is also seen in the growing emphasis on business-led forms of social inclusion, and on moves to contrast inclusive business with "charity"—marking out a distinction that implies hierarchy (in which profit generation is the lens through which relative value is assessed). These narratives stand in contrast with, and further silence, the observed preference among and benefits to smallholders from growing independently; the prevalence of adverse forms of incorporation of local land and labor; and the significant gains to employees and smallholders that stem from consistent *public* support in the form of higher labor standards and the strategic use of government finance and gatekeeper functions to align investment with rural development objectives (see German et al. 2020).

In advancing the notion that industrialized agriculture and neoliberal policies are not just compatible with, but necessary for, rural livelihoods, several silences are created. The first is land grabbing itself as a phenomenon and site of activist intervention, as profiled in Chapter 2. If large-scale land acquisitions are the very means through which opportunities in rural areas are generated, concerns over land grabbing are effectively muted. The concept also obscures the challenges faced by smallholders and employees under current policies, markets, and value chain governance—with smallholders and their market share,

> surviving *despite* increasingly unfavorable policy and market conditions . . . While market liberalization and efficiency logics are a key reason behind declining opportunity, it is now seen as the solution—with larger firms not the risk, but the only opportunity. (German et al. 2020: 16)

The structuring of global value chains seems instead to be working at cross-purposes with truly inclusive forms of territorial ordering and economic relations, and yet what is centered in the international development imaginary is the compatibility between these distinct aims. Evidence for trade-offs rather than compatibility is widespread. Bill Vorley, Senior Associate in the Shaping Sustainable Markets program of the International Institute for Environment and Development and someone who has clearly put in his time to understand the dynamics of agricultural markets, explains this as follows (Vorley 2016, emphasis added):

> Food manufacturers and retailers want what they have ordered. Small farmers' reliability to fulfil orders will always fluctuate, as they have to manage risk in the face of climate variability and creaky infrastructure. The goodwill of a progressive company will stretch to a few failed consignments, but it is unreasonable to expect them to adjust to the vagaries of smallholder agriculture. *There is a fundamental issue of business compatibility* . . . These issues of business incompatibility crop up across multiple projects. Successes may look distinctly shaky once donor funds and NGO support are withdrawn. But little gets written up, so what gets cemented into the business and development literature is almost entirely positive. Scratch the surface, however, and there is evidence from Nicaragua to Nairobi of dynamic informal markets trumping inclusive business . . . If we are to combine inclusion and business in a more grounded and scalable way, driven less by wishful thinking and more by evidence, *we need to look beyond big business*. The irony is that inclusive business needs to be approached more inclusively. In many countries, the informal economy dominates food trading, processing and vending. But those actors may be subject to harassment and downright hostility from officials who see them as illegal, unhygienic, tax avoiding and anti-progress. There is tremendous scope for improving the economic, social and environmental performance of the informal economy at scale, without pushing people out of jobs.[5]

This view is not fringe. Similar evidence for incompatibilities is found from the agribusiness sector itself. A review of IFC's experience with inclusive business by the Independent Evaluation Group of the World Bank states, "interviews with IFC staff and clients indicated a perception of higher risk with inclusive business models because of the complexities and challenges of integrating many smallholders in the projects' supply chain and ensuring proper capacity building and quality" (IEG 2018). A set of guidelines advanced by FAO for improving linkages between producers and buyers of agricultural produce and based on pilot experiences carried out in Africa, the Caribbean, and the Pacific also advances as its core contribution "the guidance it provides to practitioners on the *trade-offs between the 'inclusive' and 'business' elements* of an inclusive business model" (FAO 2015: vi). While the final report presents nuanced lessons for how to strengthen the linkage between producers and first buyers, it states that, "Trade-offs sometimes have to be made if a business model, inclusive of small actors, is expected to generate profits and grow as an enterprise" (FAO 2015: viii). They further summarize the limitations of inclusive business as an engine of rural development as follows:

> The integration of smallholders into value chains should only take place when there is a viable business case. However, promoting viability and competitiveness alone cannot be depended upon to reduce poverty. Indeed, overreliance on the private sector can result in poorly coordinated markets and further exclusion of marginalized groups . . . Supporting the development of business models that integrate smallholders into value chains is not a strategy for the poorest of the poor or a panacea for all development ills. (FAO 2015: vi, xii)

And yet such efforts continue to frame development interventions, and the inclusive business concept remains firmly entrenched in corporate responsibility discourses and public perception. As explored more in the concluding chapter, this likely has more to do with the political economy of land than the potential for inclusive business to alleviate poverty in rural areas.

Also obscured by the inclusive business concept and surrounding discourses is the extent to which legal frameworks and public finance are propping up agribusiness—from agricultural subsidies in industrialized nations to bilateral investment treaties, fiscal and policy support to transnational corporations and industrial-scale farms, and public investment in agricultural infrastructure. The US federal government spends more than $20 billion a year on subsidies for farm businesses, most of it going to the largest producers of corn, soybeans, wheat, cotton, and rice, and the EU spends three times that amount.[6] These subsidies directly undercut farmers from Africa and elsewhere, many of whom would otherwise be able to produce these products more cheaply (Oxfam 2002; Watkins 2007). Other examples include reforms, carried out often at the behest of international financial institutions, to streamline land acquisitions and business operations—from market-based land reforms to enable foreign firms to acquire and hold land securely, to land banks whereby governments negotiate the reclassification of customary land and/or its transfer out of the customary domain, and business climate reforms that are minimizing the transaction costs for incoming investors (Brown 2005; Daniel and Mittal 2010; German, Schoneveld, and Mwangi 2013; Maganga et al. 2016; Mousseau 2019). This is occurring alongside discourses emphasizing the limited public finance available to support smallholders and other local land users, and the judgements leveraged on these forms of direct support.[7] Advancing a concept suggesting the interests of agribusiness and rural land users are aligned in effect masks the more frequent alignment between (and, some social theorists would argue, the inseparability of) government and business actors and interests. With a large body of multidisciplinary scholarship calling for direct (public) support to smallholders as the means to enhance agricultural production, food security, and rural livelihoods, is it not time to redirect public efforts and finance toward this end?

A final set of silences created by the inclusive business debate concern alternative sites of governance and alternative rural futures. While the inclusive business debate places the onus of responsibility on individual corporations and the actors working to support their efforts at social inclusion, other possible sites of governance and intervention that might mitigate risk to rural livelihoods or provide more empowering forms of support are obscured. Yet the above evidence suggests the need to shift our gaze from individual firms to economic and investment policies themselves as crucial objects of governance and to the wider political economies in which land and its governance are embedded. And the move to sideline social enterprise-type programs and farmer-led initiatives from the inclusive business concept's semantic domain begs the question of what other visions of rural futures are being sidelined in the process—a topic addressed more fully in Part III. This question is crucial, since the primary approach to addressing the inherent tensions between the "inclusive" and the "business" elements of IB seems to be use of additional public development finance to mitigate these trade-offs, rather than exploring options inherently compatible with rural livelihoods and logics.[8]

CONCLUDING REFLECTIONS

This chapter has profiled the central role played by the inclusive business concept in reframing the "global land grab" and incoming investment not as threats to customary land users, but as a grand opportunity for lifting people out of poverty. The divergence between discourses and lived experiences on the one hand, and the clear patterning in what is foregrounded and silenced in related discourses, clearly positions inclusive business as a central piece to the "complex cultural work" being done to assemble land as a resource for commercial investment (Li 2014: 592).

The evidence presented from comparative studies and wider reviews appears more aligned with the alternative framings profiled above than with the narratives advanced within mainstream development thought. Inclusion is not the panacea it is claimed to be, but more often than not appears to advance adverse forms of incorporation and deepen vulnerability for both workers and small-scale producers. Social inclusion is also far less prevalent than one would think based on the ink spilled on it and the sheer volume of initiatives devoted to advancing it and proving it exists. Inherent incompatibilities between the "inclusive" and the "business" aspects of inclusive business, inherent barriers faced by smallholders to market entry,[9] and market shifts to ever greater production and processing efficiencies and ever-tighter control over (the traceability of) supply chains, are key factors in the identified trends toward more *ex*clusive business. Where significant inclusion is found, it is often where civil society has pressured governments to raise labor standards (Friedemann-Sanchez 2006); where governments themselves have strongly guided or regulated the sector for smallholder inclusion (McCarthy 2010; Zen et al. 2016); where certification has created niche opportunities and inclusive exceptions to predominantly exclusive value chains (Bassett 2010; Fridell 2007); and where public investment and political will align to enable smallholders not just to grow more, but to add value locally (Dammert Belo 2017). This is a far cry from the vision of agribusiness as the key to rural inclusion and the market liberalization ideologies of most inclusive business advocates.

So how might we explain the fact that inclusive business discourses and interventions are reaching a fever pitch at a time when the trend is toward growing smallholder *ex*clusion rather than inclusion? I would argue that these discourses and practices are necessary for our ability to imagine large-scale land acquisitions as anything other than a form of dispossession of the most vulnerable actors. By shining light on the benefits of this investment and deflecting attention from the wider trends toward growing exclusion from agribusiness supply chains (and landscapes), land grabs are legitimated and the strategic functions of public policy and finance in propping up big business rather than poor smallholders is effectively obscured.

REFERENCES CITED

Amanor, K. 2018. Global value chains and agribusiness in Africa: Upgrading or capturing smallholder production? *Agrarian South* 8(1–2): 30–63.

AU, AfDB, and UNECA. 2014. *Guiding Principles on Large-Scale Land Based Investments in Africa*. Addis Ababa, Ethiopia: African Union, African Development Bank and United Nations Economic Commission for Africa.

Bassett, T.J. 2010. Slim pickings: Fairtrade cotton in West Africa. *Geoforum* 41(1): 44–55. https://doi.org/10.1016/j.geoforum.2009.03.002.

Bienabe, E. and H. Vermeulen. 2007. *New Trends in Supermarket Procurement Systems in South Africa: The Case of Local Procurement Schemes from Small-Scale Farmers by*

Rural-Based Retail Chain Stores. London: International Institute for Environment and Development.

Borras, S.M. Jr. and J. Franco. 2012. Global land grabbing and trajectories of agrarian change: A preliminary analysis. *Journal of Agrarian Change* 12(1): 49.

Brown, T. 2005. Contestation, confusion and corruption: Market-based land reform in Zambia. In: S. Evers, M. Spierenburg and H. Wels (Eds.), *Competing Jurisdictions: Settling Land Claims in Africa*, 79–102. Leiden, Netherlands: Brill Academic Publishers.

Carney, J.A. 1988. Struggles over crop rights and labour within contract farming households in a Gambian irrigated rice project. *The Journal of Peasant Studies* 15(3): 334–349.

CFS. 2014. *Principles for Responsible Investment in Agriculture and Food Systems of the Committee on World Food Security*. Rome: Committee on World Food Security.

Chamberlain, W. and W. Anseeuw. 2018. Inclusive businesses and land reform: Corporatization or transformation? *Land* 7(18), doi: 10.3390/land7010018.

Chamberlain, W. and W. Anseeuw. 2019. Inclusive businesses in agriculture: Defining the concept and its complex and evolving partnership structures in the field. *Land Use Policy* 83(2019): 308–322.

Chinsinga, B. 2016. The Green Belt Initiative, politics and sugar production in Malawi. *Journal of Southern African Studies* 43(3): 501–515.

CIPS and Tradecraft. 2008. *Win/Win: Achieving Sustainable Procurement with the Developing World*. Stamford, UK and London: The Chartered Institute of Purchasing & Supply and Tradecraft.

Cooke, F.M. 2012. In the name of poverty alleviation: Experiments with oil palm smallholders and customary land in Sabah, Malaysia. *Asia Pacific Viewpoint* 53(3): 240–253.

Cooke, F.M., S. Toh, and J. Vaz. 2011. *Community-Investor Business Models: Lessons from the Oil Palm Sector in East Malaysia*. London: International Institute for Environment and Development.

Cotula, L. and R. Leonard. 2010. *Alternatives to Land Acquisitions: Agricultural Investment and Collaborative Business Models*. London, Bern, Rome andMaputo: International Institute for Environment and Development, Swiss Development Corporation, International Fund for Agricultural Development and Centro Terra Viva.

Dammert Belo, J.L. 2017. *Contested Booms: The Politics of Oil Palm Expansion in the Peruvian Amazon*. Doctoral Dissertation, Clark University. Available at: https://pqdtopen.proquest.com/pubnum/10600663.html.

Dancer, H. and E. Sulle. 2015. Gender implications of agricultural commercialization: The case of sugarcane production in Kilombero District, Tanzania. *Future Agricultures Working Paper* No. 118. Available at: https://www.future-agricultures.org/download/fac-working-paper-118-pdf/ (retrieved May 22, 2021).

Daniel, S. and A. Mittal. 2010. *(Mis)Investment in Agriculture: The Role of the International Finance Corporation in Global Land Grabs*. Oakland, CA: The Oakland Institute.

Dolan, C. and J. Humphrey. 2004. Changing governance patterns in the trade in fresh vegetables between Africa and the United Kingdom. *Environment and Planning* 36(3): 491–509.

Fairhead, J., M. Leach, and I. Scoones. 2012. Green Grabbing: A new appropriation of nature? *The Journal of Peasant Studies* 39(2): 237–261.

FAO. 2015. *Inclusive Business Models: Guidelines for Improving Linkages between Producer Groups and Buyers of Agricultural Produce* (by S. Kelly, N. Vergara and H. Bammann). Rome: Food and Agriculture Organization of the United Nations.

FAO and CIFOR. 2002. Towards Equitable Partnerships between Corporate and Smallholder Partners: Relating Partnerships to Social, Economic and Environmental Indicators. Rome and Bogor: Food and Agriculture Organization of the United Nations and Center for International Forestry Research. Available at: http://www.fao.org/DOCREP/005/Y4803E/y4803e00.htm#TopOfPage (accessed Dec. 8, 2020).

FAO, IFAD, UNCTAD, and World Bank Group. 2010. *Principles for Responsible Agricultural Investment that Respect Rights, Livelihoods and Resources*. Rome and Washington, DC: Food and Agriculture Organization of the UN, International Fund for Agricultural Development, UN Conference on Trade and Development Secretariat and World Bank Group.

Ferguson, J. 2006. *Global Shadows: Africa in the Neoliberal World Order*. Durham, NC: Duke University Press.

Fridell, G. 2007. *Fair Trade Coffee: The Prospects and Pitfalls of Market-Driven Social Justice*. Toronto, Canada: University of Toronto Press.

Friedemann-Sanchez, G. 2006. Assets in intra-household bargaining among women workers in Colombia's cut-flower industry. *Feminist Economics* 12(1–2): 247–269. https://doi.org/10.1080/13545700500508551.

G20. 2015. *G20 Inclusive Business Framework*. G20 Development Working Group. Available at: http://www.g20.utoronto.ca/2015/G20-Inclusive-Business-Framework.pdf (retrieved June 19, 2020).

German, L. and G. Schoneveld. 2012. Review of the early legal and institutional framework for biofuel investments in Zambia. *Review of Policy Research* 29(4): 467–491.

German, L., G. Schoneveld, and E. Mwangi. 2013. Contemporary processes of large-scale land acquisition in sub-Saharan Africa: Legal deficiency or elite capture of the rule of law? *World Development* 48(2013): 1–18.

German, L., E. Cavane, A. Sitoe, and C. Braga. 2016. Private investment as an engine of rural development: A confrontation of theory and practice for the case of Mozambique. *Land Use Policy* 51(2016): 1–14.

German, L.A., A.M. Bonanno, L.C. Foster, and L. Cotula. 2020. "Inclusive business" in agriculture: Evidence from the evolution of agricultural value chains. *World Development* 134, October 2020, 105018.

German, L.A., L. Cotula, K. Gibson, A. Locke, A. Bonanno, and J. Quan. 2018. *Land Governance and Inclusive Business in Agriculture: Advancing the Debate*. LEGEND State of the Debate Report 2017. London: Overseas Development Institute.

GRAIN. 2008. "SEIZED! The 2008 Land Grab for Food and Financial Security." *GRAIN Briefing*, October 2008.

Hall, D. 2013. Primitive accumulation, accumulation by dispossession and the global land grab. *Third World Quarterly* 34(9): 1582–1604.

Hall, R., I. Scoones, and D. Tsikata. 2017. Plantations, outgrowers and commercial farming in Africa: Agricultural commercialization and implications for agrarian change. *The Journal of Peasant Studies* 44(3): 515–537.

Hart, S.L. 2007. *Capitalism at the Crossroads: The Unlimited Business Opportunities in Solving the World's Most Difficult Problems*. Upper Saddle River, NJ: Wharton School Publishing.

Hart, S.L. and C.M. Christensen. 2002. The great leap: Driving innovation from the base of the pyramid. *Sloan Management Review* 44(1): 51–56.

Harvey, D. 2003. *The New Imperialism*. Oxford, UK: Oxford University Press.

Herrmann, R. and U. Grote. 2015. Large-scale agro-industrial investments and rural poverty: Evidence from sugarcane in Malawi. *Journal of African Economies* 24(5): 645–676.

Hickey, S. and A. du Toit. 2007. Adverse incorporation, social exclusion and chronic poverty. *CPRC Working Paper* No. 81. Chronic Poverty Research Centre.

Humphrey, J. and O. Memedovic. 2006. *Global Value Chains in the Agrifood Sector*. United Nations Industrial Development Organization. Available at: http://www.ruralfinanceandinvestment.org/node/296 (retrieved Dec. 8, 2020).

Hystra. 2015. *Smallholder Farmers and Business: 15 Pioneering Collaborations for Improved Productivity and Sustainability*. Paris: Hybrid Strategies Consulting.

IEG. 2015. *Investment Climate Reforms: An Independent Evaluation of World Bank Group Support to Reforms of Business Regulations*. Washington, DC: The World Bank.

IEG. 2018. *IFC's Experience with Inclusive Business: An Assessment of IFC's Role, Outcomes, and Potential Scenarios*. Washington, DC: Independent Evaluation Group, World Bank Group.

IFC. 2011. *Accelerating Inclusive Business Opportunities: Business Models that Make a Difference*. Washington, DC: International Finance Corporation.

IFC. 2014. *Shared Prosperity through Inclusive Business: How Successful Companies Reach the Base of the Pyramid*. Washington, DC: International Finance Corporation.

IFC. 2016. *Built for Change: Inclusive Business Solutions for the Base of the Pyramid*. Washington, DC: International Finance Corporation.

Kelly, S., N. Vergara, and H. Bammann. 2015. *Inclusive Business Models: Guidelines for Improving Linkages between Producer Groups and Buyers of Agricultural Produce*. Rome: Food and Agriculture Organization of the United Nations.

Li, T. 2011. Centering labor in the land grab debate. *The Journal of Peasant Studies* 38(2): 281–298.

Li, T. 2014. What is land? Assembling a resource for global investment. *Transactions of the Institute of British Geographers* 39(2014): 589–602.

Maganga, F., K. Askew, R. Odgaard, and H. Stein. 2016. Dispossession through formalization: Tanzania and the G8 land agenda in Africa. *Asian Journal of African Studies* 40(August 2016): 3–49.

Mamonova, N. 2015. Resistance or adaptation? Ukrainian peasants' responses to large-scale land acquisitions. *Journal of Peasant Studies* 42(3–4): 607–634.

Matenga, C.R. and M. Hichaambwa. 2017. Impacts of land and agricultural commercialisation on local livelihoods in Zambia: Evidence from three models. *The Journal of Peasant Studies* 44(3): 574–593.

Mausch, K., D. Mithöfer, S. Asfaw, and H. Waibel. 2009. Export vegetable production in Kenya under the EurepGAP standard: Is large "more beautiful" than small? *Journal of Food Distribution Research* 40(3): 115–129.

McCarthy, J. 2010. Processes of inclusion and adverse incorporation: Oil palm and agrarian change in Sumatra, Indonesia. *Journal of Peasant Studies* 37(4): 821–850.

McKersie, B. and M. Hichaambwa. 2011. *Feasibility Study for the Enhancement and Extension of Kaleya Smallholder Scheme, Final Report*. Thame, UK: Cardno Emerging Markets Ltd.

Mehta, L., G.J. Veldwisch, and J. Franco. 2012. Water grabbing? Focus on the (re)appropriation of finite water resources. *Water Alternatives* 5(2): 193–207.

Monson, J. 2009. *Africa's Freedom Railway: How a Chinese Development Project Changed Lives and Livelihoods in Tanzania*. Bloomington, IN: Indiana University Press.

Mousseau, F. 2019. *The Highest Bidder Takes It All: World Bank's New Scheme to Privatise Land in the Global South*. London: Bretton Woods Project.

Moyo, S., P. Yeros, and P. Jha. 2012. Imperialism and primitive accumulation: Notes on the new scramble for Africa. *Agrarian South: Journal of Political Economy* 1(2): 182.

Mujenja, F. and C. Wonani. 2012. *Long-term Outcomes of Agricultural Investments: Lessons from Zambia*. Lusaka, Zambia: International Institute for Environment and Development.

NEPAD. 2002. *Declaration on Democracy, Political, Economic and Corporate Governance*. Midrand, South Africa: New Partnership for Africa's Development.

Oberlack, C., L. Tejadaa, P. Messerli, S. Rist, and M. Giger. 2016. Sustainable livelihoods in the global land rush? Archetypes of livelihood vulnerability and sustainability potentials. *Global Environmental Change* 41(2016): 153–171.

Obidzinski, K., R. Andriani, H. Komarudin, and A. Andrianto. 2012. Environmental and social impacts of oil palm plantations and their implications for biofuel production in Indonesia. *Ecology and Society* 17(1): 25. http://dx.doi.org/10.5751/ES-04775-170125.

Oxfam. 2002. Cultivating poverty: The impact of US cotton subsidies on Africa. *Oxfam Briefing Paper* 30. Washington, DC: Oxfam.

Plank, C. 2013. Land grabs in the black earth: Ukrainian oligarchs and international investors. In: J. Franco and S. M. Borras (Eds.), *Land Concentration, Land Grabbing and People's Struggles in Europe*, 198–204. Amsterdam: Transnational Institute.

Potter, L. 2015. Managing oil palm landscapes: A seven-country survey of the modern palm oil industry in Southeast Asia, Latin America and West Africa. *CIFOR Occasional Paper* No. 122. Bogor, Indonesia: Center for International Forestry Research.

Prowse, M. 2012. Contract farming in developing countries: A review. *A Savoir* 12. Paris: Agence Française de Développement.

Schoneveld, G., L. German, and E. Nukator. 2011. Land-based investments for rural development? A grounded analysis of the local impacts of biofuel feedstock plantations in Ghana. *Ecology and Society* 16(4): 10.

Smalley, R., E. Sulle, and L. Malale. 2014. The role of the state and foreign capital in agricultural commercialisation: The case of sugarcane outgrowers in Kilombero District, Tanzania. *Future Agricultures Working Paper* No. 106. https://media.africaportal.org/documents/FAC_Working_Paper_106_1.pdf.

Sulle, E. 2016. Social differentiation and the politics of land: Sugar cane outgrowing in Kilombero, Tanzania. *Journal of Southern African Studies* 43(3): 517–533.

Taruvinga, M. 2011. Commercialising subsistence farmers: A benefit or detriment to the poor? MA thesis, Faculty of Humanities, University of Witwatersrand, Johannesburg, South Africa. https://core.ac.uk/download/pdf/39669239.pdf.

Technoserve and IFAD. 2011. Outgrower schemes: Enhancing profitability. *Technical Brief*, September 2011.

Tinsley, E. and N. Agapitova, Eds. 2018. *Private Sector Solutions to Helping Smallholders Succeed: Social Enterprise Business Models in the Agriculture Sector*. Washington, DC: The World Bank.

UN. 2015. *Addis Ababa Action Agenda of the Third International Conference on Financing for Development*. New York: United Nations.

UNDP. 2013. *Realizing Africa's Wealth: Building Inclusive Businesses for Shared Prosperity*. New York: United Nations Development Program.

UNECA and AU. 2016. *African Inclusive Markets Center of Excellence (AIMEC) Concept Note*. Ninth Joint Annual Meetings of the African Union Specialized Technical Committee on Finance, Monetary Affairs, Economic Planning and Integration and the Economic Commission for Africa Conference of African Ministers of Finance, Planning and Economic Development. Addis Ababa, Ethiopia, 31 March to 2 April, 2016.

Van den Broeck, G. and M. Maertens. 2016. Horticultural exports and food security in developing countries. *Global Food Security* 10: 11–20.

Vermeulen, S. and L. Cotula. 2010. *Making the Most of Agricultural Investment: A Survey of Business Models that Provide Opportunities for Smallholders*. Rome and London: Food and Agriculture Institute of the United Nations and International Institute for Environment and Development.

Vermeulen, S., J. Woodhill, F. Proctor, and R. Delnoye. 2008. *Chain-Wide Learning for Inclusive Agrifood Market Development*. London and Wageningen, Netherlands: International Institute for Environment and Development and Wageningen International.

Vorley, B. 2016. "Big brands like Unilever aren't the answer to helping Africa's farmers." *The Guardian*, 31 August 2016. Available at: https://www.theguardian.com/sustainable-business/2016/aug/31/unilever-africa-farmers-inclusive-business-agrifood-development (accessed Apr. 13, 2022).

Vorley, B., M. Lundy, and J. MacGregor. 2008. Business Models that are Inclusive of Small Farmers. Paper prepared for FAO and UNIDO as background to the Global Agro-Industries Forum, New Delhi, 8–11 April 2008. Available at: https://pubs.iied.org/pdfs/G02340.pdf (accessed Dec. 8, 2020).

Watkins, K. 2007. Northern agricultural policies and world poverty: Will the Doha "Development Round" Make a Difference? In: F. Bourguignon, P. Jacquet and B. Pleskovic (Eds.), *Economic Integration and Social Responsibility*, 9–90. Washington, DC: The World Bank.

WBCSD. 2016 *Delivering on the Sustainable Development Goals: The Inclusive Business Approach*. Geneva: World Business Council for Sustainable Development.

Wendimu, M.A., A. Henningsen and P. Gibbon. 2016. Sugarcane outgrowers in Ethiopia: "Forced" to remain poor? *World Development* 83: 84–97.

White, B., S.M. Borras, Jr, R. Hall, I. Scoones and W. Wolford. 2012. The new enclosures: Critical perspectives on corporate land deals. *Journal of Peasant Studies* 39(3–4): 619–647.

Wolford, W., S.M. Borras Jr, R. Hall, I. Scoones, and B. White. 2013. Governing global land deals: The role of the state in the rush for land. *Development and Change* 44(2): 197.

Woodhill, J. 2016. *Inclusive Agribusiness: The State of Play*. Background Working Paper prepared for the Global Donor Platform for Rural Development.

World Bank. 2014. The practice of responsible investment principles in larger-scale agricultural investments: Implications for corporate performance and impact on local communities. *Agriculture and Environmental Services Discussion Paper* No. 8. Washington, DC: World Bank.

Zen, Z., C. Barlow, R. Gondowarsito, and J.F. McCarthy. 2016. Interventions to promote smallholder oil palm and socio-economic improvement in Indonesia. In: R. Cramb and J. F. McCarthy (Eds.), *The Oil Palm Complex: Smallholders, Agribusiness and the State in Indonesia and Malaysia*, 78–108. Singapore: NUS Press.

PART III

Prospering in Place

CHAPTER 7

Rethinking Land and Rural Futures

> It appeared to me that anthropology could be an entry into the contemporary: precisely because it took ontology seriously at last. Not as symbolic representation. Not as those beliefs left on the wrong side of the modernizing frontier. But as life and death struggle to have the right to stand in one's own time and place.
>
> —Bruno Latour (2014: 15)

> The opposite of dispossession is not possession, it is deep, reciprocal, consensual *attachment*.
>
> —Leanne Simpson (Nishnaabeg) (2017: 43, emphasis in original)

In writing this book, I have endeavored to "provincialize" (Chakrabarty 1992) the land governance orthodoxy that has consolidated on the heels of the late 2000s financial crisis and the outcry over global land grabs, through the tools of ontology. Through a careful and critical reading of the concepts and discourses employed by multilateral agencies investing in knowledge production surrounding "what land is" and "how it should be governed," together with a reading of counter-truths and other ways of knowing land from the ethnographic literature, I sought to bring to light the shaky evidentiary grounds and situated ontological assumptions on which the theories of change justifying land governance interventions rest. This work has revealed radically distinct ways of knowing and being with "land" (broadly conceived) that contrast sharply with dominant constructs, robbing them of their universalizing and modernizing gaze. Seen in their entirety, the land governance discourses of the World Bank and allied multilateral and bilateral development agencies emerge not as a universal prescription for how land should be used and governed, but as a very particular (and peculiar) project firmly situated in a particular time, place, and *cultural*[1] tradition.

From the chapter on women's land rights, we see how women are not made uniformly insecure through relations of custom and conjugality, nor are they uniformly supported by laws enacted in the name of gender equity or by organs and agents of the state. The diversity of women's experiences under distinctive systems of descent, inheritance, and conjugality, and the diverse ways in which women participate in land use and governance or exercise their capacity to claim, stand in sharp contrast to discourses of uniform dispossession. Securities conferred through matriliny, descent-based landholdings, conjugality, and the *responsibilities* enshrined in the customary domain are obscured through discourses treating custom as a threat to women's empowerment. The evidence also shows how claims related to the benevolence of the state, and the benefits of state-sanctioned title, are upended by evidence of gender bias within the state, the refusal to formalize entitlements of women in informal or polygamous unions, and the erosion of former rights and securities under formalization as they are consolidated in the hands of a few. The assumption that land titling and transferrable titles will enhance tenure security for women also fails to acknowledge how titling simplifies the entitlement structure, dispossessing some as it recognizes the rights of others, and obscures the diverse ways in which tenure security may be undermined under formalization *due to* the enhanced transferability of title and the vibrancy of informal land markets. The diversity of women's experiences with land, custom, and relationality profiled in this volume discredits the notion that "women" share some singular condition of insecurity that calls for outside intervention or Western saviors.

In the case of collective title, while Indigenous peoples undoubtedly face mounting pressure over their territories and autonomy due to a suite of economic, political, and technological factors (FAO and FILAC 2021), the issuance of collective title and procedural rights to FPIC are not panaceas for addressing vulnerability to displacement and unregulated extraction or for fostering Indigenous self-determination. As the case studies from Mozambique and Peru show, formalization does not only recognize but may also curtail collective rights (whether to contiguous Indigenous territories, to valuable resources, or to consent); may codify rights in ways that enable the subdivision, commodification, and alienation of communal land; and may enable achievements to be reversed over time as the rights formerly recognized run counter to the interests of economic and political elites. One might argue that as practiced, rights amount to the procedural legitimation of dispossession in Mozambique, and the whittling away of Indigenous territories and identities in Peru. Such ongoing precarity of collective tenures tends to be met with calls for *more* titling and stronger *procedural* rights (in the form of

FPIC). However, we need to shift our gaze to how these practices are *compatible with* ongoing dispossession—from the formalization of collective rights that are spatially and substantively circumscribed, conditional, reversible and alienable, to procedures for transacting in collectively held land. These insights resonate deeply with critical theories of law and property that show the law not as a neutral arbiter or protector of rights, but as deeply embedded within and reflective of broader power relations in society. They also reveal the ongoing commitment by the World Bank and its multilateral, bilateral, and nongovernmental allies to the subdivision and alienation of collective lands and territories in spite of seemingly progressive discourses of customary rights recognition. As with individual titles, the recognition of Indigenous and collective land rights is a double-edged sword: on the one hand seen as necessary to safeguard collective territorial rights, and on the other fundamentally changing (eroding, fragmenting, commodifying) customary entitlements and land relations while reinforcing state territorial authority.

Chapter 5 further shows how ontologies of tenure security are not stable essences, but deeply situated constructs. The World Bank and allied multilateral and nongovernmental organizations have advanced ideas about the threats posed by social relations (e.g., with male relatives or custom), and argued for the benefits of private (and ideally individualized) rights to land and for the very peculiar notion that alienability confers security. Land itself within these constructs is rendered as a discrete entity that may be abstracted from its surrounding social and ecological relations. Those constructs may seem natural in the absence of ethnographic evidence on alternative ontologies of land and security, which are not just embedded in and uniquely adapted to the exigencies of distinct livelihood systems but exhibit features *in direct contrast* with dominant constructs. For sedentary agriculturalists, ontologies of land emphasize interpersonal and intergenerational *responsibilities* and the agential qualities of land and the ancestral realm attached to it; they thus stand in stark contrast with ontologies of security-as-*rights*. They also emphasize attachment, belonging, and the inseparability of people and place, and thus the fundamental inalienability of land *from the landholding group*. For pastoralists, livelihood and ecological resilience rests on mobility, and conceptions of tenure security grounded in neatly bounded territorial units and identities or exclusivity of rights can only be conceived of as *undermining* pastoralist tenure and livelihood security. Here, the emphasis on security through relationality (with people, place, ancestors, spirits), responsibility (to group members, the unborn), and care across African ontologies of land stands in sharp contrast with an ontology that conceives of the severance of all forms of relationality and of alienability as the way to advance tenure security and restrictions on personal entitlements as threats to that security. Clearly, something is amiss.

It is also possible to provincialize "inclusive business"—a concept that stands alongside land governance as a key object of development programming in the post-2008 era. This can be done not only against alternative notions of inclusiveness from farmers' organizations and rural dwellers, as was done for the other themes, but through a detailed look at the work that was done in re-framing "land grabs" as a grand opportunity for rural development. This analysis, in Chapter 6, exposed how what is centered in the public imaginary—agribusiness firms as the key to rural opportunity and much-needed finance, technical expertise, and markets—silences other realities, such as the threats this investment poses to the territorial and livelihood interests of rural land users; the value of informal markets to small-scale farmers, pastoralists, and fisherfolk; farmers' own visions for rural futures; or how the structuring of global value chains is working at cross-purposes with truly inclusive forms of territorial ordering and economic relations. Inclusive business constructs, while somewhat diverse, center the notion that local people are to be "included" in projects conceived of by outsiders while normalizing agribusiness-led growth. As stated before, these are neither endogenous visions of rural futures being advanced, nor the values, expertise, and productivity of rural communities being centered. Furthermore, as argued by Kojo Amanor, "far from constituting a dynamic system of entrepreneurship that facilitates acquisition of new skills by farmers, upgrading of production, and higher incomes," what has been sold as inclusive business may instead be "value capture in which transnational corporations extend their control over production and marketing through takeovers and contractual arrangements that control farmers' production" (Amanor 2019: 30).

What does this all mean? Do competing ontologies of land simply mean there are multiple cultures, multiple constructs that populate the human imagination—that the world is flatter than we once thought, having dethroned Western constructs of land and security from their claimed position of universal relevance? Or is that difference far more meaningful to the shaping of rural futures at local and global scales? Before turning to these questions for the land arena, it is worth re-visiting some of the insights from ontological scholarship. Most writings associated with the "ontological turn" in anthropology and related disciplines emphasize the deep connections between the ontological and material—whether for how the concepts through which we think the world bring that very world into being, or for the inseparability of the two (Blaser and de la Cadena 2018). Yet the debate over whether ontological scholarship is apolitical or *inherently so* is a subject of ongoing debate. Bessire and Bond argue that the turn to ontological questions in anthropology shifts our gaze away from 'operations of domination and struggles that lay claim to what is, [towards] a principled assertion of how things could be,' thereby dampening critique and diverting attention from the "actually existing politics of nature and culture" (Bessire and Bond 2014: 441, 449).

This volume comes down on the side of ontological questions—the questions about what things *are* and *might be*—being inherently political. This may be seen first in the uneven power relations in the pluriverse: the world is no flatter for having upended the universalist assumptions of modernity, as the ability and will to impose one-world conceptions onto others is unevenly shared. Those in positions of power continue to insist that not all cultures or ways of knowing the world "have the same standing in rational politics, the arena *where decisions affecting a territory and its population* are debated" (Blaser 2013: 15, emphasis added). With many contemporary conflicts surrounding "land" and "the environment" involving the very definition of the 'things' that are at stake (Blaser 2013: 14), this uneven terrain of recognition and legitimation matters deeply to the relationships and actions that play out on land. And if we are willing to accept the premise that concepts are meaningful in world-making, then ontological questions are also political in the way in which advanced specification of the concepts through which the world is to be known (by those able to invest in this complex cultural work of constructing the world in these ways and not others) has the power to normalize certain world-making projects and conditions of possibility while foreclosing others. As Lila Abu-Lughod argues, without the Western construct of "Muslim women" as a uniformly oppressed category, geopolitical struggles carried out under the "War on Terrorism" may have been less tenable (Abu-Lughod 2002). Ontology is no less than a "life and death struggle to have the right to stand in one's own time and place" (Latour 2014: 15).

ONTOLOGY AND MATERIALITY: LOCATING THE POLITICS OF THE POWER/KNOWLEDGE/LAND NEXUS

> Vision is always a question of the power to see—and perhaps of the violence implicit in our visualizing practices. With whose blood were my eyes crafted?
> —Donna Haraway (1988)

> Modernization is a war cry that has to be resisted everywhere.
> —Bruno Latour (2014)

In this section, I set to the task of clearly locating the politics and materiality of the world-making project of "land governance." The findings from Part II of this volume, as sketched out briefly above, provide evidence of a plurality of ontologies of land, of security, and even of the conditions and value of rural peoples and landscapes of the global South. Perhaps more importantly, they point to a clear patterning of dominant discourses across themes: land is being made into a good that can be abstracted from the web of relations in which it is embedded and exchanged in the marketplace. In so doing, land is not just re-made as commodity, but as property. This undoubtedly involves the recognition of rights, but is it not of a particular form of rights—akin to Westbrook's notion of "the right to exclude without further connection" (Westbrook 2004: 88)? Rather than embodying objective, universal ideas—"views from above, from nowhere" (Haraway 1988: 589), the land governance orthodoxy that has consolidated within international development circles in the post-2008 era is squarely aligned with the shifting interests in Africa's farmland and the political economic interests behind those shifts that were sketched out in the Introduction. The power/knowledge or power/ontology nexus, when it comes to land (as with so many other things), is thus deeply implicated in and reflective of deeper material and political struggles over Africa's farmland, and the values (current and future, productive and financial) and possible futures linked to it.

What does it mean for land governance discourses to "align with" the political economy of land? What forms of interaction, of causality, are involved? While Foucault tends to give historical-analytical primacy to knowledge *(logos)* over the constitution of things (Pellizzoni 2015), he has also called for specifying both the conditions which give rise to concepts and the conditions that these concepts in turn sustain. For the former, while some of the land governance instruments (such as legal mechanisms for formalizing exclusive entitlements to land and providing security for foreign investors) and constructs (such as individualism) profiled in this volume have histories that pre-date the contemporary land governance era, other concepts and discursive-ontological practices can be traced to more recent conditions—the post-2008 scramble for land, the growing trends toward the financialization of farmland, and the need to legitimate land takings by reframing "land grabs" as a long-awaited opportunity for rural development.

The primary conditions of interest that these concepts in turn sustain are the ongoing alienation of customary land to agribusiness firms, and the growing concentration of land rights, access, and control at local, national, and global scales. This has been enabled by the cover of legitimacy these discourses extend to land takings, and to the legal constructs and mechanisms through which land rights—both individual and collective—are circumscribed, privatized, and rendered alienable in the context of their recognition. This has also been enabled through the "complex cultural work" (Li 2014: 592) involved in establishing and bounding our field of vision and action. There are reasons for the vast investment in knowledge production surrounding land and its governance: efforts to get ahead of the "land grab" critique and establish a semantic field through which the world is brought to think about things in certain ways (while foreclosing others) yields fruit.[2] Taming diverse and unwieldy place-based ontologies of land—what it *is* and what it *can do* (Li 2014)—is crucial to this project.

Property was until recently considered infertile academic terrain, subject to such extensive theoretical debate across multiple academic fields as to be a settled object or fact. As commonly understood, property was a socially recognized relationship between people consisting of rights and corresponding duties surrounding objects, resources, or benefit streams (Bromley 1991; Benda-Beckmann, von Benda-Beckmann, and M.G. Wiber et al. 2006). Yet in the past few years, an emerging body of critical scholarship has unsettled property once again—showing that it is "never merely about the allocation of 'stuff'" (Prudham 2015: 440). These works reveal property relations not just beyond social/material dichotomies and human-human relationality, but also as linked to political economy, processes of state building and racialization, and struggles over authority and citizenship (Bhandar 2018; Fontein 2011; Moreton-Robinson 2015; Prudham 2015; Shipton 2009; Sikor and Lund 2010). Several of these works coalesce around arguments framing property and its relation to the customary not through the emancipatory language of rights, but rather commodification and theft. In a 2020 book entitled *Theft Is Property!*, political theorist Robert Nichols analyzes the genealogy of dispossession and Indigenous property rights in the Anglo settler world, and finds dispossession to be a process in which new property relations are generated but "under structural conditions that demand their simultaneous negation" (Nichols 2020: 8). This is found to occur by combining two processes often thought of as distinct—the transformation of nonproprietary relations into proprietary ones, and the (systematic) transferal of control and title of this newly established property. Aileen Moreton-Robinson's *The White Possessive: Property, Power and Indigenous Sovereignty* also explores property in Anglo settler contexts, profiling the difficult cultural and legal work required "to maintain Canada, the United States, Hawai'i, New Zealand and Australia as white possessions" (Moreton-Robinson 2014: xi). Both authors provide clear evidence for settler colonialism's ongoing operations in the present (see also Wolfe 2006), in the form of legal and regulatory mechanisms for Indigenous dispossession as well as forms of rationalization investing in "reproducing and reaffirming the nation-state's ownership, control, and domination" (Moreton-Robinson 2014: xii).

In line with these works, this volume has revealed knowledge/ontology, the law, and political economy as entwined instruments enabling the ongoing dispossession of customary land users, which works to prop up a world order rooted in global hierarchies and relations of coloniality. While the geographies of focus are not ones recognized as settler colonial or even Indigenous, parallels with the colonial histories of African countries and the settler colonial present are difficult to ignore—from discourses of *terra nulius* and populations in need of intervention and improvement, to the need to destroy (the Indigenous/local) to re-make (the settler/modern), and knowledge production at the service of imperialism (Mignolo 2007; Said 1978; Wolfe 2006). To again paraphrase Tania Li, this is deep cultural work, indeed.

LAND AND RURAL FUTURES "OTHERWISE"

Clearly, there is need to issue a no confidence vote for the World Bank and its allies, and their presumed authority to broker global poverty alleviation through the institution of property. Yet if both land and its governance are understood as having not singular essences, but manifold potentials for what they might be, how might we think of land and its governance "otherwise" (Povinelli 2012)? What alternative visions might be advanced for reimaging rural futures? Since these questions are in no small part ideological, and a question of values, this task is likely to attract staunch criticism.[3] It is therefore worth taking a moment to interrogate some of the most deeply held assumptions on which modernization ideologies rest—assumptions that have (mis) guided development policy since the colonial era, and which continue to fuel the outright dismissal of other ways of knowing and being with land. With this cleaner ideological slate, I will set to the task of exploring other possibilities for land and rural futures.

Decentering Ideologies of Deficiency

Whether interventions in rural areas are advanced in the name of conservation or development, modernization or improvement (Escobar 1988; Li 2007; Quijano 2007), or "the woman question" (Abu-Lughod 2002), a few core assumptions tend to stand out. The first is that there is a global hierarchy of value. This hierarchy imbues the authority of some nations (the "developed" or "first world") and their technocrats with the authority to speak for others—establishing the semantic terrain through which aspirations are established and operationalized (what development *is*, and the techniques through which it is to be institutionalized and measured); and deploying the expertise through which it is to be brokered. A second core assumption is that small-scale farmers, pastoralists, and fisherfolk are backwards, inefficient, unproductive, and environmentally destructive, and thus incapable of feeding the world while safeguarding crucial environmental values. These two assumptions are two sides of the same coin, and often coupled together within the narrow prescriptions that are advanced for development, conservation, and climate mitigation. While a deep interrogation of these ideas has been the life work of many and lies beyond the scope of this volume, it is important to name them, as whether they are taken as universal truths or historically and culturally situated projects will shape the generosity with which one will approach alternatives to the status quo.

Let us take a minute to consider the second of these premises. The literature on smallholder productivity and efficiency is extensive. It also tends to be more sophisticated than the simple metrics deployed in the 2011 World Bank report on land grabs (Deininger et al. 2011), where productivity is measured in terms of "yield gaps" for five key agricultural commodities, and cultivated and forested land are the only land uses recognized. Embedded in such concepts and metrics are the assumptions that current land users are underperformers (read "gaps"); that productivity is best or adequately evaluated through single commodities grown as monocultures; that "land for nature" is separate from agricultural land (see, e.g., Lambin and Meyfroidt 2011); and that sedentary agriculture is the only relevant or productive land use. With corporate agriculture increasingly being framed by land use change scientists and policy makers as a key solution to feeding the world's population while saving nature, this suite of assumptions matters deeply to the land question.

Crop yield remains the dominant indicator of agricultural productivity for development planning purposes (Reynolds et al. 2015). Here, despite common assumptions, the relationship between farm size and productivity has long been recognized as an inverse relationship—with smaller farms producing *higher* crop yields and gross returns per hectare on average. Recent efforts to scrutinize this further and improve on measurement have tended to re-affirm and even strengthen these findings (Carletto, Savastano, and Zezza et al. 2011; Kagin, Taylor, and Yúnez-Naude et al. 2016; Larson et al. 2014), and the call to use total output rather than yields of a single crop in developing productivity and efficiency metrics for (often diverse) smallholder farming systems suggests that those productivity and efficiency benefits are likely to exceed the findings from these studies (Altieri 2008). These findings undermine discourses using "yield gaps" or even "land sparing"[4] as rationales for investment in large-scale, commercial farming. Other researchers have also found evidence for an inverse relationship between farm size and *efficiency*—with Mexican smallholders found to use inputs in a more technically efficient manner (Kagin, Taylor, and Yúnez-Naude et al. 2016) and small farms typically achieving higher productivity with lower capital intensities (Hazell 2011; Hazell et al. 2007) and energy (Pimentel 1980) than large industrialized farms. The inadequacy of crop yield as a proxy for smallholder productivity has led some to propose land productivity, labor productivity, and total factor productivity as alternatives for measuring "agricultural progress" (Reynolds et al. 2015: 2).

If we look beyond these conventional metrics to other ways of valuing small-scale farming (or pastoralism), still other options for representing their value emerge—from the number of people nourished or supported per hectare (Cassidy 2013; Dove 1983), to the diverse social, livelihood, food security, equity, and environmental benefits of diverse smallholder and pastoralist land use systems. The diversity of crops, varieties, and land uses on smallholder farms and farming landscapes have has been linked to livelihood resilience in the face of various stressors; to household dietary diversity; and to a suite of local and global environmental values (e.g., biocontrol, pollination, soil fertility, and disease regulation, to name a few) (Frison et al. 2006; Iverson et al. 2014; Jones,

Shrinivas, and Bezner-Kerr et al. 2014; Kennedy et al. 2013; Letourneau et al. 2011; Mäder et al. 2002; Power 2010; Power and Flecker 1996; Remans et al. 2011). Smallholders have been shown to underpin food security beyond rural communities, with small farms (≤20 ha) and very small farms (≤2 ha) found to produce more than 75% and 30%, respectively, of most food commodities in sub-Saharan Africa, and South and Southeast Asia (Herrero et al. 2017; see also Samberg et al. 2016). The diversity of agricultural and nutrient production also diminishes as farm size increases, with the majority of global micronutrients (53–81%) and protein (57%) produced in more diverse agricultural landscapes (Herrero et al. 2017)—pointing to the crucial role smallholder agriculture plays in underpinning global nutritional quality. Peasant agriculture and food sovereignty, and the de-coupling of agriculture from financialization, have also emerged from the Covid-19 pandemic as "indispensable ingredients" for the stability of the global food system (van der Ploeg 2020). And from an equity and poverty standpoint, there is "a strong case for preferring small to large farms"—from the ability to absorb labor, to their more favorable expenditure patterns for promoting growth of the nonfarm economy (Hazell et al. 2007: 12; see also Mellor 1976; Hazell and Roell 1983). For pastoralists, there is also need to look beyond narrow metrics of growth rates and meat produced/sold per unit area, to the multiple products (e.g., milk, blood, calves, hides) and values (e.g., nutritional, subsistence, security, ecological) sustained by pastoralism (Homewood and Rodgers 1987). The broader you cast your indices, it seems, the greater the relative and absolute value accorded to smallholder farming systems. There is clearly a need to move beyond debates over "whether there is a future of smallholder farming systems" (see, e.g., Hazell 2005)[5] and to broaden the metrics used to comprehend and evaluate their worth.[6]

Conceptualization

> Political ontology wants to enable political thought and practice beyond the onto-epistemic limits of modern politics and what its practice allows.
>
> —Blaser and de la Cadena (2018: 6)

One of the core tools of the ontological anthropologist is conceptualization, or deep consideration of "what concepts we use to think concepts" (Blaser and de la Cadena 2018: 6). If ontological assumptions are assumptions about what something *is*, then ontological questions are those concerning "what things *might be*" (Holbraad and Pederson 2017: 10, emphasis added). Much of the methodological writing surrounding conceptualization concerns tools for the ethnographer to step outside of the concepts they use to translate and interpret other worlds to ask, "how might X be thought otherwise?" Here, I begin to sketch what "might be" in two ways. I begin by using the dominant constructs of the land governance orthodoxy from Part I as a basis for decentering the ontological assumptions therein, exploring how we might move beyond the constructs and theories of change that have been offered up for our consumption. Secondly, I draw on the broad array of ethnographic evidence in Part II to identify alternative possibilities for what land *might be* by drawing on what land *is* across differently situated practices.

Beginning with Part I, where the dominant knowledge regime is laid out, we might begin by shifting the burden of responsibility for global land grabs away from developing countries (in the "good land governance" vein) to the policy and market forces that have aligned to enable land to be sold to the highest or most savvy bidder—market liberalization coupled with pro-business reforms, market-based land reforms, investment promotion, and bilateral and multilateral aid programs advancing a market-based, pro-business vision of agriculture[7] and other land-based sectors (Brown 2005; Daniel and Mittal 2010; Martin-Prével and Mousseau 2016; Mousseau et al. 2020). This, in turn, allows us to shift our gaze from land governance and the problem of corrupt and sexist public officials in Africa, to political economy and *how to govern economies in ways that are more inclusive of the rural poor, agricultural laborers, and those practicing diverse ways of life*. It also calls upon us to ask what other futures are foreclosed in the efforts of the World Bank and others to advance very particular conceptions of land and its governance. If we were to transition away from the codification of "rights" and "tenure security" as legal certainty of all rights holders, rights, and uses, we might begin to see the value of relational tenures consisting of shared and overlapping rights, or of conceiving of land in terms of responsibilities for collective well-being rather than exclusive rights. Or if we were to decenter rights as the object of intervention, transactional conceptions of rights, or the state as the rightful authority in manners pertaining to land, other possibilities for *property relations as responsibility, care, and connection* come to the fore; so too does the possibility for other authorities—or the absence of centralized authority (see, e.g., Conway and Singh 2011)—in matters pertaining to land.

From the ethnographic evidence reviewed in Part II, yet other possibilities emerge for what land is and might be. From Chapter 3, the category "women" and their presumed vulnerabilities within the customary domain might be de-centered to expose other sources of vulnerability linked to the political economic relations profiled above, or from earlier waves of land titling. It might also reveal *forms of security that are deeply embedded in customary land relations* or are derived from the agencies exhibited by differently positioned (or, better yet, individual) women; other gender constructs beyond the male/female binary or its imposed symbolic referents; or *a diversity of experiences with land, custom, and relationality that upends the notion that "women" share some singular condition in need of outside intervention or Western saviors*. And if we were to decenter dominant conceptions of collective title, as discussed in Chapter 4, we might re-envision formalizations that do more to safeguard local and Indigenous interests in land (e.g., along the lines of Indigenous territory and sovereignty), or begin to see the limitations of formalized title (or of rights as its conceptual-ontological twin) in securing local lifeways or advancing collective visions for the future. Forms of political organizing oriented towards reasserting Indigenous sovereignty over territory and livelihoods, and the place-based ethics that flow from this, may come to the fore as the unique condition under which land governance might finally be decolonized (Coulthard 2010; Burow, Brock, and Dove et al. 2018). And from Chapter 5, we might begin to envision securities that lie beyond the severance of ties to place and to variably defined collectivities, to embrace a diversity of ways of understanding, enacting, and relating to those complex realities lumped under the label "land" (and forest, fisheries, or rangeland). Finally, if we were to decenter the dominant notions of "inclusive business" whose contours were profiled in Chapter 6, we might move beyond commercial viability, profitability, and scalability as the defining features of desirable business relations to equity and inclusivity as embodied in social enterprise-type programs. We might also see how social inclusion on the terms set by industry has dispossessed, marginalized, constrained freedom of choice, offloaded risk, and enhanced the vulnerability of smallholders, laborers, and customary land users, and begin to envision pathways for inclusive economies centered on the aspirations and initiative of local land users (farmers, fisherfolk, pastoralists, and others) rather than multinational corporations and their government backers.

Yet perhaps the most obvious point of departure for imagining "what might be," based on the ethnographies reviewed here, are relational orientations to land and security: the sense of belonging and social identities that connect people to place; the securities derived from diverse forms of relationality; and the inseparability of people and place. To those who would dismiss these ontologies as backward or as mere cultural beliefs that have no bearing on reality, or would center land as tradable resource or commodity as the only "real," I would ask, "Does attachment to place, as diversely as it might be conceived and enacted across geographies, serve no purpose?" While such attachment may work at cross-purposes with outside interests in land, it has clearly served the interests of rural people themselves in spite of aggressive efforts to dismantle it.

Prospering in Place

The vision advanced here is one of prospering in place. This is not a question of traditionalism or resistance to change, but about rooting processes of change in local aspirations and demand-driven innovation rather than in the interests and ideologies of the international development community or its lenders. It is also about giving value to local ways of relating to "land" and to one another, and to the multifaceted social, ecological, and economic values this contributes to—free of charge to the governments and global constituencies that derive benefit from them. Lest the reader interpret the ontological orientations profiled herein as relics of the past, it is important to also center the political visions of rural people themselves—from populist movements to African farmers on the modernizing frontier who wish not just to remain in place, but to prosper economically.

For visions of place-based futures grounded in local ways of being and doing, insights may be drawn from traditions of radical democracy and resistance within subaltern and Indigenous social movements, or from the vision set out by La Via Campesina (2017, 2018). Efforts to document the political aspirations of subaltern social movements and the writings of Indigenous scholars tend to center a vision of autonomy and self-government (Couthard 2010, 2014; Esteva and Prakash 1998; Rosset 2013; Tuck and Yang 2012). This is about people governing themselves "autonomously, well rooted in the spaces to which they belong and that belong to them" (Esteva and Prakash 1998: 27); "reclaiming land and life ways, defending and enlarging spaces of communal self-reliance" (Conway and Singh 2011: 699); and centering "place-based understanding of what constitutes proper relations—relations between people, relations between humans and their environment, and relations between individuals and institutions of authority" (Coulthard 2010: 81). These political projects are often rooted in resistance to state authority and to the capitalist relations that threaten local values and ways of life. For subaltern social movements, these political projects are interpreted as efforts to safeguard the commons against "escalating dynamics of enclosure, extraction and exploitation" and to "enlarge domains of autonomous action from the state and neoliberal economies" (Conway and Singh 2011: 699). For Indigenous scholar Glen Coulthard (Yellowknives Dene), it is instead understood as resistance to "power relations that threaten to erase or destroy our senses of place" (Coulthard 2010: 79). They are also struggles for *self-reliance* which free local people from "the illusion that governments, the FAO and other international institutions will fix the mess they continue engineering and promoting" (Esteva and Prakash 1998: xvi). For these scholars and social movements, the only hope for shifting the one-world metaphysics of "land" and "development" does not lie in the ongoing articulation with the nation-state or global development institutions, but on radical, plural, and place-based alternatives to them. Here, people are asking for neither "charity" nor "inclusion" in ever-more-global value chains; they simply want to be allowed to "govern themselves in their own cultural terms" (Conway and Singh 2011: 699).

La Via Campesina, on the other hand, centers a vision of popular agrarian reform within the framework of food sovereignty.[8] Their vision is also framed in part by what they are fighting against—namely, "the growing imposition of financial and market paradigms on every facet of their lives," whether in the form of the privatization and commercialization of land, water, and seed; enclosures of the commons; or policies that favor large-scale production systems (La Via Campesina 2017: 4). The alternative they envision involves the defense and reconstruction of territory within a food sovereignty framework[9]; the strengthening of agroecological production[10]; the democratization of knowledge; social relations free of oppression; and a land governance and political system that favors the common good and guarantees personal security (La Via Campesina 2017: 5). While intervention in public policies may be necessary, this process is to be driven by grassroots action linking the urban and rural poor.

The third and final vision I will consider here is that most closely aligned with a modernization agenda, namely, farmers' federations who tend to represent the voices of the so-called "progressive" farmers most likely to succeed under the conditions imposed by the contemporary restructuring of the global agri-food regime. Here, I return to the view articulated in the Introduction by the East African Farmers' Federation (EAFF 2010), who calls for smallholder farmers, fisherfolk, and pastoralists to be recognized as "the key investors on land and in agriculture in Africa," and for "sound investments in African farmers that increase their productivity on the land." Investments in agriculture and African farmers are seen as an "opportunity to reduce poverty, eradicate food insecurity, create wealth, ensure sustainable economic development in Africa, and restore the dignity of the African people." This vision for productivity enhancement is one in which land is secured *for smallholders* and supplemented by the provision of business support services (e.g., credit, access to inputs, market facilitation, value addition, processing), preferably through downwardly accountable farmers' organizations. This is a vision not only of place-based self-governance, but of economic prosperity. Yet this prospering is one that values farmers and supports them in becoming the primary engines of growth and global food security.

What emerges from these political visions? Each of these projects calls for putting brakes on moves to commodify customary land and on predatory forms of extraction and enclosure, and for creating political space for place-based alternatives. They also call for forms of self-determination that center place-based values (of land, life, reciprocity, and connection), and for valuing local contributions to economic development and to addressing the global social, ecological, and climate unravelling linked to advanced capitalism. Finally, they call for rural futures on their own terms—not where small-scale farmers and pastoralists are asked to deliver goods and services to boost national economic indices or global environmental services (though they will continue to do so), but things valued locally; not where they must sever attachments to community and to place, and their very history and identity, to access healthcare or a livelihood; and not where they must engage in market relations that promise to deliver ever-lower rewards and ever-greater uncertainties as a condition for remaining in place or for being seen and valued.

Yet there are also important differences between these projects in the roles envisioned for engaging with outside actors. While the first vision calls more or less for being left alone, the last two call for some form of articulation with market and policy forces—with wider regimes of governance. What pathways exist for realizing these visions without falling prey to one-world ontologies of land and rural futures and the unbridled commodification and precarity this gives rise to? How might national and local economies be governed in ways that are more responsive to the interests of the rural poor and those practicing diverse ways of life? A few key reorientations seem necessary.

A key starting point seems to be avoiding the scope of vision being set exogenously, and instead centering the visions and aspirations of local land users—of place-based imaginaries. This is not the same as the decentralization reforms being imposed on African nations over the past 30 years, which have "as a premise a notion of power which centralizes it at the top—delegating it from the top down through levels of competence" (Esteva and Prakash 1998: 39). Rather, it roots development within local institutions, initiatives, and aspirations, building local capacity outwards and perhaps "constructing from the bottom-up mechanisms for delegating limited functions to the state for concerting the harmonious coexistence of local units" (Esteva and Prakash 1998: 39). There is no one size fits all strategy, but as many strategies as there are ontologies and visions for land and rural futures.

This starting point, in turn, calls for a very different kind of relationship with the market than the one centered in Part I of this volume—one that does not rest on universal prescriptions, leave rural development at the mercy of global market forces governed purely for profit, rely on highly demanding foreign markets, or center the interests and leadership of agribusiness firms. A more "human economy," perhaps, one that emphasizes well-being and "the satisfaction of all human needs, not just those that can be met through private market transactions, but also the need for public goods" (Hann and Hart 2011: 8). Inspiration for what it might look like can be drawn from those working to understand market relations from the smallholder perspective.

Research carried out by scientists at the Overseas Development Institute (ODI) and the International Institute for Environment and Development (IIED), while often ideologically grounded in modernization ideologies, Malthusian crisis narratives or an abiding faith in the ability of markets to lift farmers out of poverty (see, e.g., Wiggins and Keats 2013; Biles 2008), nevertheless exposes the shortcomings of dominant constructs on land governance and inclusive business. Three key findings stand out.

First are the limitations of high-value export markets for smallholders. Wiggins and Keats (2013), for example, find that these are an option for only a minority of smallholders. Dynamic informal markets, while often treated with hostility by governments, tend to dominate food trading, processing, and vending; serve as a better fit with smallholder needs and constraints; and often provide greater value to farmers (Vorley, Fearne, and Ray et al. 2007). Fast-growing urban markets (domestic or regional) were also found to be less demanding and more dependable for most smallholders (Wiggins and Keats 2013). With the market moving closer to the farm, farmers now have more choice of what to produce and where to market; thus, "contract farming and exports to the global market are no longer the only games in town."[11] According to Bill Vorley, Senior Associate for Sustainable Markets with IIED, there is also "tremendous scope for improving the economic, social and environmental performance of the informal economy at scale, without pushing people out of jobs."[12] A related finding is the limitations of larger firms and private action in supporting smallholder farmers. While Vorley highlights business incompatibilities, Wiggins and Keats (2013) emphasize the limitations of private initiatives in enhancing smallholder access to markets for the staple crops traditionally grown.

A second key finding is that interventions, if they are to work, must respond to the variable needs of small-scale farmers rather than the needs of agribusiness. These needs may include improvements in yield or pricing, but may also mean reducing the risks associated with credit, production, and marketing. This means enabling and facilitating (pastoralist-, fisherfolk- and) smallholder-led or -responsive learning and innovation rather than replacing what people currently do with other models, or trying to replicate isolated successes to a larger area. Such approaches would build on the established productivities and multifaceted values supported by rural land uses and lifeways, while supporting smallholder aspirations. An ethos of *enabling* rather than *replacing*.

Finally, market linkages often fail to reach or to help the poorest and most vulnerable households, who instead require public support to access healthcare and education, build assets, and secure social protection.

Supporting more plural ways of organizing local life and livelihoods and supporting markets more favorable to smallholders also call for a very different kind of state and civil society. From these alternative visions for land governance, the state factors in but in ways that legitimate local efforts to assert land and food sovereignty (see Borras and Franco 2012 for examples). The law would be deployed not as a tool of dispossession and replacement, but in ways responsive to local demand to supplement customary law in the mediation of disputes or to sanction transactions among customary users (see, for example, Lavigne-Delville 1999). Inspiration can also be drawn from visions emanating from the development establishment itself, but marginalized by dominant interests.[13] The views of Olivier de Schutter, the UN Rapporteur on the Right to Food; the views of civil society expressed through the Civil Society Mechanism of the CFS (CSM)[14]; and the views of the international scientific community expressed in the reports commissioned through the International Assessment of the Role of Agricultural Knowledge, Science, and Technology for Development (IAAKSTD)[15] in the context of the 2006 International Conference on Agrarian Reform and Rural Development (ICAARD) (McIntyre et al. 2009) are particularly instructive.

The views of the CSM can be concisely summarized in their call for "special policies and strategies targeted at small-scale and traditional fishers and farmers in rural areas," and for inscribing the role of private sector participation to the areas of human capacity development and "removal of constraints to agricultural production, marketing and distribution" (CSM 2018, Article 3.7). This vision clearly situates the private sector within stages of the value chain that do not compete with, but instead add value to, smallholder farming—thereby ruling out the need to transfer large land areas out of the customary domain. In his 2009 report entitled "Agribusiness and the Right to Food," Olivier de Schutter largely supports these prescriptions, laying out the responsibilities of governments for safeguarding local food security (UN 2009). These included actions to expand the choices for smallholders to sell their products at a decent price; efforts to strengthen the bargaining power of smallholders to equalize their relationships with the agribusiness sector; and re-engaging in public regulation of global food chains.

The orientations emanating from the Final Declaration (FAO 2006) and Synthesis Report (McIntyre et al. 2009) of ICAARD are equally unrecognizable within the contemporary dynamics of agricultural production and marketing. The reports acknowledge the negative social and environmental consequences of the exclusive emphasis on productivity enhancement and individualized action in the agricultural sector; call attention to inequality and the limited opportunities faced by the poorest and most vulnerable; and note the pattern of North American and European domination of value chains and agricultural exports—which they equate to the uneven pace of technology development. They also call for retooling AKST and for "nonhierarchical development models" to address poverty and environmental degradation through the valuation of local knowledge systems and collaboration between local and scientific knowledge systems. Solutions to the pressing problems of food insecurity, poverty, and environmental decline are located firmly within diverse agriculture and food systems and the multifunctionality of agriculture, rather than industrial agriculture and land sparing strategies—thereby making smallholder agricultural practices part of the solution to biodiversity conservation, climate mitigation, and water conservation and recognizing farming households/communities "as producers and managers of ecosystems" (McIntyre et al. 2009: 4).

The reports call for concerted action and governance across scales to move beyond a logic of individual benefit, and place the responsibility for economic and social development back in the hands of States states rather than the private sector—noting the "crucial role of the State to provide fair and equal opportunities and promote basic economic security." They also call for rural development policies, laws, and institutions that are downwardly accountable, responsive "to the needs and aspirations of rural people";[16] and for re-writing agricultural and trade policies to enable developing countries to "minimize trade-related dislocations," increase value capture by small-scale farmers, tax externalities, and remove resource use-distorting subsidies. While 58 countries lodged their approval of the Synthesis Report, Australia, Canada, and the United States were not among them, and none of the preparatory or background documents for the High-Level Expert Forum on "How to Feed the World in 2050" convened by FAO in 2009 made reference to the IAAKSTD.[17] While the scientific evidence appears to support the political visions "from below" (Indigenous nations, place-based social movements), the political will from above is clearly lacking or being sidelined by dominant interests.

If Foucault is correct in giving historical-analytical primacy to *logos* over the constitution of things, then new narratives for describing the value of rural people and their land uses, new metrics for appraising them, and new platforms for popularizing them, are urgently needed. For only this, it seems, in communion with radical place-making from below (Coulthard and Simpson 2016; Heynen and Ybarra 2020; Stahelin 2017), will enable us to move beyond the language of inherency through which small-scale farmers, pastoralists, and fisherfolk are viewed as deficient rather than the very antidote to the world's ills. Perhaps this, together with scholarship to decenter received dogmas surrounding land and rural development—revealing them as a political project both situated within and uniquely suited to the current political economic moment, rather than a universal prescription for development—will help the world apprehend the unique value of prospering in place to local people . . . and to the world.

REFERENCES CITED

Abu-Lughod, L. 2002. Do Muslim women really need saving? Anthropological reflections on cultural relativism and its others. *American Anthropologist* 104(3): 783–790.

Altieri, M. 2008. *Small Farms as a Planetary Ecological Asset: Five Key Reasons Why We Should Support the Revitalisation of Small Farms in the Global South*. Kuala Lumpur, Malaysia: Third World Network.

Amanor, K.S. 2019. Global value chains and agribusiness in Africa: Upgrading or capturing smallholder production? *Agrarian South: Journal of Political Economy* 8(1–2): 30–63.

Benda-Beckmann, F., K. von Benda-Beckmann, and M.G. Wiber. 2006. *Changing Properties of Property*. New York: Berghahn Books.

Benin, S., S. Babu, S. Odjo, A.A. Gado, and N. Paul. 2020. Political economy of national agricultural statistics: The case of Niger. *IFPRI Discussion Paper* No. 01929.

Bessire, L. and D. Bond. 2014. Ontological anthropology and the deferral of critique. *American Ethnologist* 41(3): 440–456.

Biles, J.J. 2008. Regoverning markets: A place for small-scale producers in modern agrifood chains? *Journal of Economic Geography* 8(1): 127–129.

Bhandar, B. 2018. *Colonial Lives of Property: Law, Land and Racial Regimes of Ownership*. Durham, N.C.: Duke University Press.

Blaser, M. 2013. Notes towards a political ontology of "'environmental'" conflicts. In: L. Green (Ed.), *Contested Ecologies: Dialogues in the South on Nature and Knowledge*, pp. 13–27. Cape Town, South Africa: HSRC Press.

Blaser, M. and M. de la Cadena. 2018. *A World of Many Worlds*. Durham, NC: Duke University Press.

Borras, S.M. and J.C. Franco. 2012. A "'land sovereignty'" alternative? Towards a peoples' counter-enclosure. *TNI Agrarian Justice Programme Discussion Paper*.

Bromley, D. 1991. *Environment and Economy: Property Rights and Public Policy*. Oxford: Basil Blackwell.

Brown, T. 2005. Contestation, confusion and corruption: Market-based land reform in Zambia. In: S. Evers, M. Spierenburg, and H. Wels (Eds.), *Competing Jurisdictions: Settling Land Claims in Africa*, pp.79–102. Leiden, The Netherlands: Brill Academic Publishers.

Burow, P.B., S. Brock and M.R. Dove. 2018. Unsettling the land: Indigeneity, ontology and hybridity in settler colonialism. *Environment and Society: Advances in Research* 9: 57–74.

Carletto, C., D. Jolliffe, and R. Banerjee. 2015. From tragedy to renaissance: Improving agricultural data for better policies. *The Journal of Development Studies* 51(2): 133–148.

Carletto, C., S. Savastano, and A. Zezza. 2011. Fact or artefact: The impact of measurement errors on the farm size-productivity relationship. *Journal of Development Economics* 103(2013): 254–261.

Cassidy, E.S. 2013. Redefining agricultural yields: From tons to people nourished by hectare. *Environmental Research Letters* 8(3): 3.

Chakrabarty, D. 1992. Provincializing Europe: Postcoloniality and the critique of history. *Cultural Studies* 6(3): 337–357.

Chauveau, J.-P. 2003. Plans fonciers ruraux: Conditions de pertinence des systèms d'identification et d'enregistrement des droits coutumiers. *Dossier* no. 122. London: International Institute for Environment and Development.

Conway, J. and J. Singh. 2011. Radical democracy in global perspective: Notes from the pluriverse. *Third World Quarterly* 32(4): 689–706.

Coulthard, G.S. 2010. Place against Empire: Understanding Indigenous Anti-Colonialism. *Affinities: A Journal of Radical Theory, Culture, and Action* 4(2): 79–83.

Coulthard, G.S. 2014. *Red Skin, White Masks: Rejecting the Colonial Politics of Recognition*. University of Minnesota Press.

Coulthard, G. and L.B. Simpson. 2016. Grounded normativity/place-based solidarity. *American Quarterly* 68(2): 249–255.

CSM. 2018. *Civil Society Report on the Use and Implementation of the Right to Food Guidelines*. Rome: Working Group on Monitoring of the Civil Society Mechanism for relations with the Committee on World Food Security.

Daniel, S. and A. Mittal. 2010. *(Mis)investment in Agriculture: The Role of the International Financial Corporation in Global Land Grabs*. Oakland, CA: The Oakland Institute.

Deininger, K. and D. Byerlee with J. Lindsay, A. Norton, H. Selod and M. Stickler. 2011. *Rising Global Interest in Farmland: Can it Yield Sustainable and Equitable Benefits?* Washington, DC: The World Bank.

Dove, M. 1983. Theories of swidden agriculture and the political economy of ignorance. *Agroforestry Systems* 1: 85–99.

EAFF. 2010. *The Entebbe Declaration on Large Foreign Land Acquisitions*. Nairobi, Kenya: East African Farmers' Federation. Available at: https://www.landcoalition.org/sites/default/files/documents/resources/EAFFPositionLargeLandAcquisitions_3.pdf (Oct 18, 2019).

Escobar, A. 1988. Power and visibility: Development and the invention and management of the Third World. *Cultural Anthropology* 3(4): 428–443.

Esteva, G. and M.S. Prakash. 1998. *Grassroots Postmodernism*. London, UK: Zed Books.

FAO. 2005. *Voluntary Guidelines to Support the Progressive Realization of the Right to Adequate Food in the Context of National Food Security*. Rome: Food and Agriculture Organization of the United Nations.

FAO. 2006. *International Conference on Agrarian Reform and Rural Development, Porto Alegre, Brazil, 7–10 March, 2006, Final Declaration*. Rome: Food and Agriculture Organization of the United Nations.

FAO and FILAC. 2021. *Forest Governance by Indigenous and Tribal Peoples. An Opportunity for Climate Action in Latin America and the Caribbean*. Santiago, Chile: Food and Agriculture Organization of the United Nations.

Fontein, J. 2011. Graves, ruins and belonging: Toward an anthropology of proximity. *The Journal of the Royal Anthropological Institute* 17(4): 706–727.

Frison, E.A., I.F. Smith, T. Johns, J. Cherfas, and P.B. Eyzaguirre. 2006. Agricultural biodiversity, nutrition, and health: Making a difference to hunger and nutrition in the developing world. *Food and Nutrition Bulletin* 27(2): 167–179.

Hann, C. and K. Hart. 2011. *Economic Anthropology: History, Ethnography, Critique*. Cambridge, UK: Polity Press.

Haraway, D. 1988. Situated knowledges: The science question in feminism and the privilege of partial perspective. *Feminist Studies* 14(3): 575–599.

Hazell, P. 2005. Is there a future for small farms? *Agricultural Economics* 32(1): 93–101.

Hazell, P. 2011. Five big questions about five hundred million small farms. Conference on New Directions for Smallholder Agriculture, 24–25 January, 2011, Rome, Italy.

Hazell, P. and A. Roell. 1983. Rural growth linkages: Household expenditure patterns in Malaysia and Nigeria. *Research Report* No. 41. Washington, DC: International Food Policy Research Institute.

Hazell, P., C. Poulton, S. Wiggins, and A. Dorward. 2007. The future of small farms for poverty reduction and growth. *Discussion Paper* No. 42. Washington, DC: International Food Policy Research Institute.

Hazell, P. and A. Roell. 1983. Rural growth linkages: Household expenditure patterns in Malaysia and Nigeria. *Research Report* No. 41. Washington, DC: International Food Policy Research Institute.

Herrero, M., P.K. Thornton, B. Power, et al. 2017. Farming and the geography of nutrient production for human use: A transdisciplinary analysis. *Lancet Planet Health* 1(1): e33–e42.

Heynen, N. and M. Ybarra. 2020. On abolition ecologies and making "freedom as a place." *Antipode* 0(0): 1–15.

Holbraad, M. and M.A. Pederson. 2017. *The Ontological Turn: An Anthropological Exposition*. Cambridge, UK: Cambridge University Press.

Homewood, K. and W.A. Rodgers. 1987. Pastoralism, conservation and the overgrazing controversy. In: D. Anderson, and R. Grove (Eds.), *Conservation in Africa: People, Policies, and Practice*, 111-128. Cambridge, UK: Cambridge University Press.

IEG. 2010. International assessment of Agricultural Knowledge, Science and Technology for Development. *Global Program Review* 4(2). Washington, DC: Independent Evaluation Group of the World Bank. 72p.

Iverson, A.L., L.E. Marin, K.K. Ennis, et al. 2014. Do polycultures promote win-wins or trade-offs in agricultural ecosystem services? A meta-analysis. *Journal of Applied Ecology* 51: 1593–1602.

Jerven, M. 2014. Political economy of agricultural input subsidies: Evidence from Nigeria and Malawi. *Journal of Agrarian Change* 14(1): 129–145.

Jones, A.D., A. Shrinivas, and R. Bezner-Kerr. 2014. Farm production diversity is associated with greater household dietary diversity in Malawi: Findings from nationally representative data. *Food Policy* 46(2014): 1–12.

Kagin, J., J.E. Taylor, and A. Yúnez-Naude. 2016. Inverse productivity or inverse efficiency? Evidence from Mexico. *The Journal of Development Studies* 52(3): 396–411.

Kennedy, C.M., E. Lonsdorf, M.C. Neel, et al. 2013. A global quantitative synthesis of local and landscape effects on wild bee pollinators in agroecosystems. *Ecology Letters* 16: 584–599.

La Via Campesina. 2017. *Struggles of La Via Campesina for Agrarian Reform and the Defense of Life, Land and Territories*. La Via Campesina.

La Via Campesina. 2018. *Food Sovereignty Now! A Guide to Food Sovereignty*. Brussels, Belgium: European Coordination Via Campesina.

Lambin, E.F. and P. Meyfroidt. 2011. Global land use change, economic globalization, and the looming land scarcity. *PNAS* 108(9): 3465–3472.

Larson, D.F., K. Otsuka, T. Matsumoto, and T. Kilic. 2014. Should African rural development strategies depend on smallholder farms? An exploration of the inverse-productivity hypothesis. *Agricultural Economics* 45(2014): 355–367.

Latour, B. 2014. Anthropology at the time of the Anthropocene—A personal view of what is to be studied. Distinguished Lecture, American Association of Anthropologists, Washington, DC, December 2014. 16p.

Lavigne-Delville, P. 1999. *Comment Articuler Droit Positif et Droits Fonciers Locaux: Expériences Récentes et Perspectives en Afrique de l'Ouest Francophone*. London: International Institute for Environment and Development.

Letourneau, D.K., I. Armbrecht, B.S. Rivera, et al. 2011. Does plant diversity benefit agroecosystems? A synthetic review. *Ecological Applications* 21: 9–21.

Li, T. 2007. The Will to Improve: Governmentality, Development, and the Practice of Politics. Durham, NC: Duke University Press.

Li, T. 2014. What is land? Assembling a resource for global investment. *Transactions of the Institute of British Geographers* 39(2014): 589–602.

Mäder, P., A. Fließbach, D. Dubois, L. Gunst, and P. Fried. 2002. Soil fertility and biodiversity in organic farming. *Science* 296: 1694–1697.

Martin-Prével, A. and F. Mousseau. 2016. *Unholy Alliance: Five Western Donors Shape a Pro-Corporate Agenda for African Agriculture*. Oakland, CA: The Oakland Institute.

McIntyre, B.D., H.R. Herren, J. Wakhungu, and R.T. Watson, Eds. 2009. *International Assessment of Agricultural Knowledge, Science and Technology for Development: Synthesis Report*. Washington, DC: Island Press.

Mellor, J. W. 1976. *The New Economics of Growth: A Strategy for India and the Developing World*. Ithaca, NY: Cornell University Press.

Mignolo, W.D. 2007. Delinking. *Cultural Studies* 21(2–3): 449–514.

Moreton-Robinson, A. 2015. *The White Possessive: Property, Power, and Indigenous Sovereignty*. Minneapolis and London: University of Minnesota Press.

Mousseau, F., A. Currier, E. Fraser, and J. Green. 2020. *Driving Dispossession: The Global Push to "Unlock the Economic Potential of Land."* Oakland, CA: The Oakland Institute.

Nichols, R. 2020. *Theft Is Property!* Durham, NC and London, UK: Duke University Press.

Ouédraogo, H.M.G. 2004. *Etude Comparative de la Mise en Oeuvre des Plans Fonciers Ruraux en Afrique de l'Ouest: Bénin, Burkina Faso, Côte d'Ivoire*. Ouagadougou: LandNet West Africa.

Pellizzoni, L. 2015. *Ontological Politics in a Disposable World: The New Mastery of Nature*. Farnham, UK and Burlington, VT: Ashgate.

Pimentel, D. 1980. *Handbook of Energy Utilization in Agriculture*. Boca Raton, FL: CRC Press.

Povinelli, E.A. 2012. The will to be otherwise / The effort of endurance. *South Atlantic Quarterly* 111(3): 453–457.

Power, A.G. 2010. Ecosystem services and agriculture: tradeoffs and synergies. *Philosophical Transactions of the Royal Society of London (Series B, Biological Sciences)* 365: 2959–2971.

Power, A.G. and A.S. Flecker. 1996. The role of biodiversity in tropical managed ecosystems. In: G.H. Orians, R. Dirzo, and J.H. Cushman (Eds.), *Biodiversity and Ecosystem Processes in Tropical Forests*, pp. 173–194. New York, NY: Springer-Verlag.

Prudham, S. 2015. Property and commodification. In: T. Perrault, G. Bridge and J. McCarthy (Eds.), *The Routledge Handbook of Political Ecology*, pp. 430–445. London and New York: Routledge.

Remans, R., D.F.B. Flynn, F. DeClerck, et al. 2011. Assessing nutritional diversity of cropping systems in African villages. *PLoS ONE* 6(6): e21235.

Reynolds, T.W., C.L. Anderson, E. Slakie, and M.K. Gugerty. 2015. How common crop yield measures misrepresent productivity among smallholder farmers. Paper presented at the annual conference of the International Association of Agricultural Economists, August 9–14, 2015, Milan, Italy.

Rosset, P. 2013. Re-thinking agrarian reform, land and territory in La Via Campesina. *Journal of Peasant Studies* 40(4): 721–775.

Said, E.W. 1978. *Orientalism*. New York, NY: Pantheon Books.

Samberg, L.H., J.S. Gerber, N. Ramankutty, M. Herrero, and P.C. West. 2016. Subnational distribution of average farm size and smallholder contributions to global food production. *Environmental Research Letters* 11, 124010.

Shipton, P. 2009. *Mortgaging the Ancestors*. New Haven, CT: Yale University Press.

Sikor, T. and C. Lund. 2010. *The Politics of Possession: Property, Authority and Access to Natural Resources*. Hoboken, NJ: Wiley Blackwell.

Simpson, A. 2014. *Mohawk Interruptus: Political Life Across the Borders of Settler States*. Durham, NC: Duke University Press.

Simpson, L. 2017. *As We Have Always Done: Indigenous Freedom through Radical Resistance*. Minneapolis: University of Minnesota Press.

Stahelin, N. 2017. Spatializing environmental education: Critical territorial consciousness and radical place-making in public schooling. *The Journal of Environmental Education* 48(4): 260–269.

Stein, H. 2020. Institutional transformation and shifting policy paradigms: Reflections on land reform in Africa. In: C.M. Obote Ochieng (Ed.), *Rethinking Land Reform in Africa: New Ideas, Opportunities and Challenges*, pp. 85–110. Abidjan, Nigeria: African Development Bank.

Tuck, E. and K.W. Yang. 2012. Decolonization is not a metaphor. *Decolonization: Indigeneity, Education & Society* 1(1): 1–40.

UN. 2009. *Report of the Special Rapporteur on the right to food, Olivier De Schutter: Agribusiness and the Right to Food, A/HRC/13/33*. 13th Session of the Human Rights Council. New York, NY: United Nations.

van der Ploeg, J.D. 2020. From biomedical to politico-economic crisis: The food system in times of Covid-19. *The Journal of Peasant Studies* 47(5): 944–972.

Vorley, B., A. Fearne, and D. Ray, Eds. 2007. *Regoverning Markets: A Place for Small-Scale Producers in Modern Agrifood Chains?* Boca Raton, FL: CRC Press.

Westbrook, D.A. 2004. *City of Gold: An Apology for Global Capitalism in a Time of Discontent*. New York and London: Routledge.

Wiggins, S. and S. Keats. 2013. *Leaping and Learning: Linking Smallholders to Markets.* London: Imperial College and Overseas Development Institute.

Wolfe, P. 2006. Settler colonialism and the elimination of the native. *Journal of Genocide Research* 8(4): 387–409.

NOTES

INTRODUCTION

1. With the exception of the pandemic years of 2020 and 2021.

2. Several of these visions were also articulated in a March 16, 2017 interview with Steve Muchiri, CEO of EAFF.

3. While the evidence on which the arguments in this volume stand derive from terrestrial ecosystems, most of the political economic (and ontological) trends engulfing Africa's farmland also apply to forests and fisheries (see, e.g., DePuy et al. 2021; Fairhead et al. 2012).

4. At least 331 human rights defenders were killed in 2020, 69 percent of whom were defending land, environmental, and Indigenous Peoples' rights (Front Line Defenders 2020). For details on the preceding years, see: https://www.frontlinedefenders.org/en/location/global (accessed Feb. 18, 2021).

5. I include this reference with some reservations, noting both the often limited traction of anthropological writings to wider social fields, and the complicity of anthropology with colonialism, the cold war, and the construction of global hierarchies that have long underlied the imperialist project.

6. "U.N. Food Chief Warns on Buying Farms," *Wall Street Journal*, Sept. 10, 2008.

7. GRAIN is a "small international non-profit organisation that works to support small farmers and social movements in their struggles for community-controlled and biodiversity-based food systems" (see https://grain.org).

8. See LDPI Working Paper Series (https://www.iss.nl/en/research/hosted-iss/land-deal-politics-initiative/ldpi-working-papers-series); IIED's Land, Investment and Rights series (https://pubs.iied.org/search/?s=LIR); and ILC and AGTER's Commercial Pressures on Land series (formerly available here: https://www.landcoalition.org/en/resources/commercial-pressures-land-worldwide).

9. A special Forum on Global Land Grabbing in the Journal of Peasant Studies and international conferences on global land grabbing in 2011 and 2012 served as platforms for bringing the academic community into dialogue with the issue and with prominent voices in international development—including Olivier de Schutter, UN Rapporteur on

the Right to Food, and Klaus Deininger of the World Bank. See: https://www.tandfonline.com/toc/fjps20/38/2; https://www.future-agricultures.org/category/events/international-conference-on-global-land-grabbing/.

10. See: https://landportal.org/book/sdgs (accessed July 19, 2019).

11. While I led the production of this LEGEND report, constraints on length, nuance, and freedom of expression led us to publish a subsequent journal paper in *World Development* (German et al. 2020).

12. See special issue in *Ecology and Society* at: https://www.ecologyandsociety.org/issues/view.php?sf=68.

13. For full special issue on biofuels sustainability in *Energy Policy*, see: https://www.sciencedirect.com/journal/energy-policy/special-issue/1030D0K4LN9.

14. See: "Examining the impact of Covid-19 on tenure rights" (http://www.fao.org/tenure/news/news-articles/examining-the-impact-of-covid-19-on-tenure-rights/en/); "How COVID-19 puts women's housing, land, and property rights at risk" (https://blogs.worldbank.org/sustainablecities/how-covid-19-puts-womens-housing-land-and-property-rights-risk); "Intimate partner violence and land tenure" (https://www.land-links.org/document/intimate-partner-violence-land-tenure/); "Secure land rights and climate change resilience go hand in hand: Here's why" (https://www.landesa.org/blog-secure-land-rights-climate-change-resilience-go-hand-in-hand/), accessed May 30, 2021. See also Landesa (2012).

15. See, for example, Eve Tuck and K. Wayne Yang (2012); Patrick Wolfe (2006).

16. Settler moves to innocence are defined by Tuck and Yang as "strategies or positionings that attempt to relieve the settler of feelings of guilt or responsibility without giving up land or power or privilege" (Tuck and Yang 2012: 10).

17. The latter figure includes all reported deals, with the former figure derived from what they deem reliable sources.

18. According to David Harvey (2010), the era has its roots in neoliberal policies introduced in the 1970s.

19. The 2016 Land Matrix report estimates that government entities account for only 6% of land deals and 4% of land area (Nolte et al. 2016).

20. Although they may also be found here, from the use of market instruments to verify feedstock compliance with the Renewable Energy Directive to policy-induced markets for bioethanol and biodiesel (German and Schoneveld 2012; Kristoufek et al. 2012).

21. In the Canadian case, the 1982 Constitution Act recognizes Aboriginal title.

CHAPTER 1

1. See also: "The Second Scramble for Africa Starts", Inter Press Service News Agency, April 20, 2009. Available at: http://www.ipsnews.net/2009/04/development-the-second-scramble-for-africa-starts/ (Oct. 12, 2019).

2. The 2016 report from the Land Matrix finds evidence of 42.2 million hectares of concluded deals, 26.7 million hectares of which was under contract for large-scale agriculture, and an additional 20 million hectares of intended deals—with Africa the

most targeted continent (Nolte et al. 2016). Yet the Land Matrix received significant criticism for the methods used in earlier estimates, causing them to adopt a far more onerous burden of proof in the inclusion of deals in their database. Earlier estimates suggested a far larger area—"as large as 51 to 63 million ha" (Friis and Reenberg 2010), with summaries of deals reported in the media of up to 56.5 million ha over a one-year period from 2008 to 2009 (Deininger et al. 2011) and 83.2 million ha in the 2000 to 2012 period (Anseeuw et al. 2012). With limited transparency, uneven reporting metrics and definitional challenges complicating any effort to gain an accurate estimate of area, such estimates are best used as reflections of trends rather than spatial extent.

3. Available at: https://www.economist.com/international/2009/05/21/outsourcings-third-wave (Sept. 25, 2019).

4. Following manufacturing in the 1980s and information technology in the 1990s.

5. Other optional modules include forestry and tenure regularization.

6. The report is also said to have benefited from intellectual exchanges with Klaus Deininger and Derek Byerlee at the World Bank and from linkages with a parallel study led by the World Bank and involving IIED and FAO (Cotula et al. 2009: iii).

7. Available at: https://www.worldbank.org/en/topic/land (Sept. 27, 2019).

8. Available at: https://www.worldbank.org/en/topic/land (Oct. 16, 2019).

9. Available at: https://www.worldbank.org/en/news/press-release/2019/03/25/women-in-half-the-world-still-denied-land-property-rights-despite-laws (Oct. 16, 2019).

10. See also: http://www.worldbank.org/en/topic/land (June 7, 2018).

11. See: https://sustainabledevelopment.un.org/sdgs (Oct. 18, 2019).

12. See: https://www.donorplatform.org/news-land-governance/putting-land-high-on-the-international-development-agenda-developing-the-state-of-land-tenure-and-governance-report.html (accessed Apr. 6, 2022).

12. Available at: https://landportal.org/book/sdgs/142/sdgs-indicator-142 (May 10, 2019).

13. Discourses on voice and representation varied on their endorsement of free, prior, and informed consent, and for whom it should apply; and whether procedural norms were adequate or particular outcomes achieved through these processes should be emphasized. For fair value chain relations, divergent opinions were observed on the question of who should lead and own value chains, whether agribusiness or smallholders; who is to be included, whether only smallholders or small and medium-scale enterprises throughout the value chain, or even consumers; and whether the poorest of the poor should be supported or only those with the capacity to succeed in commercial farming (while providing pathways out of agriculture for the rest). For land rights, while widespread endorsement of (procedurally just) land transactions was observed, emphasis on securing ongoing control and access for customary rights holders was found in some circles. Differential emphasis on procedural vs. substantive interpretations rights during land acquisitions was also noted. There was a notable absence of Pillar 4 (employment) among regional farmer federations, presumably because of the view that smallholders are to be the main producers. In discourses on food security, visions for agribusiness-driven productivity increases to feed the world's growing population contrasted with those centered on smallholders serving as the backbone to rural and urban, local and global food security. Given the slipperiness of these concepts and the high

variability in interpretation across actor groups, it is unclear whether further efforts will be advanced to further stabilize this concept—or whether that ambiguity itself will be embraced as most conducive to advancing the diverse political projects obscured by this term.

14. This reform expanded participation to non-governmental actors (civil society, the private sector, international agricultural research institutes and others) and established a High-Level Panel on Experts to advance evidence-based policy making (CFS 2009: 1).

15. Available at: https://www.worldbank.org/en/topic/land (Sept. 27, 2019).

16. The term used by the Bank in this instance is "secure property rights".

17. http://www.worldbank.org/en/news/feature/2017/03/24/why-secure-land-righ ts-matter (June 5, 2018).

18. A causal linkage that finds some support for Indigenous territories (Blackman et al. 2017), but is clearly refuted for individualized title (Probst et al. 2020).

19. https://www.worldbank.org/en/topic/forests#2 (Oct. 18, 2019).

20. See also: "Peruvian Guru Holds Key to Crisis" by N. MacEarlean, *The Guardian*, March 14, 2009; and "Hernando De Soto Revolutionized Thinking on Poverty," by D. Freddoso, *Investor's Business Daily*, March 4, 2015. Available at: https://www.theguardian.com/business/2009/mar/15/hernando-de-soto-credit-crunch and https://www.investors.com/news/management/leaders-and-success/hernando-de-soto-revolutionized-world-thinking-poverty/ (Oct. 18, 2019).

21. World Bank land titling projects around the world can be found at: https://proje cts.worldbank.org/en/projects-operations/projects-home.

22. https://www.worldbank.org/en/topic/land#2 (Sept. 27, 2019).

23. See: https://www.worldbank.org/en/news/feature/2017/03/24/why-secure-land -rights-matter (Oct. 18, 2019).

24. See: "Table A1—Environmental and Social Safeguard Policies—Policy Objectives and Operational Principles," Available at: http://web.worldbank.org/archive/websi te01541/WEB/0__CO-11.HTM (accessed Apr. 6, 2022).

25. http://www.worldbank.org/en/news/feature/2017/03/24/why-secure-land-righ ts-matter (accessed June 6, 2018).

CHAPTER 2

1. Other bilateral donors such as the UK's Department for International Development are arguably better choices given their active involvement in relevant international fora and the prominence of land in their lending portfolios, but their online presence provided little basis for this analysis.

2. This was done by using the terms in quotations, limiting the search to the organization's websites ("site: —xxx.org"), and specifying time ranges under Google's Tools tab.

3. To cater for the different number of organizations covered under each category, category averages are used rather than total number of hits.

4. "To end deforestation, we must protect community land rights," June 4, 2018.

Available at: https://www.weforum.org/agenda/2018/05/end-deforestation-protect-community-land-rights-interlaken/ (accessed Feb. 11, 2020).

5. In a google search for her, the first link to appear is a World Bank blog profiling her work: https://blogs.worldbank.org/team/nana-ama-yirrah (July 15, 2020).

6. While the private sector also exhibits limited engagement with procedures for consultation and consent, low numbers may be explained as much by their lesser investment in knowledge production as by their level of engagement with these concepts; the focus should thus be on trends.

7. Available at: https://www.landesa.org (Dec. 7, 2019).

8. Available at: https://indepth.oxfam.org.uk/land-rights/key-issues/#indigenouscommunity (Nov. 24, 2019).

9. See: https://www.landesa.org/press-and-media/joint-statement-iaeg-sdgs-land-rights/ (June 1, 2019).

10. State recognition of "rights over productive resources, instead of mere access" is also said to best support "the connection between food sovereignty and smallholder livelihood" (CSM 2018: 19).

11. In reference to a research project and 2014 symposium by this name hosted by MIT and *Université Catholique de Louvain*, available at: https://dusp.mit.edu/idg/project/property-rights-below-rethinking-property-rights-over-natural-resources (accessed Apr. 7, 2022).

12. "Alternatives to individual land titling" available at: https://www.dailymaverick.co.za/article/2018-08-29-alternatives-to-individual-land-titling/ (accessed Apr. 7, 2022).

13. While some view the "*plans ruraux fonciers*" or rural land maps of francophone West Africa as having potential to strike a balance between recognizing local land use practices and renegotiating them to address inequities, this view seems to rest on faith in the interests and ability of the state to mediate in the spirit of "guaranteeing fundamental rights and freedoms of citizens" (Ouédraogo 2004). Further, this research shows that clarity does not imply security (Chauveau 2003), which begs the question of who benefits from the enhanced legibility and legal certainty achieved through formalization (see, e.g., Scott 1990). This research has also highlighted the futility of efforts to formalize all land rights given the tendency for reversion to informality, questions of cost, and incompatibilities between customary and de jure property systems—leading some to suggest formalization only in arenas in which custom is perceived as inadequate in governing land transactions (Lavigne-Delville 1999).

14. See: https://viacampesina.org/en/power-and-impunity-of-transnational-corporations-stifles-people-s-voices/ (accessed June 1, 2019).

15. https://viacampesina.org/en/the-guidelines-on-the-responsible-governance-of-tenure-at-a-crossroads/ (accessed June 6, 2018).

16. They also note the inherently ambiguous nature of the VGGTs themselves in their observation that, "Governments, and bilateral and international agencies interested in promoting an agenda that focuses on economic growth, boosting land markets

and profiting from commercial interests will also find useful references for these purposes in the text" (IPC 2016: 19).

17. See: *People's Manual on the Guidelines on Governance of Land, Fisheries and Forests* (IPC 2016), which received technical support from the FAO and is advanced "to support the use of the Voluntary Guidelines on the Responsible Governance of Tenure of Land, Fisheries and Forests in the Context of National Food Security." Available at: https://www.forum-synergies.eu/docs/peoplesmanual.pdf (retrieved Mar. 16, 2021).

18. See: "VGGT: The global guidelines to secure land rights for all," by Jorge Muñoz, Oct. 5, 2017. Available at: https://blogs.worldbank.org/voices/vggt-global-guidelines-ensure-secure-land-rights-for-all (accessed Dec. 4, 2019). Fora where the VGGTs were formally endorsed, such as the Committee on World Food Security, also have systems in place for multi-stakeholder engagement. Their structure of members, participants, and observers and Advisory Group, for example, provide a mechanism for input from representatives of five categories of actors: representatives of UN agencies and bodies; civil society and non-governmental organizations and their networks; international agricultural research systems; international and regional financial institutions (the World Bank, IMF, WTO and regional development banks); and representatives of private sector associations and private philanthropic foundations (see: https://www.fao.org/cfs/about-cfs/cfs-structure/en/).

19. In the World Bank blog cited above, this is framed as advancing the "consensual recognition" that states must protect more than just legally recognized rights, yet it also falls short of recognizing customary or de facto rights and of defining what exactly "legitimate" means—leaving this responsibility to states.

20. Its efforts to bring together the voices of members (over 50 international and national NGOs), and to consult "academic experts" as well as farmers' organizations and human rights groups from across the global South, in the process of providing written input into the CFS process allows for a detailed retrospective look at the concerns and aspirations expressed by civil society and the established mechanisms for bringing their voice into international normative frameworks on land governance and food security (https://www.csm4cfs.org).

21. A 2018 report evaluating the use and implementation of the RTF Guidelines calls the right to food "arguably the most violated human right"; highlights the alarming growth in the number of food insecure and violence against human rights defenders; and calls attention to resistance within the CFS of its human rights mandate under the declining authority of public policy-making to the benefit of private sector interests (CSM 2018: 9, 11). It also calls for greater democratic control and accountability and monitoring of the RTF Guidelines and related international instruments and interpretations.

22. "CSM Opening Statement on the Negotiations of the Guidelines on Food Systems and Nutrition," Jan. 25, 2021. Available at: http://www.csm4cfs.org/csm-opening-statement-negotiations-voluntary-guidelines-food-systems-nutrition/#opening (accessed Mar. 18, 2021).

23. Available at: http://www.fao.org/tenure/resources/collections/governanceoftenuretechnicalguides/en/ (retrieved Mar. 13, 2021).

24. Among the criteria for becoming a partner of the network is agreement with the values and approaches of GLTN and an interest in the advancement of GLTN's strategic plan. The list of partners that have made this commitment is impressive—consisting of 18 bilateral and multilateral organizations; 15 international professional bodies (mostly geoinformatics, land survey and land taxation organizations); 29 international research and training organizations (universities, land tenure institutes); and 18 civil society organizations—including Oxfam, ILC, and ActionAid (for a list of partners, see: https://gltn.net/gltn-partners-3/#1458850937352-8f0ffb84-8953). Yet what are they all signing up to? Aside from the strong interventionist logic, the Strategic Plan provides little evidence of how their work plays out on the ground (GLTN 2018). The Plan advances a suite of crisis narratives surrounding tenure, stating that "the world faces housing, land and property rights challenges of critical proportions," that the situation is "particularly dire in developing countries" and the SDGs cannot be achieved without "a seismic change in tenure security and land governance" (GLTN 2018: 5). The Plan talks of accelerating reforms in the land sector, and institutionalizing land tools to scale up tenure security interventions. It also endorses claims and theories of change long advanced by the World Bank—from how individuals are currently denied equitable access to land and secure tenure in rural areas, to the linkages between tenure security and a suite of goods (from development to environmental resilience, sustainable land use, self-determination, peace and livelihood security for the vulnerable)—with limited evidence to back them up. Citations used to back up claims are limited in number and drawn almost exclusively from UN agencies. Their involvement in and endorsement of the land indicators in the SDGs through their Global Land Indicators Initiative (GLII) provides the best evidence of how these ideas are advanced in practice. Here, despite their discursive support for a continuum of land rights and recognition of the need for the form that rights take to be matched to context (GLTN 2018: 10), they are advocating for global uptake of the narrower conceptions of rights enshrined in the SDGs (see: https://youtu.be/noZvslRhUug), including formalization. In a box entitled, "The scale of the land governance problem" in GLTN's 2018–2030 Strategic Plan, for example, tenure security is equated with formalization (GLTN 2018: 9). And their strong interventionist logic suggests that protecting the suite of "existing social networks and arrangements that do offer security" (Bromley 2008: 20) is not high on the agenda.

25. See: https://landgov.donorplatform.org (accessed Mar. 13, 2021).

26. See: https://www.donorplatform.org/land-governance.html (accessed Mar .13, 2021).

27. https://rightsandresources.org/en/the-coalition/#.Xefuc7GZPow (accessed Dec. 4, 2019).

28. The "business turn" involves a shift from adversarial tactics to one in which social advocates seek to make common cause with multinationals in a growing number of issue-areas (Hall et al. 2016).

29. The Interlaken Group is a self-described informal network of individual leaders from influential companies, investors, CSOs, government, and international organizations working to expand and leverage private sector action to secure community land rights. It is co-chaired by Andy White of RRI (an NGO) and Mark Constantine of the IFC, and its members include NGOs (Global Witness, Landesa, Oxfam), multilateral financial institutions and banks (IFC, European Investment Bank, Rabobank), governments (DfID, CDC Group), and private firms (e.g., Coca-Cola, Nestle, Olam, Unilever). See: https://www.interlakengroup.org (Nov. 11, 2019).

30. See: https://www.landesa.org/seniorship-level/board-of-directors/ (Dec. 6, 2019).

31. See: https://rightsandresources.org/en/the-coalition/#.XeqGdrGZPox; https://www.omidyar.com/news/cadasta-foundation-democratize-land-and-resource-rights-partnership-uk-aid-uk-government; https://www.landcoalition.org/en/donors (Dec. 6, 2019). A brief look at Oxfam International's financials for 2017–2018 also reveals "occasional funding" from public or corporate bodies; $1.2 million in funding from the EU and Dutch Ministry of Foreign Affairs "to support women's access to and control over their land resources across Africa" and additional funding from the Dutch Ministry of Foreign Affairs for their GROW campaign (Stichting Oxfam International 2018: 58).

32. I have reflected much on the work these conferences do. They undoubtedly surface emergent issues and foster debate, but they also seem to serve the purpose of alignment through the knowledge ecosystems they create, and the opportunities they provide to harness and domesticate critique. A full accounting, however, lies beyond the scope of my research.

33. Consultancy firms have a financial incentive, if not an explicit mandate, to provide evidence in support of funding agencies' theories of change. A 2018 request for proposals by a member of the Global Donor Working Group on Land, for example, specifies "identifying knowledge gaps" in the agency's theory of change and "filling gaps in the evidence that designers used when creating the activity" as a desired deliverable. The process of producing evidence for a donor agency may also involve strong control over the substance of resulting knowledge products, as was evident in the push-back received against my efforts to report on the diversity of extant visions for rural futures, in a report prepared for another member of the Working Group.

34. This has included the Land Portal Foundation, a public benefit organization registered in the Netherlands working to improve land governance through open-access data and cross-sectoral collaboration that hosts an online thesaurus designed to create a "controlled vocabulary for land information" (Land Portal 2019: 11); Cadasta, an NGO founded in 2015 to provide technical tools and services to support the documentation of land and resource rights; Resource Equity, a non-profit working to advance women's land and resource rights through training and support to "governments, donors, private sector companies, NGOs, local advocates and others to develop new legal, policy, and programmatic solutions that address the gap between law and practice for women"; and Landesa, a US-based non-profit working "to advance durable land rights to bring

transformational changes on a large scale." Available at: https://landportal.org/who-we-are; https://cadasta.org/about-us-3/; https://resourceequity.org; https://www.landesa.org/who-we-are/ (accessed Mar. 18, 2021).

35. See, for example, the 2018–2030 Global Land Tools Network Strategy (GLTN 2018), and the number of prominent international organizations (bilateral, multilateral and non-governmental organizations; professional, training and research institutions) endorsing them (https://gltn.net/gltn-partners-3/#1458850937352-8f0ffb84-8953). See also the number of actors and initiatives supporting land titling and regularization: https://www.omidyar.com/news?type=&initiative=Property+Rights&date%5Bvalue%5D%5Byear%5D=&search=#filter; https://landportal.org/news/2019/09/statement-sdg-land-momentum-group-response-political-declaration-sdg-summit (accessed Dec. 7, 2019).

CHAPTER 3

1. See the Global Land Tool Network's "Gender Evaluation Criteria for Large-Scale Land Tools" (https://gltn.net/2016/11/09/gender-evaluation-criteria-for-large-scale-land-tools/) and website (http://gltn.net/crosscutting-issues/) (accessed May 9, 2019).

2. For a few examples, see the UN's 2013 publication *Realizing Women's Rights to Land and Other Productive Resources*; FAO's 2018 publication, *Realizing Women's Rights to Land in the Law*; Cadasta's *Guide for Cadasta Partners on Women's Land Rights* (https://cadasta.org/womens-land-rights/); Landesa's Center for Women's Land Rights (https://www.landesa.org/what-we-do/womens-land-rights/); the World Bank's blog on women's land rights (https://blogs.worldbank.org/tags/womens-land-rights); *Her Land, Her Story*, a media campaign led by the Cadasta Foundation and the Land Portal Foundation; and the emergence of non-profits dedicated exclusively to advancing women's land and resource rights (e.g., Resource Equity).

3. The Global Land Indicators Initiative (GLII) of UN-Habitat, for example, is a self-described "laboratory for land indicators, data protocols and tools linked to the SDGs and other global land governance and development frameworks" that works to support to efforts to generate data for tracking progress on land governance issue at country level.

4. One key document (World Bank et al. 2008) was produced in collaboration with FAO and IFAD.

5. The first two NGOs to appear under a Google search on "women's land rights" (10 May 2019).

6. It should be noted that identities linked to livelihood systems other than sedentary farming are poorly covered in this review, but receive some attention in Chapter 5.

7. This narrative is widespread in the international development arena, and often based on questionable evidence. Landesa, for example, has sought to quantify the problem by drawing on an OECD database of countries with "some customary, traditional or religious practices that discriminate against women," using this evidence to declare that

there are 90 countries where "customs inhibit women's access to land" (https://www.landesa.org/resources/property-not-poverty/). This narrative has been picked up by a host of organizations on the front lines of efforts to advance tenure security worldwide, with *Her Land, Her Story*—a campaign organized by the Cadasta Foundation and Land Portal in partnership with ten other organizations (including ILC, Landesa and Oxfam)—framing women's vulnerability as a problem of "laws or customs [that] undermine or block women's rights to own, manage, or inherit land or property" (http://herlandherstory.com).

8. "The attainment of gender equity with regard to land rights . . . depends not only on legal recognition of those rights but also on overcoming social and cultural constraints" (World Bank et al. 2008: 130).

9. See: http://www.worldbank.org/en/topic/land (accessed June 7, 2018).

10. https://cadasta.org/about-us/ (10 May, 2019).

11. Available at: https://cadasta.org/about-us-3/ (accessed Apr. 7, 2022).

12. See: https://cadasta.org/womens-land-rights/ (10 May, 2019).

13. See: https://www.landesa.org and https://www.landesa.org/what-we-do/womens-land-rights/ (10 May, 2019).

14. See: http://www.fao.org/sustainable-development-goals/indicators/5a1/en/ (May 8, 2019).

15. Available at: http://www.fao.org/sustainable-development-goals/indicators/5.a.2/en/ (May 10, 2019).

16. See, for example: https://devtracker.dfid.gov.uk/projects/GB-1-204252/transactions (accessed 10 May 2019).

17. The campaign is organized by the Cadasta Foundation and Land Portal in partnership with ten other organizations (including ILC, Landesa and Oxfam), and frames women's vulnerability as a problem of "laws or customs [that] undermine or block women's rights to own, manage, or inherit land or property" (see: http://herlandherstory.com, accessed June 6, 2018).

18. Cadasta's annual report lists DfiD, IFAD, Habitat for Humanity, Landesa, and Omidyar Network as "donors and supporters" (among a few lesser-known entities), and a generic category of "international institutions" is listed as providing over half of their funding in the 2017–2019 period (Cadasta 2019). Landesa lists the Ford Foundation, Omidyar Network and a host of foundations as among their supporters, with one contributor simply listed as "anonymous" (https://www.landesa.org/annual-report-2020/).

19. In one ruling on inheritance, Magaya vs. Magaya, the five judges ruled that it is the "nature of African society that women are not equal to men. Women should never be considered adults within the family but only as a junior male or teenager" (Goebel 2005: 154).

20. The degree of a woman's incorporation into her husband's group and the strength of her natal kin ties has since been recognized as a continuum (Parkin 1980).

21. On the role of these reforms in exacerbating conflict and unequal access to land, see Attwood 1990; Besteman 1994, 1996; Coldham 1978; Davison 1988; Haugerud 1989;

Okoth-Ogendo 1976; Pala Okeyo 1980; Shipton 1994, 1988; and Shipton and Goheen 1992. On the growing livelihood precarity, inequality and environmental degradation produced by privatization in livestock and range management schemes, see Baxter and Hogg 1990; Behnke et al. 1993; Galaty 1992, 1994, 1999; Horowitz 1986; Mwangi 2007; and Peters 1994.

22. Social scientists studying customary land tenure and authority have come to view the "customary" domain not as an unchanging relic of a pre-colonial past, but as relations forged through colonial and post-colonial negotiations between local and state authority—often forged through efforts to prop up indirect rule (Peters 2010; Schmidt 1990; Ubink and Amanor 2015).

23. Through processes such as information asymmetries, the scramble for land, barriers to access and corruption.

CHAPTER 4

1. The declaration recognized the rights of peasants and other people working in rural areas "to have access to and to use in a sustainable manner the natural resources present in their communities that are required to enjoy adequate living conditions" and to participate in the management of these resources, and gives States the responsibility of ensuring "equal access to, use of and management of land and natural resources" for peasant women. It further calls on States to take measures to ensure that any exploitation of "natural resources that peasants and other people working in rural areas traditionally hold or use" be subject to an environmental and social impact assessment, good faith consultations, and fair and equitable sharing of the benefits of such exploitation on mutually agreed terms (UN 2018, Articles 4, 5).

2. See, e.g., "Collective rights are human rights—what the world should learn from John Chau and the Sentinelese" (Hannah Storey, 10 Dec 2018), available at: http://www.forestpeoples.org/en/news-article/2018/collective-rights-are-human-rights-what-world-should-learn-john-chau-and (accessed July 29, 2019); ILC (2012); "Why indigenous and community land rights matter for everyone," available at: https://www.oxfam.org/en/take-action/campaigns/stand-land-rights/why-indigenous-and-community-land-rights-matter-everyone (accessed May 21, 2020).

3. The term was coined by Richard White in his study of relations between the French and their Algonquian trading partners (White 1991).

4. Available at: http://www.fao.org/new-york/fao-statements/detail/en/c/1118557/ (Aug. 1, 2019).

5. Mongabay has a series on "Indigenous Peoples and Conservation" under their "Global Forests" series, that regularly covers news on this topic. See, for example, the July 2018 article entitled, "Investing in indigenous communities is most efficient way to protect forests, report finds," available at: https://news.mongabay.com/2018/07/investing-in-indigenous-communities-most-efficient-way-to-protect-forests-report-finds/.

6. Such rights are unable to be taken away from or given away by the possessor.

Even stronger protections are rights which are indefeasible (not able to be annulled/overturned); imprescriptible (unable to be taken away by prescription or by lapse of time); and nonforfeitable (not subject to forfeiture, or to loss as a penalty of wrongdoing).

7. It is defined by FAO as "an international human rights standard that derives from the collective rights of indigenous peoples to self-determination and to their lands, territories and other properties" (FAO 2014: 4).

8. See https://undocs.org/E/C.19/2005/3, para. 14, 16, 17, 18, 43 (retrieved Aug 3, 2019).

9. See: https://ic.fsc.org/en/news-updates/technical-updates/id/254; https://rspo.org/news-and-events/announcements/free-prior-and-informed-consent-guide-for-rspo-members-2015-endorsed (retrieved Aug. 2, 2019).

10. See: https://documents.worldbank.org/pt/publication/documents-reports/documentdetail/649591473352354755/executive-summary (accessed May 28, 2021).

11. In Africa, political push-back has centered on the ambiguities in the definition of Indigeneity and the notion that all Africans are Indigenous as well as fears of ethnonationalism and threats to state sovereignty, while support for Indigenous recognition has rested on the similarities in the political struggles of marginalized ethnic groups in Africa with those of recognized Indigenous peoples (Hodgson 2009). Underlying these contestations in sub-Saharan Africa, however, are tensions over authority in land (Hodgson 2009).

12. A 2016 study by Cabral and Norfolk reiterates this distinction between good law and bad practice, stating, "The law may be progressive, but government politics are not" (Cabral and Norfolk, 2016: 3).

13. Simon Norfolk and Christopher Tanner (2007) relate this to the invisibility of customary rights on cadastral maps and the local awareness that is often created through the formalization process.

14. While often translated as simply "customary authority" or "chief," *régulos* were the creation of the colonial administration. They included traditional chiefs who collaborated with the colonial administration whether voluntarily or under duress, and those with no connection to customary leadership and therefore lacking any legitimacy in mediating between the administration and rural life (Åkesson et al. 2009).

15. Executive Director of the Nampula Delegation of ORAM, a Mozambican NGO working to defend the rights and interests of peasants.

16. June 28, 2013 interview with the director of the *Serviço Provincial de Geografia e Cadastro* of Nampula Province.

17. While title is defined as "the document issued by Cadastre Services confirming the right of land use and benefit" (*Technical Annex to the Land Law Regulations*, Art 2.13), undocumented customary rights are recognized as equivalent to a DUAT—creating some ambiguity on the protections afforded by each arrangement.

18. It also establishes as one of its guiding principles guaranteed land access and use for the population and women, and investment without harming the local population.

19. The Technical Annex to the Land Law Regulations states that, "delimitation and/or demarcation of areas occupied by local communities does not impede the realization

of economic activities or other ventures, as long as they obtain consent of the communities" (Republic of Mozambique 2000, Art. 3). Despite this reference to consent, the mechanism is codified in the Technical Annex, and practiced, as the *consulta comunitária* (community consultation).

20. The form provides five lines of text for each of seven community members to express their "opinion" surrounding "the request to occupy the land concerned"; four blank lines to document the "agreement"; and five blank lines to document "the type of existing infrastructure and improvements," with no specification of why this information is being requested.

21. Even the benefits of employment itself must be questioned, give its use as a powerful negotiation tactic to get communities to cede land and the subsequent preference often shown by investors for migrant labor.

22. These include forms of deception, pressure to acquiesce, and playing upon people's emotions to achieve strategic aims (Arnall 2019), as well as a widespread tendency to emphasize project benefits rather than factual information on the project's features and expected impacts.

23. These distinctions are in large part a product of the historical and ideological milieu under which these new categories took shape. Growing social unrest in the Peruvian Andes toward the end of the 1950s led to an integrationist strategy that resulted in the conversion of the Indigenous population of the Andes into peasants "in national conceptualization and idiom" (Hvalkof 2002: 90). By transforming Indigenous people into peasants in cooperatives, the state sought to overcome their presumed backwardness. Subsequent legislation has maintained a distinction between *comunidades campesinas* (peasants) of the highlands and *comunidades nativas* (native communities) of the Amazonian lowlands. In the highlands, "land rights are granted as communal rights and a means of production, not as a territory. The legal unit is the *Comunidad Campesina*. The political ideology on which this model is based is the . . . notion that 'we are all Peruvians,' a nationalist and populist idea that is constantly propagated as 'democracy,' indicating that no special rights should be granted to any particular social or ethnic group" (Hvalkof 2002: 90).

24. Other countries such as Colombia and Bolivia had previously enacted administrative norms (sectoral regulations) on consultation over specific activities, such as hydrocarbon; Peru's law thus stands out for its generalized, cross-sectoral character (Merino, personal communication).

25. Peru ratified ILO 169 in 1994 and became a signatory to UNDRIP in 2007.

26. Between 1974 and 1975, a total of 133 communities were titled covering 766,758 hectares (Chirif Tirado and Garcia Hierro 2007; cited by Monterroso et al. 2017).

27. These efforts were furthered with the passage of *The Law of Private Investment in the Development of Economic Activities in the Lands of the National Territory and of the Peasant and Native Communities* (Law No. 26505) in 1995, through which new legal options were provided to allow peasant and native communities to divide collective land into individual parcels (Monterroso et al. 2017).

28. *The Law of Private Investment in the Development of Economic Activities in the*

Lands of the National Territory and of the Peasant and Native Communities (Law No. 26505).

29. This number has since increased to 75%.

30. The case was reportedly resolved through a 2015 settlement whose terms are non-disclosed (see: https://earthrights.org/case/maynas-v-occidental-petroleum/#documentsff69-1a905f26-f4b6).

31. In total, 99 legislative decrees were passed in 2008 aimed at opening the Amazon to mining, logging, and oil drilling (Monterroso et al. 2017), and to formalize the subdivision of communal land (Bebbington 2009).

32. https://www.iwgia.org/en/peru; see also Merino (2019, 2021a).

33. Personal communication with representatives of two Indigenous communities during the "Multistakeholder Dialogue on Community Consultation and FPIC," held on July 5, 2019 in Lima during the meeting of the International Association for the Study of the Commons.

34. See: https://www.iwgia.org/en/peru/3265-wampis-nation-peru (accessed Sept. 7, 2019).

35. At this time, Hvalkof declared "The local struggle for territorial rights and the social enactment of the indigenous territory may be one of the most powerful instruments for social and political change in Latin America today," changing "the entire power structure of the region." A good working relationship and rapport with Indigenous communities was declared "a must" for gaining access to resources on Indigenous lands (Hvalkof 2002: 94, 104). He goes on to declare that, "If democracy consists of active participation in policy and decision making by a culturally mixed population creating common instruments for dealing with differences and conflicting interests, this has been achieved in this part of Peru's Amazon. The irreversibility of the process not only confronts the existing power structure in the region, it also challenges the very process and concept of development" (Hvalkof 2002: 111).

36. See: https://www.un.org/development/desa/dspd/2018/04/unpfii17-adopted-recommendations-on-collective-rights-to-lands-territories-and-resources/ (July 29, 2019).

37. This has been variously described as a "meritocratic ideology," "hyper-responsibilization" (Hilgers 2010) and "the trope of individual responsibility at the service of commodification" (Wacquant 2012: 66).

38. See, for example: https://news.mongabay.com/2018/09/forests-and-indigenous-rights-land-459m-commitment/ (accessed July 29, 2019).

39. These sentiments were echoed by Indigenous participants at a multi-stakeholder dialogue on community consultation and FPIC held in Lima in July, 2019.

40. With the proposed Indigenous territory overlapping "with the concession rights of national and transnational oil and mining corporations, settlers' property rights, and the ambiguous administrative competences of *centros poblados*, district municipalities, provincial governments, regional governments, and even the national government" (Merino 2021a: 146), the challenges include reshaping the form of the state itself to a

plurinational state; the rearticulation of administrative competencies over the territory at diverse levels; and reshaping the firmly extractivist political economy.

41. Of internal institution-building to establish shared norms and procedures for governing and defending Indigenous territories vis-à-vis outside interests, such as that recently undertaken by the Wampis Autonomous Territorial Government.

42. See, for example, Faustin Maganga et al. (2017).

43. In reference to Hernando de Soto's theory on formalization of customary tenures.

CHAPTER 5

1. See, for example: https://www.donorplatform.org/land-governance.html (accessed Feb. 6, 2019).

2. https://landportal.org/blog-post/2018/05/why-measuring-land-tenure-matters-sdgs-impact-evaluation (Feb. 6, 2019).

3. According to its 2019 Financial Report, while the Foundation benefits from donations from a host of organizations active in the global land governance arena (e.g., FAO, Omidyar, PRIndex, GLTN, Transparency International), the main contributor is the UK Department for International Development.

4. https://landportal.org/book/sdgs/142/sdgs-indicator-142 (accessed Feb. 6, 2019).

5. https://www.landesa.org/resources/property-not-poverty/ (accessed Sept. 28, 2018).

6. http://herlandherstory.com (accessed Sept. 28, 2018).

7. Available at: http://www.worldbank.org/en/topic/land (accessed June 7, 2018).

8. Such an assumption leads the World Bank to declare, "For the majority of the world's poor, secure property rights are a rare luxury. Only 30% of the world's population has a legally *registered* title to their land." From "Why Secure Land Rights Matter," Mar. 24, 2017; available at: https://www.worldbank.org/en/news/feature/2017/03/24/why-secure-land-rights-matter (accessed Apr. 12, 2022).

9. See: https://landportal.org/blog-post/2019/02/status-sdgs-land-indicators-overcoming-barriers-and-bridging-yawning-data-gaps (accessed 3 May, 2019) and https://www.landportal.org/blog-post/2017/12/what-counted-will-count-why-getting-sdg-land-indicators-tier-i-matters (accessed Apr. 12, 2022). By the time of publications, the land indicators had moved from Tier III to Tier II status. For an up-to-date status of SDG indicators, see: https://unstats.un.org/sdgs/iaeg-sdgs/tier-classification/.

10. https://landportal.org/blog-post/2018/05/why-measuring-land-tenure-matters-sdgs-impact-evaluation (accessed Feb. 6, 2019). At the time this book went to press (July 2022), these core land indicators remained at Tier II status.

11. Here, states are given the mandate to establish recording systems "to increase tenure security and to reduce the costs and risks of transactions" (CFS and FAO 2012: 20).

12. Chaveau and Colin describe what is at stake in variable interpretations of "the cognitive, cultural and social constructions of objects of exchange (what objects are legitimately transferred?), of parties to exchange (who can legitimately transact with whom?) and of norms of exchange (how do people conceptualize the transactions?)" (Chaveau and Colin 2010: 83). They also argue that "it is illusory to try to secure land rights independently of the socio-political embeddedness of these rights" (Chaveau and Colin 2010: 100).

13. These are said to include processes of legitimation through which farmland investments are said to create benefits to focal countries while closing food, yield, and energy gaps; efforts to construct farmland as an alternative asset class by translating "the world of crops and farms into frames, calculations and codifications that make sense to finance" (Williams 2014: 422); specialized industry intelligence; farmland investment conferences—sites of sociality and calculation where uncertain futures are made tangible through "storytelling" (Tarim 2012); efforts to address reputational risks through the revision of internal economic, social, and governance criteria and launching or subscribing to principles for responsible investment; and the development of new financial instruments to enable more financial capital to be channeled into risky frontiers such as African agriculture (Ouma 2018).

14. Described by Keith Hart as "the ability of an individual owner to command exclusive rights over something against the rest of the world" (Hart 2005: 44).

CHAPTER 6

1. These efforts have taken shape through diverse partnership models linking businesses, NGOs and donor programs.

2. In the context of a consultancy report led by me, but integrating ideas of co-authors closely linked to the development establishment.

3. This refers to the roughly 4.5 billion people living on less than $8 per day (Hart and Christensen 2002). As "a $5 trillion consumer market," it is used by those framing inclusion as targeting not just producers, but small-scale suppliers, distributors, retailers and consumers (see, e.g., https://www.ifc.org/wps/wcm/connect/news_ext_content/ifc_external_corporate_site/news+and+events/news/howsuccessfulcompaniesreachthebaseofthepyramid).

4. A market structure in which a single buyer substantially controls the market, limiting competition and smallholder choices.

5. "Big brands like Unilever aren't the answer to helping Africa's farmers," available at: https://www.theguardian.com/sustainable-business/2016/aug/31/unilever-africa-farmers-inclusive-business-agrifood-development?CMP=share_btn_tw (retrieved June 28, 2020).

6. See: https://www.downsizinggovernment.org/agriculture/subsidies; https://www.nytimes.com/2019/11/03/world/europe/eu-farm-subsidy-hungary.html (retrieved June 27, 2020).

7. The UNDP, for example, contrasts inclusive business with "charity" by emphasizing the foundations it lays for "profit and long-term growth" (UNDP 2013: 8).

8. Jim Woodhill's report to the Global Donor Forum on Rural Development finds that inclusive approaches will "require the matching of public and private investments to achieve both commercial and public good outcomes" (Woodhill 2016: 2).

9. Smallholders were found by German et al. (2020) to face a host of inherent barriers to market entry that place them on an uneven playing field relative to larger-scale operators: limited access to key production factors (land, labor, capital); inefficiencies or "diseconomies" associated with their small scale; limited voice; and the frequent misalignment of local and national interests and values.

CHAPTER 7

1. I use this term very purposefully in light of the tendency to construct Indigenous and subaltern peoples as quaint and "cultural" while advancing white settlers, "moderns," or development professionals as civilized and "knowledgeable," and the tendency to define this culture "by its proximity to difference, not its sovereignty"—a difference "defined against the sameness and omniscience of a stable ontological core, an unquestioned 'self'" (Simpson 2014: 101–102; see also Blaser 2013; Burow et al. 2018; Coulthard 2014; Dove 1983; Wolfe 2006). This book points not to the stability and universality of dominant ontologies of land, but to their cultural specificity.

2. This suggests an intentionality that may well be over-stated. Whether these constructs emerged from a place of omniscient intentionality on the part of key knowledge brokers, the "growing domination by neoclassical economics and its convergence with donor priorities and international capital" within the World Bank (Stein 2020: 108), or the workings of power within neoliberal, multi-stakeholder modes of governance is not entirely clear. Yet the advancement of ontologies of security in direct contrast with the evidence (e.g., that titling disadvantages women) and with relational ontologies of security from across the continent are strongly suggestive of some intentionality to advance interests other than those of African smallholders.

3. This statement derives less from the academic scholarship than a personal history of interactions with colleagues and acquaintances within the development establishment.

4. Land sparing refers to the setting aside of land for biodiversity conservation. If it is assumed that commercial farms are better able to intensify output per unit area than smallholders are, they would be favored in land sparing strategies.

5. Many journal papers now include the phrase "the future of small farms," and a 2005 workshop was dedicated to the topic (see: https://citeseerx.ist.psu.edu/viewdoc/download?doi=10.1.1.474.8402&rep=rep1&type=pdf#page=362 (retrieved Apr. 26, 2021).

6. There is a growing literature critiquing the quality of agricultural statistics and acknowledging how they are shaped by political economic factors (Benin et al. 2020; Carletto et al. 2015; Jerven 2014; Reynolds et al. 2015).

7. For example, technical assistance and advisory services (Daniel and Mittal 2010) and the Enabling the Business of Agriculture project (Martin-Prevel and Mousseau 2016).

8. Their view of what this involves is set out in detail in a 2018 publication entitled, "*Food Sovereignty Now! A Guide to Food Sovereignty*": farmers retaining their land and freedom of choice, rather than being made laborers in someone else's business or bound by long-term contractual agreements; food that is produced by smallholders rather than by agribusiness firms; food that is not exported, but consumed within households, nationally and regionally; an agri-food system in which individuals have direct, democratic control over how they feed and nourish themselves and use land, water, seed and other resources; and sustainable and agroecological production models (La Via Campesina 2018).

9. Put simply, "we must determine by ourselves what to eat; and we must produce it" (Esteva and Prakash 1998: xv).

10. Which is seen as compatible with natural processes and capable of halting climate change, maintaining biodiversity and reducing contamination.

11. "Big brands like Unilever aren't the answer to helping Africa's farmers," *The Guardian*, August 31, 2016.

12. "Big brands like Unilever aren't the answer to helping Africa's farmers," *The Guardian*, August 31, 2016.

13. The debates surrounding the CSM have already been profiled in Chapter 2 and are not re-visited here. The political dynamics surrounding the IAASTD can be seen most clearly in a Global Program Review carried out by the Independent Evaluation Group of the World Bank (IEG 2010), in which the program outcome was rated "moderately unsatisfactory" for the questionable robustness of policy-relevant information for decision-makers; for underestimating the potential of new technologies relative to existing technologies; and for the "undercurrent against new technology" (IEG 2010: xiii).

14. The CSM has lobbied around the idea of "the right to food" as codified in the Voluntary Guidelines to Support the Progressive Realization of the Right to Adequate Food in the Context of National Food Security (FAO 2005), which emphasize small-scale farming systems over corporate agriculture. Their vision for rural futures involves "small-scale agroecology" and "sustainable production practices" that promote diverse, more nutritious and culturally acceptable diets, protect biodiversity and ecosystems and help mitigate climate change, based on the principles of peoples' sovereignty over natural resources, the right to livelihood, the right to food and food sovereignty (CSM 2018).

15. The World Bank and FAO initiated a global consultative process in 2002 to determine whether an international assessment of agricultural knowledge, science and technology (AKST) was needed. While stimulated by an interest in biotechnology and transgenics, the consultative process resulted in a recommendation to undertake a broad assessment of the role of AKST in "reducing hunger and poverty, improving rural livelihoods and facilitating environmentally, socially and economically sustainable development" (McIntyre et al. 2009: vii).

16. This includes women and vulnerable groups; forest, fishery, Indigenous, and traditional rural communities; and those producing under individual, communal and collective land tenure systems.

17. Civil Society open letter to FAO regarding the High-Level Expert Forum on "How to feed the world in 2050," September 2009. Available at: http://www.agassessment-watch.org/docs/IAASTD_letter_to_FAO_and_reply.pdf (retrieved Apr. 30, 2021).

INDEX